THE FUNDAMENTALS OF SPEAKING

THE FUNDAMENTALS OF SPEAKING

SECOND EDITION

WILBUR E. GILMAN/*Queens College of The City University of New York*

BOWER ALY/*University of Oregon*

HOLLIS L. WHITE/*Southern Illinois University*

THE MACMILLAN COMPANY, NEW YORK
COLLIER-MACMILLAN LIMITED, LONDON

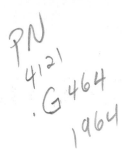
First Printing

Library of Congress catalog card number: 64–10587

The Macmillan Company, New York
Collier-Macmillan Canada, Ltd., Toronto, Ontario

Printed in the United States of America

PREFACE

The ability to speak well is frequently taken for granted; yet how many times in a day do we find ourselves baffled because our speech is inaccurate, incomplete, or unsatisfactory? Speechmaking is far more difficult and complex than most people realize, because they think of it as just an everyday activity developed from early childhood.

This book attempts to make speeches more accurate, more complete, and more satisfactory. Whether we are informing, persuading, impressing, or entertaining; whether the occasion be professional, deliberative, ceremonial, or social; whether the audience be old or young, large or small, friendly or hostile, homogeneous or heterogeneous; whether we are experienced or inexperienced in using the techniques of public address for inquiry or advocacy, we can do a great deal to improve the quality and effectiveness of our speaking. By studying and applying the principles of analysis, adaptation, and composition in preparing to speak and by acquiring competence in interpreting and presenting meaning accurately and fully with control of voice, articulation, and pronunciation and with appropriate poise and physical expression, we can make our speech more useful to ourselves and to others.

The order of chapters represents a sequence of steps in utilizing the principles of preparation and delivery, but each chapter is a self-contained unit that can be used at whatever point it fits into a plan of study. In every chapter the authors have endeavored to provide the illustrative material necessary to make the application of principles clear.

Although this book is a revision, the material is so completely reorganized and rewritten that in many respects the result is a new book. The authors have condensed, combined, and omitted sections of the first edition, have introduced new sections where needed, have supplied many different illustrations, and have sought to make the treatment as concise as possible and yet as comprehensive as seems desirable. The chapters on professional speaking and on evaluation and criticism present the development of important concepts and principles that received very little attention in the first edition.

WILBUR E. GILMAN
BOWER ALY
HOLLIS L. WHITE

ACKNOWLEDGMENTS

In the revision of this book, the authors have utilized the suggestions and criticisms of many teachers who have used the first edition in their classes. They are still heavily indebted to the long list of individuals in the acknowledgments of the first edition. They wish to express special appreciation to Loren D. Reid, a co-author of the first edition, for his permission to use material from that edition.

For advice and help in the preparation of this manuscript and for contributing at illustrations, the authors are especially indebted to Arthur J. Bronstein, Eleanor DiMichael, Jon Eisenson, Beatrice Jacoby, Robert G. King, John Newman, Mardel Ogilvie, and Norma Rees of Queens College of the City University of New York, to Frances McCurdy of the University of Missouri, to Jean Ervin of the Arlington County Public Schools, Arlington, Va., and to Lucile Aly of the University of Oregon. For editorial and secretarial assistance, the authors wish to thank Mrs. Frances Pine, Mrs. Peggy Erickson, and Mrs. Bea Gardner. For invaluable practical guidance, the authors acknowledge the experience gained from hundreds of students in their speech classes.

WILBUR E. GILMAN
BOWER ALY
HOLLIS L. WHITE

CONTENTS

I. PREVIEW: Concepts, Responsibilities, and Background   1
   1. INTRODUCTION: *Speaking and Listening in a Democratic Society*   3

II. SPEECH PREPARATION: Analysis, Disposition, and Composition   23
   2. INVENTION: *Topics, Materials, and Support*   25
   3. EXPOSITION AND PERSUASION: *Forms and Principles*   62
   4. ADAPTATION: *Audience and Plans*   109
   5. COMMUNICATION: *Thought, Language, and Style*   146

III. SPEECH DELIVERY: Problems, Methods, and Means   177
   6. MEANING: *Comprehension and Presentation*   179
   7. UTTERANCE: *Voice, Articulation, Pronunciation*   199
   8. ACTION: *Poise and Physical Expression*   236

IV. SPEECH TYPES: Opportunities, Occasions, and Forms   257
   9. SOCIAL SPEAKING: *Entertaining*   259
   10. CEREMONIAL SPEAKING: *Impressing*   278
   11. PROFESSIONAL SPEAKING: *Specializing and Popularizing*   302
   12. DELIBERATIVE SPEAKING: *Inquiry and Advocacy*   323

V. KNOWLEDGE AND SKILLS: Principles and Application   369
   13. EVALUATION AND CRITICISM: *Understanding and Judgment*   371
   14. CONCLUSION: *Uses and Abuses*   386

APPENDICES   391
   I. A SPEECH FOR STUDY   393
   II. A SPEECH FOR CRITICISM   403
   III. PARLIAMENTARY PROCEDURE   416

vii

SPEAKING IS INTERNATIONAL

Meetings of the United Nations are often occasions for speeches that influence the course of history.

Part I PREVIEW:
Concepts, Responsibilities, and
Background

*Men are never so likely to settle a question
rightly as when they discuss it freely.*
　　　　　　　　—T. B. Macaulay

1 INTRODUCTION:
Speaking and Listening in a Democratic Society

All life comes back to the question of our speech, the medium through which we communicate with one another.
—*Henry James*

People do more speaking and more listening to day than formerly: more buyers talk to sellers, more public servants address their constituents, more employers instruct their employees. In an atomic age national and international problems are more perplexing than they were in a simpler day. Every thoughtful person wants to speak well enough to do credit to himself as he discharges his professional and civic obligations.

College and university students today find the ability to speak well a major asset. As they become better informed about their fields of study, they are called upon more frequently to participate in group discussion, to report the results of their investigations, and to demonstrate processes. Engineers explain an exhibit of high-voltage equipment; members of a livestock judging team defend their score card; students of municipal government report on a study of the city-manager plan.

Many students take part in well-established programs of dramatics, debating, and public speaking found on every campus. They also find opportunities for speaking outside the classroom. They preside over meetings, appear on various programs, participate in campus politics, and make speeches of presentation, acceptance, installation, and commemoration. They talk to field representatives of corporations and confer with superintendents and college presidents about teaching positions.

3

Young men and women who are establishing themselves in a community find equally important opportunities for responsible communication: interviews with officials, boards of directors, or purchasing and planning committees; participation in the activities of the company or the union; membership in a service club, the Junior Chamber of Commerce, or the League of Women Voters; attendance at various kinds of party, political, and civic meetings. These responsibilities of young men and women are typical. As for speaking activities of older people, a glance at any newspaper will suggest their great variety and scope.

Teachers of adult extension classes in public speaking report that members of every conceivable business and profession cheerfully pay for instruction because they feel the need to speak effectively. Every student should study the relation of speechmaking to his chosen field. The prospective engineer, for example, should not visualize his life as centered wholly upon problems of design and construction; he will be called upon to present his ideas orally to civic and professional groups. The recommendations of the American Society for Engineering Education, supported by a study of the activities of graduate engineers, indicate that speech is as important in the engineer's career as mathematics and the basic sciences. Students of education, law, and the ministry usually understand the need for learning to speak; but this need should be recognized also by students preparing for careers such as accountancy, banking, medicine, physical education, and journalism. Any student who doubts the need to learn speechmaking should confer with successful practitioners in his chosen profession.

A day-by-day survey of the citizen's activities shows that he is engaged in one speech problem after another. As a speaker, he may make pleas for local school taxes, for a city charter, or for national labor legislation. As a listener, he must evaluate similar pleas.

BASIC CONCEPTS IN SPEECHMAKING

In every field of knowledge the speechmaker should know that his art is not merely an appendage to other studies but is a discipline in itself. Just as medicine is concerned with the human body in sickness and in health, and law with the statutes and with equity, so speechmaking is concerned with its own special principles: how to find and use the means of gaining a response. It is thus one of the applications of an art of which rhetoric is the theory. As such, it is a social force comparable to military power and economic control. Military means enable men to impose their will upon others by violence. Economic means enable men to obtain goods and services by exchange. Rhetorical means enable men to obtain responses by influencing human behavior.

SIGNIFICANCE OF SPEECHMAKING

Speechmaking is a significant form of power. Only the uninformed identify it exclusively with some of its more trivial and unworthy uses. Only the superficial fail to observe its major function of creating, maintaining, and expressing the great forces of public opinion. Today, as for ages past, suasion and dissuasion are instruments in determining expediency or inexpediency of policies looking toward the future; accusation and defense are the means of dispensing justice concerning acts committed in the past; eulogy and censure are methods of determining honor and dishonor within the present. Happiness, security, even life itself may depend upon the ability to make or to respond intelligently to arguments or appeals in speeches. Woodrow Wilson, campaigning for the League of Nations; Laval, the traitor, pleading for his life; Winston Churchill, eulogizing Franklin D. Roosevelt, exemplify the uses of speechmaking in questions of policy, justice, and honor.

SPEECHMAKING AS PROBABILITY

The speechmaker is primarily concerned with probability. Characteristically he deals with questions that do not permit scientific demonstration. An attorney presenting circumstantial evidence cannot prove the absolute truth of the indictment. A legislator advocating a policy cannot predict precisely the effect of his measures.

That the speaker cannot establish certainty is no disparagement of speechmaking. The fundamental questions of human life are often not susceptible to scientific answer. Nor does the concern of rhetoric with probability rather than with absolute truth place less responsibility on the speechmaker; knowing well the hazards, he must make the best judgment he can and demonstrate the expediency of that judgment. Probability is the special business of the rhetorician.

USES OF SPEECHMAKING

Speechmaking is primarily a useful art, resembling engineering more than music. But a speech may achieve notable and permanent beauty, as well as usefulness, and thus become a part of the literary tradition of a people. Just as the George Washington Bridge is universally admired as a work of beauty as well as a thoroughfare across the Hudson, so Lincoln's inaugural addresses are widely accepted as great literature as well as excellent speeches. Nevertheless, speechmaking is rightly considered a useful art, and its impulse springs characteristically from practical affairs. Four major uses of speechmaking are commonly described.

Speechmaking has a normative use. In a society where questions may be decided by free inquiry and advocacy, sound judgments have a tendency to prevail. Since free men do not easily continue to accept fallacies, those who advocate unworthy causes are under a handicap. Since the probable is usually easier to establish than the improbable, those who advocate worthy causes have an advantage. But the proponents of good causes must equip themselves in the art of speechmaking; for if their causes fail, they will have themselves to blame.

Speechmaking has an instructional use. Some people do not learn easily; others cannot learn without instruction. Great numbers of men and women require the simplification of knowledge. If all men could understand a logical demonstration of probabilities, a speaker would be required only to make a statement and to prove it; but since men are moved by passions as well as reasons, effective instruction must deal with attitudes and prejudices.

Speechmaking has a technical use. The rhetoric of speechmaking may be employed to find the arguments for and against a proposition. As a means of analyzing a proposal, it is a useful instrument for testing assumptions, evidence, and reasoning. The drawing of a brief is an excellent way to discover what inferences the facts support and where the probabilities lie. This application of rhetoric is essential in discussion, conference, and debate and is highly desirable in persuasion.

Speechmaking has a defensive use. If a man or his cause be attacked, he should be able to offer a persuasive case. Since men in a free society must always be prepared to sustain themselves and their measures, the art of rhetoric is never without employment.

ETHICS OF SPEECHMAKING

Speechmaking may be used to advance either good or evil designs. As an army may be employed either by free men to defend their country or by a dictator to enslave a people, so speechmaking may stir up citizens against a tyranny or incite a mob to a lynching. As a sum of money may be used either by a gangster to corrupt a judge or by a philanthropist to build a hospital, so one speech may arouse interest in going to the polls and another may help to elect an incompetent legislator. To note that all the arts may be employed for good or evil is not an apology for speechmaking, nor a warrant for its abuse, but merely an observation that speechmaking is no exception to the general rule. The character and judgment of the public speaker are therefore of first importance.

THE NECESSITY FOR SPEECHMAKING

Doubtless moved by the abuses of speechmaking, philosophers have often inveighed against it. Although they have sometimes been eloquent in their denunciations, they have not succeeded in abolishing speeches, nor are they likely to do so; for speechmaking of some sort appears to be necessary wherever men congregate. Even the philosophers use rhetoric when they attack rhetoric, as did Plato himself.

Different societies have called for different kinds of speechmaking. The type approved by one generation may be discredited by the next; the style of one region may be frowned upon in another. The flamboyant oratory of the 1890's has been generally replaced by a more functional speechmaking today. No matter how the standards may differ, however, the art itself is universal.

PERSISTENT QUESTIONS IN SPEECHMAKING

The arts of speechmaking are not limited to any single field, but on the contrary may be applied to all kinds of knowledge. Some questions occurring again and again become associated in the popular mind with speechmaking. The reason is not that speeches can be employed only within limited areas, but is rather that people tend perennially to be involved in the same problems requiring the agency of the speaker.

Among the persistent questions giving rise to speeches today, as in centuries past, are: Should the tariff be raised or lowered? Should taxes be increased? If taxes are increased, should the heaviest burden fall upon the rich or the poor? Should war be declared? Under what conditions should peace be negotiated? Should military training be compulsory? Should subsidies be paid to agriculture? Should the condition of the poor be ameliorated by grants from the public treasury? Every area of life has its own persistent questions.

LISTENING TO SPEECHES

In communication, every citizen has not only the function of presenting his ideas but also the parallel function of receiving the ideas of others. For the welfare of a democratic society these functions are equally important. Increasing the desire to listen critically to speeches and improving the listening habits of the citizens can do much to raise the level of

LISTENING COMPLEMENTS SPEAKING
Increasing the desire to listen and improving the listening habits of citizens can do much to raise the level of public thought and action. Good habits of listening should be stimulated in children.

public thought and action. Especially in a democracy, every student of speaking should be personally interested in becoming not only a more persuasive speaker but also a more discriminating listener.

The criterion of listening to understand is accuracy; that of listening to decide is judgment. The listener should be able to comprehend a systematic explanation and distinguish valid inferences from spurious arguments. He should find the meaning intended and decide what it signifies. No one can have the background for critical listening on every question; few have the ability for intelligent listening on abstruse matters. But on familiar topics everyone should strive to be an accurate listener; and on controversial issues everyone should try to be critical, at least to the extent of knowing when a speaker has made a reasonable case.

ACCURATE LISTENING

Accurate listening is essential in communication. Absent-mindedness is as defeating to listening as it is to speaking. Incoherence in composition or indistinctness in delivery may prevent communication. But if composition and delivery are both acceptable, what can account for misunderstanding? Are not faults to be found in listening as well as in speaking?

Hindrances to Accurate Listening

Some of the common difficulties in listening are familiar to everyone, but overcoming them requires intelligent practice. Six major hindrances should be considered.

Distraction. Although the listener may expect speakers to be interesting, he must contribute an effort to follow a line of thought. He cannot devote his attention to personal problems and still attend to what is being said. He must even resist the temptation to trace the speaker's thinking into interesting bypaths remote from the sequence of ideas. Although he should relate what he hears to his own experience, he should not allow his thoughts to wander by uncontrolled association—he must not go woolgathering. In listening as in speaking, he should stay close to the central idea.

Boredom. A listener may be forced into boredom before a speaker has finished, but if he is bored at the outset, he is allowing a pose to interfere with his thinking. He need not be eager, but he should be receptive. Thoughtful listening requires effort. A supercilious resistance to the speaker's efforts to hold attention deserves only censure. Posing for effect is as troublesome for listening as affectation is for speaking.

Intolerance. Good listening does not require that fools be suffered gladly, but unless a speaker is patronizing or presumptuous, a hearing is not too much to grant. Forbearance is wiser than impatience.

Captiousness. The good listener does not expect perfection; he is charitable toward minor faults in composition and delivery. He is not diverted from the speaker's ideas by mannerisms and details of language. Losing his sense of proportion, the hypercritical listener is likely to miss the full import of what is said and to discount the speech as inconsequential simply because the speaker has failed in some minor point.

Stolidity. Good listening requires all of the hearer's mental activity. To acquire a superficial impression of a speech is not rewarding. The listener should strive to understand the speaker, to follow the connotations intended, and to analyze the thought structure. Comprehending the speaker's supporting ideas as well as his central thought, the listener should be able to give an adequate summary of what he has heard.

Impatience. The speaker constructs a speech; the good listener reconstructs it—not as he would have given it, but as the speaker gave it. Many people, however, tend to hear what they *think* they are going to hear. Instead of waiting until the speaker completes his thought, they rush on to their own conclusions and may thus pervert the meaning. A speaker deserves to be understood before he is interpreted. The time for comparing what he actually said with what he might have said is after the speech is over.

Suggestions for Accurate Listening

Constructive suggestions may facilitate accurate listening. At the outset the listener should choose the best available place to see and hear the speaker; he should free himself from worries and distractions. Since much depends on achieving the right mental attitude, the listener should make up his mind to listen. Recalling related experiences, observing the speaker's facial expressions, responding to his attitudes, analyzing his ideas, and summarizing the discourse from time to time will enable him to participate actively.

CRITICAL LISTENING

In the democratic process, critical listening is even more important than forceful speaking. Just as the dupe emboldens the swindler, so the credulous audience encourages the shyster. Accepting ideas without question is like signing a document without reading it.

With disastrous results, the German people allowed themselves to be captured by the ranting Nazis. In this striking example, Americans find confirmation of their strong belief that the citizen must be educated for active participation in public policy. Unfortunately, however, some evidence supports the view that Americans are becoming more and more susceptible to appeals dissociated from valid reasoning. If the American nation is to endure both strong and free, every citizen must be as well informed as his opportunities permit; every voter must be as judicious as his obligations require. To approve uncritically what we hear is to forfeit the fundamental privilege of citizenship—that of forming well-considered judgments for the good of the state. What difficulties prevent our being critical listeners?

Hindrances to Critical Listening

Since critical listening implies evaluating as well as understanding what is said, any interference with the fair judgment of a proposition is an obstacle. The removal of obstacles requires intellectual and emotional self-control of a high order.

Prejudice. In a matter of policy the listener normally should be ready to modify his opinion according to the evidence. He should be willing to receive new facts and relate them to those he already has. Certainly he has a right—even a duty—to demand acceptable proof before he changes a well-grounded opinion; but he should beware of trying uncritically to maintain the *status quo*. An open mind entertains propositions on their merits and revises previous judgments in accordance with new information.

Distortion. A listener who distorts the speaker's meaning is dishonest. Altering the thesis to fit one's own point of view interferes with communication. Deliberate unwillingness to comprehend is perverse; listening merely to confirm beliefs already held is stultifying.

Passivity. The submissive listener accepts uncritically all that the speaker tells him. If he thinks, reads, or observes at all, he should be able to compare and contrast the content of the speech with what he already knows; he should have some basis for reaching a judgment on the validity of each assertion. To allow a speaker to dominate one's thought and feeling is sheer mental laziness. A good listener must be alert.

Indiscrimination. The listener who fails to distinguish between what is merely asserted and what is actually proved neglects his chief responsibility. The unscrupulous speaker can deceive him with all kinds of shams: a pompous manner, smooth delivery, appeals to prejudices, fictitious illustrations, glittering generalities, pseudo erudition, false allusions, gross inconsistencies—the whole bag of tricks used to hide the lack of evidence. The indiscriminating listener should study speechmaking to resist imposition.

The listener should also remember that sometimes a good speaker advocates an unworthy cause, and a poor speaker a worthy one. The integrity of the speaker is a factor in reaching a judgment, but not the only one. The sophisticated listener distinguishes between the cause and the speech.

Suggestions to Improve Critical Listening

The technique of critical listening can be acquired just as surely as the technique of effective speaking; indeed, each has much to contribute to the other.

If you do not already know enough about the topic to evaluate the speech you are to hear, you should acquire as much information as circumstances permit. The more relevant knowledge you bring to the analysis, the more likely you will be to judge it competently. Read as much of the best material available on the topic as time permits, and discuss it with others. If the topic is controversial, you should ascertain the reasons for each point of view maintained, and, from your own weighing of evidence, reach a tentative conclusion. In other words, you should know what you think and why.

Even though your information may be more limited than the speaker's, you are justified in using it as a standard as far as it goes. Recognizing its limitations, you should accept better information when it is presented. Your own knowledge may enable you to determine how much the speaker knows about his topic and how well he uses the available facts. You may be able to discover whether his ideas are original, plagiarized, or paraphrased. You may recognize his sources and know their relative value. Your knowledge may prevent your being misled by the superficial; it should enable you to distinguish the important from the trivial.

Ask yourself whether the speaker's assumptions are generally held and whether you are willing to accept them. Is the speaker assuming a great deal that he needs to prove? Is he allaying your suspicion of unacceptable premises by associating them with assumptions you believe?

Each assertion should be supported with enough evidence to make it acceptable. Does the speaker generalize without proof? Does he direct his proof toward his proposition or does he state one proposition and prove another?

You should keep in mind the standards of valid evidence and raise questions about each item presented. Is it consistent with what the speaker has said or what you know? Is it reasonable? Is the authority cited competent and unprejudiced? Can the source be checked? Is the evidence recent? These and other questions help you to judge the validity of evidence.

You should check the reasoning to assure yourself that the speaker is making sound inferences. Has he given enough instances? Are these instances typical? Are negative instances being overlooked? Are the facts accurate? Is the necessary causal connection established? Has the speaker proceeded logically from premises to conclusion? A knowledge of the requirements for sound reasoning is essential to competent criticism.

You should be on guard against the loose thinking shown in careless exaggerations, dubious figures, bold assertions, and startling predictions. Such expressions as "it is generally known," "the facts of history prove," and "beyond the shadow of a doubt" should make you suspicious of the proof. You should recognize appeals to prejudice, witticisms substituted for evidence, and lack of information concealed by emotional display. In your analysis of the support for the proposition, you should not be diverted by a straw-man argument or a red-herring device.

After listening to the speaker, you should be able to form a judgment about his integrity. Is he exploiting his audience, or does he seem to have your interests at heart? Is he fair to those who differ with him? Does he use good sense in what he says and in the way he says it? Does he inspire your confidence by the thoroughness of his treatment of the material and the forthrightness of his presentation?

Listeners may be too stubborn. In urging the desirability of a future policy, the speaker can offer only presumptive proof; therefore, the listener must not expect absolute proof. While being critical of what the speaker asks you to believe, you should nevertheless accept the weight of probabilities. In some instances, considering the alternatives to accepting the proposal is helpful in reaching a judgment. More may be lost by inaction than by the wrong action. Even when you look back upon an action taken, you may not know whether it was more or less wise than the alternatives. With an open mind you should ask yourself whether the speaker's proposal is probably the best course to follow in the light of the evidence and reasoning he can offer and in the absence of stronger arguments for inaction or for a different course.

In order to develop your critical powers, take advantage of opportunities to use them. Follow the announcements of radio and television programs and of public meetings and discussions for opportunities to hear outstanding speakers representative of current thought and opinion. You should listen to speakers whose opinions are different from your own. When a speaker develops a theme counter to your traditions, you should be able to listen to his arguments objectively and to evaluate them by the standards you have set up for judging reasoning and evidence. If you are a conservative, listen to a liberal; if you are a liberal, listen to a conservative. Try to find what is sound or unsound in the other person's thinking. Consider what the speaker has done well and what he has failed to do. In the classroom you may apply these principles of listening to student speeches; in doing so, you should develop the same objectivity as in judging speeches off the campus.

Remember that speaking is a means, not an end; and utilize your training not merely as a judge of speech preparation and delivery, but as an intelligent member of the audience. Although you may wish sometimes to listen as a critic of the techniques of speechmaking, normally you should think of yourself simply as a specially qualified person evaluating the information and arguments presented. The primary responsibility of any listener is to find the speaker's full meaning. A knowledge of the principles of speechmaking should help you to fulfill this function more competently than would otherwise be possible. With your experiences in speechmaking as a practical standard and your knowledge of principles as an ideal, you should know a good speech from a poor one. One way to tell a good speech from a poor one is to be well grounded in the tradition of speechmaking.

THE TRADITION OF SPEECHMAKING

In the first age of language primitive men communicated by cry, action, and gesture. Spoken language, much older than written, began when man uttered his first meaningful sounds. After the invention of writing initiated the second age of language, the visual symbols increased in importance at the expense of the audible symbols of speech. Men put down on stone, clay tablets, or papyrus their laws, histories, and holy books. They preserved the sayings of their prophets, warriors, and wise men. After the invention of printing in the fifteenth century, printed words could be reproduced cheaply and easily, and the ability to read became widespread in the Occident. For a while Western civilization was to depend for information and persuasion relatively less upon the spoken and more upon the written word.

In 1837 Morse's invention of the telegraph ushered in the third language age. The laying of transoceanic cables followed the discovery of telegraphy; the telephone followed the cable. Impressions of the sounds of speech on wax cylinders provided a new kind of spoken record for posterity. The wireless telegraph, followed by the wireless telephone, astonished a world grown accustomed to the sending of language by wire. Constant research improved techniques: sensitive microphones were constructed; public-address systems were improved; sound equipment was invented for motion pictures; radio and television were perfected. Speech synthesizers are now being developed. Today, a hundred thousand listeners are but a handful, and a million people following the same speaker form a new kind of audience.

Only the discerning appear to realize that the third age of language is well advanced; that the spoken word has now increased in importance relative to the written word; that henceforth educated men will have an increasing obligation not only to read and write but also to speak and hear with accuracy and understanding. Now as never before the welfare of the human race depends on the competent use of language.

ANCIENT GREECE

In the Occidental tradition Corax, who lived in the Greek colony of Syracuse in the fifth century B.C., first considered speechmaking systematically. His principles, carried to Greece, were received with great interest, especially at Athens, where any citizen called into court was required to present his own case. Moreover, since Athens was a democracy, the citizens needed to speak well in order to exert their influence in making the laws. Both the theory and the practice of speechmaking, sustained by the social order, thus reached a high level of development. Outstanding among the Greek orators is Pericles (495?–429 B.C.), the statesman who delivered the funeral oration honoring the Athenian heroes of the first Peloponnesian War. Lysias (450?–380? B.C.), who brought the practice of oratory to the common man, is justly praised for his simplicity and vigor. Of all the Greek orators, however, the most famous is Demosthenes (384–322 B.C.), whose oration "On the Crown" remains a model of eloquence.

More important to succeeding generations than the speeches of their orators is the theory of speechmaking developed by the Greeks. So well did they understand the four basic attitudes toward oratory that these concepts can still be described in terms of the Greek theorists: Sophistic, Platonic, Isocratean, and Aristotelian.

Originally the term *sophist* was applied to teachers. Some were of good and some of doubtful character, but Plato (427–347 B.C.) damned them all as teachers of the devious art of making the worse appear the better reason. Even those who were interested in the whole of education have suffered because their characteristic concern for technique has put them under suspicion.

The followers of Plato have often been antagonistic toward speechmaking. As idealists, they distrust the eloquent speaker and question his value in the social order. Paradoxically, in their attacks upon persuasion, they employ the very methods they have professed to despise.

The third attitude, exemplified in the School of Isocrates (436–338 B.C.), comprehended the arts of discourse as the means to a truly liberal education and the way to participation in all public affairs. The point of view of Isocrates influences democratic citizenship today.

The fourth attitude was developed in the *Rhetoric* of Aristotle (384–322 B.C.), who heartily disapproved of the shallow theories of his time; but unlike Plato, he proceeded from the realistic view that speechmaking is necessary in society. Instead of attacking or praising rhetoric, Aristotle systematically determined its principles.

The four attitudes developed in ancient Greece are still prevalent. Some men, like the sophists, regard speechmaking as a private concern; others, like Plato and his followers, distrust the art profoundly, but are nevertheless constrained to use it. The followers of Isocrates regard rhetoric, by one name or another, as the core curriculum; and others, like Aristotle, view it as a powerful social force, capable of being used for good or evil.

ANCIENT ROME

The Greeks became the teachers of the Romans and taught their pupils the principles of eloquence. But where the Greeks had used speech-making in the face-to-face democracy of small city-states, the Romans employed it in the developing and governing of a great empire. In the courts and in the Senate during the time of the Roman republic, the requirement of effective speaking brought eminent orators to the fore-front of public life. The Romans contributed practice as well as theory to the art of speechmaking in government. In practical affairs they were supreme: the name of Cicero (106–43 B.C.) survives as witness. Aristotle looked upon speechmaking with the mind of a scientist, but Cicero viewed it with the experience of an orator. As a lawyer and a politician, Cicero was the pre-eminent public speaker of his day. Moreover, as the author of *De Oratore,* he is one of the few great speakers to leave a valuable account of his rhetorical theory.

As Cicero was the great practitioner, so Quintilian (A.D. 35?–100) was the great teacher of public speaking. In his *Institutes of Oratory,* published A.D. 95, he set forth a complete system for the orator's education. Since, in his view, the orator requires the finest possible training, his treatise is rightly regarded as a fundamental contribution to education as well as to speechmaking. Quintilian declared that the orator is "the good man speaking well." In his preface he observes:

> Let the ideal orator, then, be such as to have the genuine title to the name of philosopher: it is not sufficient that he should be blameless in the point of character (for I cannot agree with those who hold this opinion); he must also be a thorough master of the science and the art of speaking, to an extent that perhaps no orator has yet attained.

The influence of Cicero and Quintilian, like that of Isocrates, Plato, and Aristotle, is pervasive and continuing. The Romans established the following canons of rhetoric: (1) *inventio,* discovering materials; (2) *dispositio,* planning arguments; (3) *elocutio,* choosing language; (4) *memoria,* mastering ideas; and (5) *pronuntiatio,* presenting the speech.

In perspective, the Romans perhaps contributed most in exemplifying the usefulness of oratory to the statesman. Since the days of the Roman republic men have understood that the statesman should be an orator and the orator a good man.

THE MIDDLE AGES

During the decline and after the fall of the Roman Empire, speech-making, as the instrument for converting nonbelievers to Christianity and for resolving differences among sects, underwent a change in form and content. St. Augustine (354–430), eminent father of the church, was renowned both as an author and as an orator. His work, *On Christian Doctrine*, which adapted the theories of Cicero to the propagation of Christianity, was widely used as a manual in the art of preaching.

Throughout the Middle Ages intellectual questions generally concerned faith and doctrine. Since these questions were peculiarly suited to treatment by the arts of rhetoric and dialectic, instruction in speech-making flourished. For generations the *trivium*, consisting of grammar, logic, and rhetoric, was so fundamental a part of the curriculum that every man educated in the schools was versed in it. The term *rhetoric*, as employed in the Middle Ages, has diverse meanings. Even before Peter Ramus (1515–1572) departed from the Aristotelian concept of rhetoric, and increasingly after his influence became widely felt, rhetoric tended to lose the canons of *inventio* and *dispositio* and to become chiefly an art of adornment and of presentation. The emphasis on the arts of discourse, however, was maintained throughout the Middle Ages. William Shakespeare, attending the grammar school at Stratford in 1577, probably received an education grounded in rhetoric. A generation later, John Milton probably received at St. Paul's School in London an education essentially similar to Shakespeare's.

In the Middle Ages the respect accorded to the *trivium* was perhaps comparable to that given to science and to the scientific spirit today. In view of the basic assumptions of the Middle Ages, the concepts of grammar, logic, and rhetoric were well suited to serve the time. They became the means of resolving major intellectual problems—for example, the reconciliation of the teachings of Aristotle with those of the Christian religion. Anyone who has difficulty in understanding the high place given to the arts of discourse in the schools of the Middle Ages should recall the preoccupation of that era not only with the propagating of faith but also with the determining of doctrine. The problems of life and death and earth and heaven were no less genuine for being metaphysical: they challenged the greatest intellects and the finest spirits of Christendom. In so far as the problems were amenable to solution, they were solved by the theory and practice of the arts of discourse. Such men as

Alcuin, Abelard, Bernard of Clairvaux, Thomas Aquinas, and Albertus Magnus, with many a forgotten monk, carried on in convocation and disputation the intellectual life of Western Europe.

BRITAIN

As the preoccupation with religion and metaphysics declined, the institutions of the Middle Ages became less relevant to the life of the time. Eventually the term *scholastic* became a reproach. Speechmaking, revived as a part of the growing interests of trade, of business, and of the rising national states, returned to the employment it had taken in ancient Rome—the governing of men and women.

In the early Renaissance, the study of rhetoric was an intellectual enterprise common to all European states, but a modified classical tradition of rhetoric was transmitted to the New World chiefly from Great Britain. For centuries Britain has been governed by a parliament whose functioning requires conference, discussion, and debate. Such a government was likely to produce notable speakers, as indeed it did among the British from the earliest times. The Golden Age of British oratory, however, began in the eighteenth century with such masters of the art of speechmaking as Lord Chatham, a vigorous and imaginative orator; Charles James Fox, called by Edmund Burke "the most brilliant and accomplished debater the world ever saw"; and with Edmund Burke himself, eloquent speaker and many-sided man. Chatham, Fox, and Burke are the most famous of the British orators; but Sheridan, Pitt, Erskine, and Brougham—and in later years Cobden, Bright, Disraeli, and Gladstone—also illustrate the genius of the British for government by discussion and debate. Winston Churchill, modern exemplar of British oratory, stood before the Congress of the United States and said with justifiable pride, "I am a child of the House of Commons."

In Britain, moreover, as in Greece and Rome, the practice of oratory has been accompanied by a study of its principles. The first English treatise on the theory of speechmaking, Leonard Cox's *Arte or Crafte of Rhethoryke*, published about 1529, was chiefly a practical commentary. Thomas Wilson's *Arte of Rhetorique*, first published in 1553, includes a systematic and comprehensive treatment of all the phases of rhetoric in the classical pattern, with suitable adaptation for the Englishman of his day.

Britain is indebted to Francis Bacon for his concept of rhetoric as the application of reason to imagination for the better moving of the will; to Thomas Sheridan for his insistence on spontaneous and easy delivery of speeches; and to Hugh Blair for his interpretation of the basic theories of public address. Outstanding are contributions to modern theories of speechmaking made by George Campbell, whose *Philosophy of Rhetoric* was published in 1776, and Richard Whately, whose *Rhetoric* appeared in 1828.

The most significant contribution of the British to the art of speechmaking is to be found, however, not in the great orators, theorists, and teachers but in the common people of Britain. The free play of speechmaking was at once a cause and a result of representative government. The British people taught the world that a nation can be both responsible and free.

UNITED STATES

The English who crossed the Atlantic as settlers continued the practice of speechmaking in their daily affairs. In every colony efforts were made to establish schools and colleges to teach the liberal arts, including public address. The courts, the legislatures, and the pulpits perpetuated British institutions. The theory of speechmaking in early America followed the British pattern, but the practice was American. Jonathan Edwards, the eminent preacher and theologian; Patrick Henry, the eloquent Virginian; and Samuel Adams, the New England agitator, are doubtless the best known of the early American orators; but many other speakers were respected in their own day. James Otis and John Adams of Massachusetts, James Wilson and Benjamin Franklin of Pennsylvania, Richard Henry Lee and George Wythe of Virginia are representative. The leading characteristic of speechmaking in colonial America was the interest taken in it by all classes of people. Americans in general, according to Jonathan Boucher, were "eminently endowed with a knack of talking; they seem to be born orators." [1]

Following the Revolution the drafting and adopting of the new Constitution and the founding of a new government required high talents in deliberation and debate. Among the speechmakers, Alexander Hamilton and James Madison supported the new Constitution, while Patrick Henry and Melancton Smith opposed it. Taken as a whole, the debates fairly represent the Americans of 1788; and they offer convincing evidence not only of superlative political ability, but also of proficiency in speechmaking.

During the early national period, the Americans, preoccupied with gaining and holding the land, with building up the country, and with establishing institutions, were a vigorous, even a rowdy, people greatly given to talk. The vital issues of public lands, of slavery, of the fundamental structure of the federal government developing among the ener-

---

[1] *Reminiscences of an American Loyalist*, p. 61. Quoted from George Bohman, "The Colonial Period," *A History and Criticism of American Public Address*, W. Norwood Brigance, ed., New York: McGraw-Hill Book Company, 1943, Vol. I, p. 17.

getic people gave occasion for lively public discussion and debate that produced such persuasive orators as Henry Clay, Daniel Webster, John C. Calhoun, and Thomas Hart Benton.

The Civil War, arising out of issues too delicate for settlement in the public forums, developed Abraham Lincoln as America's representative orator. Following the Civil War, the westward movement began again; and as new commonwealths were established, debates proceeded on local and national issues.

The conclusion of the Spanish-American War left the United States a continental nation and a world power facing problems of world magnitude. Such orators as William Jennings Bryan, Albert J. Beveridge, and Champ Clark confronted and debated questions of imperialism, isolationism, and internationalism. These issues, together with pressing domestic problems, were still unresolved in 1917 when a reluctant nation under the leadership of Woodrow Wilson, the very type of classic orator, engaged in the First World War. A generation later, under the presidency of Franklin D. Roosevelt, who was an outstanding speaker, the New Deal gave way to the crisis of the Second World War. Following this war, the aggression of communism resulted in the action of the United Nations in Korea. In the decade following Korea, world problems still dominated the political life of the country as the nations of the free world sought to win the cold war and to establish a lasting peace. Many significant speeches influenced national and international affairs.

The American experience suggests that in a free country the life of the state and the conduct of affairs are inextricably bound up with speechmaking, that oratory is not the diversion of the few, but an enterprise important to everyone. Moreover, the experience suggests that the high significance of oratory does not lie chiefly in the orator but in the audience and in the pervasive quality of speechmaking in the lives of the people. By the free interchange of ideas in churches, courts, legislatures, town meetings, and conferences, Americans have become accustomed to hearing speeches before making up their minds on public questions.

Along with the practice of speechmaking, Americans have given some attention to its theory and teaching. John Witherspoon probably made the first contribution with his lectures on rhetoric, published after his death in 1794. John Quincy Adams' *Lectures on Rhetoric and Oratory,* delivered at Harvard University (1806–09), was published in 1810. During succeeding years the interest of American scholars was chiefly in style and delivery rather than in the fuller concepts of analysis and composition.

During the latter part of the nineteenth century the art of speechmaking taught in the schools was largely elocution.[2] The major part of

[2] See Everett Hunt's review of *The Copeland Reader, Quarterly Journal of Speech,* XIII, 205–206, April, 1927.

rhetoric was neglected, and as the demand for instruction in writing increased, rhetoric came to be chiefly an adjunct of written composition. Although the principles of rhetoric were derived from oral discourse, they were generally applied, if at all, in the writing of themes and essays. John F. Genung, Fred Newton Scott, and Charles Sears Baldwin were outstanding among the American scholars who influenced the teaching of writing through the application of the ancient principles of rhetoric. Thomas C. Trueblood was instrumental in re-establishing the formal study of speechmaking in colleges and universities.

Among the first Americans in modern times to discard the elocutionary concept of public address was George Pierce Baker, who based his *Principles of Argumentation* (1895) on the older concept of logical proof. Some years later Charles Henry Woolbert related the available body of psychological literature to speechmaking. But the outstanding contribution of modern times was made by James A. Winans, who not only set forth his concept of conversational quality, but also elaborated a theory of public address that turned decisively from the methods of elocution. The restoration to speechmaking of its ancient prerogatives culminated in 1932 with Professor Lane Cooper's translation of the *Rhetoric* of Aristotle, the first by an American.

THE PRESENT TENDENCY

No present tendency suggests a decrease in the influence of speechmaking in America. The development of instruction in the schools and the scholarly interests of the universities are responses to an obvious need for more intelligent understanding and more effective communication of ideas. The constant demand of a vigorous society for making and listening to speeches, for conference, for discussion, and for debate suggests that Americans will be more and more concerned with speechmaking in the future. Indeed, one might express as a hope for America today what Richard Jebb declared to be true of ancient Athens:

The glory of Attic oratory, as such, consists not solely in its intrinsic excellence, but also in its revelation of the corporate political intelligence to which it appealed: for it spoke sometimes to an Assembly debating an issue of peace or war, sometimes to a law-court occupied with a private plaint, sometimes to Athenians mingled with strangers at a festival, but everywhere and always to the Athenian Demos, everywhere and always to a paramount People, taught by life itself to reason and to judge.[3]

[3] *The Attic Orators from Antiphon to Isaeus,* London: Macmillan and Co., 1876, Vol. I, pp. cxxxvi–cxxxvii.

Part **II** SPEECH PREPARATION: Analysis, Disposition, and Composition

True eloquence consists in saying all that is necessary and nothing but what is necessary.
—*La Rochefoucald*

2 INVENTION:
Topics, Materials, and Support

*No man can be eloquent on a subject that
he does not understand.*

—Cicero

Anyone who undertakes to prepare a speech is
faced immediately with three problems: (1) What shall I talk about?
(2) Where can I find the materials to develop the content of my speech?
(3) How can I organize the content of the speech in a meaningful way?
These three problems will be the subject of this chapter.

CHOOSING A SPEECH TOPIC

According to common observation, the two kinds of speakers are those
who have something to say and those who have to say something. Yet,
even for those who have something to say, deciding what to talk about
may be a problem. Experienced speakers may know so much that they
cannot tell it all. They may be forced to choose from a multitude of
possibilities.

A good topic will repay the time and effort spent in its selection.
Those who speak only because they "have to say something" should use
the opportunity to advantage. Even though they have no burning message, they may be justified in speaking because not to do so may be
impolitic or rude. Moreover, the man who thinks he has nothing to say
may discover on inquiry that he has more to say than he thought.

The reasons for a systematic choice of topic apply especially to students. The way to learn is to make speeches; yet, ordinarily the student
must gain his experience by talking to a classroom audience that has not

25

specifically invited him to speak. In these circumstances an idea is not always demanding utterance; the beginner must look for something to say. He will need to choose a topic, a general concept from which a speech may be developed.

Sometimes a student says, "I don't know anything to talk about; nothing has ever happened to me." Questioning reveals that he is mistaken: much has happened to him. One student to whom "nothing had ever happened" disclosed under questioning that he had once herded mules across the Atlantic, that his arm had been broken during a storm en route, and that, after jumping ship at Barcelona, he had been arrested by the police and had spent a night in jail before being rescued by the American consul. Yet the student was entirely honest in his original statement. He meant, "Nothing has ever happened to me *that belongs in a speech*," for he held the misconception that speeches are mostly bookish, that they must deal with weighty questions, and that personal experiences should be barred. The speaker's systematic choice of a speech topic should reveal his resources in the materials of speechmaking and encourage him to use them.

PROCEDURE FOR CHOOSING A SPEECH TOPIC

A senior in civil engineering was invited to represent his university at a student convention. When he consented to address a sectional meeting devoted to highway engineering, he was confronted with a number of problems: (1) what preparation he should make, (2) what special assets he could employ, (3) what purpose he could achieve, (4) what topic would interest the group, (5) what kind of listeners he would face, and (6) what the occasion would require. He decided to talk about recent experimentation in highway construction because (1) he had tested unusual materials, (2) he would represent a university known for research in road building, (3) his audience would want to be informed about his experiments, (4) the theme of the sectional meeting was "New Developments in Highway Engineering," (5) his audience was limited to students of highway engineering, and (6) the occasion was a convention devoted to new techniques.

The problems of the student engineer are typical. Like him, you may need to consider what topics are indicated by the preparation you already have made or can make, what kind of topic is appropriate for you to develop, what purpose is suitable, what subjects are available, what ideas can be adapted to the audience, and what the occasion requires. With reference to these six problems, two steps should enable you to make a final choice: (1) finding possible topics, and (2) testing their suitability.

Finding Possible Topics

Speakers who have read extensively, traveled widely, or observed closely should have no difficulty in finding topics. A girl who worked as a ticket seller made a lively speech on the foibles of theatregoers. A sophomore who worked as a waiter convinced his classmates that working students are underpaid. A striking treatment of your personal experience may be well adapted to speechmaking. Not every experience merits the attention of an audience, it is true; a trivial topic will neither inform nor interest listeners, but a speaker can easily assume that experiences so familiar to him that they seem trivial may be informative and interesting to others.

Everyone can widen his horizons through reading. A professor of philology whose hobby was the history of polar exploration once held the close attention of a critical audience by telling how he explored the Arctic from an armchair. Versatile speakers have often devoted a great deal of time to reading. Wendell Phillips gave a year of his college life to reading about the English Revolution of 1640. He searched out everything related to it—memoirs, speeches, plays, novels, and histories. He studied closely the Dutch struggle for independence. He read French literature and examined the ideas of Tocqueville, the great commentator on American institutions.[1] All his knowledge was put to use when he became the great advocate of human freedom. Your own store of topics will be enlarged by systematic reading; such an enrichment of your own experience will be invaluable when you must decide what to talk about. And even if your topic is assigned, your reading will enable you to interpret it.

The speech preparation. You should consider first those topics for which you have the best resources. When you know of some readily available material, you should consider the topics that can be drawn from it.

DOES YOUR COMMUNITY OFFER SUGGESTIONS? Perhaps a noteworthy public forum or an efficient city government will be a good topic. A visitor from Salt Lake City captivated his audience with an account of what the Mormons have done for their people.

CAN YOU SPEAK ON PLACES, PROCESSES, METHODS, OR ORGANIZATIONS YOU HAVE OBSERVED? Speakers sometimes overlook the topics they are best qualified to discuss. The Wall Street stenographer can talk about the New York Stock Exchange, the Amarillo rancher can tell how to raise beef cattle, and the Detroit machinist can explain the activities of a labor union.

---

[1] Raymond H. Barnard, "The Freedom Speech of Wendell Phillips," *Quarterly Journal of Speech*, XXV, 598, December, 1939.

CAN YOU TALK ABOUT THE PECULIAR MANNERS, CUSTOMS, OR TRADITIONS OF YOUR REGION? Like Nathaniel Hawthorne's traveler who went to the Green Mountains, speakers are sometimes blind to their own surroundings. The Bostonian was astonished that the farmer had never gone into the next valley to see the Great Stone Face; the farmer was equally amazed that the Bostonian had never been to Bunker Hill. The Ozark boy thought his dialect commonplace, but at his university, five hundred miles away, Ozark dialect was perhaps the most interesting topic he could choose.

DOES YOUR LIBRARY HAVE RESOURCES ON SPECIAL TOPICS? The Folger Shakespeare Library in Washington, D.C., is famous for its collection of Elizabethan literature, and the Widener Library at Harvard is known for American history. After you have searched the card catalogue, you may be encouraged to speak on one of the topics for which your local library is best known. At a college noted for its collection on slavery, a student gave an excellent speech on the underground railroad.

DOES THE AVAILABILITY OF AN EXPERT SUGGEST A TOPIC? In any community you will find professional people whose ideas will interest an audience. A real estate agent may have a solution for the housing problem, a judge for juvenile delinquency, or a nurse for emergency hospitalization. A conversation with one of these people may be the starting point for a speech. The son of an airline official gave an excellent talk on plans for more comfortable travel.

DO THE INTERESTS OR EXPERIENCES OF YOUR FRIENDS POINT TO AN UNUSUAL TOPIC? If your neighbor has a collection of clocks, perhaps you should talk about them. If your neighbor's mother knew William Faulkner, perhaps you should talk about her—or him.

The speaker. You should consider closely the relation of the topic to your own interests, competence, and background. Sometimes a student will develop a special interest in a topic as he prepares; normally he can acquire some competence in dealing with new ideas within the time available for speech preparation. The wisest policy is to begin early with a topic in which you already have a background both of interest and of competence.

DO YOUR APTITUDES SUGGEST A TOPIC? An elderly man made a living demonstrating and discussing the potter's wheel. A Minnesota fisherman talked about making artificial trout flies. A saleswoman explained the designing of greeting cards.

HAVE YOU HAD AN UNUSUAL EXPERIENCE? Admiral Byrd lectured upon his adventures at the South Pole. Colonel John Glenn spoke about his experience as an astronaut. A television cameraman described his experience as a captive of the Communist Pathet Lao. Everyone has had some experience that could hold the attention of an audience.

CAN YOU TALK ABOUT YOUR HOBBY? A high school audience was pleasantly surprised when a professor of geology talked about feats of magic. A business executive told of his experiences with a sailboat. Photography and stamp collecting may have been overworked, but the young man whose hobby was railroad signaling had exceptionally good material for a speech.

DOES YOUR RELATION TO YOUR AUDIENCE OR TO THE OCCASION INDICATE A POSSIBILITY? The man who has held a government appointment may be invited to relate his experiences to his fellow club members. An eminent economist who spent three critical years in Europe discussed the formation of the European Economic Community.

CAN YOU REPRESENT SOME SPECIAL GROUP IN YOUR CHOICE OF A TOPIC? Booker T. Washington spoke at the Atlanta Exposition as the representative of the Negro race. William Lyon Phelps frequently appeared before popular audiences as a representative literary critic.

The purpose. The speaker's purpose for addressing an audience may be influenced by the occasion. A society at a banquet may expect to be entertained; at the dedication of a new club building, to be impressed; at a program meeting, to be informed; and at a business session, to be persuaded. Factors other than the occasion and the purpose may influence the choice of topic. At the business session, the stated objectives of the organization may limit the number of topics to be discussed. The business of the speaker and the audience defines the purpose and indicates the topic. A physician who is able to inform students about an adequate health program may not be successful in persuading the school board to appropriate money for it. Frequently a speaker has more than one purpose. An engineer who developed a new method of tunnel construction may want to inform the directors of his corporation about his discovery and to persuade them to adopt it.

WHAT TOPICS ARE APPROPRIATE FOR ENTERTAINING? A suitable topic for entertaining can frequently be derived from your own experience. One girl talked about the disadvantages of being a minister's daughter, another about the problems of a bookworm, and a third about her reasons for remaining a wallflower.

The kind of audience sometimes suggests the best theme for entertainment. At the annual banquet of the Mortgage Bankers' Association, Harvey T. Harrison, an attorney, speaking on farm mortgages, used the clever title "Whither Midst Falling Due?" Joseph H. Choate talked to the New England Society of New York about the pilgrim mothers.

Often a beginning speaker, thinking that topics must be novel or bizarre, tortures his imagination to find an idea that nobody ever thought of before. He should look a little more sharply at what goes on around him; the instructor who is always talking about his lily garden, the trials of a freshman in a fraternity house, or the perils of waiting on tables. Topics seemingly commonplace can be given unusual treatment—for example, "Waiting for a Woman," "Traffic Cops," "How to Get Through the U.S. Customs."

WHAT TOPICS ARE APPROPRIATE FOR IMPRESSING? If you are to celebrate the founding of an institution, you will be expected to impress your audience with its achievements. The occasion determined the purpose and the topic when a senior, on Founder's Day, paid tribute to the self-sacrificing men who chartered the college; and a statesman, at a Lincoln's Birthday dinner, praised the courage and the vision of the Great Emancipator. The recipient of an honorary degree impressed his hearers with the peculiar opportunities of educated men; the retiring business executive impressed his employees with his appreciation of their loyalty; the visitor from abroad impressed his hosts with the joint achievements of his nation and theirs.

WHAT TOPICS ARE APPROPRIATE FOR INFORMING? The specialist may be called upon to inform either professional or lay audiences about his research. The physician lectures on the untoward effects of thalidomide; the scientist explains atomic structure.

Animal life, as one aspect of nature, illustrates the possibilities for speech topics: the distribution of animals throughout the world; the habits of insects, birds, or mammals; the life cycle of individual species, such as the housefly, the quail, or the salmon.

Even more interesting than animal life are human institutions: home and family, school and college, church and state. Since our welfare depends upon the way we are governed, we are concerned with political parties, primaries, and conventions. Every institution that touches us receives some of our attention: the press, the pulpit, and the theatre; hospitals, asylums, and prisons; libraries, galleries, and museums.

The various aspects of the college may be explained: history, alumni, governing board, administration, faculty, students, curriculum, instruction, extracurricular activities, buildings, and grounds. For the student, many campus topics are available, such as the grading system, the drama group, or the plan of student government. Comparisons are possible between the state and the endowed university, the liberal college and the professional school, the junior college and the first two years of the university. College presidents and students alike have interpreted the college curriculum, the ideals of the founders, the traditions of the alumni, and the needs of the freshmen.

Any one of these topics may be broken down into subtopics for informing. The college curriculum yields the elective system, the honors college, preprofessional training, and comprehensive examinations.

In discovering topics for informing, the speaker should consider his own experience. His interests may prepare him to talk about an occupation, a symphony, or an invention. His opportunities may qualify him to discuss an adventure, a recent event, or a public program. Special training may equip him to speak about a theory, an organization, or a sport.

WHAT TOPICS ARE APPROPRIATE FOR PERSUADING? The persuasive speaker attempts to show that of all the possibilities, his proposal is the best. He is dealing not with what is demonstrably true, but with what is probable. He uses the evidence at his command to prove that a certain course of action should be adopted by his hearers.

Of all controversial topics, those from the field of foreign policy are perhaps the most lively and persistent. Informed speakers on foreign affairs are in great demand. Because the nation is constantly confronting world problems, no set list of topics could prove half so valuable as the headlines of the daily newspaper.

The adult who is a taxpayer, and perhaps a parent as well, may have become familiar with some of the controversial aspects of education. As a member of a college community, the student is entitled to an opinion on academic issues. Among the persistent problems in education are the following:

- What should be the role of the federal government in education?
- Should the privileges of higher education be limited to students of exceptional ability?
- Should the list of required courses be decreased?
- Should a college education be primarily vocational or liberal?
- Should colleges adopt one of the year-round plans?
- Should student publications be censored?
- Should athletes be placed on the university payroll?
- Should students grade instructors?

If you consult the current periodicals and the controversial speeches reported by the newspapers, you will discover many questions about economic, social, and political conditions. The single field of government regulation illustrates possibilities: utilities, railroads, merchant marine, aviation, insurance, and trade unions. At the community level some problems concern municipal regulation of restaurants, dairies, stores, transportation, utilities, and the sale of tobacco and liquor. College students have spoken well on such questions as air pollution, the contamination of the water supply, and the effect of wage and hour legislation on student labor.

The subject. To know what is going on in the world is to have ideas from which topics may be drawn. Speeches may come from reading, listening, and observing.

CAN YOU DERIVE A TOPIC FROM THE NEWS? A political crisis, an industrial collapse, or a new discovery may be in the public eye. A change in
leadership, a paralyzing strike, or a new method of manufacturing may
supply an idea.

HAVE YOU RECENTLY HEARD A SPEECH OR READ A BOOK THAT LEADS TO A
TOPIC? A lecture or a sermon may stimulate your thinking; so may such
a book as *War and Peace, The Decline of the West,* or *Andersonville.*

DOES SOME RECENT DECISION SUGGEST AN IDEA? When policies are
changed, interpretations of the changes are necessary. The speaker who
talked about prayer in the public schools, following the decision of the
Supreme Court in the case of *Engles v. Vigale,* chose a timely topic.

DOES A SCHEDULED EVENT SUPPLY A TOPIC? The athletic coach talks to
businessmen about the conference track meet; the astronomer speaks of
the coming partial eclipse; the statesman discusses the problems of the
next international congress. All three take advantage of the interest of the
audience in events to come.

DOES A PERSISTENT CONTROVERSY LEAD TO A TOPIC? The treatment of
racial minorities, the participation of labor in politics, and methods of
taxation are timeless subjects. Speeches on topics drawn from them should
develop their current significance.

DO YOU CARE TO SUPPORT SOME REFORM? The movements and organ-
izations of reform provide topics for speeches. Outstanding examples are
CARE, the Peace Corps, and the American Society for Prevention of
Cruelty to Animals.

DO YOU BELIEVE THAT SOME CONDITIONS SHOULD BE CHANGED? Speeches
and newspaper articles have aroused public opinion sufficiently to bring
about the widening of streets, urban-renewal plans, and the abatement of
the smoke nuisance in some cities. You may be concerned with bad living
and working conditions or poorly managed homes for the aged. You may
believe that the college should keep the library open longer, that the
city should reorganize the police department, or that the state should
protect wild life.

CAN YOU TREAT AN OLD SUBJECT IN A NEW WAY? The dullest classroom
speeches are often on subsidizing college athletes; the dullest commencement addresses are sometimes on the responsibilities of the college graduate. Yet excellent speeches have been made on topics drawn from these
subjects.

Some students planning to talk to their classmates may profitably
choose a topic concerning parliamentary procedure. Every member of the
audience is potentially interested in the topic; if the speaker is not an
authority, he has strong incentives for becoming one. Good speeches on
parliamentary procedure give members of the class information they

need, and improve the speaker's special knowledge of some phase of the subject.

The audience. If the potential audience does not inspire the ideal speech, at least it should suggest a topic worthy of further consideration.

DOES THE AUDIENCE EXPECT TO HEAR A SPEECH ON A PARTICULAR TOPIC? People often expect an expert to talk about his specialty. Farmers who would be well satisfied to hear a professor of agricultural economics talk about the marketing of farm crops might be disappointed if he spoke on the future of Alaska. College students often have their specialties: local history, photography, music, painting, tennis.

DOES THE LOCALE SUGGEST A TOPIC? A speaker may develop a topic involving the place in which the speech is given, particularly if the place be noteworthy. When Jules Jusserand, Ambassador from France to the United States, dedicated the bust of Abraham Lincoln in the Hall of Fame, he observed that in future times pilgrims from all parts of the United States and many parts of the world would come to visit the Hall of Fame.

DOES THE ASSOCIATION OF THE AUDIENCE WITH A HISTORICAL EVENT PROVIDE A TOPIC? You may develop the story of some famous occurrence, perhaps with modern applications. An architect, addressing a Chicago audience, contrasted the inflammable buildings at the time of the great Chicago fire with the fireproof structures of today. Woodrow Wilson spoke at Independence Hall in Philadelphia on the meaning of the Declaration of Independence.

DO THE PROFESSIONAL INTERESTS OF THE AUDIENCE SUPPLY A SUITABLE TOPIC? A banker addressing businessmen touched upon their professional interests by discussing the relation between taxes and the discount rate. A college professor talking to insurance men was well received when he told them how to sell insurance to college professors. A physician talking to physicians would doubtless find them interested in medicare, in immobilization of fractures, and in chloromyacin.

CAN YOU DERIVE A TOPIC FROM THE BELIEFS OF THE AUDIENCE? The curiosity of a convention of investment counselors was aroused by the announcement of a speech on the possibilities for the survival of capitalism. When a university professor addressed a conference of newspaper editors, he talked about the responsibilities of editors to evaluate measures to aid education.

DOES THE SEX OF THE AUDIENCE SUGGEST A TOPIC? A gathering of men may give special attention to speeches about sports, wages, or investments. Women may also be interested in these topics, but an audience of housewives might prefer to hear about low-calorie menus, modern home decoration, or the care of children. At a national forum on "The American Woman and Her Responsibilities" the following were the topics of major addresses: the problems of the average American home, the effect of current world affairs on the American woman, and the changed conditions of marriage and the family.

DOES THE AGE OF THE AUDIENCE INDICATE A SUITABLE TOPIC? The interests of youth sometimes differ greatly from those of older people. The choosing of a career might be a suitable theme for high-school students; retirement incomes would be more appropriate for people past fifty. Admiral Harold R. Stark considered the age of his audience when he told college students at Bucknell University what America expects of today's youth.

DOES THE BACKGROUND OF THE AUDIENCE PROVIDE A TOPIC? Society women may enjoy hearing a discussion of etiquette at the Court of St. James. Bankers will doubtless be interested in maintaining adequate interest levels; factory workers will want to hear about stabilizing wages. When a businessman addressed a general audience in an industrial city, he asked employers and workers for a moratorium on industrial strife.

DO THE POLITICAL AFFILIATIONS OF THE AUDIENCE HELP THE SPEAKER IN FINDING A TOPIC? While Republicans speak about the origin of the Grand Old Party, Democrats talk about the Jeffersonian or Jacksonian tradition. A speech on civil rights may have a special appeal for minority groups.

DOES THE RELIGION OF THE AUDIENCE SUPPLY A TOPIC? In planning a talk for the members of a religious group, you should consider the beliefs they hold in common. Then you should examine your own experience to find a topic that will interest them as Catholics, Protestants, Jews, or simply as believers in religion. In 1960, John F. Kennedy, a Catholic campaigning for the Presidency, spoke in Houston to Americans of all faiths about intolerance.

DOES THE PURPOSE OF THE ORGANIZATION SUGGEST A TOPIC? A welfare organization is concerned with problems of poverty, ill health, and social maladjustment. A taxpayers' association is presumably interested in economy. A chamber of commerce seeks ways of attracting new industries to the city.

The occasion. Speeches are delivered on many special occasions: anniversaries, dedications, convocations. You may be able to find an excellent topic simply by studying the occasion.

DOES THE OCCASION INDICATE THE TOPIC? When Daniel Webster spoke on the death of Adams and Jefferson, the most suitable theme was the one he chose: an evaluation of their contributions to their country. The attack on Pearl Harbor required Franklin D. Roosevelt to address Congress on the national crisis. Less significant occasions also dictate the topic: the bonfire before the homecoming game, the alumni banquet, the presentation of an award to a classmate.

CAN THE OCCASION BE SO TREATED AS TO MAKE A TOPIC APPROPRIATE? Occasions may be adapted to give recognition to a man or an institution. A company official who has completed twenty-five years of service or a congressman who has been elected to a fifth term may be the subject for tribute. The Boy Scouts of America or the Community Chest may be honored.

DOES THE OCCASION SUGGEST A RELATED IDEA? A topic peculiarly associated with the occasion gives vitality to the speech. Dr. Carroll V. Newsom, who spoke on the future of higher education at commencement exercises in 1962, chose a topic of lively interest at that time.

CAN SOME SPECIAL EVENT RELATED TO THE OCCASION PROVIDE A POSSIBILITY? Some occasions are so common that they suggest no vital topic. The speaker in search of an idea may refer to files of the local newspaper, to biographies and histories, and to *Anniversaries and Holidays*.[2] Every day is an anniversary: August 3 is the day that Columbus first set sail for the New World; November 19 is the date of "The Gettysburg Address"; December 16 is the birthday of Beethoven.

Testing a Topic

Sometimes a speaker considers only one aspect of the problem and is thus tempted to choose an unfortunate topic. The choice of topic should be dictated by a consideration of *all* the factors together. In one instance the critical question may be, Can I find sufficient material in the time available? In another it may be, In discussing this topic, would I be handicapped by youth, inexperience, or previous identification with opposing views? You must decide whether your topic is compatible with your purpose: a professor of political science might give an informative speech analyzing a party platform in circumstances that would permit a governor seeking re-election to give a persuasive address on economy in government. You must apply the subject tests by such questions as the following: Is the subject matter too difficult or involved for oral presentation? Before reaching a final decision, you must certainly consider the interests, attitudes, and abilities of your audience. You must be sure that your topic is developed for an audience prepared to hear you and to deal with the problem you have to present. Finally, a good topic must always be measured by the occasion. An audience at a college anniversary expects to hear speeches praising the progress made by the institution rather than caustic criticism showing how selfishness has hindered it. The speaker who chooses to go against the spirit of the occasion should ask

[2] Mary E. Hazeltine, *Anniversaries and Holidays*, rev. ed., Chicago: American Library Association, 1944.

himself whether he has the ability to be effective in spite of the obstacles he sets up for himself.

The following list of questions offers a convenient means of testing the topic against the factors that should be considered before a final choice is made:

I. THE PREPARATION TEST

1. Can I find sufficient material in the time available?
2. Is the material authoritative?
3. Will I have time to develop my ideas?
4. Will I have opportunity to find the examples needed to clarify the topic?
5. Can I give my personal judgments?
6. Can I relate this speech to the experiences of the audience?
7. Can I make the speech original?
8. Do the opportunities for preparation indicate the possibility of an effective speech?

II. THE SPEAKER TEST

1. Do I have any handicap, such as youth, inexperience, previous identification with opposing views, which would make my choice of a topic unfortunate?
2. Will the audience be willing to hear me speak on the topic?
3. Will the audience expect me to speak on the topic?
4. Will I be able to develop the topic adequately?
5. Am I better fitted than my hearers to speak on the topic?

III. THE PURPOSE TEST

1. Is my topic in keeping with my purpose?
2. Have I translated my general purpose into specific terms?
3. Can my purpose be made clear to my audience?
4. Can I accomplish my purpose by proper treatment of the proposed topic?
5. Is my purpose suited to the occasion?
6. Is my purpose suited to the audience?

IV. THE SUBJECT TEST

1. Is the topic too difficult for oral presentation?
2. Is the topic worthy?
3. Is the audience already so familiar with my topic as to make my discussion seem naive?
4. Can the topic be properly adapted for adequate treatment?

V. THE AUDIENCE TEST

1. Is my topic suited to the specialized interests of the audience?
2. If the topic is already familiar to my audience, can I treat it with sufficient freshness to hold attention?
3. Is my topic designed to change belief into action?
4. Is the audience in a position to accept the view, to adopt the plan, or to follow the course of action I propose?
5. Will the size of the audience affect the choice of the topic?
6. Does the audience already know my views?
7. Can I foretell how the audience will receive the topic?
8. Does the audience have prejudices which would make the speech futile?
9. Can I easily relate my topic to the fundamental interests or accepted beliefs of the audience?

VI. THE OCCASION TEST

1. Is the topic suited to the spirit of the occasion?
2. Can I relate the topic to the occasion?
3. Will others speak on the same topic, the same phase of the problem, or the same side of the question?
4. Do circumstances such as the time of day, preceding events, or the environment make the presentation of the subject a special problem?

ESSENTIALS IN DECIDING ON A TOPIC

After a little experience you will be able quickly to apply suggestions and tests to select a good topic. You should not expect always to find the perfect topic; you may have to be content with the best you can find within a reasonable length of time.

An ordinary topic chosen in good time may serve you and your audience better than an excellent topic chosen in frantic haste. If you choose your speech topic soon enough, you will gain the advantage of maturing your thought; you will acquire almost effortlessly some attitudes and ideas about your speech simply because your attention has been directed toward the topic. *The beginning speaker can receive no better advice than to choose his speech topics as early as possible.* The ambitious and thoughtful student will make a complete speech calendar early in his course.

As a final check, remind yourself that the most critical questions exist in the minds of your hearers. These questions are:

- What has this topic to do with me?
- What does this speaker know about the topic?

Unless you can demonstrate the immediate relation of the topic to your hearers and to yourself, you should consider other possibilities.

FINDING MATERIAL

The work of the speaker requires time for ideas to mature. Problems that can be dealt with only clumsily at first may be solved easily on reflection; an idea that is shadowy today may become sharp tomorrow. In no phase of preparation is time more important than in surveying the materials available for the speech.

CONSIDERING RELATED PERSONAL EXPERIENCE

In exploring what you know, consider all possibilities. If your speech is about honesty, recall events: a clerk followed you a block to return your briefcase; a travel agent saved you money in planning your trip. On the other hand, do not become so preoccupied with your personal observations that you neglect ideas gained from conversation, speeches, books, and periodicals.

The speaker's primary sources of personal information are his stock of remembered experiences and his collection of speech material. A classified file of ideas, quotations, illustrations, stories, and references makes available material that might otherwise be forgotten. Books are no substitute for a personal file: they lack the vividness of your own record. Reviewing the file from time to time will refresh your memory.

MAKING AN OUTLINE

As an architect prepares a sketch, so a speaker may prepare an outline indicating, in their order, the divisions of his topic. If you decide to use your personal experience in selling as a source for a speech, your preliminary survey may result in the organization of your ideas in this form:

QUALITIES OF A GOOD SALESMAN

1. Perseverance
   a. Danger of being too easily discouraged
   b. Success on fifth call
2. Confidence
   a. In himself
   b. In the product

3. Knowledge of human nature
   a. Want what others have
   b. Like bargains but not cheap goods
   c. Subject to flattery

An outline is a trial to be modified, reconstructed, or discarded. The preceding example may be the beginning of a well-planned speech: the three principal divisions are clear, mutually exclusive, and representative of the qualities of all good salesmen. The outline could be improved by the addition of supporting ideas; it needs authoritative factual support and lively illustrations. If the speaker cannot supply this material from personal experience, he must go to other sources. Further investigation may also reveal important omissions, even of major divisions.

FINDING NEW MATERIAL

The chief sources of additional material are observation, conversation, inquiries, speeches, and books and periodicals.

Observation

A good speaker must be a good observer. A botanist examined growing plants before reporting on an experiment in cross-fertilization. A safety expert studied the responses of workmen during a test period. A college student watched a number of television news programs in preparation for a speech on national elections. Henry Ward Beecher gathered striking illustrations for his sermons during his walks through New York City and the surrounding country. These sermons are filled with references to everyday events: trout fishing, squirrel hunting, teaching, checker playing, draying, drafting, and blacksmithing. Beecher declared on one occasion that he used fifty times as many illustrations in his later life as he did in the early years of his ministry.[3]

Conversation

Speakers do not practice sufficiently the art of learning from others. If possible, you should confer with experts, who should be able not only to provide facts but also to evaluate sources of information. You need not limit yourself to interviews with them; on some topics the opinions of your friends may be useful. Interviewing them may be an excellent method of collecting ideas on such a topic as the honor system.

Talking with your friends tests your ideas. If you are planning to speak on the honor system, you may lead the conversation into this topic

[3] *Yale Lectures on Preaching*, New York: J. B. Ford and Company, 1872, pp. 175–200.

SPEAKING REQUIRES IDEAS

Fact finding is essential for all kinds of speaking—public speaking, discussion, and debate. A presidential committee, headed by Senator Paul Douglas of Illinois, holds a meeting in Charleston, South Carolina, to gather information on the problems of depressed areas.

and by a little questioning obtain added information, new points of view, and helpful examples. By presenting your own ideas, you may draw out confirmations, objections, and opposing arguments. After such a conversation, you may approach the problem in a different way by choosing different lines of reasoning or by strengthening your case with convincing illustrations.

Great men have often used conversation as a means of speech preparation. Even Woodrow Wilson, commonly regarded as unusually self-reliant, declared, "I not only use all the brains I have, but all I can borrow." He prepared speeches several weeks before their delivery and revised them in the light of comments he received from his associates.

Inquiries

Inquiries may be made by letters to individuals or by forms circulated to special groups. Correspondence with campus leaders, labor organizers, or business and professional men often yields useful items. Members of Congress, who have a natural interest in their constituents, are able to supply valuable information from official sources. You need not hesitate to write letters to prominent citizens; usually they are prompt in answering their mail. Most authors are willing to reply to letters concerning their books.

Current Speeches

Choosing your topic early may enable you to hear speeches that might otherwise escape your notice. News analysts, government officials, and experts in business, science, and economics are frequently on the air. For further study you can often obtain an electrical transcription of a public address. You may want to study the text of a speech. Some metropolitan newspapers report important addresses. *The Congressional Record* prints all speeches delivered in Congress, many given elsewhere, and some that were written but never spoken; *Vital Speeches* publishes many current addresses. The intelligent use of other men's speeches in your own preparation will require you to analyze their ideas and develop your own conclusions. You will thus avoid the slavish following of their argument as well as the borrowing of their language.

Books and Periodicals

Few speakers have all the references they need. Books and periodicals are so essential to certain forms of speechmaking that you will find yourself making frequent use of the resources of libraries.

USING THE LIBRARY

Using the library requires patience, but the task seems less formidable when compared with the opportunities presented. Some annoyances you must face philosophically; others will disappear as you become more competent. Asking relevant questions helps you; most librarians, realizing that the public needs assistance, take pride in answering inquiries.

The Card Catalogue

The card catalogue is the alphabetical directory to the resources of the library. Each item usually is represented by one or more cards: author, title, and subject. For example, the book *Blood, Sweat, and Tears,* by Winston S. Churchill, is represented by an author card in the C's (Churchill), by a title card in the B's (Blood), and by cards under a variety of subject headings such as "Great Britain—Foreign Relations," "Europe—Politics," and "World War, 1939—Great Britain." If you know the full name of the author, you should look for the author card. If you know only the title of the book, you should consult the title card. If you need to determine the available resources upon a potential speech topic, you should turn to the subject cards.[4]

Readers' Guide to Periodical Literature

In consulting magazines, you should refer to the *Readers' Guide to Periodical Literature,* a complete cumulative index to articles published in more than a hundred selected periodicals. Entries are alphabetized according to author and subject and, infrequently, according to title as well.[5] The foregoing description suggests that the *Readers' Guide* will answer two questions arising in your preparation:

WHAT MAGAZINE ARTICLES HAVE BEEN PUBLISHED ON MY TOPIC? By looking under the appropriate subject headings of issues of the *Readers' Guide,* you may find a list of pertinent articles. The usefulness of the *Readers' Guide* is obviously limited to the periodicals indexed.

WHERE DID I SEE A CERTAIN ARTICLE ABOUT MY TOPIC? You may recall reading an article you need. You should search for the title, the author, or the subject heading in the *Readers' Guide.* You may find an entry similar to the one on page 43.[6]

Special Indexes

Various references enable speakers to find information on special topics. *The International Index to Periodicals* analyzes a selected list of journals of the world. *The Bulletin of the Public Affairs Information Service* indexes new books, current periodicals, government documents, and pamphlets published in English-speaking countries. *The Industrial Arts Index, The Agricultural Index,* and *The Education Index* are designed for publications in the fields indicated by their titles. All

---

[4] For an excellent discussion of the card catalogue, see Ella V. Aldrich, *Using Books and Libraries,* rev. ed., New York: Prentice-Hall, 1946, pp. 14–24.

[5] *Readers' Guide* has been published since 1900. *Poole's Index,* similar to *Readers' Guide,* with its supplements covers periodicals from 1802 to 1906.

[6] *Readers' Guide to Periodical Literature,* Vol. 63, No. 4, April, 1963, p. 12. Copyright 1963 by The H. W. Wilson Company, New York 52, New York. Reproduced by permission of The H. W. Wilson Company.

ATOMIC bombs—Testing, Suspension of—_Cont._
  Monitoring a test ban. M. Sands. Bul Atomic
    Sci 19:12-15 Mr '63
  Negotiating with Communists: a test case;
    excerpts from address, February 21, 1963.
    T. J. Dodd. Nat R 14:184 Mr 12 '63
  Playing the numbers; on-site inspection. Nat
    R 14:220-1 Mr 26 '63
  Primary test; the people's decision. N.
    Cousins. Sat R 46:28-9+ Mr 30 '63
  Secretary Rusk's news conference of Feb-
    ruary 1, 1963. D. Rusk. Dept State Bul
    48:235-43 F 18 '63
  Test ban: Kennedy-Khrushchev exchange. J.
    F. Kennedy; N. Khrushchev. Bul Atomic
    Sci 19:32-7 Mr '63
  Test ban: prospects for agreement may be
    dim, but in Cuban aftermath they appear
    brighter. D. S. Greenberg. Science 139:739-
    41 F 22 '63
  Thin but important opening. N. Cousins. Sat
    R 46:26-7 Mr 2 '63
  U.S. and U.S.S.R. exchange views on nuclear
    test ban; exchange of letters; with Depart-
    ment statement of January 20, 1963. N.
    Khrushchev; J. F. Kennedy. Dept State
    Bul 48:198-202 F 11 '63
  What goes on here? Nation 196:189 Mr 9 '63

libraries have most of these special references, and large libraries have aids organized to serve particular purposes.

Often a speaker wishes to consider a topic reported in the daily newspapers. The news of a strike, for example, may have been set forth more fully in newspapers than in any other source. To find the story needed, you should examine _The New York Times Index_,[7] which may also be used as a guide to newspaper articles appearing in other daily newspapers. For _The London Times_ two indexes are available. _Palmer's Index_ covers the issues since 1790, while the more comprehensive _Official Index_ covers the issues since 1906.

Bibliographies

The speaker may save himself much work by finding a bibliography on his topic. The card catalogue and the various indexes to periodicals are helpful.[8]

The _Bibliographic Index_ is issued frequently and is cumulated. Boyd's _United States Government Publications: Sources of Information for Libraries_ lists bibliographies issued by the federal government. The _Document Catalog_ covers the sessions of Congress. The field of speech is served by Thonssen and Fatherson's _Bibliography of Speech Education_ and its supplement. Similar bibliographies are available in other fields.

Other Reference Books

Mudge's _Guide to Reference Books_ [9] lists 4,000 titles. The following works of reference are commonly used:

[7] _The New York Times Index_ has been published since 1913. For the period of 1875 to 1906, the speaker may refer to _The New York Herald Tribune Index._

[8] The abbreviation _bibliog_ following the title of an article means that a bibliography is included.

[9] Sixth ed., Chicago: American Library Association, 1936. Supplements are published every two or three years to keep the work up to date.

Dictionaries. Pronunciations, etymologies, illustrations of word usage, antonyms, and synonyms, as well as definitions, may be found, for example, in *Webster's New International Dictionary, Second Edition.* The third edition, following a different editorial policy, omits some of the information found in the second. A good dictionary provides much assistance beyond the actual scope of a definition, as in the description of the Mannheim slide rule, sketches of the insignia of the United States Army, and pages of illustrative photographs. Special sections alphabetize foreign words and phrases, biographical data concerning famous people, and geographical information. Sir James Murray's *A New English Dictionary*, sometimes called the *Oxford Dictionary*, is invaluable for its meanings and etymologies; information not in the original volumes may be found in the supplement. *A Dictionary of American English*, edited by Sir William A. Craigie and James R. Hulbert, is the American counterpart of the *Oxford Dictionary. An American Pronouncing Dictionary*, by John S. Kenyon and Thomas A. Knott, represents American pronunciation by international phonetic symbols.

Wordbooks. Several books are available to aid the speaker in choosing the right word. Roget's *Thesaurus* suggests related words and phrases. Among numerous citations under *homeliness*, for example, are listed such nouns as *ugliness, deformity, inelegance,* and *disfigurement,* and such adjectives as *ordinary, unsightly, unseemingly,* and *misshapen.* Crabb's *Synonyms* helps to distinguish between words of similar meaning: *relinquish* and *abandon, inmate* and *inhabitant, transparent* and *translucent.* Webster's *Dictionary of Synonyms* groups together words of like meaning and differentiates them by its discriminating definitions and illustrations of usage.

General encyclopedias. Topical surveys are available in *The Encyclopaedia Britannica, The New International Encyclopedia, The Encyclopedia Americana,* and their supplementary yearbooks. If your topic concerns art, athletics, education, or other fields of human activity, you can orient yourself with the encyclopedias. *The Columbia Encyclopedia,* published in one volume, is a collection of concise and accurate summaries. *The Catholic Encyclopedia* is especially valuable for church history and ecclesiastical matters.

Biographies. Frequently the speaker will need to identify an authority or to investigate a career. Although biographical articles are provided in dictionaries and encyclopedias, more specialized sources of biographical data are available in Lippincott's *Universal Pronouncing Dictionary of Biography and Mythology* and in Webster's *Biographical Dictionary.* The limited works are the *Dictionary of National Biography,* with supplements, for deceased persons prominent in the British Empire; the *Dictionary of American Biography* for deceased Americans; *Who's Who,*

Who's Who in America, and similar publications for distinguished living people; and various classified compilations such as *Living Authors, American Men of Science,* and *Directory of American Scholars.*

Sources of facts. The speaker should know how to find specific facts. Who is the chief executive of Brazil? *The Statesman's Yearbook* gives the answer. How many Moslems are there in the world? *The World Almanac* gives the answer. How much cotton is exported from the United States? *The Statistical Abstract of the United States* gives the answer. In any library are numerous other books of special information concerning the many fields of human knowledge. *Facts on File* is a weekly digest of world events, each issue containing a cumulative index of preceding numbers.

Books of quotations. Whenever the speaker needs a quotation or wishes to identify an author, he may refer to such works as Bartlett's *Familiar Quotations,* Mencken's *A New Dictionary of Quotations,* *The Oxford Dictionary of Quotations,* Stevenson's *Home Book of Quotations,* or Hoyt's *Cyclopedia of Practical Quotations.*

USING BOOKS AND PERIODICALS EFFICIENTLY

A little research on almost any topic will soon produce many pertinent references. You can study these references most efficiently if you begin with those offering general treatment and proceed to specialized articles. Encyclopedias usually contribute compact and well-organized surveys which sometimes conclude with a short bibliography. Since you often need to know the source of your information, note that the authoritative encyclopedias usually initial the important articles and provide a list of contributors. If your topic is concerned with a rapidly changing field, you should discover when the article was written.

The typical reader has difficulty in determining the best books in·a given field. The surest way is to obtain the advice of someone who is familiar with the subject. Lacking this guidance, you must judge as best you can. From the card catalogue you can determine the year of publication, the name of the publisher, the number of pages, and sometimes even the titles of chapters. By reading the preface and by glancing at the footnotes and the bibliography, you can survey the book. By means of the table of contents and the index, you can soon locate those parts of the book that have a direct bearing on your topic.

Current magazines are probably the most common source of material for short talks on popular subjects. By looking under promising headings in the periodical indexes, you can accumulate a list of titles. From the name of the author, the length of the article, the date of publication, and the standing of the magazine, you should be able to predict the usefulness

Reinhardt, 228
       Students frequently change their opinion of
teachers whom they once thought good. The following
reasons are given for such changes of opinion:
       "The teacher was too easy and permitted pupils
to do a poor quality of work."
       "The teacher used poor methods."
       "The teacher was lax in discipline."
       "The teacher did not know his subject matter."
       "The teacher was partial."

A SAMPLE NOTE CARD

of the articles. *Time, The Saturday Evening Post, Harper's,* and *Foreign Affairs,* for example, give entirely different editorial treatments to articles of international significance. Among the other helpful magazines are *Vital Speeches, New Republic, Newsweek, Atlantic Monthly,* and *Current History.*

For news events of national or international importance, you should read the dispatches of the different news services and the comments by special correspondents and analysts. For accurate and comprehensive treatment, consult outstanding newspapers of the caliber of *The New York Times, The New York Herald Tribune, The Christian Science Monitor, The Baltimore Sun, The Atlanta Constitution, The St. Louis Post-Dispatch,* and *The Louisville Courier-Journal.*

RECORDING MATERIAL

Taking notes saves the speaker from duplicating his research. All systems of note taking have basic principles in common. For easy filing and handling, make your notes on cards of the same size. Use headings taken from your outline to classify your notes: the main heading in the upper left-hand corner of the card, and the subheading in the upper right-hand corner. Put the name of the author and the page reference on each card referring to a book or article. Record each idea on a separate card; follow the standard practice of placing quotations within quotation marks and interpolated explanations within brackets. If you omit words within a sentence, indicate your omission by three dots. If your research is to continue for sometime, adopt a filing system.

The speaker should be on the alert for interesting material: an epigrammatic statement that suggests an appealing title, illustrations for specific use, compelling assertions by well-known authorities, summaries of sound reasoning, and other kinds of supporting evidence. In preparing a talk on coeducation, a student selected the following items:

- Marriages resulting from acquaintance in college are likely to endure.
- Men who have gone to college with women are less likely to feel that whatever men do is important and whatever their wives do is unimportant.
- In 1900 one divorce occurred for every twelve marriages; in 1929 one for every six marriages; and in 1962, one for every four marriages.

The student placed each of the foregoing statements on a separate card with the appropriate heading and subheading, the identification of the source, and the page reference. (See page 46.)

PREPARING A BIBLIOGRAPHY

When you are collecting material for speeches requiring accuracy of citation, you should record your references. In the long run you will save time and trouble by following the basic principles of bibliographical form: accuracy, completeness, and consistency.

Accuracy requires that the bibliography be correct as to spelling of names, wording of titles, place of publication, name of publisher, date of publication, number of pages, and any necessary citation of the edition, revision, and volume.

Completeness requires that all information be given. "Jones, *Ideas in America*" is insufficient. The entry should state the name of the author or editor, the title, the place of publication, the publisher, and the date of publication: "Jones, Howard Mumford, *Ideas in America* (Cambridge: Harvard University Press, 1944), xi + 304."

Consistency requires a single form of punctuation and arrangement. The bibliography on page 48 provides a standard.

Form for a Bibliography

Although bibliographic customs differ, the generally accepted practice is to list the items in this order: name of author (last name first), title of book, place of publication, name of publisher, year of publication, number of pages. If the reference is to a magazine article, the title, enclosed in quotation marks, is followed by the name of the magazine, the volume number, the month and the year, and the pages.[10] The entries are usually arranged in alphabetical order. The title of a book and the name of a magazine are conventionally italicized in print and underscored in manuscript.

[10] Many special problems arise concerning bibliographic form. For further information, see *A Manual of Style*, Chicago: University of Chicago Press, 1949, pp. 66–67, 70, 150–153.

Annotating a Bibliography

Annotating a bibliography increases its value. The annotation may give the main idea, set forth the particular point of view, describe special features, or point out some peculiar merit. Annotations should be brief, clear, specific, and consistent in form.

Illustration of a Bibliography

Most bibliographies consist of items from a variety of sources, including books, periodicals, and newspapers. The following bibliography illustrates the three common types of entries, with annotations.

AMERICAN TRADE POLICY

Belaunde, Victor A., "The Economic Basis of Politics in Latin America," *The Annals* of the American Academy of Political and Social Science, 342, 54–58 (July, 1962). A timely treatment of politico-economic problems in Latin America.

Benoit, Émile, *Europe at Sixes and Sevens* (New York: Columbia University Press, 1961), 275 pp. An authoritative study of the problems of the European Economic Community and the European Free Trade Area.

Curtiss, W. M., *The Tariff Idea* (Irvington-on-Hudson, New York: The Foundation for Economic Education, 1953), 80 pp. A lucid explanation of the basic arguments for free trade among nations.

King, Seth S., "Commonwealth Faces Dilemma on 'Six,'" *The New York Times*, September 9, 1962, E 5. An analysis of the problems facing the British Commonwealth of Nations in respect to the European Economic Community.

Mayne, Richard, *The Community of Europe* (New York: W. W. Norton & Company, Inc., 1963), 192 pp. A brief history of the movement toward European unity, with emphasis on the Common Market.

ORIGINALITY IN SPEECHMAKING

After you have accumulated a body of facts, statistics, quotations, examples, and illustrations, you must determine how to use this material in an original speech. You will avoid plagiarism (1) by recalling your own experiences, (2) by consulting a variety of sources, (3) by giving due credit, (4) by using your own language, (5) by presenting your own point of view, and (6) by relating your own thought to your investigation.

RECALLING YOUR OWN EXPERIENCES

The starting point of every speaker's investigation should be his own storehouse of ideas and experiences. Even though you have gathered data from many sources, you should not permit the material from books and magazines to dominate your thinking. Your speech may include material from borrowed sources, but you must assimilate the ideas. Illustrations from your own experience are especially interesting to an audience.

CONSULTING A VARIETY OF SOURCES

True originality can come only from reflective thinking based upon a broad foundation of knowledge obtained from many sources. Some speakers, either through misunderstanding or indolence, derive a talk from a single magazine article. The least original of all speeches is the one summarizing a magazine article that is itself a summary.

GIVING DUE CREDIT

Sometimes another person's language may be so incisive that you wish to quote his exact words, but whether you quote his words or present his ideas, you should give him credit. You gain influence when you demonstrate that your speech is based upon reliable and authentic sources. Instead of hiding behind such meaningless generalities as "Statistics show . . ." or "It is a well-known fact that . . . ," you may say, as Walter Lippmann did concerning universal and compulsory education, " 'No other sure foundation can be devised,' said Jefferson, 'for the preservation of freedom and happiness.' " [11]

USING YOUR OWN LANGUAGE

When you use material in books or periodicals, you should avoid merely copying the words of the author. The author's language was designed for writing, not for speaking; furthermore, his vocabulary and syntax are suited to his personality, not yours.

PRESENTING YOUR OWN POINT OF VIEW

Since the speaker usually deals with current ideas, his originality must consist primarily in his selection and arrangement of subject matter and particularly in his interpretations and conclusions. The facts them-

[11] A. Craig Baird, ed., *Representative American Speeches: 1940–1941*, New York: The H. W. Wilson Company, 1941, pp. 294–295. Copyright 1941 by The H. W. Wilson Company.

selves are accessible to anyone, but you, as a speaker, make them available and show what they mean. In addition, by your skillful use of language, you may make them clearer, more interesting, or more significant than they were in their original form. Especially in persuasion, you should consider arguments *against* as well as *for* your central idea.

RELATING YOUR OWN THOUGHT TO YOUR INVESTIGATION

Every part of the speech should result from your own thought and experience. You should use ideas gathered from available sources and give due credit for them. The selection, arrangement, interpretation, and composition should be your own. The dullness resulting from the presentation of hurriedly compiled, unassimilated material, and the dishonest practice of borrowing ideas without acknowledgment, can be prevented. Relate what you find to what you think.

ANALYZING AND ORGANIZING THE MATERIAL

At this point you should take a mental inventory of your available material. You have your original notes as well as your file of ideas for speechmaking, the trial outline that guided your investigation, and the memoranda you made during your reading, observing, and interviewing. If your inventory reveals a need for further information, you should fill in the gaps; but if you have gathered material systematically, you should now have an abundance of evidence, details, and illustrations for every heading and subheading in your trial outline. You may enlarge and revise your outline to provide for developments you did not foresee. You probably have some material you will not use.

ANALYSIS A CONTINUING PROCESS

The analysis and organization of your speech begin as you choose your topic and discover material. As the prospective speech takes form, you make certain decisions affecting the final structure. When you make your trial outline, you indicate possible divisions of your speech. The trial outline is thus roughly comparable to an architect's preliminary sketch of a floor plan. Just as the architect abandons the preliminary sketch in favor of a more accurate working drawing, so the speaker proceeds from the key-word trial outline to the more accurate complete-sentence analysis.

Confusion sometimes arises from the use of the single term *outline* to describe a variety of types having different functions. In this book the preliminary listing of key words or phrases is called the *outline*. The logical setting forth of the material in sentence form, with a statement, divisions, and subdivisions, is called the *analysis*. The final arrangement of the material, showing the title, the introduction, the body, and the conclusion, is called the *plan*.

PRELIMINARY ANALYSIS

Analysis is essentially self-questioning. In discovering your material, you have asked these questions: (1) What material do I have? (2) Do I have all I need? (3) Is it systematically arranged and coordinated?

For further orientation, you may ask yourself another series of questions:

WHY SHOULD THIS MATTER BE DISCUSSED? The circumstances that make your topic timely should give point to your analysis. If a specific plan for governmental reorganization has been offered, that plan, rather than governmental reorganization in general, should direct your thinking.

WHAT IS GENERALLY KNOWN ABOUT THIS FIELD? Popular impressions about your topic should help you in considering its various aspects. The reports about county poorhouses and the stories told about the treatment of the aged should give you an approach to an explanation of old-age insurance.

WHAT IS THE HISTORICAL BACKGROUND? A knowledge of the origin and history of a problem will orient your thinking. An acquaintance with the history of the press will help you organize your ideas about censorship.

WHAT ARE THE AREAS OF KNOWLEDGE INVOLVED? The departmentalizing of knowledge has tended to limit our concepts. The improvement of the American diet is not solely a problem in home economics; it touches on chemistry, biology, agriculture, economics, government, and sociology. Although you could not discuss all of these areas in a single short talk, your knowledge of the range and complexity of the problem would qualify you to speak intelligently.

WHAT IS THE PRESENT STATE OF THE DISCUSSION? The current state of public opinion on your topic should affect your treatment of it. If you are analyzing material on labor problems, the public reaction to recent strikes should influence your analysis.

WHAT TERMS MUST BE DEFINED? Defining terms at the outset avoids confusion. If you are to tell your audience how to build a house, you may need to check your understanding of *joist, façade,* and *cornice.* If you are to argue in favor of changing the immigration laws, you should know the precise meaning of *citizen, alien, quota,* and *naturalization.*

WHAT CONCESSIONS MUST BE MADE?   Progress in analysis and organization depends largely on distinguishing between essential ideas and those
that may be safely admitted, waived, or conceded. In defending the
achievements of labor unions, you might need to waive consideration of
the constitutionality of certain legislation, to concede that certain unions
were once infiltrated by communists, and to admit that some union practices have been contrary to the public interest. You are thus free to concentrate on the remaining issues basic to your defense of the unions.

THE COMPLETE-SENTENCE ANALYSIS

In proceeding with the analysis you will need to ask:

- What is the statement?
- What are the divisions?
- What are the subdivisions?

The answers to these questions, properly phrased, will give you the approved means of setting forth your ideas for examination—the complete-
sentence analysis.

Although the short, descriptive phrases of the trial outline are suitable
for the preliminary purpose of classifying the materials of your speech,
they are not adequate to prevent confusion in your thinking. To check
the relevancy of ideas, you should make a sentence analysis consisting
of a statement with its divisions and subdivisions.

Statement

The first essential of organization is to determine your statement, the
formal phrasing of your central idea—not, as inexperienced speakers
sometimes suppose, the writing of an introduction. You should leave the
preparation of the introduction to the last, when you will know what
you have to introduce. Moreover, the introduction is not a part of the
analysis, but a means of adapting the speech to the audience (and, accordingly, is discussed in detail in Chapter 4). The statement is the
key to your analysis and must be completed before any other part of the
work can be undertaken profitably.

Phrasing the statement.   Since the statement is the key to your whole
speech, you should make it as definite as you can. Consider first the
general purpose you wish to accomplish with your topic. Ask yourself,
With what idea do I want to entertain, to impress, to inform, or to persuade my listeners in this speech? The answer to this question in the
form of a complete sentence will be your statement. For example:

- The college professor may be naive in fields outside his specialty.
- Benjamin Franklin was the first American.

- The majority of the native inhabitants of the Malay archipelago belong to two races.
- Medical care for everybody should be a responsibility of the government.

Your specific, as well as your general, purpose should control your statement. Instead of saying, "The need for safety in industry has increased," when your specific purpose is to persuade your hearers to protect themselves, you should phrase your statement, *The workers in this plant should use the prescribed safety equipment.* If your specific purpose is to persuade your hearers to seek legislative action, your statement should be, *Every citizen should urge his assemblyman to vote for the bill to increase safety in industry.* Similarly, instead of saying, "The federal government should adopt a plan of subsidized housing," when your specific purpose is to persuade your listeners to obtain better homes for themselves, you may say, *You should support the pending housing bill.* If your specific purpose is to persuade party leaders to push one particular plan, your statement should be, *The Senate plan for federal housing deserves immediate enactment.*

Testing the statement. Your statement, supremely important in your organization, should meet exacting tests. It should be (1) complete, (2) declarative, (3) affirmative, (4) purposive, (5) functional, (6) unified, (7) limited, (8) clear, (9) direct, (10) concise, (11) objective, and (12) accurate. Time devoted to testing your statement will be well spent.

COMPLETENESS. Use a sentence, not a fragment. Say, *The need for an efficient traffic system has increased,* not "The increased need for an efficient traffic system."

DECLARATION. Use an assertion, not a question. Say, *The United Nations should control all nuclear weapons,* not "Should the United Nations control all nuclear weapons?" Even for a speech of inquiry, the statement should be a declaration. For example, *There are advantages and disadvantages to having the United Nations control all nuclear weapons.*

AFFIRMATION. Make your statement affirmative. Say, *Our state should adopt the unicameral legislature,* rather than "Our state should not reject the unicameral legislature." Affirming a negative is a difficult and confusing task. Hence the speaker should find a wording that will permit him to make a positive attack on his problem.

PURPOSE. Determine whether your statement is consistent with your purpose to entertain, to impress, to inform, or to persuade. Word it to suggest a theme, to establish a fact, to justify a conclusion, or to defend a policy. If your purpose is to inform, say *The technique of examining includes three recent developments,* not "The system of final examinations should be revised."

FUNCTION.   Make the statement for an informative speech susceptible of systematic treatment. Say, *The manufacture of rubber involves three phases,* not "The manufacture of rubber is a single process." The statement for a persuasive speech should be open to proof—that is, in itself it should not be obviously true or false. You should be able to prove it either probably true or probably false. Say, *Television should be owned and operated by the federal government,* not "Television is supervised by the Federal Communications Commission."

UNITY.   Present one idea, not two or more. Say, *The federal government should adopt a plan of reducing taxes,* not "The federal government should adopt a plan of reducing taxes, and the state governments should cooperate in it."

LIMITATION.   Limit the scope of your statement. Say, *The United Nations policy in the Congo is justified,* rather than "The United Nations policy is justified."

CLARITY.   Avoid general and ambiguous terms. Say, *Non-Communist nations should form reciprocal trade agreements,* not "Somebody should do something about Communism."

DIRECTNESS.   Make your statement definite and direct. Say, *The team should win the game next Saturday,* not "It is necessary to say a few words about the athletic situation."

CONCISENESS.   Word your statement concisely. Say, *This anniversary marks a decade of achievement,* not "This anniversary, the tenth in a series, represents a period of progress toward a goal yet to be realized."

OBJECTIVITY.   Exclude unnecessary personal references. Say, *Grover Cleveland was a great president,* not "I want you to know what a great president I think Grover Cleveland was."

FAIRNESS.   Avoid prejudicial terms. Say, *Socialist tendencies should be discouraged,* not "These un-American socialist tendencies should be discouraged." Any biased wording will usually be obvious, will arouse the hostility of many listeners, and will damage the speaker's cause at the outset.

To make a sound analysis, you must begin with a statement that conforms to a standard of accuracy. To include in the statement a question-begging term is self-defeating.

Changing the statement.   At the outset your statement may have been vague. As your study proceeds, your thinking should become sharper. Perhaps you began, *The treatment of prisoners should be more severe.* You became convinced by your study of the problem that your phrasing should be, *The treatment of prisoners should be more intelligent.* If your investigation reveals that the material you have collected does not support the statement you intended to use, you should rephrase it to express your modified point of view.

Divisions

After you have formulated your statement, you should list the principal ideas that support it. These ideas, called divisions, develop your thought structure. Put them into clear, complete-sentence form, and check them thoroughly.

Wording of divisions. Parallel wording of divisions is desirable because a ready checking of relations between units is simple. Variety in style is recommended in the composition of a speech, but consistency should be the guiding principle in analysis.

Relation of divisions to statement. Since each division is a part of the general idea presented in the statement, your sentence analysis enables you to check the relation of the divisions to the statement. Unless you keep this relation constantly in mind, you may find that you have gone on a tangent in one or more of your divisions.

Sometimes an inexperienced student will prepare a first draft of his analysis with only one division. Since a division into one part is an anomaly, he needs to re-examine his material. The difficulty may be that he has merely repeated his statement in different terms instead of dividing it. If the second version of the statement is more explicit than the first, it is preferable and should replace the first. Any subdivisions will then become divisions. The first anomalous draft might run as follows:

STATEMENT

An economic community of non-Communist nations is necessary.

DIVISIONS AND SUBDIVISIONS

I. An economic community of non-Communist nations should be established.
   A. It will bring the free world closer together.
   B. It will bring the world to a higher standard of living.

The anomalous first draft might be amended and corrected as follows:

STATEMENT

An economic community of non-Communist nations should be established.

DIVISIONS AND SUBDIVISIONS

I. It will bring the free nations of the world closer together.
   A. It will create conditions of mutual advantage.
   B. It will settle difficulties in the marketplace.
II. It will bring to the world a higher standard of living.
   A. It will encourage more efficient production.

    B. It will release new resources.

    C. It will open new markets.

    D. It will stimulate legitimate competition.

Subdivisions

You should find the subdivisions in the way that you have found the divisions. If your analysis is elaborate, the subdivisions may present general ideas requiring more development in further subdivisions. If your analysis is simple, the subdivisions will embody the development needed to make the divisions clear or logical. When much explanation or reasoning is required, the support may be carried to the fourth step or even further. Each step in the division is indicated by a different kind of symbol as shown in the analyses on pages 57–60. The first step is indicated by Roman numerals I, II, III; the second step by capital letters A, B, C; the third step by Arabic numerals 1, 2, 3; and the fourth step by lower-case letters a, b, c.

For the informative speech, you should ask, What ideas will develop each of the divisions? These subdivisions will bear the same relation to the divisions that the divisions bear to the statement. In this way you may carry the analysis through as many steps as necessary.

For the persuasive speech, you should ask, What reasons support each of the divisions? These reasons are the subdivisions. You may test the logical relation by inserting a causal connective after the division. You may carry the analysis as far as necessary.

A METHOD OF ANALYSIS

In method, the expository and persuasive analyses have much in common. Each has two elements: (1) a carefully constructed statement to be elaborated or proved, and (2) the development of that statement into divisions and subdivisions. In format, expository and persuasive analyses are subject to the same rule.

The Informative Analysis

Suppose that a student of speechmaking finds that the topic best suited to him and to his audience, as well as to the other factors involved, concerns the construction of a systematic sentence analysis for an informative speech. After he has fulfilled the preliminary obligation to prepare, he is ready to analyze the subject systematically. What does he do? His first problem is to phrase and test the statement.

First step: Statement. After studying the material, he decides to explain that "There are four steps in making a sentence analysis."

Second step: Divisions. Each division of the analysis is directly related to the statement. By answering the question "How?" or "In what ways?" you may discover the divisions:

I. The first step is determining the statement.
II. The second step is determining the divisions.
III. The third step is determining the subdivisions.
IV. The fourth step is checking for the minimum essentials of the analysis.

Third step: Subdivisions. The analysis moves from the general to the less general, or specific. Each step in the subdivisions makes the thinking more detailed; an examination of the completed analysis will show the progression of ideas. In the first division below, for example, the subdivisions are carried two steps: *determining the statement* and *testing for accuracy*. The second division is divided into two, the third division into three, and the fourth division into eight steps. The subdivisions are variously divided, as the subject matter requires.

SYSTEMATIC SENTENCE ANALYSIS FOR SPEECHMAKING

STATEMENT

There are four steps in making a sentence analysis.

DIVISIONS AND SUBDIVISIONS

I. The first step is determining the statement.
   A. The statement is worded to indicate the speaker's purpose.
      1. He may wish to persuade his audience.
      2. He may wish to inform his audience.
      3. He may wish to impress his audience.
      4. He may wish to entertain his audience.
   B. The statement is tested for accuracy.
      1. It must be a complete sentence.
      2. It must be an assertion.
      3. It must be affirmative.
      4. It must be consistent with the speaker's purpose.
      5. It must be consistent with its own function.
      6. It must be confined to one idea.
      7. It must be sufficiently limited.
      8. It must be clear.
      9. It must be direct.
     10. It must be concise.
     11. It must be objective.
     12. It must be fair.

II. The second step is determining the divisions.
   A. The divisions are the principal ideas supporting the statement.
   B. The divisions differ according to the speaker's purpose.
      1. The divisions may be expository.
         a. They may follow a time-order development.
         b. They may follow a space-order development.
         c. They may be of the classification type.
         d. They may be of the specific-instance type.
         e. They may indicate similarities.
         f. They may indicate dissimilarities.
      2. The divisions may be persuasive.
         a. They may express evaluations.
         b. They may express reasons.
         c. They may exclude other arguments.
         d. They may indicate necessity.
         e. They may indicate practicability.
         f. They may demonstrate principles and make applications.
      3. The divisions may employ combinations of sentences expository and persuasive.

III. The third step is determining the subdivisions.
   A. The subdivisions embody the development needed to make the divisions clear or logical.
   B. The subdivisions may embody the development needed to make further subdivisions clear or logical.
   C. The relationship of the subdivisions to the divisions is the same as that of the divisions to the statement.
      1. They may be expository.
      2. They may be persuasive.
      3. They may employ combinations of sentences expository and persuasive.

IV. The fourth step is checking for the minimum essentials of the analysis.
   A. Except for the two headings STATEMENT and DIVISIONS AND SUBDIVISIONS, only complete sentences must be used.
   B. Each sentence must contain only one essential idea.
   C. Each division must directly support the statement.
   D. All subdivisions must directly support the division or subdivision under which they stand.
   E. Divisions or subdivisions bearing symbols of the same order must hold an equal relationship to the sentence they clarify or support.
   F. The use of symbols must be consistent.
   G. Second and third lines of a single division or subdivision must be indented in block form.

    H. Symbols of the same order must be placed directly under each other.

The Persuasive Analysis

The foregoing analysis is designed for an informative speech. It assumes an audience willing to hear the speaker without prejudice. In many respects the persuasive analysis does not differ from the informative analysis, but in one respect it is quite different: it is designed for a topic that is or may be controversial, one on which the audience may require evidence and reasoning beyond information. Whereas the analysis for the informative speech may answer only the question "How?" the analysis for the persuasive speech may have to answer, in addition, the question "Why?"

Suppose a student hopes to persuade an audience of university students that general education is important. Having discovered, tested, and partially prepared his topic, he is now ready to analyze and organize his material.

First step: Statement.   In determining the statement for a persuasive analysis, the speaker must first make up his own mind. As soon as he has taken a position, he must frame a statement making that position unmistakably clear. He completes the first step in his analysis by deciding to support the statement, "Professional men should complete the requirements for the A.B. degree before taking up specialized studies." Every sentence in the body of the analysis has a definite, logical relation to this statement.

Second step: Divisions.   In a persuasive analysis, the reasoning of the speaker is the reverse of that by which he formed his opinion. In his first steps of preparation he examined facts to see what conclusion should be drawn from them. Now, having reached his conclusion, he surveys the support he has for it. He clarifies the reasons and presents them as the divisions of his analysis. He now asks himself, what are the reasons why this statement is true? Why should professional men complete the requirements for the A.B. degree before taking up specialized studies? After reflection, he answers these questions with two reasons:

  I. The current trend in specialized education is to require more general education in the early college years.

 II. Requirements for the A.B. degree permit the development of a field of concentration.

The foregoing reasons form the divisions in the analysis. Each one answers the question "Why?" with reference to the statement. The student should test each division for logical relation by making it a subordinate clause connected with the statement: *Professional men should complete the requirements for the A.B. degree before taking up specialized studies,* because the current trend in specialized education is to require more general education in the early college years; or again, *Professional men should complete the requirements for the A.B. degree before taking up specialized studies,* because requirements for the A.B. degree permit the development of a field of concentration.

Third step: Subdivisions. The third step is to put the question, What reasons support each of these divisions? The speaker finds the reasons for the first division to be:

A. Engineering schools recently have increased their requirements in the liberal arts.
B. Journalism schools recently have increased their requirements in the liberal arts.
C. Universities are stressing the need for more general education.
D. Men in public life have urged the need of broader training.

Any reason not found, on testing, to bear a logical relation to the division it supports is either irrelevant or ambiguous. The four reasons should be coordinate; together they constitute the support for the division.

The same procedure will serve to work out the reasons for the other divisions and also to carry the analysis another step—that is, to find the reasons to support all of the subdivisions. This process may be continued as many steps as necessary to establish the statement.[12]

MINIMUM ESSENTIALS OF ANALYSIS

The following items should be checked in every sentence analysis:

COMPLETE SENTENCES.   Every item following a symbol must be a complete sentence.

UNITY.   Each assertion is single—that is, it contains only one essential idea, not two or more.

STRUCTURE.   Supporting ideas, if divided, must have at least two parts.

RELATION.   All the divisions directly support the statement either as explanations or as reasons.

CLARIFICATION.   All subdivisions clarify or support the divisions under which they stand.

COORDINATION.   Divisions are coordinate. Subdivisions within the same division or subdivision are coordinate when they bear symbols of the same order.

---

[12] Examples of the complete-sentence analysis will be found in: Wilbur E. Gilman, Bower Aly, and Hollis L. White, *An Introduction to Speaking,* New York: The Macmillan Company, 1962, pp. 26 and 27, 33, 39, 67 and 68, 81, 92 and 93, 102, 112–114. Copyright 1962 by The Macmillan Company.

CONSISTENCY. The use of symbols is consistent: first Roman numerals, then capital letters, then Arabic numerals, then small letters (I, A, 1, a). If more steps are needed, the next symbol should be the Roman numeral in parentheses, and so on.

INDENTATION. All second and third lines should be indented evenly in block form in order that all of the symbols will stand out clearly.

PLACEMENT. Symbols of the same kind should be kept directly under each other so that there will be no possibility of confusing divisions with subdivisions.

THE USES OF ANALYSIS

If your analysis succeeds only in eliminating rambling and disordered thought, your time will be well spent. But analysis, more than a technique of avoiding incoherence, is a process of choosing, testing, rejecting, and restating your ideas until you are confident that they are sound and closely related to each other. Your analysis is your thought structure for your speech.

3 EXPOSITION AND PERSUASION:
Forms and Principles

To be truly eloquent is to speak to the purpose.

—Hugh Blair

In former times no great distinction was made between informing and persuading. Today, however, the distinction is common, and certain other arts of discourse are also considered as ancillary to the primary concern with persuasion. To make this distinction between informing and persuading is sometimes difficult. As Herbert J. C. Grierson observed:

> In some fields instruction passes at once into persuasion. In dealing with ethical, religious, and political topics, writers [and speakers] instruct as a rule in order that they may persuade.[1]

INFORMING

The audience—always the end and object of the speech—determines whether the speaker must go beyond exposition of the case to gain their adherence to his proposition. The problem of exposition versus persuasion may thus be considered as one of adaptation. Yet, in learning to speak, students and teachers often find useful the distinction between the informative speech, in which the audience requires only demonstration, and the persuasive speech, in which the audience may require extensive proof.

[1] *Rhetoric and English Composition*, Edinburgh: Oliver and Boyd Ltd., 1945, p. 25.

Systematic study should reveal the leading characteristics of informing and the principal obstacles to its accomplishment, as well as its rationale and its methods.

THE CHARACTERISTICS OF INFORMING

Five essential characteristics of the art and practice of informing serve to describe it. It is distinctive, prevalent, universally applicable, significant, and difficult.

Distinctiveness

The distinction between informing and persuading is often enforced by time, place, and prevailing opinion. The element of controversy distinguishes persuasion: a speech of information immediately becomes one of persuasion when the speaker is confronted with opposition either from another speaker or from members of his audience. Information is conveyed only when the audience is receptive. A speaker who talks today about the circulation of the blood assumes that the principle is accepted. Since no prejudices exist, he proceeds with complete freedom to report the result of scientific inquiry. Before Harvey discovered the circulation of the blood, however, the same speech might have endangered the reputation, if not the actual person, of the speaker; anyone who seriously proposed that the blood circulated was obviously silly.

Sometimes the speaker must remove prejudice before sympathetic understanding is possible, or he may need to entertain his hearers in order to gain their attention. But these necessities do not alter the distinctive function of informing once the audience is ready to receive information. Circumstances may determine the purpose a speech serves with some or all of the hearers. An explanation of freshman rules may be important information to entering students, but it would be entertainment to alumni. A speech on the civil service may be informative to new government employees, but persuasive to career-minded seniors in high schools.

Prevalence

Speaking to inform is a common type of discourse. At every turn, information is the mainspring of thought and action. Airlines, factories, business offices, and governments establish agencies to supply information. Some professions are devoted almost exclusively to informing; in no profession can the function be neglected. Whether patients get well may depend upon how fully a nurse understands the doctor's directions about food, medicine, and care. Whether an astronaut completes his mission may depend on how well he understands the instructions received from the ground stations. Whether an army wins a battle may depend upon how well the soldiers understand the orders of their officers. Information must be provided for everyday problems; it must also be transmitted to oncoming generations. Civilization depends in part upon the ability of one generation to convey to the next all that it has learned about highly complicated processes in science, art, and technology. Our elaborate systems of education depend upon skills in the transmission of knowledge.

Applicability

The techniques of informing apply to all kinds of knowledge. Whether the subject is momentous or trivial, simple or complex, limited or comprehensive, the principles of informing are used in reporting facts, observations, ideas, opinions, and theories for the evident benefit of others. Informing is thus a means essential to human knowledge and activity. Yet the process is not a mere adjunct to government, law, or medicine; within its own right it is a discipline governed by principles that may be applied to any ideas whatsoever. If a speaker is to inform other people about the principles of psychiatry, he must know not only psychiatry but also the art of informing. Some men presumably understand a body of subject matter, but they do not know how to explain it to others.

Significance

Those who deprecate knowledge for its own sake often say, "Oh, that is mere information." They are right to say that much of what people know may not be strictly useful in practical affairs. Knowing who was king of England in 1474 or who first made papyrus may be of little value to most people. But the process of informing does not deal merely with isolated facts. Concerned chiefly with imparting coherent information, it is thus one of the most highly significant of all the arts employed by man, and it grows in significance as society becomes more and more complex. Schools are foolish indeed to identify the process with such topics as "How to Make Chocolate Fudge." Simple exercises may be useful as first trials for children; they are not suitable for adults.

Difficulty

To the naive person, nothing seems easier than saying what he means. To the mature person, however, deciding exactly what he means may present a formidable task. "Do you understand me?" Robert Louis Stevenson once wrote to a friend. "God knows, I should think it highly improbable." The talkative lady was wiser than she knew when she exclaimed, "How can I know what I think until I've heard what I've said?" Speaking or writing often helps a person determine what he means.

Since the speaker must not only clarify his knowledge but also communicate it to a group of hearers with varying capacities for understanding, the task of informing becomes difficult. Even when the topic is closely related to the experience of the listeners, making it clear to them requires skillful application of the principles of informing. But when the topic is remote or involved, choosing the appropriate technique will require the closest study. Driving a locomotive may be explained by systematic comparison and contrast with driving an automobile, but the application of more elaborate principles of informing may be required for explaining the mechanism of the Diesel engine.

THE RATIONALE OF INFORMING

Like any other discipline, informing is subject to certain basic principles. These principles form a rationale that includes classification and development.

Classification

An understanding of a means for examining and classifying ideas is desirable, if not indispensable, in transmitting information. In speaking to inform, as in any other meaningful discourse, the first requirement is an order and system appropriate to the subject. The speaker should so thoroughly understand the subject he wishes to present that he can see it in its various elements. While comprehending it as a whole, he should also see it in its several parts; and he should be able to classify them. Poor informative speaking results from disordered thinking; good informative speaking is a consequence of the division of a problem into its elements. Such, for example, was the method employed by Huxley in his lecture "On a Piece of Chalk."

Classification should not be considered in theory and neglected in practice. Every experienced speaker knows the necessity for dividing his material into units that can be taken up one at a time. In an interesting exposition entitled "The Geography of the Pacific," E. S. C. Smith made the following analysis:

In discussing the islands of the Pacific we find that we must at once separate them into two categories, first, those islands which may be said to be continental in character, and second, those which are true oceanic islands.[2]

In his discussion of meaning, I. A. Richards began at once with the following division into parts:

It is plain that most human utterances and nearly all articulate speech can be profitably regarded from four points of view. Four aspects can be easily distinguished. Let us call them *sense, feeling, tone,* and *intention.*[3]

[2] *Vital Speeches,* VIII, 283, Feb. 15, 1942. Copyright 1942 by City News Publishing Company.

[3] *Practical Criticism,* New York: Harcourt, Brace and Company, Inc., 1929, p. 180. Copyright 1929 by Harcourt, Brace and Company, Inc.

In an address entitled "How Can We Stop Rising Prices?" Robert A. Taft analyzed his material as follows:

Remedy Number One is to cut expenses. . . .

Remedy Number Two is to increase taxes. . . .

Remedy Number Three is to persuade the people to save the additional income they are receiving and to invest it in government bonds. . . .

Remedy Number Four seems to me a determined attempt to stabilize prices voluntarily. . . .

Remedy Number Five should be an attempt to stabilize wages so that during the emergency period they do not increase faster than the cost of living. . . .

Remedy Number Six is to control the inflation of private credit and currency. . . .

Remedy Number Seven [is] . . . compulsory price control as embodied in the bill now before Congress.[4]

Development

After the elements of the process or the problem are classified, the speaker seeks a unifying idea that will enable him to select and fuse the relevant parts. Classification and development enable both speaker and listener to view the topic as a whole. In building a unified whole, the speaker should consider what underlying principle can be found, what theme runs through all the parts, or what common idea binds the segments together. He develops the material as he gains perspective on it, just as a critic judges a painting by standing off to study it.

Sometimes the relationship between the parts is set forth throughout the speech. James F. Byrnes used this method of development in his speech on United States policy in Germany. The unifying principle of his speech to disclose American plans and policies to his audience of Allied and German officials was revealed in such assertions as:

We have learned that peace and well-being are indivisible and that our peace and well-being cannot be purchased at the price of peace or the well-being of any other country.

We intend to continue our interest in the affairs of Europe and of the world.

What we want is a lasting peace.

. . . the United States is not unmindful of the responsibility resting upon it and its major allies to maintain and enforce peace under the law.

. . . the United States will not agree to the taking from Germany of greater reparations than was provided by the Potsdam agreement.

[4] *Vital Speeches,* VIII, 90, Nov. 15, 1941. Copyright 1941 by City News Publishing Company.

We favor the economic unification of Germany.

The principal purposes of the military occupation were and are to demilitarize and denazify Germany, but not to raise artificial barriers to the efforts of the German people to resume their peace-time economic life.

It is our view that the German people should now be permitted and helped to make the necessary preparations for setting up of a democratic German government. . . .

As long as an occupation force is required in Germany, the Army of the United States will be a part of that occupation force.

The American people hope to see peaceful, democratic Germans become and remain free and independent.

The United States cannot relieve Germany from the hardships inflicted upon her which the war leaders started. But the United States has no desire to increase those hardships. . . .[5]

Sometimes a speaker begins with a development of his ideas as Brander Matthews did in his lecture on "American Character":

. . . we find this Frenchman alleging, first, that we Americans care chiefly for making money; second, that we are hostile to art and to all forms of beauty; and thirdly, that we are devoid of ideals. These three allegations may well be considered, one by one. . . .[6]

A good development contributes to the conclusion of a speech. It provides a survey and review, as Charles W. Eliot demonstrated in his lecture on "Five American Contributions to Civilization." Near the close he said:

These five contributions to civilization—peace-keeping, religious tolerance, the development of manhood suffrage, the welcoming of newcomers, and the diffusion of well-being—I hold to have been eminently characteristic of our country. . . .[7]

OBSTACLES TO INFORMING

Some obstacles to informing exist in the limitations of the hearers, others in the intention of the speaker, the novelty and complexity of the subject, and the limitations of language. Recognition of these natural and artificial impediments should help the speaker to eliminate them, to avoid them, or to adapt his material in accordance with them.

[5] *The New York Times*, September 7, 1946, p. 5. Copyright by *The New York Times*. Reprinted by permission.
[6] Alexander M. Drummond and Everett Lee Hunt, eds., *Persistent Questions in Public Discussion*, New York: Century Company, 1924, p. 27.
[7] *Ibid.*, p. 24.

Ignorance

A formidable barrier to the conveying of information is the ignorance of the hearer, or of the speaker, or of both. For a college senior to talk to an audience of high-school freshmen about Spinoza's metaphysics would be unprofitable. The hearers would doubtless lack the background to comprehend an involved metaphysical problem. Even a mature audience would require a well-planned explanation. If the speaker himself were only beginning to understand metaphysics, the likelihood of his informing any audience would be slight. To be competent to inform, the speaker needs a reserve of knowledge. In order to know his topic in its relation to a whole subject and in relation to the information the audience already possesses, he needs a comprehensive understanding. To know Spinoza, he should know the history of philosophy, not just Spinoza's own treatises. To popularize Spinoza to an uninformed audience would be difficult even for an exceptionally able student of human experience.

The thoughts and even the vocabulary of one generation are not those of another. The high school student has difficulty explaining to his parents not only his social affairs but even his scholastic problems. He assumes information they do not have.

In a day when almost no fact is indispensable to everyone, a speaker cannot be sure what knowledge his hearers hold concerning his topic. A distinguished audience of botanists, for example, may know little about the history of art in the Renaissance. Renowned statesmen may be novices in the field of entomology.

Stupidity

A primary fact about the human race is the magnitude of individual differences. The ability to learn is not the attribute of any single race, nor is any people entirely free from an inheritance of stupidity. The problem of the speaker is to inform the unintelligent without boring the intelligent. He must be both clear and interesting. He must use imagery that is familiar to all. The need for simplification and illustration is greater than he may assume.

Indifference

Indifference may be a more difficult obstacle than stupidity, because it involves an unwillingness to listen. The individual who says, "Oh, that isn't worth knowing," cannot be informed until he is persuaded that the facts are worth having. To interest an indifferent audience in a topic, the speaker must consider fully the approach, the choice of principles, and the method of treatment. Some students who were indifferent to physics changed their attitude when they discovered that the atomic bomb is an application of nuclear fission. To overcome indifference, the speaker may need to demonstrate that the supposedly impractical subject is practical, the supposedly unfamiliar problem is familiar, or the supposedly unimportant topic is vital.

Inertia

Lack of necessity for information is a great deterrent to keen interest in the speaker's explanation. In peacetime, prospective bomber crews may not heed the elaborate directions given them, whereas in wartime they listen intently because they know that they will be called upon immediately to take a bomber aloft for active combat. Their lives depend upon their knowledge. The speaker who overcomes inertia makes his listeners understand the value of the information he presents.

Beliefs

The human race has an inheritance of superstitious beliefs. If the audience and the speaker hold superstitions in common, technical difficulties in imparting information may be avoided; the speaker and the audience are mistaken in the same ways. When the speaker and his audience do not share the same beliefs, however, a problem of informing arises. In giving information, the speaker may need to take into account habits, customs, and opinions based on beliefs. An audience of farmers who have planted their crops in traditional ways may have to relinquish fixed beliefs before they are ready to receive information about balanced farming.

Taboos

Among every people certain ideas, subjects, and words are forbidden. In the Victorian era polite people did not use the word *leg;* the proper word was *limb.* Until recently the taboo on venereal diseases hampered physicians in their efforts to inform the public. What is acceptable depends upon the circumstances, the community, and the specific audience. Age, sex, and education; inhibitions and repressions; travel and experience —all shape mental attitudes. Discovering what the audience considers proper may be a major problem in the giving of information.

Complexity

Because they are abstract, novel, or technical, some subjects are so complex that they demand the speaker's best efforts. Topics from mathematics, semantics, or electronics may be simple for the expert, but they are difficult for many listeners. Simplification and clarification will challenge the speaker's ingenuity.

Unavailability

Because of remote location or of restrictions placed on them, sources for some topics are not available. Other sources are so technical that effective use requires too long a time; still others do not provide the necessary facts. The constantly increasing store of knowledge is useless to the speaker unless he can determine quickly what information is available and where to find it. The physician discussing multiple sclerosis would know that the cure has not been found. He could give information only on how to treat the disease.

Wishful Thinking

None are so blind as those who will not see. No matter how clearly a speaker demonstrates the validity of his inquiry, those who are opposed to his conclusions may be unwilling to understand them. On the other hand, a pleasant hope is easier to believe than a mournful expectation. "Everything is going to be all right" are words that may deceive speakers and audiences as well as the makers of polls. The bearer of bad news is seldom welcome. Furthermore, speakers are themselves subject to wishful thinking. They may not realize that they are coloring the facts and adding to the difficulties of conveying accurate, reasonable, and sensible reports.

Vested Interest

The interests of the speaker may impede the conveying of accurate information. One who talks about safety legislation may find his inquiry colored and his report biased by his ownership of shares in a mine. Human beings find difficulty in coming to conclusions which would react to their own disadvantage. Yet information is constantly being conveyed by persons who have a stake in the outcome of their reports.

Censorship

Even in free countries some restrictions are placed on the release of information, especially in time of war. Furthermore, standards of taste and reasons of safety may require the speaker to be discreet. On the other hand, what passes for information may be propaganda. The facts may be distorted, exaggerated, minimized, or withheld. The speaker giving a factual report on the relations between labor and management may have difficulty in obtaining information because one side or the other does not want publicity; or he may be misled by the propaganda of both sides.

Imperfections of Language

Language itself is an imperfect instrument for stimulating and conveying thought. We have not created new words as rapidly as we have created new objects. Frequently, therefore, an old word for something new is a makeshift. The word *speech*, now used to designate a field of study including voice, articulation, pronunciation, interpretation, dramatics, public speaking, discussion, debate, rhetoric, and oratory, basically means the faculty of uttering articulate sounds or words to express thoughts. Since the new meaning has not become universally known, the term may need definition when used in the new sense.

The designation of the same object with different words in different parts of the English-speaking world is sometimes confusing. What the British call a *lorry*, Americans call a *truck;* and what the British call a *wireless*, Americans call a *radio. Lumber* means *timber* in the United States, but in England it means *discarded furniture.*

The various languages men employ further complicate the process of informing. In the Western world the word *democracy* means self-government, but in Russia it means something else. Translation must be supplemented with interpretation. Time and again a translator can find no English equivalent for a French word. The German tongue is the German mind, and the translation of a German speech into English may be like an orchestra concert without the string section.

At times the English language has so many words that the choice is confusing. Choosing among *similarity, resemblance, likeness, similitude, semblance, affinity, approximation, parallelism,* or *agreement* requires a nice discrimination.

Unfortunately, words tend to become stereotyped, so that the glib speaker may utter fiery nothings. Such terms as *liberty, justice, free enterprise*, and *human rights* are used so loosely as to be almost meaningless. Without definition, they do not convey exact information.

Finding the word that expresses identical meaning for both speaker and listener is an indispensable requirement for accuracy. To say *scholar* when the context means *student* may distort the thought.

METHODS OF INFORMING

Having studied systematically the characteristics and the rationale of informing, and having recognized the obstacles to its accomplishment, the speaker may choose the method or methods best designed to make his presentation clear, interesting, and pointed. Some of the most useful methods are: (1) authority, (2) definition, (3) division, (4) narration, (5) description, (6) negation, (7) explication, (8) exemplification, (9) statistics, (10) interpretation, (11) criticism, (12) demonstration.

Authority

The simplest means of informing is to quote from an authoritative text; for many people the printed word carries such weight that the quotation is sufficient. The minister, for example, may make his meaning perfectly clear by a reading of the Scriptures.

In his informative address on "The Function of the Leader in Scholarship," Lane Cooper made much use of quotation from authority. At one point he said:

If a specific instance is needed of a man who was a great teacher because he was a great and tasteful scholar, we may take the Latinist who taught the foremost popularizer of classical literature in our day. Says Andrew Lang: "It was extraordinary to see the advance which all who cared to work made under Mr. Sellar's instructions; . . . the stimulus of competition was needless to all who were able to feel the inspiration of [his] educational influence. It is not easy for his biographer to refrain from saying that, having come to St. Andrews with no purpose of working, he left it in another mind, and that to Mr. Sellar he owes the impulse to busy himself with letters. . . . No less important than his work as an author, important as that is, was his example as a scholar, and as a man; his loyal, honorable, simple and generous life. . . . He loved his studies entirely for their own sake; he dwelt with the great of old because he enjoyed their company." [8]

Definition

Although an adequate definition is difficult to formulate, it is prerequisite to understanding. The difficulty frequently arises because the speaker must first define clearly the words employed to denote the objects themselves. The average audience would not understand *memory* defined as "the functional retention of any psychological modification of structural behavior resulting from the organism's activity, environment, or mnemonic processes." When William James gave his talk to the teachers at Cambridge, he provided a more helpful definition in the following terms:

Memory proper, or secondary memory as it might be styled, is the knowledge of a former state of mind after it has already once dropped from consciousness; or rather it is the knowledge of an event, or fact, of which meantime we have not been thinking, with the additional consciousness that we have thought or experienced it before. [9]

Definition is often used as a device not for gaining clarity but for making points, for presenting paradoxes, or even for misleading hearers. Many of the brilliant aphorisms of Oscar Wilde, James McNeill Whistler, George Bernard Shaw, and others depend for their brilliance upon an unexpected twist of definition. Ambrose Bierce, for example, in *The Devil's Dictionary*, defined *dictionary* as "a malevolent literary device for cramping the growth of a language and making it hard and inelastic."

---

[8] *Two Views of Education,* New Haven: Yale University Press, 1922, pp. 195–196. Copyright 1922 by Yale University Press.

[9] *Briefer Course in Psychology,* New York: Henry Holt and Company, 1930, p. 287. Copyright 1930 by Henry Holt and Company, Inc.

Discussion, according to Bierce, is "a method of confirming others in their errors." These definitions are obviously devices to expose perversions. But in more subtle cases definitions may be misleading—that is, they may not be an accurate representation of the object.

A good definition (1) should state the essential attributes of the object to be defined, (2) should avoid use of the name to be defined or any word synonymous with it, (3) should not be too broad or too narrow, but exactly equivalent to the class of objects defined, (4) should be expressed in readily understandable terms, (5) should be precise.

John G. Winant made considerable use of definition in his address on "Security for a People: A Creative Life of the Spirit." He said, in part:

> But what is security? . . . It is no abstraction too nebulous for definition. It is a making sure of something; and that something without which security is only an empty word—is a way of life and the means to its realization.
>
> Security for the people begins with bread and butter. An opportunity to earn a living, to be a member of the community, to have a part in the government, is fundamental. But a mere subsistence is no security for the American citizen. . . . Living should, as times go on, become more and more adequate to the expanding needs of a richer life. But security is more than a condition of material well-being. It is a state of mind, the antithesis of fear, the creative life of the spirit that enables men and women to face the future with glad hearts and free minds. It is the hopeful urge to provide, to build, to plan, to look ahead—to make the most of ourselves and our opportunities.[10]

Division

Following the divisions of the analysis, as retained in the synthesis, is a good method of development. A systematic treatment enables the listener to see where he has come from and where he is going. The method is especially helpful with a long or involved problem.

Since divisions often indicate groups of objects, they frequently involve classification. Sometimes subdivisions represent classifications even when the divisions do not.

A satisfactory division (1) should be made on the ground of difference fundamental to all members of the whole, (2) should be based on only one principle, (3) should consist of mutually exclusive groups, (4) should be so exhaustive that the groups, taken together, make the whole.

In his lecture on "Work," John Ruskin used divisions and subdivisions. His divisions of the industrious are:

- Between those who work and those who play.
- Between those who produce the means of life and those who consume them.

---

[10] Lew Sarett and William Trufant Foster, eds., *Modern Speeches on Basic Issues,* Boston: Houghton Mifflin Company, 1939, pp. 328–329. Copyright 1939 by City News Publishing Company.

- Between those who work with the head, and those who work with the hand.
- Between those who work wisely, and those who work foolishly.

Ruskin's subdivisions of his last division are three tests of wise work: (1) It is honest; (2) it is useful; and (3) it is cheerful.[11]

Narration

Sometimes the telling of a story will serve as a means of informing. A connected sequence of events involving people and places will unfold the information in vivid language that appeals to the imagination. When used with other methods of informing, it may provide needed relief because it holds attention easily. The narrative should clarify and develop either the central idea or a subordinate division. It should further the purpose of the speech and in no way distract from the idea being explained.

In showing the relation and importance of gaiety to the serious life of a scholar, Stuart Sherman, in a Phi Beta Kappa address, cites the case of Dr. Samuel Johnson, usually melancholy but extremely gay at times. He makes his point by quoting one of Boswell's stories:

One night [says Boswell] when Beauclerk and Langton had supped at a tavern in London, and sat till about three in the morning, it came into their heads to go and knock up Johnson, and see if they could prevail on him to join them in a ramble. They rapped violently at the door of his chambers in the Temple, till at last he appeared in his shirt with his little black wig on the top of his head, instead of a night-cap, and a poker in his hand, imagining, probably, that some ruffians were coming to attack him. When he discovered who they were, and was told their errand, he smiled, and with great good humour agreed to their proposal: *"What! is it you, you dogs! I'll have a frisk with you."*

And, as Sherman says, the great lexicographer, the author of the *Vanity of Human Wishes,* spent the rest of the night boating on the Thames and "frisking" through the city.[12]

Description

When a scene, a person, a feeling, or a reaction is needed to develop information, description is the method to be applied. It creates a vivid impression by appealing directly to the senses in concrete and colorful language related to the experience of the listeners. It is frequently combined with narration.

[11] Ashley H. Thorndike, ed., *Modern Eloquence,* New York: Modern Eloquence Corporation, 1923, Vol. VIII, pp. 334–357. Copyright 1923 by Modern Eloquence Corporation.

[12] "The Gaiety of Socrates," William T. Hastings, ed., *Man Thinking: Representative Phi Beta Kappa Orations, 1915–1959,* Ithaca, New York: Cornell University Press, 1962, p. 9. Copyright 1962 by the United Chapters of Phi Beta Kappa.

In explaining the meaning of the assertion "we live in a changing society" in respect to family life in America, Robert J. Havighurst, a professor of education, characterizes the home of a half-century ago. He describes the various rooms as they looked then and contrasts them with the rooms in our homes today. Of the parlor and the sitting room he says:

There was the parlor, always cold and clean and quiet, with an organ which was pumped with the feet, a hard horsehair sofa, and a photographic album. The sitting room was more cheerful, with its baseburner standing in the middle of the room on a metal sheet to protect the carpet, the coals glowing red-hot through the isinglass windows of the stove, the stove pipe going straight up through the ceiling to lend a little warmth to the bedroom above; the coal scuttle beside the stove, half full of coal, and garnished with nutshells and apple cores. On the library table a big kerosene lamp shedding a yellow glow, and the latest copies of *Harper's Bazaar* and the *Youth's Companion*. Beside the table a big rocking chair, in which mother rocked the baby to sleep, singing lullabies. And I almost forgot to mention the brick sewn up in a piece of carpet, and used as a doorstop.[13]

Negation

Since impediments to understanding are frequent, the speaker must sometimes tell an audience what a thing is not. In making clear what an automobile engine is, he may need first of all to explain its limitations —that is, what it cannot do or should not be expected to do. Wherever misconception is likely, the speaker should employ the special method of negation.

In his lecture on "The Keys to Success," Edward William Bok used negation as a method of informing. After a definition of success as accomplishment, he continued:

Nor must a young man compare himself with others or measure his success by theirs. It makes no difference how other men succeed. Their success is theirs; not yours. It matters nothing to me that Edison can invent the electric light and I can't; that Kipling can write a "Recessional" and I can't; that you can plead the law and I can't. . . .

Nor must young men get the idea that if a man is known he is a success. Reputation is not success. Many a man has achieved reputation without having achieved success. . . .[14]

Explication

Explication is the elaboration of a concept, usually by the presentation of details. It is sometimes combined with enumeration or repetition.

In his lecture on "The Spoken Word," William Jennings Bryan used

[13] *Vital Speeches*, XIV, 565, July 1, 1948.
[14] Ashley H. Thorndike, ed., *Modern Eloquence*, New York: Modern Eloquence Corporation, 1923, Vol. VIII, pp. 334–357. Copyright 1923 by Modern Eloquence Corporation.

explication with division, enumeration, and repetition to explain the
kinds and advantages of faith:

> We are told that without faith it is impossible to please God, and I may
> add that without faith it is impossible to meet the expectations of those who
> are most interested in you. Let me present this subject under four heads.
>
> First: You must have faith in yourselves. Not that you should carry con-
> fidence in yourselves to the point of displaying egotism, and yet egotism is not
> the worst possible fault. . . .
>
> Second: Have faith in mankind. . . . It is better to trust your fellowmen
> and be occasionally deceived than to be distrustful and live alone. . . .
>
> Third: If you are going to accomplish anything, in this country, you must
> have faith in your form of government, and there is every reason why you
> should have faith in it. . . .
>
> Fourth: The subject presents itself in another aspect. You must not only
> have faith in yourselves, in humanity, and in the form of government under
> which we live, but if you would do a great work, you must have faith in
> God. . . .[15]

The lecture deserves study for methods of making material clear and
interesting. Bryan's use of details shows how to develop each division
until it is fully explained.

Exemplification

Because examples make abstract and general ideas concrete and
specific, they help listeners to understand. The right example will clarify
a problem for any audience.

In his lecture on "Poetry and the People," Professor William J. Courthope used several examples to explain the close connection between
national life and national poetry. In speaking of the poetry of the
eighteenth century, he says:

> Does not the characteristic poetry of the period faithfully correspond with
> the political, religious, and social state of things? . . . The aristocratic prin-
> ciple inspires poems like the *Rape of the Lock,* the *Epistles* and *Satires* of Pope,
> and *The Essay on Man;* it is still strongly felt in such works as *The Deserted
> Village* and *The Travellers;* but it becomes pompous and grotesque in Dar-
> win's *Botanic Garden,* tame and mannered in *The Pleasures of Memory.* Here,
> too, we see that the decline of the Classic style in poetry is coincident with the
> decay of aristocratic supremacy which was terminated by the Reform Bill of
> 1832.[16]

The effectiveness of examples depends upon their suitability for the
audience. Since Professor Courthope was addressing an audience of stu-

[15] *Ibid.,* pp. 96–100.

[16] *Life in Poetry: Law in Taste,* London: Macmillan and Company, 1901, pp.
130–131. Copyright 1901 by Macmillan and Company, Ltd.

dents of literature in Oxford University, he could assume acquaintance with literary history and familiarity with outstanding works of poetry.

Statistics

Closely related to exemplification is the use of statistics. Stating a problem in terms of size or quantity sometimes helps the listener to understand it. In general, however, the speaker should use figures sparingly and, whenever possible, should present them in round numbers. Accompanying explanation is usually necessary for clarity.

During a radio broadcast in 1946, Herbert Hoover, honorary chairman of the Famine Emergency Committee, explained the food crisis with statistics. He said, in part:

> There are thirteen countries where the city populations have an average intake of less than 1900 calories. Of these, six countries are at, or below, the 1500 calorie level. There are millions of people below 1000 calories. Somewhere down these various levels starvation begins. And its immediate expression is the disease rate in children and in death rates of the infants and the old people. . . .
>
> To provide this minimum (1500 calories) to the next harvest, there must be loaded on ships for the continent during each of the four months from the first of April to the end of July a total of at least 5,300,000 tons of cereals, 300,000 tons of fats, and an additional 100,000 tons of special food is urgently needed to restore subnormal children.[17]

Interpretation

To some extent, interpretation combines methods, but it emphasizes the understanding of an idea, an object, or a process in and for itself. Criticism, on the other hand, emphasizes understanding an object in reference to its class or to an ideal standard.

Interpretation may involve the simplification of the complex, translation from the unfamiliar to the familiar, or close inspection of an object. Unless the audience is composed of experts who have the same technical vocabulary as the speaker, the substitution of popular terms for technical terms is particularly necessary. A journalist talking to a general audience would doubtless mystify most of his hearers if he referred to the *ears* of a newspaper without explaining that they are the upper left and right corners of the front page, or spoke of the *bulldog* without telling his listeners that it is the early edition of the paper. A few might understand that *putting the paper to bed* means getting it ready to be printed, and still others might know that the *morgue* is the library of clippings and files of the newspaper. Translation would be a necessary part of

---

[17] *Vital Speeches*, XII, 420, May 1, 1946. Copyright 1946 by City News Publishing Company.

interpretation for most listeners. What seems commonplace to the speaker may be foreign to the audience. When the listeners really know the objects, however, the speaker needs only to identify them.

Another way to interpret is to restate the idea in the experience of the hearers. Huxley did that when he explained induction and deduction in terms of tasting hard green apples and finding them sour, and then concluding, after frequent sampling, that hard green apples are sour.

In a radio address on "Science and Religion," Arthur Compton interpreted science in terms of the technical progress that the listener can quickly recognize:

> Science has made the world a smaller place and brought all human beings closer together. As never before in human history, science and technology have made men closely dependent upon each other. We think of the Stone Age, the Bronze Age, the Iron Age, and the Machine Age, and thus in quick outline catch a view of man's technical growth. Any one of us produces only a small part of the things we require. We are specialists, each supplying his own small part to the life of the community. We depend upon the other man for most of our food, clothing, transportation, and entertainment. This sharp specialization and intense interdependence of men on each other has been made necessary in order that the achievements of the Machine Age should give us the things we want.[18]

Criticism

Criticism enables the listener to understand an idea, object, or process with reference to other ideas, objects, or processes. It involves comparison, contrast, and usually evaluation. An object to be criticized may be compared or contrasted with a real object or with an abstraction. Evaluation is usually based on comparison with an ideal, and it may be either favorable or unfavorable, or both.

In his lecture on "Roman Eloquence," Hugh Blair bases his evaluation of Cicero on comparisons with an ideal standard and with Demosthenes. After some analysis and interpretation, Blair continued with both favorable and unfavorable criticisms:

> His virtues are, beyond controversy, eminently great. In all his orations there is high art. He begins, generally, with a regular exordium; and with much preparation and insinuation prepossesses the hearers, and studies to gain their affections. His method is clear, and his arguments are arranged with great propriety. His method is indeed more clear than that of Demosthenes; and this is one advantage which he has over him. We find everything in its proper place; he never attempts to move, till he has endeavored to convince; and in moving,

[18] A. Craig Baird, *Representative American Speeches: 1939–40*, New York: The H. W. Wilson Company, 1940, p. 422. Copyright 1940 by The H. W. Wilson Company.

especially the softer passions, he is very successful. No man knew the power and force of words better than Cicero. . . .

Together with those high qualities which Cicero possesses, he is not exempt from certain defects, of which it is necessary to take notice. For the Ciceronian eloquence is a pattern so dazzling by its beauties that, if not examined with accuracy and judgment, it is apt to betray the unwary into a faulty imitation. . . . In most of his orations, especially those composed in the earlier part of his life, there is too much art; even carried the length of ostentation. There is too visible a parade of eloquence. He seems often to aim at obtaining admiration, rather than at operating conviction, by what he says. Hence, on some occasions, he is showy rather than solid; and diffuse where he ought to have been pressing. . . .

The character of Demosthenes is vigour and austerity; that of Cicero is gentleness and insinuation. In the one, you find more manliness; in the other, more ornament. The one is more harsh, but more spirited and cogent; the other, more agreeable, but withal, looser and weaker. . . .[19]

Demonstration

The best method of informing an audience is often found in the combination of speech and visual aids. In recent years business and industry, as well as the armed forces, have developed remarkably effective practices in the use of maps, charts, diagrams, photographs, and models; slides, film strips, and motion pictures have been employed to demonstrate such diverse materials as time-motion studies, analyses of engine defects, and the management of personnel. Television has been adapted to informing: a surgeon may now carry on a difficult operation before a camera while his students or colleagues elsewhere observe his actions and hear his commentary. Most informative speeches can be improved by visual aids; some informative speeches should not be attempted without them. Common sense suggests that information on the use of a tennis racket, the workings of an airplane engine, or the control of hydrostatic pressure can best be conveyed by demonstration; and extensive research on the use of visual aids has been embodied in books and monographs.[20]

Classes of visual aids. Visual aids fall into two general classes: the graphic and the three-dimensional. Graphic aids include maps, charts, drawings, diagrams, and photographs, or similar representations. The three-dimensional aids include models, schematic devices, and machines or objects actually brought before a group for demonstration.

GRAPHIC AIDS. Of the graphic aids, perhaps the oldest, and in some ways the most useful, is the map: no better way has been devised to show

[19] *Lecture on Rhetoric and Belles Lettres,* London: Thomas Tegg & Son, 1835, pp. 330–333.

[20] The literature in the field of visual aids is constantly growing. Consult the card catalogue of your library for titles.

SPEAKING EMPLOYS THE VISUAL

Except for the Russian delegate, members of the Security Council study the aerial photographs used by Ambassador Stevenson in his speech on the Cuban crisis. Demonstration with these visual aids was the speaker's most appropriate method of informing.

the relations between geographic facts. The speaker who uses maps, however, should know certain elemental facts about them: maps bear a relation to the territory described; maps are based on different projections; there is no single "right" or "wrong" map of an area. All graphic aids, including maps, will be most helpful in conveying information if they are used in accordance with approved practices, among which the following should be noted:

Graphic aids should be planned for the speech and related to it. The haphazard or perfunctory addition of a chart or a diagram may hinder rather than help.

Graphic aids should not be relied on to do the speaker's work for him. A powerful assistant to the conveying of information, the graphic aids may yet prove dull if the speaker merely introduces each picture or chart with such stilted phrases as, "And now you see on the chart phase three. We will now turn to phase four . . . ." The speaker must use the chart, not let the chart use him.

Graphic aids should be planned for a specific audience. They should be large enough for everyone to see clearly. They should be prepared with an eye to faithful representation of principle; this may require some sacrifice of detail. Colors should be used if possible, particularly in maps, and the colors should be sharply distinguished. Graphic aids should be prepared in advance; few men are equipped to speak well and draw a chart at the same time; and the act of making a chart or diagram is apt to call attention to itself, either for its skill or its clumsiness, and thus defeat the speaker's purpose to convey information.

Graphic aids should be presented with the mastery of certain simple techniques. The speaker should avoid standing between the audience and the graphic aid. He should keep his eyes on his hearers, not on the chart or sketch. He should know his material so thoroughly that he cannot be embarrassed by questions from the audience.

In the illustration on page 80, Stevenson demonstrated that the missile bases on Cuban soil were a threat to the security of the United States. His aerial photographs were well suited to the speech and to the audience.

THREE-DIMENSIONAL AIDS.   A speaker can often avoid confusion and convey the greatest amount of information in the least time by having the object, or a model of it, before him and his hearers. When the knowledge may be a matter of life or death, the audience may be eager to learn from the object itself as well as from the speaker.

Sometimes the most effective three-dimensional aids are models prepared for the purpose of instruction; the model can be designed to clarify or to emphasize points that could not be made with the object itself; or it may be made capable of manipulation during the speech to illustrate different phases of the material; or it may be produced in lieu of material that could not be brought before an audience. A scale model of the Mississippi River, for example, has been used effectively in ways that the Mississippi itself would never allow.

Some cautions should be observed in the use of any three-dimensional aid. It should be accessory to the speaker's main task of conveying information; it must not be allowed to steal the show from the speaker. It should be large enough for everyone to see clearly; it should be ready for use before the speech begins. It should be integrated into the speech: indeed, its parts may provide the obvious and discernible organization for the information to be conveyed.

Techniques of using visual aids.   Some practices in the use of visual aids, either graphic or three-dimensional, are so well established that a speaker departs from them at his peril:

The experienced speaker has learned not to pass out exhibits to members of the audience. To do so is to lose his hearers momentarily, perhaps permanently. Visual aids should be constructed so as to require the attention of all members of the audience on the same point at the same time.

The skillful use of that simple aid, the pointer, will greatly assist the audience. Observe the pointing technique in the picture on page 80.

Sometimes a series of related charts, photographs, models, or diagrams is most effective. The armed forces have been particularly ingenious in creating displays that convey a sequence of information.

The word and the object go together. Particularly in explaining a diagram or a model to persons unlearned in the material, the speaker should name and point; he should show what the object is as he describes it. The basic rules of vocabulary apply: the speaker must not use terms foreign to his hearers without clear explanation.

The visual aid is not a substitute for the accepted principles of speech composition and delivery. A poor speaker with a visual aid will be just a poor speaker with a visual aid. But properly used, a chart or a model may make the difference between confusion and clarity.

PERSUADING

Whenever the speaker finds in his hearers opposition to himself or to his proposition, the occasion changes from informative to persuasive. Hence he is well advised systematically to study the art of persuasion, which, like the art of exposition, may be considered under four heads: (1) the leading characteristics, (2) the rationale, (3) the principal obstacles, and (4) the methods.

THE CHARACTERISTICS OF PERSUASION

Of the many characteristics of persuasion, four should be emphasized: it is universal, it embodies principles, it differs from other arts, and it is unitary.

Universality

The principles of persuasion may be applied whenever men are to be influenced in any manner whatsoever. A salesman trying to sell a vacuum cleaner to a housewife may employ some phase of persuasion technically similar to an attorney's plea for the life of his client. A candidate for the legislature and a business executive may use essentially the same persuasive methods. The principles of persuasion may be employed either in writing or in speaking. Persuasion may occur when the speaker and hearer are far apart, as on radio or television; or it may occur when the speaker is near his hearers, as in a speech at a political rally, in a conference, or in a committee.

Principles

Persuasion embodies principles: it has a theory as well as a practice. Some men who understand how persuasion is accomplished are not themselves skillful in the art, just as some men who appreciate music could not replace Bernstein on the podium and some physicians who understand the anatomy could not remove a brain tumor. Other men who know little of the organized theory of persuasion are able, through intelligence and natural talents, to acquire a certain skill in practice.

Differences

Persuasion differs fundamentally from such fine arts as poetry and music because its objective is not primarily beauty or aesthetic pleasure, but effectiveness. It may be distinguished also from the subject matter with which it is involved, since the subject matter presumably exists apart from the audience to which it must be presented. The principles of arguing a given case are thus distinguishable from the law itself.

Unity

Persuasion is unitary. Especially in its practice it cannot be subdivided, for a speaker tries to accomplish his purpose without considering at the moment what the method may be called or how it may be classified. Anyone who studies persuasion, however, will observe that the art has three factors. These factors, combining in different degrees as circumstances decide, determine whether the hearers will be persuaded. Of the three factors in persuasion, the first, inhering primarily in the subject matter, may be called logical. The second, developing primarily from the hearers, may be called psychological. The third, coming primarily from the speaker, may be called personal.

THE RATIONALE OF PERSUADING

As Aristotle observed, rhetoric is useful because things that are true and things that are just have a natural tendency to prevail over their opposites, so that if the decisions of judges are not what they ought to be, the defect must be due to the speakers themselves.

Since every man who lives in society must constantly persuade other men and be persuaded by them, nothing is more useful than an understanding of the art and practice of influencing thought and conduct. Persuasion is a social force; like economic power and military strength, it is used by men of good will in honest pursuits, but it may be used also by charlatans with ulterior motives. Every competent person, therefore, should know what persuasion is and how it is accomplished. Otherwise he may be unable to respond to sound arguments or to resist all kinds of false appeals. In a free country, where every citizen has some voice in the government, persuasion is especially useful because it is employed in public as well as in private affairs. Unless the voters who form the ultimate governing body are capable of making and responding to judicious arguments and appeals, then everyone, the wise and the unwise together, will suffer.

Persuasion differs from science because science endeavors, in so far as possible, to find out what is true, or at least highly probable, without considering how to demonstrate its findings to the public. Persuasion is concerned in the main with discovering and demonstrating what is probable in terms that can be understood by men in general.

OBSTACLES TO PERSUADING

In addition to the obstacles to informing, as previously described, the speaker engaged in persuasion should be prepared to deal with other obstacles, of which the following are noteworthy: (1) prejudice against himself or his cause, (2) habits of thought that preclude acceptance of the speaker's views, and (3) previous commitment to the opposition.

Prejudice

The experienced speaker realizes that he must expect certain prejudices to be manifested against himself. Some people are prejudiced against Democrats, others against Republicans. In a farming community, a speaker from the city may be suspect. In a city, a farmer may be mistrusted. Many Americans are notably prejudiced against any proposals that may be called "socialistic" or "communistic." Others react automatically against ideas supposed to represent the views of "big business." Still others are likely to be prejudiced against proposals initiated by labor unions.

Habits of Thought

Sometimes the prevailing habits of thought may constitute an obstacle to persuasion. Some communities are loath to change any custom, to do anything in a way differing from that of former times. Some individuals—and individuals make up audiences—have often been deceived by false promises or disappointed by hopes unrealized; their experiences have made them habitually skeptical toward any proposal that promises improvement in the human condition.

Previous Commitment

Persuasion is characteristically involved in questions of probability, questions which admittedly have two, or even more, sides. The speaker must thus suppose that some persons will be committed to the opposition. A Republican speaking in a community in which the voter registration is 90 per cent Democratic would not normally expect to receive initial good will toward Republican men and measures. The previous commitment of the members of his audience to the Democratic Party would presumably put him at a disadvantage, though not always a decisive one. A Democrat speaking in a Republican community would be at a similar disadvantage.

The orator caught up in his immediate problem may be troubled by the intransigence of certain audiences, by their unwillingness to follow his counsels. In the long run, however, the resistance of thoughtful men to persuasion must be counted a blessing. Imagine what life would be like in a country in which the populace easily accepted the appeals of every speaker! In a free country, proposals for action are in constant competition with each other. The welfare of the body politic depends on the electorate's resisting sophistry as well as on its accepting sound reasoning.

METHODS OF PERSUADING

Of the three methods of persuasion—logical, psychological, and personal—that operate as a single force to induce belief or action, the most clearly intellectual is the logical. It involves cogency, judgment, and wisdom operating on evidence. The psychological aspect of persuasion involves appeals and stimulations designed to gain the speaker a full, fair, and favorable hearing. The personal aspect of persuasion involves those attributes of the speaker himself that make him appear to be worthy of belief.

Logical Persuasion

Constructing an argument may be compared to building a bridge. The engineer who constructs a bridge across a chasm has to sink piers deep into the rock. The piers must be properly designed and built of sound material. After they have been set in place, the engineer can build his roadway across the chasm. In building an argument from a state of doubt, over a chasm of inaction, and then to a state of belief, the speaker works like the engineer. The proposal for which he would gain acceptance is like the roadway of the bridge. The roadway is supported by strong piers of evidence, firmly sunk into the rock of basic human assumptions. Just as the engineer should see that the piers of his bridge are well designed to support the weight upon them, so should the builder of an argument see that his reasoning is valid to support his proposal. Just as the engineer would be foolish to employ inferior materials in the piers for his roadway, so the speech builder would be foolish to use inferior evidence to support his proposition.

The Bridge of Persuasion

Finding the statement. The first task of the persuasive speaker is to find in the mass of conflicting, confusing, and seemingly irrelevant theses the statement with which he and his audience are concerned. This statement should be put simply and clearly. The speaker must know what he proposes.

Statements are likely to be concerned with matters of fact, justification, or policy. Many of the questions dealt with in the law courts are concerned with fact: the question at issue in a felony case may be, "Is this the man who was observed at the scene of the crime on Tuesday, January 6?"

Questions of justification, or value, are likely to involve ethical matters. Many people throughout the world were disappointed when the United States failed to enter the League of Nations. The question at issue here was partly one of justification: "Was the United States justified in forsaking an organization that the President had helped to found?"

Central issues of policy involve courses of action. They have to do with principles and probabilities. Legislative bodies often consider questions of policy: for example, should corporation profits be limited to 6 per cent? Should taxes be raised in the higher income brackets? Should the United States build another canal across the Isthmus of Panama?

The issues. Every persuasive speech concerning fact, justification, or policy involves issues. These issues are always questions, and they are so related to the statement that an affirmative answer to the question must carry the statement to an affirmative conclusion. The finding of the issues requires analysis of the subject and study of the audience.

TYPES OF ISSUES. The common issues in a question of fact are these:

• Did the event occur as alleged?
• If so, is it described in correct terms?

Did this man kill the woman for whose murder he is arraigned? If so, did the killing constitute murder? Murder in the first degree, as defined by the practice of courts of law, ordinarily involves premeditation. If the act of the accused was undertaken in self-defense or without prior consideration, he may have killed the woman without having committed murder in the first degree.

The characteristic issues in a question of justification are:

- What are the criteria?
- Do the criteria fit the case?

By what principles, for example, should the United States be judged for her failure to enter the League of Nations? By the principles of the United States? Or those of Europe? Or of Asia? If the judgment is based upon American principles, does their application give reason for censure?

The essential issues in a question of policy are these:

- Is any change needed?
- If so, is the proposed change the best one?

Concerning the construction of the proposed new canal, for example, the issues might be stated: Is it necessary to increase the facilities for transportation between the Atlantic and the Pacific? Is the building of the proposed canal the best means of doing so?

DISCOVERING THE ISSUES. In so far as they relate to the subject matter, the main issues can be discovered by analysis that searches the background of the question to find the chief opposing points of view. An issue arises wherever a strong difference of opinion is found. The issues thus exist independent of the immediate participants in a controversy, and are in fact discovered rather than invented.

A single question of policy, such as, Should the United States join an economic community of non-Communist nations? may involve many special issues. A systematic analysis of the subject matter will reveal them. In the presentation of an argument, the speaker must determine the issues to be treated for each particular audience. In the foregoing question, an advocate of the policy might find the following issues:

- Is the joining of such a community in the interest of American business?
- Is the joining of such a community in the interest of American labor?

If the speaker emphasizes the latter issue, he may minimize or discard the former. His choice may depend in part on his audience.

Evidence in support of the proposition. Once he has determined what the issues are, the speaker comes to grips with proof as an adequate logical basis for accepting the proposition. Evidence is the material of proof, and its presentation affects its validity, for in a speech evidence depends not merely upon the words as they would appear on a printed page, but also upon meaning indicated by inflection or gesture.

The final test of evidence is its reception by the hearers. Ordinarily the speaker who merely says, "Prices will be higher next year," or "The administration is to blame for the coal strike," is unconvincing. The most common error in the use of evidence is the substitution of the speaker's unsupported assertion for genuine evidence based upon objective analysis.

But even here the audience is the final judge. A speaker may carry such weight that only his word is required. What would be objectionable as mere assertion in another man may, coming from him, be acceptable to his hearers. The commander of an army is not likely to quote from authority or to cite a syllogism in order to get his men to advance. Adolph Hitler found himself perfectly at ease in asserting what other speakers would be required to prove. In a free society, however, speakers cannot trespass at will upon the intelligence of their hearers. When men are accustomed to participating in decisions on public questions, persuasion requires supplementary tests of evidence.

DIRECT AND INDIRECT EVIDENCE.   Evidence may be direct or indirect. Direct evidence is testimony, presented orally or in writing, tending to offer immediate proof of the proposition. Testimony is presented either by experts or by ordinary persons. If a simple fact is involved, such as whether the accused was observed near the corner of Tenth and Ash Streets at 11:00 P.M. on the twelfth of December, the testimony of any person may be acceptable. In questions of a higher order, concerning sanity, health, or substantial assets, the testimony of an expert may be required. Such testimony may be either fact or opinion. For example, when Bruno Hauptmann was on trial for the murder of the Lindbergh baby, an expert testified that a certain piece of lumber found in the ladder used for the kidnapping had been taken from the Hauptmanns' attic. In the same trial a competent psychiatrist gave in evidence his opinion that Hauptmann was sane.

Indirect evidence is of two kinds—circumstantial and negative. Circumstantial evidence creates a pattern into which the questioned fact must fit perfectly. It should be susceptible of only one interpretation. The evidence against Hauptmann in the Lindbergh kidnapping made such a pattern.

Negative evidence is unsatisfactory as a single means of proof. However, it may tend to create a presumption, or it may be used in conjunction with other evidence. An advocate establishing the character of a witness might demonstrate that the records of the State University of Iowa, where he was a student for four years, show no instance of his having been censured for misconduct. The negative evidence is strengthened by proof that the authorities of the State University of Iowa keep an accurate record of penalties incurred.

AUTHORITY. The testimony of authority should be more acceptable to the audience than that of the speaker himself. The expert must be clearly identified, but if his prestige must be established, the speaker might do better to find another source of evidence. In assuming that the acceptability of the witness to the audience is a major requirement, however, the speaker should not suppose that just any kind of testimony will be helpful. The American nation has been held together by the common sense of the millions of people who have usually enforced at least three tests of a witness:

Is the witness competent? Intelligent audiences want to know whether the testimony comes from a person who is in a position to know. Does he have better information than other people? Has he had training or experience to justify his appearance as an authority in the field of his testimony? Henry Ford was an expert on automobile manufacturing, but not on historiography.

Is the witness fair? Other things being equal, a speaker should avoid presenting testimony from anyone who is obviously partisan. The chairman of the Democratic National Committee, for example, would not be the best person to quote in defense of a Democratic administration. An outstanding Republican would be a better witness. The speaker indicates his own fairness by using witnesses who appear to be fair, or who, if they are prejudiced, are prejudiced against his cause rather than for it.

Is the witness conclusive? The testimony should be clear and conclusive as to the point in question. Reliance on a single authority is doubtful practice even for one point; dependence on a single authority for an entire speech is inexcusable. The testimony of a single veteran would hardly be sufficient to characterize the functioning of the Navy as superior to that of the Army in an engagement.

Certain special methods in the use of testimony deserve attention: the standing of a witness for one side of a question may sometimes be validated by his having already been used as a witness for the opposition. The testimony of a reluctant witness is usually more effective with audiences than that of a witness who is eager to testify. Sometimes an admission made by a person unaware of its implications will have striking effect. The time when the testimony was given may have a bearing on its credibility. In some instances, the testimony of an eyewitness may be preferred. In others, a judicious statement constructed after the event may be less open to charges of prejudice and hence more acceptable. Citation to the authority should be so definite that everyone can understand who made the statement, for what purpose, and on what occasion. The basic requirement of authority, however, must always be, Is the witness acceptable to the audience?

Cogency. Cogency is to the establishment of a controversial statement what the proper fabrication of materials is to the building of a bridge. The materials of cogency are facts and opinions constituting evidence. Unless the facts and opinions are put together in workmanlike fashion, they will form a shoddy structure. The methods of cogency commonly employed in persuasive speech are the four kinds of reasoning: deduction, generalization, analogy, and causation.

DEDUCTION. The process of deduction, or reasoning from the general to the specific, is based upon an instrument called the enthymeme, or rhetorical syllogism, of which three kinds are recognized: the categorical, the hypothetical, and the disjunctive. All three draw a particular conclusion from a major premise and a minor premise. The categorical is stated in the following form:

> All citizens are subject to taxes.
> Kennedy is a citizen.
> Therefore Kennedy is subject to taxes.

The hypothetical is stated in the following form:

> If Kennedy is a citizen, he is subject to taxes.
> Kennedy is a citizen.
> Therefore Kennedy is subject to taxes.

The disjunctive is stated in the following form:

> Kennedy is either subject to taxes or free from taxes.
> Kennedy is not free from taxes.
> Therefore Kennedy is subject to taxes.

Categorical, hypothetical, and disjunctive enthymemes (rhetorical syllogisms) are rarely set forth formally, but their bases should be present in every speech. Inferences are frequently drawn from one premise and a conclusion, the other premise being implied. Syllogistic form is useful in analyzing and criticizing the cogency of all discourse, including your own.

The rules of the rhetorical syllogism, and the tests applied to it, are the same in speechmaking as in formal logic. Three fundamental differences, however, should be taken into account by anyone studying persuasion.

The first of these differences arises from the subject matter of the syllogism. In formal logic the syllogism may employ terms that are not controversial, whereas in speechmaking the deduction uses terms that are controversial: they are derived from the probabilities of the past, present, and future. The following deduction, for example, is concerned with future policy:

> All patriotic unions should receive public support.
> Local 343 is a patriotic union.
> Therefore Local 343 should receive public support.

The argument may hinge on the assumption in the major premise or on the question, Is Local 343 a patriotic union?

A second difference between the syllogisms of formal logic and those of persuasion is found in the people who use them. The syllogisms of formal logic are often employed by men of science or learning. The syllogisms of persuasion are often employed by speakers talking to people of little learning. Popular syllogisms are heard in the shops, the streets, the courthouses, and the factories.

A third difference lies in the fullness of the reasoning. Formal logic prefers complete chains of syllogistic thinking; popular speechmaking moves along rapidly by implying many of the premises that support the inference. The hearers are trusted to supply the missing parts.

GENERALIZATION. Generalization is both a form of reasoning in its own right and a means of creating the premises from which deductive arguments are drawn. A premise is established from similar instances or relevant facts. A generalization involves the hazard of coming to a conclusion about a great many instances upon the observation of only a few. The undergraduate, for example, notes that his friends buy their books at the university book store. From this observation he may infer, rather loosely, that students buy their books at the university book store.

A more accurate method than generalization is inspection, in which all the instances in a single class are enumerated for the purpose of the argument. Obviously, however, the method of inspection is not always possible. In coming to a conclusion about taxpayers, no speaker would be able to interview all the taxpayers in the world. He would forsake inspection and take the hazards of generalization based upon interviews with a selected number.

Since the method of generalization necessarily leaves a certain portion of the class unobserved, all generalizations are hasty; but some are hastier than others. You will need to apply certain standard tests, therefore, to discover whether your generalizations are relatively sound.

Audiences of thoughtful men in a free society are likely to insist upon the following tests:

Has the speaker observed enough instances of the class? Can the statement, "American troops in Europe are undisciplined," be proved adequately by a single instance of misconduct? No judicious audience would be satisfied with such slight support for the generalization. Since information on such a proposition should be relatively easy to obtain, additional instances should be cited if they exist.

Are the instances cited a fair sample of the class of objects observed? In a free country, where people are accustomed to hearing speeches, the members of an audience usually know that a favorite trick of the shallow speaker is to pick out exceptions to the general rule and present them as typical. Such a speaker, ignoring all the contrary evidence, chooses one instance of theft to prove that an entire city is corrupt or, in attempting to demonstrate that the city boss is a sterling gentleman, cites an exceptional instance of an action taken for the city's benefit. To satisfy the responsible audience, the instances chosen for the generalization must be fair samples.

Does the generalization accord with the other accepted facts about the phenomenon observed? The speaker must take into account the knowledge of his listeners. Many of the principles accepted in the world today were once out of accord with popular belief. Before the airplane was invented, for example, the idea of human flight was contrary to the popular concept of the world in which we live. If the speaker is able to explain the facts underlying his generalization, he may present his case adequately. If not, his material probably is unsuitable for persuasive speaking.

The speaker must test his generalization, therefore, by observing a sufficient number of instances, by taking a fair sample, and by basing his generalization upon knowledge within the understanding of his hearers. Finally, he must test his argument again by asking himself whether its whole order has been made as acceptable as possible to the people he is addressing.

ANALOGY. Analogy relies for its validity upon relevant similarities and dissimilarities.[21] A speaker advocating a new student government for Louisiana State University could show that the proposed system has been in practice at the University of California for a great many years. He would then need to show that Louisiana State University and the University of California are alike in so many relevant aspects that they should also be alike in having a similar system of student government.

Some logicians consider the argument by analogy to be inherently specious. In practice, however, it is perhaps the oldest method of inference. When used with discretion, it may induce an attitude favorable to the proposition, but at best it is a two-edged sword. In the argument concerning student government, for example, the analogy might be

---

[21] Figurative analogies are a matter of composition or style. Therefore, consideration is here given only to literal analogy.

turned to suggest that the University of California should adopt the plan of Louisiana State University.

Two tests for analogy should be employed:

Are the points of difference between the objects compared outweighed by the points of difference in significance as well as in number? To establish that Louisiana State University and the University of California both have well-kept lawns would hardly be relevant to a proposition concerning student government. To show that both institutions are coeducational, that they have a similar student body, and that they have a faculty of comparable interests might be relevant.

Are the facts alleged about the objects compared actually established? The unsophisticated assume that the unfamiliar is better than the familiar, that any highly touted project is successful. Before employing an analogy in a speech, you should determine whether the objects compared have been viewed realistically. In arguing that Louisiana State University should adopt the California system of student government, you will need to demonstrate that the proposed system has been successful.

A special form of analogy is the argument *a fortiori*, in which the speaker attempts to show that what is demonstrably true or false in one instance is even more likely to be true or false in another. The argument *a fortiori* is illustrated in the speech by Mr. Henning W. Prentis, Jr.:

> National economic planning in time of war is comparatively simple because military requirements are relatively standardized and uniform. Despite that fact, we can see right now how enormously difficult it is even to plan intelligently for war production. Yet the problems of planning to meet the demands of a free economy in times of peace would be infinitely more complicated, since peacetime demands are subject to consumer preference, personal tastes, the whims of style and the dynamics of advancing technology. . . .[22]

The reasoning in Mr. Prentis' speech is that national economic planning, difficult in time of war, is even more difficult in time of peace.

CAUSATION. As an argumentative form, causation is not strictly separable from deduction and generalization. As an application of deduction and generalization, it may best be understood by special study.

In the first kind of causation—reasoning from effect to cause—the speaker begins with a given fact and argues that some previously existing state is the cause or proximate cause. He goes from the present to the

---

[22] "Competitive Enterprise Versus Planned Economy," a speech delivered before the fiftieth anniversary celebration of the National Association of Manufacturers, held at the University of Cincinnati on Jan. 24, 1945. *Representative American Speeches: 1944–1945*, Vol. 18, New York: The H. W. Wilson Company, 1945, pp. 222–223. Copyright 1945 by The H. W. Wilson Company.

past, or from a past time to some time even more remote. Effect-to-cause reasoning is employed in the following instance:

> Why has individualism produced such notable results in America? The men who settled this country were not extraordinary people. They had a vast continent to develop, yet its natural resources were no greater than those of Asia. They had little capital to start with; in fact, they had to seek it abroad. They were not, as a rule, as skilled artisans as the workers in European industries. They believed in education but such facilities were not generally available. How then did they differ from their contemporaries in the old world? They were free. They set up a government that was legally estopped from interfering with their legitimate personal activities. They enjoyed what Justice Brandeis says is the right most highly prized by civilized men—"the right to be let alone. . . ." [23]

In the reasoning here employed, "the notable results in America" are the effect of the cause "They were free."

In the second kind of causation—cause-to-effect—the speaker begins with some known or admitted fact called the cause and concludes that the effects have resulted or may result from it. Usually such reasoning is employed from the present to the future, but it may be employed either from a relatively near future to some more distant time or from the past to the present. The following excerpt illustrates cause-to-effect reasoning:

> If we ever do lose our freedom in America, I predict that it will be due to planned economy coming as a wolf in sheep's clothing. Sad to relate, we are far closer to it than most of us realize. The shape of things to come over here is often anticipated by what happens in Great Britain. Every thinking American should read the British White Paper entitled "Employment Policy," . . . and ponder the program there outlined with real concern. For only a short time ago—with little or no publicity in our newspapers in the United States— the policy advocated in that document was enacted into law by the British Parliament under the frank title of "Planned Economy for Great Britain." [24]

The cause in this line of reasoning is "planned economy," the effect is "loss of freedom."

Causation is difficult as well as hazardous to employ, either in the abstract or in speechmaking. Nevertheless, speechmakers constantly resort to causative reasoning as a means of establishing proof. In so far as they deal with propositions of policy, they must do so.

The constructively valid tests of causal relation may be developed from the five principles set forth by John Stuart Mill:

1. The method of agreement. If the instances of a phenomenon under study have a single factor in common, then that factor is either the cause or the effect of the phenomenon. A military investigator studying the per-

[23] *Ibid.*, pp. 219–220.
[24] *Ibid.*, p. 226.

formance of ten battalions which were outstanding in maneuvers found that the only feature they all had in common was a longer and more effective period of training in the basic skills of a soldier. The conclusion of the investigator was that the superior performance of the ten outstanding battalions resulted primarily from the longer and more effective basic training.

2. *The method of difference.* Whatever is present when a phenomenon occurs and absent in another instance when the phenomenon does not occur (all the other factors being the same) is either the effect or the cause, or directly associated with the effect or the cause, of the phenomenon. The administrator of a naval training program wished to find out why one naval training unit was remarkably more successful by all objective measures than another similar unit. He discovered that the two units had identical ratings on performance and intelligence, that the textbooks in the two units were identical, that the instruction was comparable. He discovered upon further investigation, however, that in the highly successful unit every man was tested every day. In the other unit the men were tested only at the end of their period of training. The conclusion of the naval administrator was that the daily testing produced a consistently higher performance from the sailors in training.

3. *The joint method of agreement and difference.* This test is an elaboration of the methods of agreement and of difference. A cause-or-effect relation is more conclusively established in the following circumstances: (a) a number of instances of a phenomenon are observed; (b) the instances of agreement have only one factor in common; (c) the instances of difference are dissimilar, save for the absence of the same factor. If, for example, the naval administrator just mentioned had extended his study to include all naval training units in the United States and had found that the *presence* of daily testing was the common factor in high-rating naval units and that the *absence* of the daily testing was the common factor in low-rating naval units, his conclusion concerning the value of daily testing would have been strengthened.

4. *The method of residues.* The method of residues is employed when so many causes are operating that a cause-effect relationship is difficult to establish. If we subtract from a given phenomenon the effects for which causes are known and agreed on, then the remainder of the phenomenon may be attributed to the remaining causes. To determine the effect of an increase in taxes upon price changes, for example, note the effects of all other elements—wages, materials, dividends, etc. The residue of price change may be attributed to increase in taxes.

5. *The method of concomitant variations.* If variation in any single phenomenon is consistently accompanied by variation in another, the two phenomena are considered to have some causal relation. Sociologists employ the method of concomitant variations to illustrate the relationship

between unemployment and such social disorders as crime, suicide, prostitution, and revealed insanity. Since coincidental resemblance is possible, the method of concomitant variations must be used with caution, but it may support the other valid tests of causal relationship.

Errors.   The capacity for human error is so great, and the ability of human beings to classify error is so limited, that no complete catalogue of fallacies has ever been made. Indeed, errors in reasoning exist in reference to their context and can hardly be listed. Moreover, whether a line of argument is fallacious will sometimes depend upon external factors. Some of the errors ordinarily described are fallacious only in name. For example, the argument *ad hominem,* commonly referred to as the fallacy of reference from the conduct or profession of an individual to the truth or falsity of a general proposition, may not be fallacious rhetorically, however it may appear logically. Audiences are skeptical of men whom they believe to be wicked even when these men advocate good measures.

In these circumstances most public speakers should center their attention on ways in which men fall into error. Fallacies are likely to occur in (1) the assumptions or (2) the cogency or (3) the evidence of a speaker or of his opponent. Errors in assumption occur when the speaker proceeds on assumptions that the audience is unwilling to accept. A speaker who takes for granted that an audience of Americans desires the rule of a dictator would be mistaken. Yet speakers sometimes fall into this kind of error or tend toward it. Errors of cogency occur in the violation of one or more of the principles of deduction, generalization, analogy, or causation. The speaker who infers that a change in the administration of the government is the cause of improved economic conditions merely because one followed the other draws an invalid inference. Errors of evidence frequently result from failure to obtain the facts, from the use of assertion rather than substantiation of fact, or from the citing of facts or opinions not available to, or not understood by, the audience. The student who states that one university is better than another should demonstrate specifically the essential ways in which the superiority is evident.

Refutation.   Refutation is the attempt to answer an opposition either present or absent. The first task is selection. The speaker does not hope to answer all the charges levied against his assumptions, his cogency, and his evidence. He must decide which opposing arguments to ignore and which to attack. The basic rule is to refute the arguments most likely to affect the audience. Generally, speakers take up too many arguments rather than too few. A good refutation is like the rifle fire that hits the bull's eye on the target rather than like the shotgun fire that scatters over the landscape. Having determined which arguments in his own view and the view of his audience are significant and decisive, the speaker limits his attack to them.

RULES OF REFUTATION.   Refutation has three essential rules. First, the speaker should state fully and fairly the argument under attack. Even if the twisting of the opponent's argument were honest, it would not usually be effective. The opposing point of view should be quoted accurately. The second step is to state the evidence and the full position in refutation clearly and cogently. Allusion to an argument developed in a previous speech is not enough; the proof should be detailed. The third step is to demonstrate the effect of the refutation on the opposing argument. Too many speakers follow the first two steps in refutation and neglect the third. The refutation is not complete, however, until you have shown what has happened to your opponent's argument under your attack.

POINTS OF ATTACK.   In refuting an opposing argument, the speaker has the choice of three elements to attack: the assumptions, the evidence, or the conclusions. If he attacks the assumptions, he goes beyond the argument of his opponent to see from whence the argument derives. He must be sure of the ground attacked, and should be fairly confident of the state of opinion among his hearers. If he attacks the evidence, he denies the validity of the testimony or the facts alleged in behalf of his opponent's premises. If he attacks the conclusions, he will presumably have found some major error in the reasoning of the opposition.

SPECIAL PLANS OF REFUTATION.   Refutation should be planned as thoughtfully as constructive argument. Four ways are available to the speaker in organizing his attack on his opponent's position. These special plans are: reduction to absurdity, residues, exposing inconsistency, and turning the tables.

Reduction to absurdity. In reduction to absurdity, the speaker assumes, for the sake of argument, the validity of the proposition and then extends it to its ultimate but apparently absurd conclusion. The value of this method is diminished if it is pushed too far. Counter-refutation can be used against it, as Abraham Lincoln demonstrated in the Lincoln-Douglas debates. Lincoln was having to meet the argument that the logical extension of his case required intermarriage between the white and black races. He declared:

I do not understand that because I do not want a Negro woman for a slave I must necessarily want her for a wife. My understanding is that I can just let her alone. I am now in my fiftieth year, and I certainly never have had a black woman for either a slave or a wife. So it seems to me entirely possible to get along without making either slaves or wives of Negroes.[25]

[25] "Fourth Joint Debate at Charleston," by Abraham Lincoln and Stephen A. Douglas, a speech delivered by Abraham Lincoln at Charleston, Illinois, on Sept. 18, 1858. *The Political Debates Between Abraham Lincoln and Stephen A. Douglas,* New York: G. P. Putnam's Sons, 1913, part II, p. 2. Copyright 1913 by G. P. Putnam's Sons.

Residues. In the plan of residues, the speaker considers every possible conclusion and destroys all save the one he wishes to establish. The validity of this method depends upon his exhausting the possible conclusions, as well as upon his presenting acceptable evidence against the conclusions attacked. In developing an argument for public medical care, the speaker would employ the method of residues if he were to show that (1) private medical practice, (2) voluntary insurance, (3) compulsory health insurance, and (4) all other plans except public medical care are inadequate.

Exposing inconsistency. The exposing of inconsistencies rests upon the assumption that arguments should fall within a pattern of reference. A speaker who quotes William Howard Taft as having concurred in a decision of the Supreme Court in 1943 will fail to persuade those of his hearers who know that Mr. Taft was not living in 1943. The inaccuracy of the date will enable a skillful opponent to cast doubt on the whole argument. The plan of exposing inconsistency is also employed by disclosing differences between the arguments of speakers who take the same position, or between a speaker's present position and a former one.

Turning the tables. The plan of turning the tables in refutation consists of using the opponent's own argument against him. This plan is not often available, but occasionally it may be used with brilliant effect. A witness in a damage suit heard his testimony attacked by an attorney on the ground that it was hearsay. When the attorney asked him to give his age, he replied, "I don't know." The attorney demanded incredulously, "Do you mean to say you don't know how old you are?" The witness turned to the judge and said, "Your Honor, I only know what my mother told me, and that would be hearsay."

Psychological Persuasion

The engineer who constructs a bridge presumably does so to facilitate going from one point to another. The builder of an argument also wishes to get people from one point to another. But just as the existence of the bridge does not require people to travel across the chasm, so the existence of an argument leading from doubt to belief does not require people to accept it. The persuasive speaker induces people to travel his argumentative bridge. To effect a change based on even the soundest argument, he must convince his hearers that his proposal is in line with their own fundamental systems of belief, or at least not greatly at variance with them. Further, he must motivate them. In motivation, the speaker must consider (1) the use of emotional appeals and (2) the ways of gaining and holding attention. There exists in some quarters a judgment against emotion in speechmaking. In so far as the judgment operates against sentimentality, synthetic appeals, and superficiality, it is justified. Yet emotion can be as honest as intelligence, and genuine emotion has no substitute in arousing an audience to belief and action. It is most effective when it is closely identified with logical reasoning.

Emotional appeals. Since the speech must hold the attention of the hearers until the effect of the ideas is heightened in their minds, it may appeal to emotions as actively as to intelligence. Among the emotions most often aroused are sympathy, benevolence, pity, grief, fear, anger, shame, pride, and reverence.

While he was President of the United States Chamber of Commerce, Eric Johnston spoke to the Writers' War Board. He appealed to fear in seeking to impress upon his listeners the consequences of intolerance:

> The obstreperous hate-mongers and their foolish or frivolous fellow-travelers who think it is smart to rock the American boat may drown with the other passengers.
>
> If they achieve the calamity of race persecutions, they will drag our beloved America down to the barbarian level of Nazi Germany and we will pay for it in death and suffering and national degeneration, precisely as the Germans are doing today. We need to emphasize, day in and day out, that the spread of intolerance is not primarily a threat to the intended victims but to the whole country. Once the poison enters a nation's bloodstream, the entire population is doomed. Only six hundred thousand German Jews suffered through the triumph of Nazi barbarism—but the non-Jews who suffered from it include the more than eighty million Germans!
>
> If the day ever comes in this country when tolerance gives way to internal enmities and persecutions and discriminations, it will be the end of American civilization. Remember this: the dictates of intolerance cannot be enforced finally without the connivance of government. Should intolerance triumph, it will mean, as a matter of course, that free government is stamped out. Racial persecutions—whether in the old Russia or the present day Germany—have always been conducted under the protection of a tyrannical governmental regime.[26]

The emotional appeal must be absolutely appropriate to the audience, the occasion, and the speaker. The slightest hint of insincerity is likely to create an ill effect. On an occasion fraught with genuine feeling, Robert G. Ingersoll paid impressive tribute at his brother's grave:

> This brave and tender man in every storm of life was oak and rock, but in the sunshine he was love and flower. . . . He believed that happiness was the only good, reason the only torch, justice the only worshipper, humanity the only religion and love the priest. He added to the sum of human joy, and were everyone for whom he did some loving service to bring a blossom to his grave he would sleep tonight beneath a wilderness of flowers.[27]

[26] A. Craig Baird, ed., *Representative American Speeches: 1944–1945*, New York: The H. W. Wilson Company, 1945, p. 179. Copyright 1945 by The H. W. Wilson Company.

[27] James Milton O'Neill, ed., *Classified Models of Speech Composition*, New York: Century Co., 1922, pp. 466–467.

Gaining and holding attention. Common sense will tell the speaker that he must have the attention of his listeners in order to accomplish any purpose. Persuasion is impossible without communication, and communication is impossible without the attention of both speaker and audience. Yet everyone has had the experience of being physically present but mentally absent during the delivery of an address. Intermittent, divided, or lost attention means that the speaker is not communicating fully. To gain and hold attention is the first problem of psychological persuasion.

The concepts of attention and interest have long been the problem of psychologists, and some of their studies are of value to the student of public speaking. Among useful investigations are those concerning the length of the average attention span of a listener and the individual differences in capacity for attention. But the speaker is more interested in knowing how he can get people to listen to him. Psychologists have only begun to study the special problems of speechmaking, but they suggest that pausing, gesturing, repetition, and verbal emphasis tend to hold attention. Variety in force, rate, pitch, and quality is likewise effective.

The principles derived from centuries of experience in the study of speechmaking are still the chief reliance of the speaker in learning to gain and hold attention. If you will appraise each of your speeches objectively, your own experience in applying these principles should teach you a great deal. You should be able to improve your technique from one speech to another.

How can a speaker win attention? The systematic study of speechmaking will provide the extended answer to this question. A more immediate reply may be given in a classified list of practical suggestions. Most of the ways seem simple and even obvious when stated; yet you must have observed how frequently speakers neglect these simple means of inducing their hearers to listen.

In order to challenge the attention of an audience, the speaker must be mindful of his hearers throughout his preparation. The material he selects, the organization he provides, and the adaptation he makes determine whether he is likely to capture attention when he faces his audience. His speech should be constructed from the outset with a view to absorbing the interest of his hearers.

Think of your hearers first. You should consider first not what *I* think, *I* believe, *I* want, or *I* feel, but rather what the hearers think, believe, want, and feel. Even though you wish to change their beliefs and desires, you must begin with the ones they have. Announcing what you expect them to do may make them only more determined not to give up their beliefs. You should remember that a good speech is a dialogue. In effect, the speaker asks and answers his hearers' questions; he carries them along with him from point to point.

Have one dominant idea. You should keep attention steadily fixed on the key idea. Through a variety of channels you should direct the attention of your listeners again and again to the one central thought. If you want your audience to believe in subsidized athletics for your campus, you will marshal reason after reason, fact after fact, example after example until your listeners focus their full attention upon the dominant idea that subsidies are necessary.

Find the most interesting approach. The speaker's opening remarks may determine the level of attention he will gain for the entire speech. The listeners are in effect asking him, "Why should I listen to you on this topic?" Within the first few minutes you must convince your audience that you have an interesting idea, that you are competent to develop it, and that you should be heard to the end. The senior in agriculture who began a speech with the assertion, "Nearly everybody eats," and followed with striking reasons why the control of soil erosion is essential for our food supply, knew how to gain and hold attention.

A story leading directly to the dominant idea may make a good beginning. The speaker who began, "You read in last night's paper about the tragic death of Emily Baden," captured immediate attention for a speech on safe driving.

An incident that is both amusing and appropriate makes an interesting approach. People enjoy a humorous anecdote, especially if the speaker tells it on himself—a predicament he has experienced, or an error he has committed. Strong initial attention must be immediately related to the dominant idea.

Hold interest by arousing curiosity. Satisfying the curiosity of your hearers at the outset may cause them to lose interest. Your development should keep them continuously looking forward to what is coming next. To arouse strong curiosity, you may even want to shock them. Some of the people in an Indiana town who heard a Catholic priest come forward and announce, "I'm going to give you the best arguments for atheism," will probably never forget the priest, his speech, nor the amazement that brought the crowd to the edge of their seats. After he had spent ten minutes seriously presenting the leading arguments for atheism, he said quietly, "You see, I have presented the best arguments because we want to deal with the best ones. Now I shall show you why they are false." Some worried people in the audience heaved audible sighs of relief.

Be concrete and specific. The speaker commands attention when he uses the concrete instead of the abstract, the specific instead of the gen-

eral. The economist who said, "Inflation threatens our economic structure," created little interest in his topic, but a labor leader got full attention when he declared to the same audience, "Eighty-nine-cent eggs,
a-dollar-and-ten-cent meat, twenty-five-cent milk, and ninety-seven-cent
butter mean that a workman cannot feed his family on ten dollars a day."

Use both the novel and the familiar. If the speaker can relate new
experiences to familiar happenings, or untried remedies to old solutions,
he can usually arouse the interest of an audience. In his speech entitled
"New Ways of Making Gold Bricks," a speaker related the new to the
old. Referring to his experiences as a detective, he revealed the latest
methods of confidence men.

Likewise, the familiar is interesting when the speaker presents it from
a new point of view. Thousands of advertising managers have told salesmen how to approach the housewife, but one advertising manager fasci-
nated an audience of housewives with a speech entitled "How to Resist
a Salesman." Thousands of students have perfunctorily presented the
hardships of working one's way through school, but one alert coed gave
a new twist to the time-worn topic. She began by telling how she longed
for the local drugstore's "Sweetheart Special," a fancy sundae costing fifty
cents, and how this expensive taste wrecked her limited budget and
threatened her college career. She explained how she decided to make
an adventure out of her financial difficulties by finding inexpensive
pastimes and held her listeners with her colorful account of familiar
experiences in reaching both a balanced budget and a new zest for living.

Appeal to fundamental interests. Winning the attention of the audience requires the speaker to determine their special interests or to appeal
to such fundamental interests as health, wealth, home, and country.
Perhaps he will never refer to these interests directly. The young man
who talked about meat inspection did not need to mention health. After
he had given details about uninspected meats and had offered to provide
a list of the local restaurants serving them, he had no cause to worry
about holding the attention of his audience.

Use illustrations. The simplest, easiest, and quickest way to get people
to listen, and the surest way to hold their attention, is to use illustrations.
Every popular speaker has understood this imperative need. Jesus Christ
revealed his message in stories: "The Figs and Thistles," "The Sower,"
"The Prodigal Son."

Talk about people. People are interested in other people—their habits,
peculiarities, fads, and fortunes. The student who tried to construct a
speech on socialism did not get along well until he decided to center it
on Norman Thomas, the American socialist leader, and to show the influence of Thomas' speechmaking on the platforms of the conservative
parties. Similarly, the undergraduate regaling alumni on the habits of

present-day college students made full use of human interest when he began, "The gentleman's schedule has no classes before eleven, none after two, and none above the second floor." He continued with a vivid account of the attitudes, beliefs, preferences, and shortcomings of his classmates. He pointed out their dislike for courses that are too difficult, for assignments that are too long, for social engagements that are too restricted, and for instructors who never miss a class.

Choose the colorful phrase. Often the colloquial phrase, the one right and colorful word, makes all the difference between tedium and interest. When the pullman porter was asked if the train was ready to go, he replied, "No, sir, but she's a-twitchin'." The protesting student speaker chose his word well when he declared, "Girls should not he *hoisted* into cabs." In his fireside chat of March, 1933, Franklin D. Roosevelt showed his fondness for the homely expression when he urged the American people to deposit their money in the reopened banks instead of continuing to hide it under the mattress.

Let your personality enliven your treatment. Listeners are interested in knowing what you are like as a person. You need not be solemn. Unless the speech calls for impersonal development, you are free to reveal your attitudes and opinions. To his fellow actors, the handsome cowboy of the western serial is "that bowlegged scene stealer." To the automobile salesman, the delighted purchaser's new secondhand car is just "four new tires, a horn, and a paint job." To the nurse in the East Pavilion, the football hero's pretty sweetheart is "that little blond appendectomy in Room 307." Some men express their judgment of women in the exclamation, "Show me a woman a man can trust." Some women express their judgment of men in the declaration, "A man is honest until he is ten years old." Your speech composition should have the benefit of your personality.

Narration and description. People who cannot follow a complicated chain of reasoning, and those who would be put to sleep by a recital of statistics, may give their full attention to a speech or to those parts of a speech that employ narration or description to amplify the proof or provide relief from the more demanding tasks of reasoning. In descriptive or narrative accounts, you can remind your listeners of pleasant or unpleasant odors, tastes, or textures. You can create in them a feeling of strain or an awareness of hunger.

The gaining of attention through sensory impressions requires that you have sufficient imagination to recreate for yourself the experience to be described and that you take the necessary pains to recreate it for your listeners. You must have the patience to search out the right details.

VISUAL IMAGERY. Attention can be gained through visual imagery. Edward R. Murrow, in his broadcast on the bombing of Berlin, chose words of sight and color to make the action vivid:

Jock observed, "There's a kite on fire dead ahead." It was a great golden slow-moving meteor slanting towards the earth. By this time we were about thirty miles from our target area in Berlin. That thirty miles was the longest flight I have ever made. Dead on time, Boz, the bomb aimer, reported, "Target indicators going down." At the same moment the sky ahead was lit up by bright yellow flares. Off to starboard, another kite went down in flames. The flares were spouting all over the sky—red and green and yellow—and we were flying straight for the center of the fireworks. "D-Dog" seemed to be standing still, and four propellers thrashing the air. But we didn't seem to be closing in. The clouds had cleared, and off to the starboard a Lanc was caught by at least fourteen searchlight beams. We could see him twist and turn and finally break out. But still the whole thing had a quality of unreality about it. No one seemed to be shooting at us, but it was getting lighter all the time. Suddenly, a tremendous big blob of yellow light appeared dead ahead, another to the right, and another to the left. We were flying straight for them.[28]

AUDITORY IMAGERY.   Attention can be gained through auditory imagery. Observe how Harry Emerson Fosdick made his listeners hear:

In this regard how like we human beings are to dogs! For one dog barks and the other barks back and the first barks more loudly and the second becomes more noisy still, in a mounting crescendo of hostility. So one man excused his terrier, to the exasperated owner of another. "After all," he said, "the dog is only human." [29]

GUSTATORY IMAGERY.   Attention can be gained through gustatory imagery. Are you talking about apple pie? Then do not be content with saying, "The apple pie tasted swell." Take time to develop the mouth-watering sensations, as did the student who delivered the speech from which the following excerpt is taken:

Mary's apple pie was no pasteboard concoction of the bakery variety. It was a confection made of early June apples, ripe, ready to be eaten, sweet-smelling, and tangy from the sun. The apples were gently smothered in sugar bubbling up in them as they cooked in a delicate, flaky crust that melted away like butter in your mouth. To the whole Mary had added a suspicion of nutmeg—not too much and not too little, but just enough. To have put ice cream on Mary's pie would have been a sacrilege and, as such, properly resented.

OLFACTORY IMAGERY.   Attention can be gained through olfactory imagery. You may need to get your hearers to smell an odor. Naming it is not enough. Describe it. Compare it with others; tell how the rich aroma

[28] A. Craig Baird, ed., *Representative American Speeches: 1943–1944*, New York: The H. W. Wilson Company, 1944, pp. 40–41. Copyright 1944 by The H. W. Wilson Company.

[29] A. Craig Baird, ed., *Representative American Speeches: 1938–1939*, New York: The H. W. Wilson Company, 1939, p. 225. Copyright 1939 by The H. W. Wilson Company.

of boiling coffee appealed to the hungry crew, how the stench of the battlefield affected the weary soldiers, how the acrid smell of the stockyards hung over the slum dwellers. The following example shows how odors may be referred to in a student speech:

When I was a little girl, I alway liked early morning because everything smelled so good. The air on the ranch was fresh and sweet before the hot winds came up, and the bedroom smelled of mother's powder and the baby's oil. Did you ever whiff coffee on the stove and bacon sizzling in an iron skillet? On fresh-bread mornings I really hurried. While I finished setting the table, the tantalizing smell of oranges mingled with the other odors. Shortly my father would appear, bearing buckets of warm, sweet, frothy milk.

TACTUAL IMAGERY. Attention can be gained through tactual imagery. Sometimes your problem is to make your hearers feel, to give them a tactile or thermal impression. You want them to know how slimy was the seaweed, how dry the desert gully, how cold the steel crowbar, or how rough the sawed timbers to the touch. You should employ detail, make comparisons, describe effectively.

OTHER IMPRESSIONS. Sometimes general sensations, either organic or kinesthetic, will provide a stimulus to attention. How does it feel to crawl and squirm through the coal chute in order to get into a locked house? How does it feel to wake in the night and find your house on fire? How does it feel to fall two thousand feet before your tangled parachute opens? These sensations and countless others have been described by students in speeches. One man recounted the battle action in which he, the target of an enemy sniper, slid down the slate roof and hung precariously on the gutter of an old church, uncertain whether to try to regain his perch on the roof or to drop the twenty feet to the ground. His hearers followed the speaker with such rapt attention that they moved forward in their seats and braced themselves unconsciously against his fall. This speaker not only had a vivid recollection of his own experience; he also employed a wealth of detail in recreating it. He did not limit his speech to one sensory impression: he told what he saw, and heard, and touched, as well as how he felt and what he did.

The various forms of imagery should be regarded as avenues leading to the attention of your audience. Since audiences differ in their responsiveness to the kinds of imagery, you would do well to approach them through more than one avenue.

Personal Persuasion

Of the three means of persuading—logical, psychological, and personal —probably the most powerful is the one derived from the speaker himself. Day after day more changes are effected by request or direction based on faith in the speaker than by an argument advanced for a proposition. Even the most exacting scientists are more likely, outside the laboratory, to rely upon statements of friends and acquaintances than they are upon objective analysis. The reason is obvious: human beings have neither the time nor the means to do otherwise.

Attributes for personal persuasion. What are the personal attributes that make a speaker persuasive? This question must be answered in terms of a specific audience. A forger, for example, might be more persuasive with his fellow inmates in a penitentiary than would an honest guard. Five attributes generally inspire the confidence of most audiences: (1) experience, (2) judgment, (3) integrity, (4) loyalty, (5) attraction. A speaker may bring to an occasion a high reputation for one or more of these attributes. As a result of his speech he may enhance or diminish this reputation.

EXPERIENCE. The advocate who has had previous experience with a proposal is more likely to be accepted by an audience than one who has not. When a street commissioner of thirty years' successful service advocates the construction of a new street, he is likely to receive a better hearing from judicious persons than is the novice who is known never to have had any related experience. If the audience is unfamiliar with this direct experience, the speaker should make appropriate reference to it as part of his support.

JUDGMENT. The speaker who has acquired a reputation for good common sense, for the exercise of judgment in difficult situations, and for restrained and measured action is likely to find his proposals well received. To a discriminating audience, his reputation for judgment will in itself carry a measure of conviction. Lacking such a reputation, he must be all the more certain that the cogency of his reasoning and the significance of his evidence are unmistakable to his listeners. His good judgment should be revealed throughout his speech.

INTEGRITY. The man who has a reputation for integrity is likely to receive the approbation of thoughtful people. On the other hand, one who is generally thought to be dishonest will be heard with suspicion. Unless the listeners believe the speaker to be trustworthy, they will not give his cause a full and favorable hearing. Indeed, he may hurt his cause by speaking for it. The man who is unknown to his audience must make special effort to establish his integrity as he speaks.

LOYALTY. A speaker may be known to have had experience, to have acquired judgment, and to be a person of proved integrity, and yet be unpersuasive because his hearers believe him to be devoted to interests other than their own. He must demonstrate his loyalty to the group he is addressing; his listeners must be confident that he is interested in their welfare.

ATTRACTION. Beyond all other qualities suggested for the persuasive speaker, he should have also a personal attraction for his hearers. Great speakers have commonly been men of compelling personality who exerted a strong influence on other people. This quality is not one of beauty, nor of size, nor of strength. It is the result of the speaker's ability to project his own mind and spirit into the wishes and hopes and fears of men and women.

Means of personal persuasion. A speaker, like any other person, may impose on the good faith of others by appearing to be what he is not. Sometimes the imposition is successful; in the long run, however, people in a free society are likely to expose dishonesty. The rule works both ways: just as a dishonest man may assume the guise of honesty, so a man of character may not know how to do himself justice as a person worthy of belief. Since audiences must judge a speaker by external signs, the unskillful man of honest purpose is handicapped by his limitations. What are the commonly accepted means to personal persuasion?

In the first place, the speaker should act as one having authority. His manner should not be overbearing, condescending, nor belligerent, but should suggest a friendly interest in the welfare of his listeners. Nor should his bearing be feeble, apologetic, or timid; it should reveal confidence in his own personal standing and in his right to be heard. The speaker should exhibit a convincing modesty, with an assurance that requires no bombast. At the same time, he must avoid even the slightest appearance of patronizing his audience. In addition to these long-time aspects of personality, he may use specific means to increase his personal effectiveness in an assembly.

IDENTIFICATION WITH THE GROUP. Since the individual who is well and favorably known to a group receives a more ready acceptance than a stranger, the speaker should be alert to identify himself with his audience either in his introduction or during the course of his speech: "I was born here in Knoxville . . . ." "My wife's people came from Atchison County, just next door . . . ." "My friends . . . ." "You and I know . . . ." The speaker strives to make the group feel, "He is one of us; he knows what we need." All experienced speakers know that the identification with the audience, although highly effective, cannot be taken for granted. Yet the speaker must not appear to be too eager in establishing himself with the group. Perhaps this means of persuasion should always be recognized but kept in the background.

FAIR PLAY. Unless the circumstances are exceptional, an audience of Americans is likely to appreciate a speaker's inclination to be fair, to give everybody a hearing, and to do full justice to his opposition. An appeal to fair play is likely to mark the speaker as worthy to be heard.

THE APPEAL TO REASON. With a judicious audience, the speaker marks himself as worthy of belief if he relies primarily upon reason and judgment. Although exceptions can be noted, American audiences are likely to distrust the perfervid appeals of the ranter. With thoughtful listeners, nothing does more to enhance the speaker's personal proof than the forthright appeal to reason.

SINCERITY. Once let an audience believe that a speaker is insincere, and he has lost them for that day and perhaps forever. Especially with an audience of simple folk, the speaker must be absolutely in earnest. Furthermore, if he employs humor, he must exercise great care lest his listeners mistake it for flippancy.

AMIABILITY. Audiences are likely to be displeased with bickering and displays of temper. A scolding or threatening attitude discredits a speaker immediately, but amiability and good nature create the atmosphere of good will usually necessary to persuasion.

SIMPLICITY AND DIRECTNESS. People sometimes distrust the man who seems to talk too well. The glib speaker appears to have spent a great deal of time learning how to say words that may not be true. The genuinely persuasive speaker conceals his art. He pleases his audience with the simplicity of his utterance and the directness of his presentation.

TACT. Although honesty and sincerity are necessary, tact is equally important. In accrediting himself, the speaker should be on guard to avoid inadvertent remarks, ill-guarded phrases, and slips of the tongue, as well as unnecessary curtness that may offend his hearers and give him a reputation for ineptitude.

THE RIGHT TIMING. Sometimes a speaker incurs the ill will of an audience by talking too long or too frequently. He monopolizes the floor in an assembly, or tries to say everything that can be said on the subject. He displeases those who would like to speak and does not endear himself to other members of the group. Good sense should tell the speaker when and how long to talk.

THE UNITY OF PERSUASION

The art of persuading has been considered as logical, psychological, and personal. In actual practice, no such easy division is possible. What the speaker says becomes as one with his person, his manner, and his bearing. The evidence he offers is fused with the attitudes and beliefs of his audience. Indeed, if the speaker is truly persuasive, all phases of his art are so fully united when he speaks to people that neither he nor they are immediately conscious of the means employed.

4 ADAPTATION:
Audience and Plans

The word eloquence, in its greatest lati-
tude, denotes "that art or talent by which
the discourse is adapted to its end."
                                    —George Campbell

If audiences were always alert, intelligent, and
fair, the speaker's problem of adaptation would be simple. The chain
of reasoning in the sentence analysis would be the speech. But audiences
are not always open to reason, and they are frequently uninterested, at
the outset, in what the speaker has to say. Consequently, even after
you have developed the substance of your speech, you should ask yourself such questions as the following:

- How can I overcome prejudice?
- How can I make my thought clear to the uninformed members of my
  audience without boring the others?
- How can I keep my hearers attentive?
- What lines of thought should I develop, and what lines of thought
  should I eliminate for this audience?
- In what order should I present my ideas?

The answers to the foregoing questions should suggest the development of a plan for your speech. The plan should be chosen as the best
means of adapting to a specific audience the materials developed in your
sentence analysis of the subject.

To make the best use of your previously determined thought structure you will need to understand your audience and to know the plans
for developing and adapting the speech to that audience. You will then be
able to determine your speech structure.

THE AUDIENCE

The diversification of modern minds, the increase in specialization, and the influence of the masses present both a notable challenge and an unparalleled opportunity to the speaker. The function of speechmaking is to deal with an audience, and one of its principal uses is so to interpret learning that laymen can understand it. The need for competent speakers is greater than ever before.

ANALYZING THE AUDIENCE

Analyzing an audience is essentially a twofold problem: to what extent are the people alike, and to what extent are they different? In the study of likenesses, or common ground, the speaker needs to consider whether his hearers share the same information, interests, beliefs, and patterns of action. In the study of differences, he needs to consider age, sex, and race; nationality, regions, and communities; occupation, economic status, and social position; religion and political belief; intelligence and education; opinions, attitudes, desires, and tensions. Fortunately, the speaker usually finds only a few of these likenesses and differences relevant to the analysis of a given audience. If the group is heterogeneous, he may find common ground in American citizenship. If the group is homogeneous, he may find common ground in the interest that binds it together.

Discovering Common Ground

In a given audience, some one attribute is likely to dominate. In periods when men emphasize religion, the church serves as a binding force. Today some audiences are bound by the religious tie. At other times men stress political beliefs. Today substantial groups are joined in political parties. The common bonds of age may give rise to youth movements or campaigns for old-age pensions. The movement for woman's suffrage exemplified an orientation based upon sex. Whatever the dominant attitudes may be, the speaker should understand them. If no common bond of unity is apparent, he must develop one.

Characteristically, the speaker wishes to give his hearers information or induce them to accept new beliefs. In order to accomplish his purpose, he must establish a common ground of information, interest, belief, or action based on the experiences of his listeners.

Common ground of information.   Schools and colleges, libraries and museums, newspapers and magazines, movies and plays, radio and television have made information more accessible than ever before. With reference to any one subject, however, the very prevalence of information may lead a speaker to assume that his listeners know more than they do. Although most people may be aware of an occurrence or a development, some otherwise well-informed individuals may have failed to hear of it. Sometimes talented people are so busy that they do not keep up with the world around them. The demands upon the time of most citizens leave them little opportunity to do all the reading they would like to do. Furthermore, what concerns some people does not concern others. Those who keep up to date on sports or the stock market may ignore science or foreign affairs.

Even the simplest facts of geography, history, and mechanics are sometimes beyond the ken of intelligent people. A well-to-do business-man did not realize that in traveling from his home in Pennsylvania to Kansas City, Missouri, he had crossed the Mississippi River. A student consistently confused President Andrew Jackson with President Andrew Johnson, and on being questioned, he admitted that he thought they were the same person. An engineer who explained the operation of a four-cycle engine was amazed to discover that most of his listeners did not know what a piston was.

Since the speaker usually cannot determine exactly what his listeners know, he must assume that their information is general. Such information may be so indefinite as to require a summary to supply the background. Without boring the informed, the speaker must develop for the uninformed the necessary common ground of information.

Common ground of interests. However much they differ, human beings are essentially alike in their basic interests. Self-preservation is generally accepted as the first law of nature. In seeking to protect himself, the individual may go to extremes, as does the miser in amassing wealth; but the general principle prevails: human conduct is directed toward self-interest, or what the individual regards as self-interest.

Self-interest takes many forms. On one level the individual may be concerned only with a day-to-day existence. On another he may want to acquire property. On still another he may be striving for personal accomplishment, either bringing primary satisfaction to himself, or winning applause from others. One musician may strive to become a great pianist because of an inner drive; another may find his chief incentive in the prestige he acquires.

Personal safety is a major form of self-interest. Since security against bodily harm is a basic concern, threatened dangers loom large in anyone's thought and action. A hunter may forego the satisfaction of his desire to shoot big game if he realizes that proceeding over treacherous ground would endanger his safety. The framers of the federal constitution were interested in personal safety of a higher order. They provided for security from tyranny by the guaranties of the Bill of Rights.

The highest form of self-interest is the welfare of the individual as represented by the family, the community, the state, or the nation; a way of life, the good of humanity, or the service of God. Whether altruism is a form of selfishness, whether group loyalty is an extension of individual personality, are irrelevant. The individual identifies his interests with those of the group to which he is most firmly devoted. The patriot who volunteers to fight for his country illustrates amplified self-interest.

Whether listeners are primarily thinking of personal advantage, a higher standard of living for their families, or the charities they would like to support, they probably share a desire for a larger income. This desire enables the speaker to establish common ground.

Common ground of beliefs. Freedom of belief is a cornerstone of American democracy. In religion, politics, and economics, an American citizen may believe what he considers right so long as he does not seek to overthrow the government by force or to interfere with the rights of his fellow citizens. An individual's beliefs may be traditional in his family, his social group, or his community; they may be freely chosen in the course of study and experience; or they may vary according to the influence that happens to prevail. With such freedom, the possibility of agreement might seem to be remote; yet commonly accepted beliefs exist in every field.

Basic assumptions are fundamental in thought and conduct. In religion most people believe that God is omnipotent; in politics, that legislative bodies should hold the purse strings; in business, that competition is the life of trade; in ethics, that everyone should respect the rights of others; in education, that every normal child should be taught to read.

The necessity of starting from basic assumptions forces the speaker to find in his audience a common ground of belief. The more diversified the listeners, the more fundamental will be that common ground. For farmers, the common ground of belief may be that they do not receive enough for their crops; for factory workers, that wages are too low; for both farmers and workers, that the American standard of living should be raised.

Common ground in patterns of action. Individuals and groups form habits that set patterns of action. Commuters read their newspapers on trains to and from work. Housewives listen to the radio as they do their morning chores. Students chat with their friends between classes. Businessmen answer their mail promptly. When habits become fixed, breaking them may be disturbing. When the papers do not arrive, the commuter may be upset for the day.

WIDE WORLD PHOTOS

J. EDW. BAILEY III

THE END AND OBJECT OF SPEAKING IS AUDIENCE RESPONSE
Prominent speakers who address large groups of people face complex problems
of audience analysis and adaptation. Presidential candidate John F. Kennedy
holds the attention of a crowd of San Diego voters. Columnist Sylvia Porter
interests a gathering of Detroit businessmen.

Some activities are agreeable; others are disagreeable. Nearly everyone likes to eat an appetizing meal and to see a good show. Businessmen like to play golf on weekends. Shoppers like to choose from a wide variety of merchandise. On the other hand, everyone dislikes to pay a high price for goods of poor quality or to be restricted in the food he can eat. Motorists dislike driving over rough roads. Soldiers dislike double-time marching.

Common sense should tell the speaker that his proposal will be less acceptable if it requires action contrary to established patterns. His problem is to suggest actions consistent with habitual responses. The chairman of the finance committee who urged his fellow club members to contribute five hundred dollars each to save the clubhouse from threatened foreclosure found in his listeners an inclination to comply with his request but a failure to act. Had he distributed five forms with return envelopes urging each member to make five monthly contributions of one hundred dollars each, his response would perhaps have been greater. The financial habits of his listeners would not permit them to make a contribution of five hundred dollars in a single month. With forms and envelopes provided, they would have been more likely to contribute.

Recognizing Differences

Differences among people require the speaker's close study. Both what to do and what to avoid depend upon knowing the composition of the audience. The information, arguments, and appeals suitable for one group may not reach another. Proof adequate for one segment of an audience may be inadequate for another. What appeals to the young may not appeal to the old; what convinces Democrats may not convince Republicans.

To list all the ways in which people differ would be tediously absurd, if not impossible; but some of the ways most significant to the speaker will serve to illustrate the problem of determining differences affecting the development of a speech.

Differences of age. The differences between age groups are important to the speaker because he must know how to talk to people in their own terms. The wisest policy is to give less attention to proverbs such as "Old men are wise" and "Young men are foolish," and to rely more upon characteristic differences in behavior that can be ascribed to sound reasons.

Generalizations about different age groups are subject to the exceptions that anyone might name—the sober young man of whom it is said, "He was born old," or the vigorous gentleman of whom it is said, "He is seventy years young." Yet everyone recognizes that, by and large, a group of old people will differ from a party of teen-agers, and that an audience of middle-aged men and women will differ from a gathering of children.

CHILDREN. Anyone speaking to an audience of children should remember that healthy American youngsters are often energetic and uninhibited. They are likely to be outspoken in approval or disapproval, and on occasion they may be noisy. Because the attention span is not well developed in children, the speaker must expect to compete with distractions. Youngsters are interested in play, in activity, and in their favorite foods.

Since the vocabulary of normal ten-year-olds is limited, they should not be expected to respond to encyclopedic diction. That children are fond of narratives is proverbial: they will listen to stories when no other discourse will reach them. Even narrative speeches, however, must be fitted into the world they live in or can imagine.

YOUTH. Young men and women often retain many childish traits, but they dislike to be treated as children. They may have reached full stature physically without having arrived at psychological maturity. Many young people are less sophisticated than they believe themselves to be. Normally youths of eighteen have not had wide experience in life; consequently, they are likely to aspire to great achievement without realizing its cost in effort and self-denial. Young people who have never been self-supporting are unlikely to understand fully the value of money or to comprehend how hard it is to earn.

Since few young people have much firsthand experience with death, the young man, in contrast with the octogenarian, looks forward to a long life, and his attitudes are colored, perhaps unconsciously, by his life expectancy. As Hazlitt said, "No young man believes that he will ever die." Perhaps for this reason young people as a group tend to be more courageous and more foolhardy than their elders. They are less cautious, more willing to take a chance. The National Safety Council reports that the number of automobile accidents in the sixteen to twenty-five age group is excessively high, not because young people are incapable of driving well, but because young drivers tempt accident by rash conduct.

Young people, as a rule, have not had to shoulder heavy responsibilities. Although exceptions should be noted, most young men and women have not had the care of a family; they have not had to provide for the welfare of others, but have themselves been provided for.

American youths are often full of high spirits. They enjoy gaiety and are disinclined to borrow trouble. Because they are having a good time with fun and excitement, they are not always willing to develop long-range plans. They tend to live more in the present than in the past or in the future. They are often unselfish, lacking in prudence, and passionate in the pursuit of their immediate goals; they are thus led sometimes to take part in riots or beach escapades that give their elders grave concern.

All these characteristics and tendencies of young Americans are natural consequences of their station. Opportunities, responsibilities, and experience determine how early in life they become mature. The speaker may sometimes have difficulty in gaining and holding their serious attention.

THE MIDDLE-AGED.   Some people grow older chronologically without maturing psychologically. By and large, however, the middle-aged tend to curb their desires, which may have become less imperious with maturity, and to let prudence govern their conduct. Hard experience has often taught men and women of middle age that strangers cannot always be trusted, that personal health and safety are of great concern, that death and taxes are twin certainties. In middle age the standards of conduct have normally become relatively fixed, and the habits of life fairly stable. If people of middle age are not likely to be ecstatic with success, neither are they too much cast down with failure. They have often come to know that neither joy nor sorrow is permanent and that the daily affairs of life tend to move in normal courses.

Men and women in middle life are likely to be aware of approaching age and, if they can, to make provision for it. They tend to judge proposals on merits, partly as to their own welfare and partly as to the general prosperity. Most American men and women of middle age have had gainful employment for a period of years: they have been working in a factory, or clerking in a store, or running a farm.

In sum, men and women of middle life tend to be in their prime, involved in adult activities of getting and spending. They often occupy the places of authority in their communities and, generally speaking, make the important decisions in the life of the nation.

Since the middle-aged are normally engrossed in making a living, in rearing a family, and in discharging community responsibilities, they may have little time to give to a proposal. They tend to judge a speech by whether it makes sense and by whether the speaker seems to be an honest man.

THE ELDERLY.   Elderly people vary widely in their characteristics. The differences depend upon their circumstances and the way life has treated them. Yet they are likely to have in common certain traits resulting from their age.

Elderly men and women tend to be less vigorous in body, even though the mind may be as keen as ever. Physical activity is less energetic, and reflexes are slower. According to a report of the National Safety Council, automobile drivers over sixty-five generally fall into accidents not because of rashness but because of physical inability to avoid them.

Elderly people are approaching, if they have not already reached, the age of retirement. Insurance data show that most of them have not acquired a competence for their old age and hence are dependent on modest pensions or on the care of others. In the American economy, the great tragedy of old age is unemployment and unemployability, for anyone over fifty who loses his job may have little opportunity to obtain another. Old people, therefore, generally are more concerned about security and the necessities of life than about developing new plans for the future.

As men and women grow older, they tend with each passing year to be the survivors of their friends and family. They sometimes live much in the past with their memories, out of touch with younger generations.

As age advances, the elderly may become timorously aware of their loss of physical and perhaps of mental vigor. When they find themselves restricted in their activities and occupied with fewer interests, they tend to become more and more disturbed by trifles. As they develop infirmities, they may become gravely concerned with their own health, well-being, and dependence upon others.

As a rule, therefore, the traits of elderly people make them a difficult group to approach with new measures or venturesome plans. Only the safest and most prudent courses are likely to recommend themselves to aged folk; and even when they approve, they may not have the vigor or the means necessary to execute a plan. Older people are often regarded, as indeed they regard themselves, as more fitted for counsel based upon experience than for the active conduct of affairs.

Differences of sex. So wide are the individual variations within the sexes that generalizations are limited in their usefulness. Certain tendencies, however, may be noted. Men tend to be concerned with business, industry, and the professions, but more and more women are learning these fields. Men tend to be more interested in economic problems, women in social problems, but exceptions are numerous. In most families women are more familiar with the needs and problems of children and with the demands of housekeeping. Food and clothing are major interests of the wife; earning a livelihood is chiefly the responsibility of the husband. In general, men are more inclined to prefer the comfortable to the artistic.

The speaker should be able to choose illustrations, arguments, and appeals suited to a masculine audience or to a feminine audience. To a group of men he might choose to show that a bond issue for new parks and streets would be a sound financial investment because improved traffic conditions would mean substantial savings to business and industry. To a group of women he might prefer to show that the proposal would be worth the cost because the children of the city would be safer and happier on the playgrounds of the new parks than on the hazardous city streets.

Differences of race.   However elaborately races may be distinguished, for the speaker they are simply groups having a common culture. In appealing to races other than his own, the speaker needs to cultivate friendly understanding. In pacifying an aroused racial group, he must solve delicate problems of language, ideas, and appeals. Understanding emotional states is essential wherever tension exists between races. Even knowing what words to use and what to avoid may be important.

Differences of nationality.   Nationality is a unity shared by people of common customs, language, and institutions. In the United States, American nationality has generally supplanted the loyalties of the foreign-born. In different areas, however, national traditions survive in local customs and celebrations. The Spanish in New Mexico, the Chinese in California, the Germans in Missouri, the Irish in Massachusetts, the French in Louisiana have preserved distinctive aspects of their original nationality.

The speaker who knows the heritage of his hearers has a great advantage in developing his arguments and appeals. In discussing a liberal education, a teacher may find illustrations from German music and philosophy provocative for an audience of German ancestry; allusions to Irish songs and folk plays may be pleasing to listeners of Irish origin.

Differences of regions.   Although the American way of life has a recognizable pattern, regional differences give color to various sections. Not only the three major areas of North, South, and West, but also such regions as Cape Cod in Massachusetts, the Ozarks of Missouri, and the Cajun country of Louisiana, have distinctive folkways. Life in the cotton belt contrasts with that of the prairies; the patterns of living in Portland, Maine, differ in some respects from those of Boise, Idaho. The mores of Charleston, South Carolina, are not precisely those of Phoenix, Arizona. The influences of the Puritan of New England, of the planter in the old South, and of the pioneer in the West are still evident in the attitudes of the people.

For the speaker, a slight but subtle regional difference may be even more serviceable than a strong likeness to the common American pattern. The speaker who manifests knowledge of a regional custom, of a local holiday, or of provincial humor may find it easy to get on common ground of good feeling with his audience.

Differences of communities.   Significant differences in habits, attitudes, and beliefs result from types of community life. The farm, the village, the town, and the city have their effects on the individual. Although the modern farmer has more contacts with other people than did the pioneer a century ago, the relative isolation of many farms still requires self-sufficiency. In the village, according to tradition, everybody knows everybody else's business. The town permits people to choose their associates and to lead their lives largely according to preferences, but the daily newspaper keeps the inhabitants aware of the diversified activities of the place. In a large city, the people in one section may know very little about those in another. Even in the same apartment house, people may live next door to each other without ever becoming acquainted.

In dealing with audiences, the speaker should ponder the characteristic traits of the farmer and the villager, of the townsman and the city dweller. The Midwestern American village, for example, has been said to retain "the grass-roots faith in good will, neighborliness, piety, and the wisdom of a good but not a hard bargain." The great American cities, on the other hand, are caught up in the driving pressures of modern times.

Differences of occupation. Since people spend much of their time earning a living, their behavior is likely to be influenced by their occupation. If they like their work, they want its contributions recognized. If they dislike it, they may wish to see it changed. The professions generally prescribe codes of ethics to discourage charlatans and to command the respect of the public. Physicians, lawyers, engineers, and journalists are usually alert to maintain their standards and to improve their public relations. Labor unions endeavor to keep wages on a level with the cost of living and to improve working conditions.

The speaker who appeals to the members of any occupational group should know their objectives. To an audience of railroad trainmen a candidate may show that he has worked for the rights of organized labor; to an audience of physicians he may point out that he supports the health plan of the American Medical Association.

Differences of economic status. Although the contrasts between poverty and wealth may be less noticeable in the United States than in some other parts of the world, wide differences exist in the American standard of living. The federal tax returns disclose the large incomes of industrial executives, motion picture stars, and Wall Street bankers. On the other hand, published investigations reveal the low incomes of government employees, teachers, and ministers. The necessity of one family is the luxury of another.

The realistic speaker recognizes the economic status of different groups. In appealing for a cancer fund, the campaigner should consider the financial ability of his listeners. A single dollar from a workman may represent a greater financial sacrifice than a thousand dollars from a manufacturer. Appreciation should be as genuine for the one gift as for the other.

Differences of social position. Democratic America does not countenance titles of nobility or classes of aristocracy, but social registers and country clubs are a part of the American scene. In many communities, being seen with the right people carries weight both with those who are accepted in the social set and with those who are not. In some circles, whether a woman does her own housework may make a world of difference.

No matter what the speaker may think of the existing social distinctions, he must deal with his audience as he finds it. To induce the ladies of an exclusive club to devote their time to sewing for the poor might prove impossible, but to persuade the same ladies to donate the proceeds of a bridge party to a local charity might be feasible.

Differences of religion. In the United States, religious freedom is a fundamental right, and the persecuted of all faiths have found refuge here. American children have been taught that many of the settlers who crossed the Atlantic were in search of religious freedom: the Pilgrims and Puritans in New England, the Quakers in Pennsylvania, the Catholics in Maryland. The Protestant denominations, the Catholic orders, the Hebrew faiths, and other congregations worship in their own way. Although religious controversies sometimes occur, interfaith organizations have helped to dissipate suspicion and to develop mutual respect.

In treating any topic with religious implications, the speaker will need to know sectarian beliefs and practices, for listeners are deeply offended by lack of respect for their faith. In pleading for Sabbath observance, for instance, a speaker should remember that some people worship on Saturday and others on Sunday.

Differences of political belief. The two-party system has prevailed in this country since the administration of John Adams. Splinter groups have flourished from time to time, but the electorate is usually divided among Republican, Democratic, and independent voters. The party members support their candidates both because of belief in party principles and because of the patronage that comes with victory. The independent voters either support one of the minor parties or make up their minds at each election as to which major party candidates they favor.

At all times, but particularly near elections, most public questions in America have close connections with party platforms and candidates for office. The speaker who wants an audience of Republicans to adopt a program of reform shows that it is consistent with Republicanism. The Democratic candidate, seeking the ballots of independent voters, identifies himself with the measures approved by his listeners—for example, low taxes on small incomes and the extension of social security.

Differences of intelligence. The capacity of the listener to think with the speaker makes a significant difference in the kind of information, arguments, and appeals employed. Since an intelligent audience understands a speaker's implications without an abundance of detail, the proof of a proposition may vary considerably with the group.

The speaker cannot afford to overestimate the intelligence of his listeners; yet to underestimate it may be costly. Perhaps he should compromise. As he appraises his hearers' intelligence, he should allow for the probable range. To avoid boring the brightest listeners, he chooses many different illustrations that are interesting in themselves. The number will be necessary for the slow-witted, and the variety for the more intelligent. With a single striking example, a minister may clarify the concept of the Golden Rule for the brilliant members of his congregation. Continuing with additional illustrations, he aids the understanding of the less intelligent. At the same time the variety holds the interest of all.

Differences of education. Some listeners are intelligent but uneducated; others are both intelligent and educated. Still others have only been exposed to schooling. The speaker's choice of arguments, illustrations, and language should be determined by the educational experience of his listeners.

If all members of the audience are well educated, or if all have a limited education, he should be able to adapt his speech to the understanding of the group. If the formal education of his listeners ranges from the grammar school to the university, he has the problem of making his material simple enough for the least educated but interesting to all.

Differences of opinions, attitudes, and desires. In forming their opinions, people are influenced by those whose judgment they respect: their clergymen, teachers, family, or friends. On some topics their opinion may derive from experience; on others it may be based on the judgment of the community. On technical matters most people are willing to rely upon experts.

Attitudes and opinions are closely linked. Rational attitudes may range from didactic and admonitory to incredulous and cynical, from questioning and doubting to critical and indignant. Emotional attitudes depend upon the kind and intensity of feeling, ranging from pleasure to pain, pride to shame, love to hate, fear to confidence, respect to contempt.

Desires spring chiefly from apparent needs. What people really want exerts a major influence upon their thought and conduct. Individual wants range from bare necessities to rare luxuries, from simple pleasures to elaborate entertainment, from minor changes to major reforms, from the easily attainable to the highly improbable. Some give first place to wealth, power, and position; others to home, family, and friends.

A speaker who knows the members of his audience can estimate their opinions, attitudes, and desires, but a stranger is limited to general information. Guided by what he knows, the speaker does not risk false appraisals. Addressing college seniors, he may safely assume their desire for rewarding careers, but he cannot properly conjecture the attitudes they have formed toward the professions.

Differences of tensions.   Whether an audience is placid or turbulent makes a great difference to the speaker. The contrast between a tranquil congregation of churchgoers and an angry mob threatening to break into a factory suggests the importance of feeling in the analysis of audiences. Whereas the minister seeks to arouse in his serene parishioners the feeling necessary to act in useful ways, the sheriff attempts to pacify the excited mob. Determining the tensions of his hearers is usually not so easy for the speaker as these extreme examples may suggest; nevertheless, he must seek to discover the basic feeling common to his audience.

Determining Relation of Audience to Preparation

All that the speaker does in determining the likenesses and the differences of his audience furthers his preparation. He should also seek to discover the size and the experience of his audience.

The size of the audience.   The size of the audience is psychologically important. Especially when the speaker wants definite action, the small audience is more difficult than the large. In a large group, suggestibility and a feeling of unity are often characteristic; in a small group, each individual tends to think and act in isolation.

The smaller the audience, the more thought the speaker should give to ways of unifying its members. If possible, he should bring his listeners close together and close to him. He should also make maximum use of the four types of common ground. In addition to well-considered arguments and appeals, he should apply the principles of unity and suggestion. Singing or laughing together tends to break down individual reserve. The signing of a petition or the adopting of a resolution helps to unify the group. Indications of approval for the proposed action may be useful: majority support, conformity with tradition, previous adoption by respected groups, rejection by individuals whom the listeners hold in contempt.

The experience of the audience.   The speaker's selection of material depends upon the maturity of his listeners. The amount of explanation needed, the kind of illustrations used, and even the reasoning introduced vary with the sophistication of the audience. What the listeners have seen and heard, where they have been, what publications they know, what opportunities they have had—all these govern the speaker in his preparation.

Essentially the speaker's problem is to find where his knowledge impinges upon the experience of his audience. He cannot use what his listeners know and he does not. He can use what he knows and they do not if he relates it to their experience at some point. A candidate clarified political problems for an audience of dairymen by drawing upon experiences from his boyhood spent on a farm.

Determining Relation of Audience to Speaker

How the hearers feel toward the speaker, what they know about him, and what they expect of him determine the initial response. If his audience is favorable toward him, if his reputation with them is good, and if he can meet their expectations, then his initial problem of accreditation is solved.

Attitude toward speaker. The attitude of the hearers toward the speaker may be well grounded upon previous acquaintance or published reports, or it may be erroneously acquired through misinformation or false inference. If the listeners are friendly toward the speaker, he may anticipate their good will in developing his theme. If they are trustful, he may count upon their confidence in his integrity. If they are respectful, he may assume their acceptance of his judgment when it does not conflict with their experience. Listeners may like a speaker without trusting or respecting him; they may trust and respect him without liking him; if he is fortunate, they may like, trust, *and* respect him.

An unfavorable attitude toward the speaker may result from a dislike of his personality, a doubt about his trustworthiness, or a lack of confidence in his judgment. If by his cordiality, good humor, and modest dignity the speaker convinces his listeners that he is really a person they can like, he may overcome their hostility. If by his fairness, his experience, and his position he shows them that he is a leader whom they can safely follow, he may gain their trust. If by his grasp of the subject, his clear reasoning, and his strong evidence he demonstrates that he is thoroughly conversant with his field, he may win their respect.

The speaker's intelligent use of common ground helps to create a favorable attitude. If through his treatment of his topic he assures his listeners that he shares their attitudes, interests, and beliefs, he makes himself one of their number. If by skillful allusion or tactful compliment he shows his appreciation of their achievements, he does not lower himself in their regard. If in using authorities and illustrations he indicates that he knows and respects the same people they do, he helps to remove doubts. If in sincere tribute he praises their heritage and their public spirit, he raises himself in their esteem.

The speaker who is arrogant, condescending, pompous, or belligerent seldom gains good will, trust, or respect. A brash manner antagonizes most listeners. Self-confidence without conceit, earnestness without insistence, and integrity without smugness create the favorable attitude the speaker requires.

Reputation of the speaker. A prominent man builds his reputation with his public activities. A man less widely known depends for his reputation upon announcement or upon the chairman's introduction. Since the speaker's usefulness depends upon what people think of him, his speech should be planned to accredit him with his immediate audience.

Expectations of the audience. Clearly, the speaker should endeavor to exceed rather than disappoint the expectations of his hearers. Although extravagant praise may create a reputation he cannot maintain, the exaggeration may suggest a clever approach that will establish good rapport. Certainly the speaker should spare no effort to make the audience feel repaid for coming to hear him.

Determining Relation of Audience to Purpose

When the speaker's purpose is only to entertain, he should discover whether his listeners are likely to be gay or serious. When he endeavors to impress, he needs to know whether they are likely to be deferential or cynical. When he seeks to inform, he should ascertain whether they are likely to be alert or dull. When he hopes to persuade, he should determine whether they are likely to be favorable, neutral, or hostile. He must not expect uniformity, but he may discern a prevailing attitude. All degrees of positive and negative feeling may be represented. A prevailing negative mood will give him most concern.

The mood to be entertained. A knowledge of the principles of entertaining should assist the speaker to create the appropriate mood. If the listeners wish to be amused, he should realize that a striking beginning is in order. If they are serious, a more deliberate approach is desirable. To avoid embarrassment to himself and his listeners, the speaker should allow their tastes as well as his own to determine his choice of material.

The mood to be impressed. The occasion usually creates the right mood for the speaker whose purpose is chiefly to impress. The audience assembles in a deferential frame of mind, and the cynical stay away. The principles of impressing assist the speaker to create a mood of respect or reverence, or to intensify the mood already created.

The mood to be informed. Listeners eager to hear a speaker make his task a pleasure. People who are present because of compulsion or chance challenge his ability to interest them. The principles of informing assist him to satisfy the curious and to stimulate the dull. At times he needs first to persuade his listeners that hearing him is to their advantage.

The mood to be persuaded. Favorable listeners may include any or all of the following. Some are ready to act, but need direction; they must be offered a specific course of action. Others are not unwilling to act, but need stimulation; they must be given strong encouragement. Still others are convinced of the desirability of the proposal but are disinclined to act; they must be convinced that action cannot be left to other people.

Neutral listeners may include any or all of the following. Some are indifferent, but their interest can be aroused; they should be given material to gain and hold attention. Others are uninformed but willing to listen; they should be supplied with information and arguments. Still others can be swayed either way, but will probably go along with the majority; they should be aroused by appeals. A few may be dubious about the proposal, but will weigh arguments; they should be offered close reasoning and evidence.

Hostile listeners may include any or all of the following. Some have misunderstood the proposal; they should be given a clear explanation. Others are predisposed against it; they should be offered proof tending to overcome the predisposition. Still others have concluded that the proposal is unsound; they must be persuaded by a stronger case than the one that induced their original decision. A special group would be adversely affected by the proposal; they must be moved by appeals stronger than the personal interest adversely affected.

The principles of persuading should enable the speaker to induce the favorable listeners to believe more strongly and to act, to make the neutral group favorable, and in some instances to overcome the opposition of the hostile. He should try to persuade all the groups in his audience, and he should not be discouraged. He should not expect miracles.

Determining Relation of Audience to Topic

The speaker should be guided by the relation of the audience to the topic. He must take into account the extent of the listeners' information, the basic assumptions they will accept, and their established attitudes.

The information of the audience. The speaker may have decided how much general information his listeners have on his topic, but he still needs to ask himself, Where can I draw the line between what they already know and what I must explain? Since he will not be able to draw a sharp line, he should review some information presumably known to his listeners. Such a review should move quickly to hold the interest of the well-informed and uninformed alike.

The speaker who explained the changes in British education since the close of the Second World War described British education before the war. In summarizing, he kept the informed listeners interested to discover whether they agreed with his description. Meanwhile, the uninformed obtained the information they needed.

Permissible assumptions. Since every argument must start with some premise that can be taken for granted, the speaker must ask himself: What will my listeners accept and what must I prove? To assume too much is to lose them at the outset. To assume too little is to waste time and effort.

The dean who assumes that teachers are influential leaders should be certain that his assumption is shared by the college freshmen whom he is seeking to interest in the teaching profession. If the listeners are skeptical, a major argument based upon that assumption would be futile.

Attitudes toward the topic. When the audience shares the speaker's feeling, he may develop the topic without hindrance, but when the listeners have mixed feelings, he meets a serious obstacle. To establish common ground may be impossible or may take more time than the speaker likes to give, but to proceed without common feeling is like sailing in a leaky boat.

The speaker who attempts to impress his listeners with the integrity of an honored citizen will not get far if they hold in contempt the man he praises. To change their feeling would require a different speech altogether.

Determining Relation of Audience to Occasion

Two questions will occur to the speaker about the relation of his listeners to the occasion: (1) what is their responsibility and (2) what is their attitude? The speaker should be able to ascertain the function of the listeners. Their attitude may not be easily predicted.

Responsibility of the audience at the occasion. On some occasions the only responsibility of an audience is to give attention. At other times, however, the audience has a special responsibility. At deliberative meetings the audience may be required to vote on a motion, a resolution, or a bill. On professional occasions the listeners may have a stated function, as does the jury at a trial. At social gatherings each member of an audience may be asked to respond in turn to the toastmaster's facetious introduction. In some ceremonies the hearers may take part in the ritual.

When a speaker contributes to the program of an organization, he should ascertain the purposes of the meeting, the customs and traditions of the body, the place he will have on the program, and especially his function and that of the audience. He should know whether he has a major responsibility to the listeners, as does the commencement speaker to a graduating class; whether the audience will be expected to take part in the meeting, as do the listeners at a forum; whether the audience will expect certain formalities of the speaker, as do the members of a fraternal order; whether the listeners expect to put the speaker's advice into immediate practice, as do salesmen called into conference.

Attitude of the audience toward the occasion. The speaker should try to determine the probable attitude of the audience toward the occasion. At a deliberative assembly he might reasonably anticipate that the responsibility for decisions will create a serious attitude. At a professional meeting he might expect dignified conduct associated with the duties to be discharged. At a social gathering he should hope for an amiable spirit accompanying the full enjoyment of good fellowship. At a ceremonial occasion he might look for a respectful mood indicating the sincere desire to pay tribute.

When the attitude of the audience is not appropriate to the occasion, the speaker has the responsibility for changing it. Since his material should be suited to the mood appropriate to the occasion, the extra care necessary to ensure the mood should not make a heavy demand upon his resourcefulness.

HOMOGENEITY AND HETEROGENEITY IN THE AUDIENCE

The more attention the speaker gives to the study of his audiences, the more deeply he should realize the infinite variety as well as the essential similarity in the groups he addresses. As he tries to put himself in the place of each listener, he should become steadily more aware of the basic needs and responses of all human beings, and more understanding of the special problems of individuals and groups. The continuing analysis of audiences should impress upon the speaker the remarkable opportunities he has to discharge his responsibilities of citizenship and, at the same time, the obligation he has to his listeners and to society as a whole to use his knowledge, his judgment, and his skill for the public good.

PLANS OF ADAPTATION

Since every honest speech is preceded by systematic analysis of the subject matter, and since every effective speech involves the adaptation of that subject matter to a living audience, one may say that the principal task of the speaker is to find a way to make his audience understand (as he understands it) the fact, truth, or policy proclaimed. The central and characteristic feature of speechmaking is thus adaptation, and the means to adaptation is the speech plan, which may be defined as a systematic procedure for choosing and presenting ideas previously analyzed into a form suitable for audiences to hear. Fortunately for the beginning speaker, the problem of adaptation in speeches is not new; the experience of speakers in the past has made possible the development of a variety of plans for presenting diverse lines of thought to many kinds of audiences.

KINDS OF ADAPTATION REQUIRED

In general, two kinds of adaptation are required of speakers. The first is that made by the man in public life who has taken a position on a controversial question and speaks from a broad background of information. His views are fairly well settled, but he does not always have complete information about his hearers. He will adapt his speech as well as he can. Senator Robert Taft, for example, discussed universal military training at Gettysburg one week and at the Town Meeting of the Air the next; a study of the two speeches reveals that he adapted essentially the same thought structure to two different audiences.

A second kind of adaptation is made by the speaker who knows his audience in advance of his preparation. He is thus able to study his audience and perhaps even to adapt his speech as he prepares it. Indeed, as you become experienced in speechmaking, you may find the twin processes of analysis and adaptation becoming more and more a single task. Just as the student of piano masters separately a series of exercises and then combines them into a single melodic pattern, so you may eventually combine the tasks of finding a reasoned basis for your speech and determining how to make it useful to your hearers.

Student speeches are generally given under conditions requiring the second kind of adaptation; and the best practice in learning is first to study the audience and occasion and then adapt to them.

Speeches ordinarily have three parts: an introduction, a body, and a conclusion. The statement, expressed or implied, determines the development of the three parts and may appear in any one or all of them. You will find it helpful first to study the statement and the analysis of your speech and then to raise the following basic questions:

- How shall I arrange and develop the material in the body of the speech?
- What is the best way to conclude?
- How shall I introduce the speech?
- What title shall I give it?

The Body

The construction of the body of the speech is the major task; all the stages of preparation contribute to it. In choosing a topic you select the ground of your discussion. In collecting material you find the substance for the body of your speech. In wording a statement you determine the direction your discussion will take. In making the outline, and later the analysis, you provide one kind of structure. For short and simple speeches this structure will often require little adaptation to become a rhetorical plan for the speech.

Principles. Two principles are basic in the development of the body of a speech: (1) it should be based on the sentence analysis, and (2) it should employ speech materials chosen, arranged, and adapted to meet the requirements of the audience.

IT SHOULD BE BASED ON THE SENTENCE ANALYSIS. A re-examination of the speech materials serves two purposes. First, it helps you to understand your topic. Second, it enables you to select appropriate ideas for development and adaptation to your audience.

IT SHOULD EMPLOY SPEECH MATERIALS CHOSEN, ARRANGED, AND ADAPTED. The speaker studies his prospective hearers to discover what factors are likely to be favorable or unfavorable in securing their attention, understanding, and approval. Concerning your own audiences you should ponder the questions raised elsewhere in this chapter and in the following list:

- How large is my audience?
- Are the members of my audience predominantly young, middle-aged, or old?
- Is my audience educated, informed, favorable, liberal, judicious, emotional?
- Is the attitude of my audience determined by race, nationality, sex, religion, party, family, health, economic position, social position, profession, membership in clubs or organizations?
- Will my audience respond to the appeals of wealth, power, honor, reputation, or career?
- Is my audience assembled for a purpose primarily political, legal, religious, academic, business, social, ceremonial?
- What is the attitude of my audience toward my topic?
- What is the attitude of my audience toward me?

The analysis can be a storehouse from which you choose ideas suited to the needs of your audience. After incorporating illustrations, examples, anecdotes, or stories, you will decide what plan to use in adapting the speech to the audience and the occasion.

Types of development in the body of the speech. You may develop the body of a speech in three ways: (1) by announcing in advance what you intend to do and then proceeding to do it, (2) by withholding the announcement of what you intend to do and presenting support leading your audience to your conclusion, (3) by combining both methods.

ANNOUNCING A STATEMENT AND SUPPORTING IT. The most common method of development is the direct approach—announcing the statement and developing serially the first step, the second step, the third step, and so on. This method has much to recommend it, especially for beginning speakers. It is clear and easy to follow. The merits of the method, however, have led unimaginative speakers to abuse it. By comparison with a somewhat more sophisticated approach, it suffers from triteness, from audience familiarity with the structure, and from lack of suspense.

PRESENTING SUPPORT LEADING TO A CONCLUSION. In the second method of development, the statement is reserved until the close of the speech. Even the title is chosen to arouse curiosity rather than to indicate the content. This method creates suspense and builds toward a high point of interest. It usually requires more speaking time than the simple announcement and support of a statement.

COMBINING TWO TYPES OF DEVELOPMENT. Experienced speakers employ the foregoing methods in combination. A preliminary narrative or series of proofs is followed by an announcement of the statement. Further proofs or generalizations are then offered, the statement is repeated, and so on.

The Conclusion

The conclusion may perform one or more of the following functions: it may review the principal ideas; it may show how the advantages of the proposal outweigh any possible disadvantages; it may leave the audience in the proper frame of mind; it may make the hearers more patriotic, more loyal, more clearly aware of their responsibilities; it may appeal to the audience to accept higher ideals or new beliefs; it may suggest a course of action.

The conclusion should not merely break off at the end of the last point in the body of your speech. Your hearers will expect you to reinterpret your ideas for clarity and emphasis. Since the final impression is likely to prevail, you should use the conclusion to reinforce your purpose.

Principles. Three principles are basic in constructing an effective conclusion: (1) it should be appropriate, (2) it should be forceful, (3) it should be well phrased.

THE CONCLUSION SHOULD BE APPROPRIATE. Your conclusion should fit into the general plan of your speech. It should not be too long, yet it must not appear abrupt. It should ask of your hearers only what they can do. It should not impress them as being strained or artificial, but should be the natural outcome of the support and the appeals used in the body of the speech.

THE CONCLUSION SHOULD BE FORCEFUL. Your conclusion should lend itself to vigorous and straightforward delivery. You should not take the apologetic attitude revealed by such a conclusion as, "Well, I'm sorry. I guess that's all I have to say." As you come to the end of your speech, you have the opportunity to intensify the impressions you have made upon your hearers. Your preparation should be designed to assure the accomplishment of your purpose in your conclusion.

THE CONCLUSION SHOULD BE WELL PHRASED. Either as a new appeal or as an epitome of your speech, your conclusion should enjoy fresh and striking treatment, avoiding cliches and meaningless repetition. The phrasing deserves special adaptation to your audience.

Types of conclusion. The foregoing principles are applied, among others, to four common types of conclusion used alone or in combination: (1) summary, (2) appeal, (3) illustration, (4) quotation.

SUMMARY. The summary conclusion reviews the *divisions*. If the speech develops the statement "Demosthenes faced three major problems," the summary might be phrased as follows:

> Demosthenes mastered three major problems in becoming the world's greatest orator. First, he overcame personal handicaps. Second, he overcame natural weaknesses in articulation. And, third, he worked hard to learn the Athenian dialect.

The summary conclusion refreshes the memory of your listeners by reviewing the principal ideas. It makes your purpose clear and definite. At best, however, the summary conclusion is neither highly original nor striking; at worst, it is mechanical and routine. To obtain the advantages of the summary and to avoid its disadvantages, you may follow it with a vivid appeal, application, or illustration.

APPEAL. Instead of concluding with a formal summary, the speaker sometimes urges his hearers to adopt a certain belief or attitude, or to pursue a suggested course of action. Winston Churchill thus ended a radio address to the American people:

> Put your confidence in us. Give us your faith and your blessing, and, under Providence, all will be well.
>
> We shall not fail or falter; we shall not weaken or tire. Neither the sudden shock of battle, nor the long-drawn trials of vigilance and exertion will wear us down. Give us the tools, and we will finish the job.[1]

ILLUSTRATION. The illustration, real or fictitious, should enforce the speaker's purpose. Elmer Davis closed a radio broadcast with an illustration designed to encourage the American people in a day of defeat:

[1] From *Blood, Sweat and Tears* by Winston S. Churchill. © 1941 by Winston S. Churchill. Reprinted by permission of G. P. Putnam's Sons. P. 462.

Those were good men who crossed the Delaware with George Washington on Christmas night, 1776, but they would have been proud to shake hands with the men who defended Wake Island or the men who are hanging on with MacArthur on the Bataan Peninsula.[2]

QUOTATION. An apt quotation may provide the best and simplest method of concluding a speech. Ordinarily it must be brief, and always it must be appropriate. Judge Learned Hand, in his address presenting a portrait of Justice Oliver Wendell Holmes to Harvard University, concluded as follows:

Another wrote these words taken from a Greek epitaph; she who for many years most closely shared that life that we have come to honor. Who could as well have said what I have tried to say?
> "A shipwrecked sailor buried on this coast
> Bids thee take sail.
> Full many a gallant ship, when we were lost,
> Weathered the gale."

I have the honor to present to the school the portrait of Holmes of the class of 1866.[3]

The Introduction

The introduction enables you to gain the confidence of your hearers, to remove their prejudices, and to evoke attitudes that will get a hearing for the body of the speech. It should make people want to listen to you, it should relate the subject directly to their personal interests, and it should help them to understand what you mean. The introduction allows you to set forth your purpose and point of view and to define your terms; it provides an opportunity to limit your topic, survey the background, state the proposition, and announce the divisions of your speech. It enables you to assure your audience of your intention to be fair, reasonable, and considerate. Since the usefulness of the introduction depends upon an understanding of the entire discourse, you should construct it after you have prepared the rest of your speech.

Whether an introduction should be long or short depends upon how well you know the members of your audience and how greatly interested they are in your topic. A long, rambling introduction defeats its purpose and consumes valuable time needed for the body of the speech. A short introduction may fail to make the audience receptive to what follows.

Principles.   Four principles are basic in the planning of the introduction: (1) it should put the speaker on common ground with the audience,

[2] A. Craig Baird, ed., *Representative American Speeches: 1941–1942*, New York: The H. W. Wilson Company, 1942, pp. 117–118. Copyright 1942 by The H. W. Wilson Company.

[3] James M. O'Neill and Floyd K. Riley, eds., *Contemporary Speeches*, New York: Century Company, 1930, p. 43.

(2) it should relate the topic to the audience, (3) it should associate the topic with the occasion, (4) it should adjust the speech to the immediate situation.

IT SHOULD PUT THE SPEAKER ON COMMON GROUND WITH THE AUDIENCE. Your introduction should be in accord with the interests, objectives, and feelings common to your hearers. Members of a college audience often have a common interest in making friends, choosing a career, and taking part in activities. Members of a community audience frequently have a tie in rearing a family, making a living, and budgeting a household.

Having discovered the bond that unites your hearers, you should find some experience or attitude common to them and to yourself. Although a veteran who returned to college differed from his audience of undergraduates in maturity and background, he was like them in being a student. His introduction utilized this common tie. A candidate reared on a farm has often used this fact in appealing for the support of farmers. Genuine bonds of interest between you and other people are seldom lacking, but you will need to seek them in common nationality, age, sex, vocation, hobbies, or regional background.

IT SHOULD RELATE THE TOPIC TO THE AUDIENCE. The introduction exploits the relation between the topic and the audience. Every listener is made to feel, "This question concerns me." Your hearers may be interested in universal fingerprinting if they can be shown that it concerns ordinary citizens as well as criminals and FBI men. In removing some of the common misunderstandings about fingerprinting, you make your hearers want more information. By giving examples illustrating its practicality, you show how it may affect the life and happiness of every citizen.

IT SHOULD ASSOCIATE THE TOPIC WITH THE OCCASION. If the occasion is the first or the last of a series, or falls on an important anniversary, or is related to some local, national, or international event, you may exploit the fact in opening your speech. Your introduction enables you to combine your interests with those of your audience in an occasion common to all.

IT SHOULD ADJUST THE SPEECH TO THE IMMEDIATE SITUATION. The introduction allows you to use circumstances in the immediate presence of your audience to put yourself and your topic in a favorable light. The remarks of another speaker, the presence of a distinguished guest, or the composition of the audience may suggest an introduction rich in spontaneity. When he spoke in Fanueil Hall, Wendell Phillips, pointing to the portraits of Adams, Hancock, and Otis, declared that they would have fought for his cause. Even a disturbance can be turned to advantage: Ingersoll remarked, when a baby started to cry during his address, "I did not suppose I could so quickly move my audience to tears."

Sometimes you can make capital of the chairman's introduction. If the remarks are humorous, you may retort in kind; if they are gracious, you may acknowledge the praise in appropriate language.

You should be alert to comment on the remarks of preceding speakers and to adapt your speech to what has gone before. You may want to agree or disagree with what some other speaker has said. If the mood of your audience is antagonistic, you may be able to change it. In Liverpool, Henry Ward Beecher, at the time of the Civil War, appealed to the British tradition of fair play to gain a hearing from an audience that included sympathizers with the Confederacy. You should not hesitate to alter your prepared introduction if by so doing you can better adapt your speech to the circumstances.

Types of introduction. The foregoing principles may be applied to at least six types of introduction: (1) assertion or question, (2) announcement, (3) quotation, (4) personal reference, (5) illustration, (6) explication.

ASSERTION OR QUESTION. Often the speaker can capture the attention of his audience by opening with a striking pronouncement: "In the first use of the atomic bomb, a Japanese city of three hundred thousand people was obliterated." "The amount of soil lost by erosion, if loaded into freight cars, would fill a train long enough to girdle the earth twenty-five times." An introduction relying upon a single question is likely to provoke an immediate response. For example, "Can democracy survive?"

ANNOUNCEMENT. A speaker may begin by announcing his statement at the outset. "I propose to prove," one speaker said, "that Negroes should have the right to attend any educational institution supported from public funds." This introduction was well received by an audience known to be friendly toward the speaker and his proposal, but it would not have served for an audience whose opposition would be aroused by such a statement. If other speakers have paved the way by giving the necessary information or stimulation, a direct announcement may be an especially apt beginning.

QUOTATION. Speakers sometimes begin with a striking quotation. William C. Sullivan, Assistant Director of the Federal Bureau of Investigation, began an address at the University of Oregon as follows: "The program adopted by the 22nd Congress of the Communist Party of the Soviet Union in October, 1961, proclaimed communism to be the 'bright future of all mankind.'" [4]

PERSONAL REFERENCE. In the beginning the speaker may identify himself with the audience or the occasion, or explain his reason for speaking. In his famous address before the Congress of the United States, Winston Churchill said:

[4] "Communism Confronts the United States," press release, February 27, 1962.

I wish indeed that my mother, whose memory I cherish across the vale of years, could have been here to see. By the way, I cannot help reflecting that if my father had been an American and my mother British, instead of the other way around, I might have got here on my own.[5]

ILLUSTRATION. An opening illustration should provide concreteness, vividness, and suspense within a simple, conversational approach. The speaker begins by saying, "Last week one of our customers called the manager and said, 'Mr. Bogard, you *must* do something about your truck drivers,' " or "Whenever I receive an envelope with a lawyer's return address on it, my first thought is, 'What have I done wrong now?' " The listeners, curious to know more about the truck drivers or the legal-appearing envelope, have their attention guided to the proposition.

EXPLICATION. An idea commanding the attention of the audience and leading directly into the development of the proposition forms a good introduction. You may introduce the statement, "The League of Women Voters should favor compulsory voting," with the historical doctrine, "Democracy was intended to be a government in which all the citizens take part"; or with the definition, "Compulsory voting means that every citizen entitled to vote must cast a ballot or pay a fine"; or with the comparison, "Compulsory voting is like compulsory registration for selective service in wartime"; or with the discovery, "Recent research shows that one ancient city compelled its citizens to vote"; or with the justification, "Compulsory voting is the only method that will make democracy work"; or with the correction, "Compulsory voting does not mean that the voter is compelled to vote in any certain way"; or with the concession, "Compulsion in a democracy is bad in principle"; or with the observation, "Only two-thirds of the eligible citizens voted in the recent election."

The Title

Although a title is not necessary, it is often advantageous. Publicized in advance, printed on the program, or announced by the chairman of the meeting, a well-phrased title arouses interest in the speech. Whether descriptive, as "The Unicameral Legislature in Nebraska," or figurative, as "The Lights Are Going Out," or humorous, as "The Fable of the Weasel and the Water Pitcher," the title should be stated briefly and appropriately. Such phrasing as "Religion and Democracy" or "Foreign Affairs" is so general that it lacks appeal. A useful title arouses the curiosity of your listeners without antagonizing them.

[5] From an electrical transcription.

THE CHOICE OF A PLAN

After studying your probable audience and your sentence analysis, you may decide that the analysis itself, with the addition of an introduction and a conclusion, will serve as a plan. If you are to explain a manufacturing process, you may find that a sentence analysis developed by time order can easily be adapted to the audience. Since the logical requirements of the subject may not coincide with the psychological requirements of the audience, however, a sentence analysis usually needs substantial modification.

The possibilities of adapting the introduction, the body, and the conclusion are unlimited. The choice of a plan is a basic decision in speech preparation.

Factors Governing the Selection of a Plan

In deciding what plan to use, you should consider the following factors: (1) your opportunities for preparation, (2) your reputation as a speaker, (3) the implications of your purpose, (4) the requirements of your subject, (5) the composition of your audience, (6) the kind of occasion.

Your opportunities for preparation. If you have an apt illustration, you may favor, other things being equal, a plan that will allow you to use it.

Your reputation as a speaker. If you enjoy the respect of your hearers, you may approach your subject directly; but if you come to them as a stranger, perhaps you will need an indirect plan.

The implications of your purpose. If you intend to inform your listeners, you may choose a plan relating new ideas to old; but if you wish to persuade them, you will need a plan of argument showing that the new ideas are sound.

The requirements of your subject. A development from an enumeration of specific instances to a general conclusion might be well suited to a speech on the evils of advertising, whereas a general statement of principles would precede specific illustrations in a speech concerning the law of supply and demand.

Not all subjects are suitable for speechmaking. If your materials are highly abstract or statistical, they may be better presented in writing. If they must be given orally, a plan permitting illustration with visual aids is essential.

The composition of your audience. If your audience is favorable to your point of view, you may choose a plan stating your proposition and offering proof. But if your audience is hostile, you should adopt a plan allowing you, first of all, to create a favorable attitude.

Of all the factors governing the selection of a plan, the foremost is likely to be the audience. The hearers will determine, for example, whether a given speech should be developed as informative or persuasive. When Jenner first discovered the principle of vaccination, he found his hearers hostile, and he therefore had to advocate a proposition. Today, however, the acceptance of his proposition is so complete that teachers explain his principle as information.

The kind of occasion. If the informality of the occasion calls for a brief speech, your plan will be simple. But if the occasion demands an extended address, your plan will be elaborate.

Types of Plans

The plans of adaptation can be classified into four groups: (1) sequence, (2) essence, (3) resemblance, and (4) motivation. These groups are not mutually exclusive. A speaker may combine a plan of sequence with a plan from any other group, or a plan of resemblance with a plan of motivation. A special plan could include elements of plans from all four groups. Plans of sequence are based on arrangement from general to specific or specific to general. Plans of essence, determined by the essential nature of the subject, serve especially the purpose of inform ing. Plans of resemblance are characterized by analogical relation or similarity in structure or idea between two or more forms, processes, objects, or arguments. Plans of motivation emphasize an appeal to the audience.

Sequence. The usual basic arrangement of ideas in any speech is either from general to specific or from specific to general. If the speech is expository, the speaker proceeds from the whole to the parts, or from the parts to the whole. If the speech is persuasive, the speaker proceeds from the statement of the proposition to the reasoned support, or from the specific evidence to the proposition.

STATEMENT TO PARTICULARS. The most common speech plan is the statement followed by the development of particulars. The plan is direct and uninvolved, but it is sometimes trite and mechanical.

In an informative speech, the plan consists of the statement of a principle followed by a number of applications. The professor of economics may begin the body of his lecture by stating the law of diminishing returns. He then explains just what the law means to the farmer who buys more cattle, to the manufacturer who builds more cars, and to the publisher who prints more books.

In a persuasive speech, the plan consists of the statement to be proved, followed by the reasons for accepting it. The speaker may say, "The federal government should adopt the sales tax." He then proceeds to develop the arguments.

PARTICULARS TO STATEMENT. Often the best plan consists of reserving the statement until the end of the speech, after the particulars have been set forth. In a speech concerning the high price of drugs, the description of individual hardships may be followed by such a proposal as, "The several states should establish public dispensaries."

With a friendly audience the plan should create suspense; with an indifferent audience it should arouse curiosity; with an unfriendly audience it should at least get the speaker a hearing. The use of illustrations may avoid the unreasoning prejudice that would have crushed an abrupt declaration of the proposal. Skillfully executed, this development can carry the audience with the speaker to the conclusion.

The plan has some disadvantages: it requires the selection of many typical and interesting instances, it may weary listeners who cannot follow the particulars, and it is relatively inefficient.

COMBINATIONS. The two preceding plans are so broad in scope that they allow an infinite variety of combinations. One possible variation is to present the statement after particulars have been advanced and follow it with more particulars. Another is to present the statement, support it with particulars, then repeat the statement and offer still more particulars. The statement may thus be repeated as often as necessary. The order may also be reversed. An advocate of uniform marriage and divorce laws developed his speech by telling stories of injustices resulting from diversity in divorce laws, presenting his statement, and following it with other evidence.

Just as the whole speech may be developed from a choice of a great many possible combinations, so may the separate divisions be elaborated from one of the various possible arrangements.

Essence. The plans of essence are concerned with the leading characteristics of the subject. These characteristics may be developed under the following heads: constituents, succession, location, enumeration, and illustration.

CONSTITUENTS. To make clear a theory, a program, a method, or even a person, the plan of constituents sets forth the essential principles, elements, or characteristics that reveal what the subject consists of. It may provide answers to the stock questions "Who?" "What?" "Where?" "When?" "How?" and "Why?" To enable his listeners to understand a new college honors plan, the speaker may tell who its sponsors are, what it is expected to accomplish, where it will be conducted, when it will begin, how it will function in the curriculum, and why qualified students should be interested in it. To know what a person is really like, the details that constitute his character and personality must be disclosed. To understand Napoleon, the facts of his life, the experiences that reveal his traits, and the qualities attributed to him by his contemporaries are needed to develop a distinct image of the man.

SUCCESSION. Chronological sequence, or time order, may provide the way to bring out the scope or development of a subject. To explain the steps in the process of manufacturing airplanes, the speaker may give the details about each step in the order in which the factory proceeded to produce the finished product. To explain the American language, the speaker may begin with its foundations in Old English and trace in chronological order the influences that have brought it to its present state.

LOCATION. Space order offers a convenient and systematic way to make clear the parts of a concrete object. To give the essentials of an ocean liner, a speaker may proceed by characterizing the parts of the ship in order of position from top to bottom, deck by deck, from bow to stern. To prepare prospective visitors to enjoy an unfamiliar city, the speaker, making reference to a map of the designated route, may take his listeners on an imaginary tour starting from the city hall and moving north, east, south, and west to observe the interesting sights in space order.

ENUMERATION. The only feasible way to present a comprehensive explanation of the essentials of some subjects is to list the areas, the items, or the details in a series. The scope of a college department may best be clarified by listing the several areas in which it offers courses and by enumerating the courses in each area. By specifying each category and each major item in a state budget, the speaker may give an audience an understanding of the need for a large annual appropriation.

ILLUSTRATION. To understand abstract, general, or complex subjects, illustration may be the best plan to make the essential characteristics or qualities evident and vivid. Either a fully developed single illustration completely typical, or a series of illustrations, each one to bring out a different aspect, may be used. To explain the Victorian era in literature, a single representative novel may be applied throughout the speech, with specific references to details of the novel to illustrate each essential characteristic of the era. To interpret impressionism in painting, particular paintings by several different outstanding artists who contributed to the movement may be described to illuminate the development of the theory and the practice. Showing large prints of the paintings as they relate to the parts of the speech would make the plan of illustration visual as well as conceptual.

Resemblance. The plans of resemblance have a common characteristic: they depend for their usefulness on the human tendency to expect things that are alike in some ways to be alike in still other ways, and to expect things that are unlike in some ways to be unlike in still others.

FAMILIARITY. This plan may be developed in two ways: from the familiar to the unfamiliar and from the unfamiliar to the familiar. Development from familiar to unfamiliar is especially useful in explaining a new process or in describing a little-known structure or place. It is also useful when the speaker wishes to persuade an audience to accept something new. When the mayor of a Midwestern city sought support for municipal ownership and operation of the electric plant, he began by describing the successful ownership and operation of the city waterworks. Only after he had focused the attention of his listeners upon the old example of municipal ownership did he turn to the new one.

Development from unfamiliar to familiar is sometimes psychologically sound. Since a new proposal commands a high level of attention, the speaker presents it first; but since any new action may arouse the fears of conservatives, he concludes by showing that he is merely advocating a new application of an old principle. A speaker supporting public medical service used this plan when he first described his program, and then proceeded to show how, in every essential principle, his new proposal was based on the old practices of public education.

LIKENESS. Speakers often need to point out the likenesses or differences between objects, processes, or policies. Each of the following five variations has advantages.

First, the speaker may point out likenesses only. Many proponents of federal world government have stressed the similarities between the American states of 1788 and the nations of the world today.

Second, the speaker may point out differences only. A young woman, arriving in the United States as a displaced person, based a talk on the differences between life in her native Lithuania and in the United States.

Third, the speaker may point out first the likenesses and then the differences. This plan allows him to appear impartial and yet to leave dissimilarity as the final impression. An art critic, for example, in discussing the misconception that a modern painter rivals Titian in the use of colors, began by pointing out similarities. "But," he continued, "the modern artist and Titian differ in this respect . . . and this . . . and this . . . ." The final impression was one of difference.

Fourth, the speaker may tell the differences and then the likenesses. A soldier returning from Australia used this plan in describing the social life of that commonwealth: Americans and Australians are different in their railways, their manufactures, and their farms, but Americans and Australians are alike in their love of sports, their insistence on fair play, and their belief in the rights of free men. The final impression was one of likeness between America and Australia.

Fifth, the speaker may employ the joint method of likeness and difference. A young Brazilian, speaking to an audience of North American college students about the celebration of Christmas, explained that the holiday is observed both in North and in South America by feasting and by religious services; but in South America the religious service is held on one day and the feasting on another. Although decorations are used on both continents, the motifs are different: North Americans emphasize

Santa Claus, snow scenes, and holly; South Americans emphasize the Magi, desert scenes, and the star of Bethlehem. Since the speaker explained the likeness and the difference for each point separately as he developed his speech, the final impression was one of clarity and balance.

Plans of resemblance can be developed around figurative as well as real likenesses and differences. Frequently such plans provide the only means of making abstractions vivid to popular audiences. The parables of the talents, of the sower and the seed, and of the house built upon the sand are all based on figurative resemblance. A modern example is found in the sermon "Bridges into a Better World," by the Reverend Charles W. Gilkey. The speech plan develops the likeness between modern steel bridges and the quality of life needed in our democracy, in our ethics, and in our religion. The speaker declared, "We must produce a quality of life like these new steels: lighter in weight, smaller in bulk, but stronger in carrying power." [6]

Motivation. The plans of motivation have in common a primary emphasis on means of disposing hearers favorably toward a proposal and on ways of suggesting a desired course of action without arousing negative or antagonistic responses.

ARGUMENT AND APPEAL. This plan may be developed in two ways. The speaker may present his argument and then end with an appeal strong enough to make his case acceptable. After offering carefully reasoned economic arguments for life insurance, he may conclude with an appeal urging the members of his audience to consider their obligations to their dependents.

The other possibility is to present alternate arguments and appeals throughout the speech. After making an economic argument for life insurance, the speaker may base a plea on self-interest. After developing a social argument, he may appeal to the desire for family security. A third and a fourth argument may be similarly developed.

The plan may have several variations. The order is sometimes reversed, or the types of appeal are varied for the successive supporting statements. The appeals may be expressed or implied, and either the appeal or the argument may be emphasized.

This plan can be used in overcoming opposition or in arousing a favorable audience to more decisive action. When logic alone might leave the listener intellectually convinced but still unmoved, the appeal may induce him to act. Whereas an appeal alone might cause the listener to rebel against a want of logic, the argument justifies the action.

[6] A. Craig Baird, ed., *Representative American Speeches: 1938–1939*, New York: The H. W. Wilson Company, 1939, pp. 234–244. Copyright 1939 by The H. W. Wilson Company.

IMPLICATION.   In a plan of implication the speaker brings his hearers to an inescapable conclusion, much as they would solve a jigsaw puzzle. Beginning at the outer edges and proceeding toward the center, the speaker and the audience progress toward the inevitable moment when one piece, and only one, will complete the picture. At no time does the speaker arouse the suspicion or the antagonism of his audience by presenting formal argument. The speech is developed primarily by narration—the simple telling of related facts and stories.

The plan is especially desirable for a neutral or unfriendly audience. Following the collapse of France in 1940, a Frenchman in America had the task of defending his country. The feeling of his American audience was that the French were weak, decadent, and unworthy of confidence. Although the speaker did not say so, he did not share the opinion of his listeners. The belief he wished to attack was that *we should censure the French.* He could have announced his stand and produced a formal series of arguments. What he did, however, was to begin far away from the center of his immediate problem by discussing unemotionally the valor of the French at Verdun and the Marne in the First World War, by showing the terrific exhaustion which France had suffered as a result of that war, by pointing out how population decreases had weakened French policy, by demonstrating how the vacillating attitude of Britain and the United States toward France had further diminished her prestige in Europe, by presenting relevant facts concerning the weakness of France in the heavy industries necessary to modern warfare, by picturing with vivid detail the unhappy position of democratic France encircled by Fascist Spain, Fascist Italy, and Fascist Germany, and by reminding his hearers of Reynaud's tragic last-minute appeal for clouds of airplanes. Story upon story, fact upon fact, picture upon picture were joined together until one blank space and one alone remained. The conclusion reached by the audience even before it was announced by the speaker was, *We are all to blame for the fall of France.*

By his skill in avoiding the negative attitudes that an early announcement of his stand would have created, the speaker obtained a hearing; and by his disarming vindication, he changed the attitude of his hearers without ever having undertaken formal argument.

Another application is to consider the possible choices first and then to show by implication the impracticability of all but the desired proposal. This form is sometimes called the "this or nothing" plan.

REVERSAL.   In the plan of reversal the speech is divided into three parts. In the first part the speaker presents the point of view against the statement which he will later announce and support. In the second part he makes a skillful transition and announces the point of view he will elaborate. In the third part he defends his position.

This plan was used to excellent advantage in 1932 by a young attor-

ney addressing a group of conservative businessmen. He began by praising and illustrating many of the excellent personal qualities of President
Herbert Hoover. Speaking with fairness and candor, he showed why he
wished to vote for President Hoover. "Respecting the President as I do
and coming from a long line of Republicans as I do," he said, "I genuinely regret that I must cast my first ballot for a Democrat." He then
proceeded to justify his decision by developing the three major reasons
that had led him to his choice in spite of his inclinations. He concluded
by predicting that on election day the overwhelming majority of young
voters would cast their ballots for Franklin D. Roosevelt, and appealed
to the older men present, particularly the Republicans, for their sympathy and understanding. His speech was effective because he avoided
antagonism and presented his case fairly.

Reversal is best suited to audiences that are judicious, indifferent,
or antagonistic. The judicious audience is likely to be favorably disposed
by the speaker's fair consideration of possible objections to his own line
of argument. The indifferent audience may be aroused by an unusual
statement of the advantages of a contrary point of view. The antagonistic
group holding strong views in opposition to the speaker's proposal will
be led by the opening of the speech to give attention to his point of view
and perhaps to follow him throughout his argument.

MOTIVATED SEQUENCE. The plan of motivated sequence has been advocated as one that "will serve as the backbone for all types of speeches." [7]
The plan in its fullest development includes five steps: securing attention,
making the audience feel a need, providing the method of satisfying the
need, helping the listeners visualize how the proposal will apply to themselves individually, and suggesting definite action. If your speech is to impress, to inform, or to entertain, you may not need all five steps.

PROBLEM SOLUTION. In applying the plan of problem solution, the
speaker (1) begins by describing the problem, (2) analyzes the possible
causes, (3) considers possible solutions, (4) indicates the preference, and
(5) enlarges upon the preferred solution, projects it into operation, and
shows that its advantages will outweigh its disadvantages. [8]

Because the problem-solution plan allows the speaker to think with
his hearers, and because it begins on ground acceptable even to hostile
members of the audience, it is sometimes more effective in persuasive
speeches than a direct statement of the speaker's point of view.

A variation of this plan may include six steps, as follows: (1) the

[7] See Alan H. Monroe, *Principles and Types of Speech*, 5th ed., Chicago: Scott
Foresman & Company, p. 282 ff.

[8] James H. McBurney and Kenneth G. Hance in *Discussion in Human Affairs*,
New York: Harper & Brothers, 1950. P. 65 gives a problem-solution plan adapted
especially to discussion. Their plan is based on John Dewey's analysis of the act of
reflective thought. See John Dewey, *How We Think*, Boston: D. C. Heath and Company, 1910, p. 72.

need, (2) possible solutions of the problem, (3) selection of the preference, (4) explanation of the preferred solution, (5) application, and (6)
appeal. Applied to the topic "Choosing a Vocation," this plan may be developed as follows:

1. *The Need.* Since only 30 per cent of college students follow the vocation for which they are trained, some kind of vocational guidance other
   than the haphazard advice of parents, teachers, and friends is needed.
2. *Possible Solutions of the Problem.* Several solutions of the problem
   have been proposed. (Discussion of advantages and disadvantages of
   these proposals.)
3. *Selection of the Preference.* Another solution, the Community Guidance Center, has been proposed.
4. *Explanation of the Preferred Solution.* This plan has three principal
   features. (Explanations.)
5. *Application.* Young people in our community could use this plan in
   finding a position.
6. *Appeal.* You should contribute toward the establishment of a community guidance center.

PROGRESSION.   In the plan of progression you first *tell a story* designed
to epitomize the entire discourse. The story should ring true. If the listeners are familiar with it, so much the better; you can develop it by re-
minder and reference.

In the second step you *make an application* of the story. If it has been
well chosen, it will be typical. You can now show the seriousness of
the evil you are attacking. If your story concerns the tragic death of a
child in an automobile accident, your application will give an account of
traffic dangers throughout the country.

In the third step you *indicate the problem* by a short and simple
statement or question—for example, "What shall we do about automobile accidents?"

In the fourth step you present the *solution* of the problem. In general,
you should prefer to advocate the plans or remedies already initiated by
competent agencies in the field of your discussion rather than to present
a new proposal. If your speech concerns automobile fatalities, you may
propose the measures already approved by highway engineers, the Red
Cross, or the American Automobile Association.

In the fifth and final step you *appeal to your listeners* to become interested, to change their attitude, or perhaps to take action. By clear reference your appeal may review the speech, even including the story you
told in the beginning, to obtain conviction and appropriate response.

The progression plan is well adapted to neutral audiences. It not only enables you to gain and hold attention, but it also allows you to develop the problem with your audience.

CLASSICAL ARRANGEMENT. The classical plan is well adapted to a weighty subject requiring extended treatment. Developed by the famous orators of the past, it is a somewhat more complicated method of arrangement than is common today, but the essential features may still be employed to advantage.

The plan may include seven parts: exordium or approach, narration or background of facts, statement or proposition, partition or divisions, proof or argument, refutation or counterargument, and peroration or conclusion.[9] The function of the exordium is to prepare the audience to listen to the speaker's argument. A good approach will gain attention and good will or arouse curiosity. The narration supplies the background of events. The statement sets forth the proposal—the point of view to be accepted or the action to be taken. The partition enumerates the main arguments in the order of their presentation. The proof, the longest part of the speech, develops the arguments in sequence. The refutation, sometimes preceding but usually following the proof, answers the opposition. The peroration is designed to dispose the hearers more favorably toward the speaker and his arguments than toward the opponents and their arguments. It should recapitulate the proof and appeal to the hearers for final acceptance of the proposition.

STRUCTURE AND PLAN

In modern as in ancient practice, a speech has an introduction, a body, and a conclusion. The plans of adaptation, used singly or in combination, provide an infinite number of possibilities for the selection and arrangement of facts, arguments, and appeals.[10]

You should select a particular plan after studying all the aspects of the speech—opportunities for preparation, reputation of the speaker, implications of the purpose, requirements of the subject, the composition of the audience, and the kind of occasion.

[9] Some famous speakers developed a part called "digression," usually consisting of a story having little or no direct relation to the sequence of thought but serving to renew the interest of the audience. A digression may occur anywhere, but characteristically precedes the proof.

[10] Examples of specific plans of adaptation will be found in: Wilbur E. Gilman, Bower Aly, and Hollis L. White, *An Introduction to Speaking*, New York: The Macmillian Company, 1962, pp. 34, 39 and 40, 68–70, 82, 93 and 94, 102 and 103, 115. Copyright 1962 by The Macmillan Company.

5 COMMUNICATION:
Thought, Language, and Style

Seeing that the truth consisteth in the right ordering of names in our affirmations, a man that seeketh precise truth had need to remember what every name he useth stands for, and to place it accordingly, or else he will find himself entangled in words as a bird in lime twigs—the more he struggles the more belimed.

—Thomas Hobbes

Those who concern themselves with scholarly and scientific problems sometimes disclose an attitude of condescension, not entirely justified, toward other people. The scholar or scientist is supposed to be searching for the ultimate truth, undefiled, whereas the speechmaker—who may be a politician, an orator, or a teacher—must be content with a different objective. In fact, however, the difference between the scientist and other persons is not so much in their objectives as in their problems and the means open for solving them. Characteristically, the scientist deals with measurable quantities. The speechmaker characteristically deals in the imponderables, in qualities and quantities not measurable by any means now known to man. Furthermore, the speechmaker is frequently concerned with determining and establishing a policy concerning the future, about which no one can be certain. Hence it is merely factual to state that the speechmaker—as orator, as legislator, as attorney, as counselor—has a task in some respects more difficult than that of the scientist.

Fortunately, one who understands the extent of the speechmaker's problems has to a degree been prepared to deal with them. In so far as the problems concern the communication of the speechmaker's ideas, they can be considered as thought, as language, and as style.

THE SPEAKER'S THOUGHT

Inasmuch as the speechmaker's problems differ from those of the scientist, his typical mode of thought is likely also to differ. One who need not concern himself with communicating the fact or the truth that he has discovered is free from certain restrictions that must instantly concern the speaker. The legislator, the orator, the counselor, who must not only formulate a policy but also communicate it, develops a habit of thought that leads him normally to consider not only how sound an idea may be but also how it can be presented. Three fundamental principles should be applied to govern three essential elements of the speechmaker's thought: (1) know the word, (2) know the object, (3) know the hearer.

KNOW THE WORD

For centuries men have been discussing the dangers in the use of words. In the Middle Ages, as well as in ancient times, philosophers debated the question of language vigorously and profitably. From the disputations of such scholastics as Abelard and Bernard of Clairvaux, men should have learned that the word itself is not the object. Yet the misuse of words has continued to bedevil mankind. As Thomas Hobbes says in his *Leviathan*, "Words are wise men's counters—they do but reckon by them; but they are the money of fools."

A word is a symbol, a picture of something else. One should ask, "Of what is this word a symbol?" To respond to a word as one responds to an object is to be like the man who tried to kill his enemy by shooting his image in a mirror.

Though the word is not the object, human mentality is largely built of words. Human history is necessarily constructed mostly from words rather than from objects. No one can see George Washington; no one now living ever received any immediate sensory impressions concerning him. Except for statues and portraits, what can be expressed of him is found in words. What is true of Washington is also true of Charlemagne, of Genghis Khan, of Cleopatra. The so-called facts of history exist chiefly in language, and the past is transmitted by some kind of language symbolism.

Just as our human past is a language phenomenon, so our future must be constructed largely of language. The objects of tomorrow's world are being created out of today's words. Next Christmas does not now exist anywhere; it cannot be experienced directly any more than George Washington can. Yet people are able to think of "next Christmas," to plan, to carry forward, and to order events. Even the scientist who wishes to be precise in his observation depends upon the symbolism of words to order his investigations and reports. The meteorologist who attempts to predict the weather must think in terms of abstractions, and one means at his command is the word, the symbol.

To the senses, parts of the present world are sometimes as inaccessible as the past or the future. Even though the Dalai Lama exists today and is occasionally seen in newsreels, he is as distant to most Americans as George Washington. For practical purposes, a town two thousand miles away may be as remote as forty years ago or as fifty years hence. Therefore, human beings depend upon language symbols to construct for themselves the world outside their immediate experience. The average American's concept of Ethiopia, of the Marne River, or of the streets of Moscow is formed not from direct experience but from report. What is true of the layman is true also even of the exact scientist. A chemist, for example, may not be able to go from place to place in order to see what is being done. For knowledge which lies beyond his own laboratory, he relies upon reports brought to him through such media as books, monographs, lectures, and convention papers.

Even in their own world men must live in part by symbols. The scientist invents a word in order to be able to think with it; the great physicists thus named the electron without ever having seen it or experienced it directly. In the same way, millions of people in their daily lives use words to represent objects which they have never seen, heard, or touched. Many people fight germs without having any sensory impressions of them. The first step in mastering the technique of informing is to know the word.

KNOW THE OBJECT

The second fundamental principle that should govern the speechmaker's thought is: know the object. An object may not be immediately perceptible to the sensory organs. On the other hand, a word is, in a way, a physical entity. Whether it be written or spoken, it exists somewhere in some amount. The spoken word is measurable in output of breath; the written word in width, breadth, and thickness. The symbol *Empire State Building* exists just as the object, Empire State Building, does. The process of language is thus, in part, the substitution of one physical object for another. The printed or spoken word, a physical object, is substituted for an idea. For the words *book, boy,* and *pen* corresponding objects exist. For the words *idea, truth,* and *hatred* no corresponding objects can be identified.

The speaker who knows intimately the object or the idea that is the topic of his discourse has a great advantage. Although knowledge is likely to bring him modesty, he can speak with authority and without the necessity of presuming beyond what he actually knows. A good example of thorough knowledge of the object is Thomas Henry Huxley's lecture delivered to the workingmen of Norwich. Huxley's son believed that this discourse, "On a Piece of Chalk," marked "the maturing of his style into that mastery of clear expression for which he deliberately labored, the saying exactly what he meant, neither too much nor too little, without confusion and without obscurity. Have something to say, and say it, was the Duke of Wellington's theory of style; Huxley's was to say that which has to be said in such language that you can stand cross examination on each word. . . ." [1]

Huxley began this deservedly famous address with the following statement:

If a well were sunk at our feet in the midst of the city of Norwich, the diggers would very soon find themselves at work in that white substance almost too soft to be called rock, with which we are familiar as "chalk."

Continuing throughout a lengthy speech, Huxley remained mindful of the object as well as the word, until finally he concluded:

A small beginning has led us to a great ending. If I were to put the bit of chalk with which we started into the hot but obscure flame of burning hydrogen, it would presently shine like the sun. It seems to me that this physical metamorphosis is no false image of what has been the result of our subjecting it to a jet of fervent, though nowise brilliant, thought tonight. It has become luminous, and its clear rays, penetrating the abyss of the remote past have brought within our ken some stages of the evolution of the earth. And in the shifting "without haste, but without rest" of the land and sea, as in the endless variations of the forms assumed by living beings, we have observed nothing but the natural product of the forces originally possessed by the substance of the universe.[2]

Huxley also uses words to inform about an abstract idea. Perhaps nothing is more theoretical than the process of induction and deduction. No physical object can be identified with it. Yet by careful construction

[1] *Discourse Biological and Geological: Essays,* New York: D. Appleton & Co., 1894, Vol. VIII, pp. 1–36.
[2] *Ibid.,* pp. 219–240.

of words from a thorough knowledge of his object, Huxley was able to make clear, even to laymen, the essence of induction:

Suppose you go into a fruiterer's shop wanting an apple,—you take up one, and, on biting it, you find it is sour; you look at it, and see that it is hard and green. You take up another one, and that too is hard, green, and sour. The shopman offers you a third; but, before biting it, you examine it, and find that it is hard and green, and you immediately say that you will not have it, as it must be sour, like those that you have already tried.

Nothing can be more simple than that, you think; but if you will take the trouble to analyze and trace out into its logical elements what has been done by the mind, you will be greatly surprised. In the first place, you have performed the operation of induction. You found that, in two experiences, hardness and greenness in apples went together with sourness. It was so in the first case, and it was confirmed by the second. True, it is a very small basis, but still it is enough to make an induction from; you generalize the facts, and you expect to find sourness in apples where you get hardness and greenness. You found upon that a general law, that all hard and green apples are sour; and that, so far as it goes, is a perfect induction. Well, having got your natural law in this way, when you are offered another apple which you find is hard and green, you say, "All hard and green apples are sour; this apple is hard and green, therefore this apple is sour." That train of reasoning is what logicians call a syllogism, and has all its various parts and terms,— its major premiss, its minor premiss, and its conclusion. And, by the help of further reasoning, which, if drawn out, would have to be exhibited in two or three other syllogisms, you arrive at your final determination, "I will not have that apple." So that, you see, you have, in the first place, established a law by induction, and upon that you have founded a deduction, and reasoned out the special conclusion of the particular case. Well now, suppose, having got your law, that at some time afterwards, you are discussing the qualities of apples with a friend: you will say to him, "It is a very curious thing,—but I find that all hard and green apples are sour!" Your friend says to you, "But how do you know that?" You at once reply, "Oh, because I have tried them over and over again, and have always found them to be so." Well, if we were talking science instead of common sense, we should call that an experimental verification. And, if still opposed, you go further, and say, "I have heard from the people in Somersetshire and Devonshire, where a large number of apples are grown, that they have observed the same thing. It is also found to be the case in Normandy, and in North America. In short, I find it to be the universal experience of mankind wherever attention has been directed to the subject." Whereupon, your friend, unless he is a very unreasonable man, agrees with you, and is convinced that you are quite right in the conclusion you have drawn. He believes, although perhaps he does not know he believes it, that the more extensive verifications are,—that the more frequently experiments have been made, the results of the same kind arrived at,—that the more varied the conditions under which the same results are attained the more certain is the ultimate conclusion, and he disputes the question no further. He sees that the experiment has been tried under all sorts of conditions, as to time, place, and people, with the same result; and he says with you, therefore, that the law you have laid down must be a good one, and he must believe it.[3]

KNOW THE HEARER

To know the word and the object profits the speaker little unless he knows the people he is addressing. He must not only understand the word and its relation to the object; he must know what the word connotes to those who hear it. The man who needs to communicate must sometimes be willing to sacrifice the minutiae of his object and even his choicest phrases in order to bring his discourse within the understanding of his hearers. Highly technical and professional vocabularies must be viewed with suspicion. Difficult words and obscure phrases must be discarded.

The discourse must be designed for the hearer. The basic principles are analysis and synthesis, two sides of the same coin; that coin is the token of clarity. Analysis is the process of seeing the parts that make the whole. Synthesis is the process of seeing the whole that is made of the parts. Analysis breaks down an object into its components; synthesis builds up the object from its components.

THE SPEAKER'S LANGUAGE

Despite the resemblances between writing and speaking, the construction of speeches is markedly different from the writing of essays, primarily because listening is different from reading. The reader may return to a difficult passage, but the hearer can hardly ask the speaker to repeat an idea. The reader may look up the meaning of an obscure word; the hearer must understand immediately or not at all. The reader may study without interruption, but the hearer must endure whatever distractions occur during a speech. The reader may look forward and gain perspective; the hearer has only such forecasts as the speaker provides. In composing speeches, therefore, you must know the fundamental laws common to writing and speaking as well as the differences between written and oral style.

BASIC PRINCIPLES

The basic principles of language for the speaker are unity, coherence, and emphasis. Unity is the selection of all that is necessary and the rejection of all that is unnecessary to the complete development of a main

[3] *Darwiniana: Essays,* New York: D. Appleton & Co., 1894, Vol. II, pp. 365–367.

idea. It results from systematic discrimination and limitation. Coherence is the connecting and relating of each part to the others. It results from intelligent arrangement of the material to be covered. Emphasis is the giving of an appropriate degree of prominence to each of the several parts. It results from making a distinction between major and minor ideas.

Unity

Perhaps you have heard rambling speakers like the one who merely wished to make a short talk explaining that a young man planning to enter business should study public speaking. He digressed presently to talk about the speakers he had heard as a boy. Before long he was comparing a boy's life today with a boy's life a generation ago. A little later he was deploring the decline of the small town. Finally, he closed by predicting the downfall of the Western World. Audience and speaker alike suffered from his lack of unity.

A speaker achieves unity by following a clearly defined system of analysis and organization. Under the discipline of the sentence analysis he includes all that is relevant and excludes all that is irrelevant to the dominant thought and feeling. The two aspects of unity are thus completeness and relevance.

Completeness. Completeness in speechmaking requires that every essential part of the speech be given its place. The speech as a whole is greater than any of its parts or even than the sum of them; yet every essential part of the speech must appear. The hearers must not go away saying to themselves, "Something was left out" or "I didn't see what he was driving at."

Every part needed to create the dominant word and thought of the speech must be understood by the hearer. The composition is thus subordinate to the final delivery. The text should be judged not as a work in its own right, but as the material from which a speech may be developed. The composition proceeds in the knowledge that the true speech is not the draft prepared for eventual presentation; it is what the listener understands. The bare text may seem unsatisfactory, but the speech is completed at the moment of delivery by the inflections of the speaker, by the response of the audience, or by the background of the occasion. Sometimes the requirement of completeness is satisfied by the speaker's personality. The man and what has happened to him are the unity. Consider Lincoln's *Farewell Address*. Early on a February morning, Abraham Lincoln stood on the platform of the train that was to carry him from Springfield, Illinois, to Washington, D. C., and said good-by to his friends and neighbors:

My friends: No one, not in my situation, can appreciate my feeling of sadness at this parting. To this place and the kindness of this people I owe everything. Here I have lived a quarter of a century and have passed from a young to an old man. Here my children have been born and one is buried. I now leave, not knowing when or whether ever I may return, with a task before me greater than that which rested upon Washington. Without the assistance of that Divine Being who ever attended him I cannot succeed. With that assistance I cannot fail. Trusting in Him who can go with me and remain with you and be everywhere for good, let us confidently hope that all will yet be well. To His care commending you, as I hope in your prayers you will commend me, I bid you an affectionate farewell.[4]

Relevance. Excluding irrelevant material is just as important as including relevant material. Your hearers must follow where you lead them. If you trace out bypaths and stop lingeringly at way stations, the audience may get lost. Yet you must not omit illustrative material. Speeches must be amplified and ideas augmented by illustration, example, or anecdote relevant to the dominant purpose and central idea. They should follow the internal logic of the occasion. If you are doubtful about a part of the speech, ask the question, How does this part contribute to the development of the main idea?

Coherence

Unity concerns the relation of all the several parts to the dominating idea; coherence describes the relation of each of the several parts to the other. The distinguishing characteristic of the coherent speech is the sense of fitness obtained by the application of three principles: continuity, transition, and reference.

Continuity. Continuity results from an orderly sequence in the development of ideas contributing to ready understanding. Nearly everyone has been embarrassed to hear a speaker interrupt the flow of his thought to go back to a forgotten point. Taking the audience back to a part of the speech already delivered is wasteful of the time and energy of the hearers and of their capacities for following the discourse. Furthermore, it is likely to weaken their confidence in the speaker.

The coherence obtained by orderly arrangement is exemplified in an address delivered by Dorothy Thompson to the people of Canada. Observe how instance follows instance without any false starts, backward looks, omitted clues, or interrupted ideas:

It seems that Germany has no quarrel with Great Britain. Hitler's quarrel is exclusively with this particular British Government and especially with its head, Mr. Churchill. If Mr. Churchill will only resign and a government come in which is acceptable to Mr. Hitler, he will be glad to make peace immediately.

[4] Mayo W. Hazeltine *et al.*, eds., *Masterpieces of Eloquence,* New York: P. F. Collier & Son, 1905, Vol. XVI, p. 6611.

He has no desire to destroy the British Empire. The man standing in the way of peace is Churchill, and the so-called fifth columnists are "only honest men, seeking peace." That is Hitler's argument.

Now, of course, we have all become familiar with this. Mr. Hitler had no quarrel with Austria, only with Mr. Schuschnigg. So the moment Schuschnigg resigned he made peace with Austria by annexing it. He had no quarrel with Czechoslovakia, only with Mr. Benes. So when Mr. Benes resigned he made peace with Czechoslovakia by turning it into a Nazi Protectorate. He had no quarrel with any of the countries he has absorbed—only with those leaders who opposed the absorption. Mr. Hitler has no quarrel with traitors in any country on earth. They are his agents, and, as his agents, are honest men seeking peace. His quarrel is only with patriots.[5]

When a speech has been thoughtfully constructed, almost any audience will be able to follow the speaker step by step to his conclusion.

Transition.   With transitions, the speaker builds a bridge of thought from idea to idea. The transition between parts of a speech may (1) summarize for the hearers what they have heard, (2) forecast what they are going to hear, or (3) accomplish both the summary and the forecast by interrelating the two.

The untrained speaker fails to provide transitions. He may suppose that he is conserving time and words. He does not realize that the elimination of transitions wastes the time and patience of hearers who cannot follow him. The careless speaker employs inadequate transitions. The words *and, well, so,* and *now* at the beginning of a new section of the speech are rarely adequate for the hearer. Frequently he requires a recapitulation of the leading ideas or a reference to points established. The pedantic speaker uses labored or obvious transitions. The dull repetition of the same word or phrase will discourage even an enterprising audience.

The effective speaker makes helpful transitions. They may be brief or expansive, depending upon the length of the address and upon the material being developed. Thomas Erskine, the famous British advocate, delivered speeches notable for their unity and coherence, yet the several ideas were often joined by the simplest transitions. In his speech on "The Rights of Juries," for example, Erskine provided the simple transition, "But another very important view of the subject remains besides." At another point, however, Erskine made a more elaborate transition, offering both a summary and a forecast:

Having established this important right in the jury, beyond all possibility of cavil or controversy [summary], I will now show your Lordships [forecast]

[5] A. Craig Baird, ed., *Representative American Speeches: 1940–1941,* New York: The H. W. Wilson Company, 1941, p. 139. Copyright 1941 by The H. W. Wilson Company.

that its existence is not merely consistent with the theory of the law, but is illustrated and confirmed by the universal practice of all judges. . . .[6]

The simple principle of transition employed by Erskine and by other effective speakers might be stated this way: The parts of a speech must be so connected that the hearers can proceed easily from idea to idea.

Reference. Reference is another means of obtaining coherence. A well-prepared speech is somewhat like a carpet in which the various figures are repeated to form a pattern. In speechmaking the pattern is made up of recurring words or phrases. Some students wrongly suppose that a word should be used only once in the same speech. Good sense and good taste alike indicate, however, that a pattern of reference ensures coherence. In a speech about liberty we would normally expect to hear the word *liberty* many times.

Another form of reference is the use of a different statement of the same idea to create a pattern. In a speech about citizenship, the idea of *obligation* may reappear in such forms as *duty, contract,* or *responsibility.* The recurring idea thus serves to bind the speech together; the variety in wording avoids monotony.

Emphasis

In every speech the ideas differ in their relative importance. Some are indispensable; others are useful; still others are helpful but strictly subordinate. Emphasis determines first what ideas should be stressed, and second what means should be employed. You should choose ideas for degrees of emphasis by comparing them with each other and by testing them against the purpose of the speech. When you have decided what is to be emphasized and what must be subordinated, you are ready to choose one or more of the means of emphasis: proportion, position, and manifestation.

Proportion. When you hear a college student spend eighteen minutes of his time talking about the football team and three minutes talking about the concert series, you are likely to conclude that he is more concerned about the team than the concerts. The amount of time given to an idea is a fair index of the significance the speaker attaches to it. If he passes over a point quickly, his hearers are likely to decide that he does not think it important; but if he lingers over the point and amplifies it, his hearers are justified in supposing it to be of some consequence.

Improper emphasis sometimes results from the lack of time sense. In developing a speech extemporaneously, a student discovered to his chagrin that he had spent all his time on his first two points and had not

[6] Chauncey A. Goodrich, ed., *Select British Eloquence,* New York: The Bobbs-Merrill Company, 1963, p. 661. Copyright 1963 by The Bobbs-Merrill Company, Inc.

even presented the point he wished to stress. Speaking overtime, he endeavored hurriedly and apologetically, but unsuccessfully, to establish the importance of his major idea. If he had observed time limits for the separate parts, he would have used his entire time to better advantage.

Position.   The different positions within a speech have varying values for emphasis. According to tradition, the place of greatest emphasis is the conclusion. Some modern studies in psychology indicate that the beginning is just as important, and a recent investigation gives some evidence that the first is a stronger position than the last. The difference between ancient tradition and modern studies may be more apparent than real. In some speeches the beginning is doubtless the place of first importance; in others, the conclusion may be critical. Circumstances alter cases.

When the speech is to be a cumulation of ideas, each point should be more telling than the one before. To the accumulated evidence the speaker adds, finally, an argument so convincing or testimony so clear that it is, in effect, irresistible. Such was the plan employed in the famous speech attributed to Patrick Henry. After reviewing in detail the history of the quarrel with Great Britain and answering objections to the appeal to arms, he finally concluded with his strongest argument: "The war has already begun."

Besides, sir, we have no election. If we were base enough to desire it, it is now too late to retire from the contest. There is no retreat, but in submission and slavery! Our chains are forged! Their clanking may be heard on the plains of Boston! The war is inevitable—and let it come! I repeat it, sir, let it come! [7]

On one point ancient tradition and modern psychology agree: the less important details should not be found either at the beginning or at the end, but should be tucked away within the speech. The same principle applies to the sentence or to any other unit of the composition.

Manifestation.   The major ways of manifesting emphasis by language are asseveration, repetition, exemplification, restatement, and the striking phrase.

Without subordination there is no emphasis. The speaker who pitches his discourse at the highest possible level for ordinary ideas has no place to go when he reaches something extraordinary. Emphasis is the result of lights and shadows; the shadows are as necessary as the lights.

ASSEVERATION.   The obvious means of manifesting emphasis is the simple, forthright, sometimes crude, but generally effective assertion, such as the following: "Now I come to the main point of my speech" or "Here is an idea of the utmost importance" or "This is the heart of the matter."

[7] Alexander Johnston and James Albert Woodburn, eds., *American Orations*, 5th ed., New York: G. P. Putnam's Sons, 1896, Vol. I, p. 23.

Experimental studies indicate the value of the method. Professors use it constantly, because they think it works.

REPETITION. Emphasis is obtained by the meaningful repetition of a word or phrase until it is indelibly impressed upon the listener's mind. The key word is not repeated for lack of a synonym; it is used because the speaker wishes to make it the point at which his ideas converge. Theodore Parker, in his memorable address delivered on the death of Daniel Webster, made the one word *mourned* his focal point:

> Do men mourn for him, the great man eloquent? I put on sackcloth long ago. I mourned for him when he wrote the Creole letter which surprised Ashburton, Briton that he was. I mourned when he spoke the speech of the seventh of March. I mourned when the Fugitive Slave Bill passed Congress, and the same cannon that have fired "minute guns" for him fired also one hundred rounds of joy for the forging of a new fetter for the fugitive's foot. I mourned for him when the kidnapers first came to Boston—hated then—now respectable men, the companions of princes, enlarging their testimony in the Court. . . .[8]

Parker achieved further effect by the repetition of the word *mourned* throughout the remainder of his speech.

EXEMPLIFICATION. Exemplification creates emphasis by adding instance upon instance in order to elaborate an idea. Since this method requires time for development, it is not often used in short speeches; but it can be used with great effectiveness in longer addresses. Excellent exemplification is found in a baccalaureate address delivered by George Barton Cutten at Colgate University. Observe that his main point could have been simply stated: "Youth is no barrier to accomplishment." Or it could have been illustrated with one or two examples; Cutten used thirty-nine, of which the following are typical:

> In the field of invention youth has been eminent. George Westinghouse invented the air brake when twenty-two; Luther Burbank produced the potato which bears his name when twenty-two. George Eastman produced dry plates at twenty-six, Alexander Bell invented the telephone when twenty-eight, Henry Ford produced his first motor car at twenty-nine. Thomas Edison invented the incandescent lamp when thirty-two and the Wright Brothers were thirty-two and thirty-six when they made their first flight. . . .[9]

RESTATEMENT. Emphasis by restatement is the phrasing of a basic idea in several different ways, with enough variation to avoid monotony, and possibly with changes designed to reach diverse groups of hearers.

---

[8] David J. Brewer *et al.*, eds., *The World's Best Orations*, Chicago: Ferd P. Kaiser, 1899, Vol. VIII, p. 3137.
[9] A. Craig Baird, ed., *Representative American Speeches: 1938–1939*, New York: The H. W. Wilson Company, 1939, pp. 211–213. Copyright 1939 by The H. W. Wilson Company.

Restatement as a means of emphasis is especially useful in persuasion when the speaker wishes not merely to make an observation, but so to illumine the whole discourse that his meaning cannot be mistaken. Yet he must accomplish the task without boring the hearers. To restate the idea, then, is to look at it again and again, to see how it would appear to someone else, to examine it in its immediate connections and its remote consequences. To restate the idea is to approach it from different avenues and show it to the hearers in varying perspectives. The flowing oral style of George William Curtis was characterized by the striking restatement of his idea. In the following selection from his speech "The Public Duty of Educated Men," he restated vigorously the same basic idea: "The failure of American politics is the fault of the honest citizen."

But let us not be deceived. While good men sit at home, not knowing that there is anything to be done, nor caring to know; cultivating a feeling that politics are tiresome and dirty, and politicians vulgar bullies and bravoes; half persuaded that a republic is the contemptible rule of a mob, and secretly longing for a splendid and vigorous despotism—then remember it is not a government mastered by ignorance, it is a government betrayed by intelligence; it is not the victory of the slums, it is the surrender of the schools; it is not that bad men are brave, but that good men are infidels and cowards.[10]

THE STRIKING PHRASE.   Sometimes a speaker can emphasize an idea by wording it into a single striking phrase that may prove more useful in the long run than elaborate means of emphasis. Such a phrase was employed by Franklin D. Roosevelt in his First Inaugural Address: ". . . the only thing we have to fear is fear itself." The striking phrase must catch the mood of the listeners, it must be short enough to be remembered, and it must express an ancient truth in new words with a present application.

DIFFERENTIATING CHARACTERISTICS

Both written and spoken discourse require the appropriate application of the principles of unity, coherence, and emphasis. Oral discourse has differentiating characteristics. The speaker must communicate instant intelligibility so that listeners will have complete understanding as he talks.

Some of these characteristics are aspects of language and others are aspects of style. Those related to language include the choice of words within the experience of the listeners, a sentence structure permitting the listeners to understand a unit of thought without the need for close analysis or reflection, and composition that commands immediate attention.

---

[10] Charles Eliot Norton, ed., *Orations and Addresses of George William Curtis,* New York: Harper & Brothers, 1894, Vol. I, p. 268.

THE SPEAKER'S STYLE

As the speaker achieves maturity, and as his needs require it, he may go beyond the elementary but necessary principles of language to achieve a style. Although the style will be his own, it is subject to critical judgment. If he is wise, he will cultivate a style that is personal and yet compatible with the rules of oral discourse. These rules would suggest the value of directness, simplicity, clarity, vigor, and distinction.

DIRECTNESS

Good speaking occurs when both the speaker and the audience sense that they have business together. The first problem of oral style, therefore, is to find language that will facilitate direct communication.

Personal Pronouns

Since a good speech is a dialogue, the personal pronouns *you, I,* and *we* are likely to appear quite often. In a speech delivered in a debate with Abraham Lincoln, Stephen A. Douglas achieved directness by immediate reference to the members of the audience and by personal pronouns in dialogue:

You cannot limit this great republic by mere boundary lines, saying, "Thus far shalt thou go, and no farther." Any one of you gentlemen might as well say to a son twelve years old that he is big enough, and must not grow any larger; and in order to prevent his growth put a hoop around him to keep him to his present size. What would be the result? Either the hoop must burst and be rent asunder, or the child must die. So it would be with this great nation.[11]

Creating a Common Feeling

The speaker has an opportunity not open to the writer: he is in the immediate presence of his audience. Even the radio speaker and his hearers have the same time-moment in common. The skillful use of this opportunity creates common feeling that the speaker can enhance. Lincoln is said to have used a striking analogy to create a common feeling within a group of visitors to the White House:

Gentlemen, suppose all the property you were worth was in gold, and you had put it in the hands of Blondin to carry across the Niagara Falls on a rope, would you shake the cable, or keep shouting out to him, "Blondin, stand up a

[11] George Haven Putnam, ed., *The Political Debates Between Abraham Lincoln and Stephen A. Douglas*, New York: G. P. Putnam's Sons, 1926, p. 269. Copyright 1926 by G. P. Putnam's Sons.

little straighter!—Blondin, stoop a little more—go a little faster—lean a little more to the north—lean a little more to the south"? No! you would hold your breath as well as your tongue, and keep your hands off until he was safe over. The Government is carrying an immense weight. Untold treasures are in their hands. They are doing the very best they can. Don't badger them. Keep silence, and we'll get you safe across.[12]

Audience Questions

The audience question recognizes the dialogue between the speaker and his hearers; it rouses the interest of the listeners and keeps them alert. The speeches of Daniel Webster, Wendell Phillips, Franklin D. Roosevelt, and others could be noted for their use of meaningful questions directed to the audience. Alexander Hamilton constructed a portion of a famous speech delivered to the legislature of New York by using question after question:

What must be the final issue of the present state of things? Will the few states that now contribute, be willing to contribute much longer? Shall we ourselves be long content with bearing the burthen singly? will not our zeal for a particular system, soon give way to the pressure of so unequal a weight? and if all the states cease to pay, what is to become of the union? It is sometimes asked why do not Congress oblige the states to do their duty; but where are the means? Where are the fleets and armies, where the federal treasury to support those fleets and armies, to enforce the requisitions of the union? All methods short of coertion, have repeatedly been tried in vain.[13]

SIMPLICITY

Young people studying the famous orations of the past or the purple passages in the speeches of the present may suppose that speechmaking must be grandiloquent. They do not know that Webster in his shirtsleeves before a jury typifies the orator just as truly as does Webster in the splendor of the Senate Chamber. Splendid phrasing is suitable for the great occasion, but speechmaking is ordinarily concerned with everyday affairs. Most good composition is unpretentious in its structure and its phrasing.

Choice of Words

The speaker should use words his audience can understand. Polysyllabic words, esoteric phrases, and erudite expressions ordinarily have no place in speechmaking. The short, familiar word is nearly always preferable to the difficult and involved phrase.

[12] Carl Sandburg, *Abraham Lincoln: The War Years*, New York: Harcourt, Brace and Company, Inc., 1939, Vol. II, p. 175. Copyright 1939 by Harcourt, Brace and Company, Inc.
[13] Harold C. Syrett, ed., *The Papers of Alexander Hamilton*, New York: Columbia University Press, 1962, Vol. IV, pp. 85–86.

Arthur Morgan, speaking before the American Society for the Promotion of Engineering Education, employed the simple, telling phrase together with a striking metaphor to clarify a conception of modern social problems:

There are very great stresses in our modern society. . . . If I see a bridge that is designed to carry a two-ton load with only a moderate factor of safety, and if I see a twenty-ton load approaching, it is not always necessary to wait until the load goes onto the bridge to know what is going to happen.[14]

Straightforward Sentences

The straightforward sentence marks a mature style. Whether short or long, such a sentence must be constructed with the audience in mind. Remember that the hearers are not readers: they must listen; they cannot look ahead; they cannot stop to consider. Note the advantage gained by the straightforward style of the following excerpt from a Scholarship Day Address delivered by William Trufant Foster:

. . . the advantage of successful men and women over all others is seldom genius; the difference is not so much brilliance of mind as persistence in the pursuit of definite aims. The prancing race-horse makes a spectacular appearance, but he fails you in the long run. He is all speed and no control.[15]

Economy

Economy is an outstanding attribute of the simple style. The mature speaker avoids loquacity, circumlocution, and tedious repetition. He is brief without being cryptic, precise without being pedantic, forthright without being abrupt. The economical speech is not necessarily short, for the length of a speech is governed by what the speaker has to say. A short speech may waste the time and energy of an audience; a long one may justify and receive faithful attention to every word. The economy of a speech is measured by its efficiency as a means of communication. In this sense, Wendell Phillips was an exemplar of economy in oral style. His speeches moved toward their conclusion without a wasted word. The following passage from his famous address on Toussaint L'Ouverture illustrates forceful economy:

Let us pause a moment and find something to measure him by. You remember that Macaulay says, comparing Cromwell with Napoleon, that Cromwell showed the greater military genius, if we consider that he never saw an army till he was forty; while Napoleon was educated from a boy in the best military schools of Europe. Cromwell manufactured his own army; Napoleon at the age of twenty-seven was placed at the head of the best troops Europe ever saw.

[14] Lew Sarett and William Trufant Foster, eds., *Modern Speeches on Basic Issues,* Boston: Houghton Mifflin Company, 1939, p. 395.
[15] *Ibid.,* p. 73.

They were both successful; but, says Macaulay, with such disadvantages the Englishman showed the greater genius. Whether you allow the inference or not, you will at least allow that it is a fair mode of measurement. Apply it to Toussaint. Cromwell never saw an army till he was forty; this man never saw a soldier till he was fifty. Cromwell manufactured his own army—out of the middle-class among Englishmen—the best blood of the island. And with it he conquered what? Englishmen—their equals. This man manufactured his army out of what? Out of what you call the despicable race of Negroes, debased, demoralized by two hundred years of slavery, one hundred thousand of them imported into the island within four years, unable to speak a dialect intelligible even to each other. Yet out of this mixed and as you say, despicable mass, he forged a thunderbolt and hurled it at what? At the proudest blood in Europe, the Spaniard, and sent him home conquered; at the most warlike blood in Europe, the French, and put them under his feet; at the pluckiest blood in Europe, the English, and they skulked home to Jamaica. Now if Cromwell was a general, at least this man was a soldier.[16]

CLARITY

The importance of clarity cannot be overestimated; you must *know* what you mean and you must *say* it to your audience, however diverse the backgrounds, interests, and prejudices may be. Of the many aids to clarity, the first is concreteness.

Concreteness

Although abstractions are of the utmost importance to the mental processes of the speaker, he must translate from the abstract into the concrete whenever possible. Sometimes a concrete word may follow immediately after an abstraction, as when the names of Eisenhower, Bradley, and MacArthur follow a reference to "American generalship in World War II." The special language of speakers and audiences is the concrete language, which typically includes "boy" or "Tommy," but not "masculinity"; "carrots" or "steak," but not "nutritional balance"; "grafters," but not "malfeasants." Helen Gahagan Douglas brought a market basket into the House of Representatives and spoke concretely on the rising cost of living:

These are the items in the housewife's basket that I priced a year ago and priced again yesterday. I want to just show you what the difference is. Here was a pound of butter. Under OPA it cost you 65 cents. Last year it cost you 82 cents, and it cost 93 cents today in the lowest-priced store in Washington.

[16] *Speeches, Lectures, and Letters,* second series, Boston: Lee & Shepard, 1894, Vol. I, pp. 493–494.

Two quarts of Lucerne milk cost 29 cents under OPA, 34 cents last year, and 38 cents today. . . .

Two pounds of Maxwell House coffee cost 60 cents under OPA, 98 cents last year, and $1.06 today in the cheapest-priced store in Washington.

Two loaves of Wright's bread cost 22 cents under OPA, 20 cents last year, and 24 cents this year.[17]

Specificity

The second aid to clarity is specificity. Although the speaker finds the general term, like the abstraction, necessary in his own thinking, he should use it with discretion in speeches, especially in those designed for a general audience. In the degrees of specificity, *knife* is more specific than *cutlery,* and *dagger* is more specific than *knife.* Since most speeches are not specific enough, you will doubtless need to look for instances to replace general terms in your speeches. *Great American inventors* is general; *the Wright Brothers* is specific. *Furniture* is general; *chair* is specific. *Atlantic* is more specific than *the ocean.* Most speakers might learn about specificity from the little girl who, on hearing her mother declare, "Thousands of children would like to have that spinach," replied succinctly, "Name two!"

In an address delivered before the Associated Traffic Clubs of America, President Fred G. Gurley of the Atchison, Topeka and Santa Fe Railway System named specifically some of the services provided free of charge to the commercial air lines:

Commercial air lines get the free use of, and are the principal users of, the beacons, radio beams, special weather services, radio and radar control towers for airports, and other special facilities of air navigation—all of which are provided, maintained and operated by the taxpayers. Such facilities are comparable to the signal and communications system and traffic control of the rail roads.[18]

In good speechmaking, concreteness and specificity are ordinarily found together. Compare the following example of an abstract and general statement with the concrete and specific language suitable for the speaker:

[17] A. Craig Baird, ed., *Representative American Speeches: 1947–1948,* New York: The H. W. Wilson Company, 1948, p. 122. Copyright 1948 by The H. W. Wilson Company.
[18] From an address "What Do You Want. . . . How Do You Expect To Get It?" Houston, Texas: Associated Traffic Clubs of America, 1949, pp. 15–16.

STYLE DETERMINES THE VALUE OF SPEAKING
Adlai Stevenson's superior style has enhanced his reputation as one of our most effective public speakers.

GENERAL STATEMENT

The general effect of war upon a population is to take from the community many of its brightest and ablest citizens. The young and able members of society are called first to serve in military situations and the casualties are higher among the physically fit. At the same time, since the demand is for young and able men in the prime of life, rather than for the aged or decrepit, a war is more likely than pestilence or famine to produce a relatively greater loss upon the males who are the heads of families and the supporters of dependent persons.

SPEAKER'S LANGUAGE

We all know what we have lost in this House. Here, sitting near me, very often sat the member for Frome [Colonel Boyle]. I met him a short time before he went out, at Mr. Westerton's, the bookseller, near Hyde Park Corner. I asked him whether he was going out. He answered, he was afraid he was; not afraid in the sense of personal fear—he knew not that; but he said, with a look and a tone I shall never forget, "It is no light matter for a man who has a wife and five little children." The stormy Euxine is his grave; his wife is a widow, his children fatherless. On the other side of the House sat a member, with whom I was not acquainted, who has lost his life; and another, of whom I knew something [Colonel Blair]. Who is there that does not recollect his frank, amiable, and manly countenance? I doubt whether there were any men on either side of the House who were more capable of fixing the goodwill and affection of those with whom they were associated. Well, but the place that knew them shall know them no more for ever.[19]

The example of oral style given above is from the speech of John Bright, a great orator. But the concrete and specific expression will not be found solely in the works of great orators; it is the stock in trade of all effective speakers.

Sometimes instances may be multiplied with good effect. William G. Carleton, in his speech entitled "What of Free Enterprise?" made use of a number of them:

Who, then, destroyed the free market? The answer is: business. Business itself. The great industrial and financial giants of the late nineteenth century. Vanderbilt and Gould and Harriman and Hill in railroading. Carnegie and Frick and Gary in steel. Pillsbury and Washburn in flour-milling. Armour and Swift in meat-packing. Havemeyer in sugar. Rockefeller in oil refining. The

[19] George Barnett Smith, *Life and Speeches of The Right Hon. John Bright, M.P.,* London: Hodder & Stoughton, 1881, Vol. I, pp. 392–393.

House of Morgan in any number of combinations effected, mergers engineered, and holding companies built. In the name of individualism these men destroyed individualism in business.[20]

Precision

The precise word is an outstanding characteristic of the mature speaking style. Do not be content with such vague pronouns as *this, these,* and *those.* Do not say *citizen* when you mean *voter;* do not say *that thing on top of the Court House* when you mean *cupola;* do not say *picture* when you mean *concept.* The speaker should not be content to use a word that is almost right. When he has the opportunity to prepare, he should seek the telling phrase that conveys his exact meaning. In this respect Mark Twain is an excellent teacher: "The difference between the right word and the almost-right word is the difference between lightning and the lightning bug."

Comparison

Figures of speech are useful not primarily for adornment, but for clarity. Sometimes the best or even the only way to explain an object or an idea is to tell what it is like. Comparisons take different forms, as in the metaphor and the simile; but whatever the form, the comparison is indispensable. Henry Ward Beecher, himself a speaker of distinction, once declared:

I have seen an audience, time and again, follow an argument, doubtfully, laboriously, almost suspiciously, and look at one another, as much as to say, "Is he going right?"—until the place is arrived at where the speaker says, "It is like—" and then they listen eagerly for what it is like. . . .[21]

In describing the distress of the Middle Western farmer to the Democratic National Convention in Houston, Claude G. Bowers chose a vivid comparison:

The hammer of the auctioneer knocking down farm lands has sounded like the continuous bombardment of a major battle in the West. . . .[22]

The successful practice of speakers in every era confirms the theory that the comparison is indispensable to communication. Anyone who wishes to speak well in public must follow the advice of Beecher: "Tell the audience what it is like."

[20] A. Craig Baird, ed., *Representative American Speeches: 1943–1944*, New York: The H. W. Wilson Company, 1944, p. 213. Copyright 1944 by The H. W. Wilson Company.

[21] *Yale Lectures on Preaching*, New York: J. B. Ford and Company, 1872, p. 158.

[22] James M. O'Neill and Floyd K. Riley, ed., *Contemporary Speeches*, New York: Century Company, 1930, p. 512.

Analogy

The analogy is an extended comparison. Monsignor Fulton J. Sheen, in his speech "Liberty and the Republic," offered a description of Communist tactics in the United States by means of what he called a parable:

One day a dozen rats got into a house and ate cheese, meat, ham, and crackers. The housewife set traps and caught six of the rats. The other six remaining rats organized a popular front with a rat-trap salesman and told him to tell the lady of the house that her greatest danger was not rats but bed-bugs; another popular front was organized with professors, who told the housewife that statistics proved that 60 per cent of children in the village of Padaowski lost their fingers in rat-traps in one year; finally the rats organized a popular front with some sentimentally inclined social leaders who told the housewife that by using rat-traps she was guilty of the reactionary crime of "rat-baiting." The poor housewife, so overcome by such influential nit-wits, gave up the use of rat-traps entirely—and now the rats run the pantry.[23]

Illustration

In his address to the members of the American Bar Association and to the Members of the Bench of the Honourable Society of the Middle Temple in the Middle Temple in London, on July 21, 1924, Roscoe Pound wished to amplify the thought that in Britain and in the United States, questions of the law are looked at judicially rather than administratively. He relied on a series of illustrations.

That is the frame of mind which led the judges in the Middle Ages to tell Edward III that, though he could pardon an offender under his Great Seal as King of England, he could not write a private letter as Edward Plantagenet to the sheriff and interfere with the due course of justice. It is that frame of mind which led the judges of Henry VII, when Parliament enacted a statute that derogated from what were then regarded as the fundamentals of the social order, to say that it was "impertinent to be observed." It was that frame of mind that led the judges to say to James I that he could not sit upon the Bench and decide in person cases affecting the fortune or inheritance of his subjects.[24]

Those who heard the speech might have forgotten a general concept, but many of them carried away the illustration, and the illustration served to recall the concept.

Parallelism

Parallelism is the fitting of various ideas into a single kind of structure. Since it frees the hearers from thinking about structure, it enables them

[23] A. Craig Baird, ed., *Representative American Speeches: 1938–1939*, New York: The H. W. Wilson Company, 1939, p. 246. Copyright 1939 by The H. W. Wilson Company.
[24] Homer D. Lindgren, comp., *Modern Speeches*, New York: F. S. Crofts & Co., 1930, p. 111.

to concentrate on idea. No one in recent times has understood the principle of parallelism better than Franklin D. Roosevelt. His address delivered at Queens University in Canada exemplifies its use:

A few days ago a whisper, fortunately untrue, raced round the world that armies standing over against each other in unhappy array were to be set in motion. In a few short hours the effect of that whisper had been registered in Montreal and New York, in Ottawa and in Washington, in Toronto and in Chicago, in Vancouver and in San Francisco. Your business men and ours felt it alike; your farmers and ours heard it alike; your young men and ours wondered what effect this might have on their lives.[25]

The repetition of the words *your* and *ours* is more than a device; it is a way of helping the listener. Note also how the parallel clauses facilitate communication:

We as good neighbors are true friends because we maintain our own rights with frankness, because we refuse to accept the twists of secret diplomacy, because we settle our disputes by consultation and because we discuss our common problems in the spirit of the common good.[26]

Periodicity

Periodicity consists of a grouping of preliminary or subordinate ideas at the beginning of a unit of discourse, and a reserving of the major thought to its conclusion. It is likely to be employed where climactic order is essential. William Jennings Bryan, in his famous speech delivered at the Chicago convention, concluded eloquently with periodic structure:

Having behind us the producing masses of this nation and the world, supported by the commercial interests, the laboring interests, and the toilers everywhere, we will answer their demand for a gold standard by saying to them: "You shall not press down upon the brow of labor this crown of thorns, you shall not crucify mankind upon a cross of gold." [27]

VIGOR

Effective speaking style is vigorous. Vigor is achieved in part by a language free from the negative, the hesitant, and the apologetic expression of ideas. But vigor is not synonymous with belligerence or pomposity. A speaker may express doubt and yet be firm. His business is to know his mind and to speak without quibbling.

[25] A. Craig Baird, ed., *Representative American Speeches: 1938–1939*, New York: The H. W. Wilson Company, 1939, pp. 26–27. Copyright 1939 by The H. W. Wilson Company.
[26] *Ibid.*, p. 27.
[27] *Speeches of William Jennings Bryan*, New York: Funk & Wagnalls Co., 1909, Vol. I, p. 249.

Of all famous speakers, perhaps Lord Chatham best exemplifies the development of vigor in style, as shown in the following excerpt from his speech delivered in the House of Lords, January 20, 1775, in favor of immediate removal of His Majesty's troops from Boston:

To such united forces, what force shall be opposed? What, my Lords? A few regiments in America, and seventeen or eighteen thousand men at home! The idea is too ridiculous to take up a moment of your Lordships' time. Nor can such a national and principled union be resisted by the tricks of office, or ministerial maneuver. Laying of papers on your table, or counting numbers on a division, will not avert or postpone the hour of danger. It must arrive, my Lords, unless these fatal acts are done away; it must arrive in all its horrors, and then these boastful ministers, spite of all their confidence and all their maneuvers, shall be forced to hide their heads. They shall be forced to a disgraceful abandonment of their present measures and principles, which they avow, but cannot defend; measures which they presume to attempt, but cannot hope to effectuate. They cannot, my Lords, they cannot stir a step; they have not a move left; they are *check-mated!* [28]

Active Voice

Since he talks directly to people, the speechmaker does not often use the passive construction. He speaks in the active voice. Note the gain when the assertion, "History has been made by the speeches of Churchill," is transposed into "Churchill's speeches have made history."

Exclamatory, Imperative, and Hortatory Expressions

Since the speaker is in direct contact with the audience, he sometimes needs to exclaim, command, or request. The wartime speeches of Winston Churchill supply examples of exclamatory, imperative, and hortatory expressions.

Exclamations. In the address broadcast on March 30, 1940, Winston Churchill exclaimed, "What a frightful fate has overtaken Poland!" and again, "Yet how tragic was their plight!" The exclamations fit exactly in their context:

All these outrages upon the sea, which are too clearly visible, pale before the villainous deeds which are wrought upon the helpless Czechs and Austrians, and they sink almost into insignificance before the hideous agony of Poland. *What a frightful fate has overtaken Poland!* Here was a community of nearly thirty-five millions of people, with all the organization of a modern government, and all the traditions of an ancient State, which in a few weeks was dashed out of civilized existence to become an incoherent multitude of tortured and starving men, women and children, ground beneath the heel of two rival forms of withering and blasting tyranny. The other day in a well-known British harbor I

[28] Chauncey A. Goodrich, *Select British Eloquence,* New York: The Bobbs-Merrill Company, 1963, pp. 130–131. Copyright 1963 by The Bobbs-Merrill Company, Inc.

inspected the crew of a Polish destroyer. I have rarely seen a finer body of men. I was stirred by their discipline and bearing. *Yet how tragic was their plight!* Their ship was afloat, but their country had foundered.[29]

Imperatives.   The imperative is a command. It issues an instruction to be followed, as Churchill did in his address "Every Man to His Post," on September 11, 1940, the eve of the anticipated German invasion:

Every man and woman will therefore prepare himself to do his duty, whatever it may be, with special pride and care.[30]

The more common form of the imperative is directly injunctive: "Vote conservative!"

Hortatory expressions.   The hortatory expression is a request made of an audience, often with a degree of urgency. In his speech delivered to the House of Commons on June 18, 1940, Churchill exhorted his hearers:

Let us therefore brace ourselves to our duties, and so bear ourselves that, if the British Empire and its Commonwealth last for a thousand years, men will still say, "This was their finest hour." [31]

Climax

Vigorous speaking is characterized by progressive development. The language, the speech plan, the rate of speaking, and the heightening of enthusiasm all contribute to producing climactic order. The speech will be climactic only if it begins on the level of the audience and moves with increasing vigor toward its conclusion. Climactic order is dependent on the right speech composition as exemplified by the conclusion of Lord Chatham's great address delivered in the House of Lords:

To conclude, my Lords, if the ministers thus persevere in misadvising and misleading the King, I will not say that they can alienate the affections of his subjects from his crown, but I will affirm *that they will make the crown not worth his wearing.* I will not say that the King is betrayed, but I will pronounce *that the kingdom is undone.*[32]

Vividness

The speaker often chooses vivid phrases and colorful words. The following excerpt from a modern sermon is a good example:

A discriminating critic of the writings of Charles Dickens accounts for their popularity in part by the numerous descriptions of appetizing meals. Lo! the

---

[29] From *Blood, Sweat and Tears* by Winston S. Churchill. © 1941 by Winston S. Churchill. Reprinted by permission of G. P. Putnam's Sons. P. 245. Italics supplied for this text.

[30] *Ibid.*, p. 368.

[31] *Ibid.*, p. 314.

[32] Chauncey A. Goodrich, *Select British Eloquence*, New York: The Bobbs-Merrill Company, 1963, p. 132. Copyright 1963 by The Bobbs-Merrill Company, Inc.

steaming puddings, the meats roasted to just the right turn, the delicious fruits, and the frosted cakes—no wonder Dickens is popular. The point made by this critic might apply with equal weight to the Bible. The flavor of hospitality permeates its pages. Bible characters, whether kings, peasants, sages, seers, apostles, are seen many times as hosts and guests, and often at the family meal. Jesus Himself moves amid such scenes very much at home. Many of His parables were spoken at the table. He has been called the Greatest of Table Talkers. He was a guest, not only in the home of friends, but of enemies as well. As for His parables, a number of them have for theme some phase of feasting—the host, guests, food, and drink.[33]

Strength

An energetic speaking style should give a total impression of strength in restraint. A good example of a strong, restrained style is found in Lincoln's Second Inaugural Address:

With malice toward none; with charity for all; with firmness in the right, as God gives us to see the right, let us strive on to finish the work we are in; to bind up the nation's wounds; to care for him who shall have borne the battle, and for his widow and his orphan—to do all which may achieve and cherish a just and a lasting peace among ourselves and with all nations.[34]

DISTINCTION

In any language a good oral style will be simple, direct, clear, and vigorous. A superior oral style will be characterized also by distinction attained through unquestioned propriety, unusual felicity, appropriate diction, and judicious flexibility.

Propriety

In speechmaking the language must be suited to the audience and to the occasion. The easy style of a student addressing a mass meeting would be inappropriate for a minister delivering a funeral sermon. Since proper style is determined by the mood and feeling of the hearers, the speaker should suit his language to their mood.

Triteness. Triteness is likely to displease the judicious audience. The threadbare word, the hackneyed phrase, the time-worn simile have no place in good speeches. They may once have been powerful or provocative, but long use has reduced them to stereotypes. Such a hackneyed

[33] From the sermon "Life's Foolish Rivalries" by Edgar DeWitt Jones, *Best Sermons 1925*, Joseph Fort Newton, ed., New York: Harcourt, Brace and Company, Inc., 1925, p. 159. Copyright 1925 by Harcourt, Brace and Company, Inc.

[34] Thomas B. Reed, ed., *Modern Eloquence,* Philadelphia: John D. Morris & Co., 1900, Vol. VIII, p. 776.

expression as "plays its part" conveys neither image nor idea; you must find a fresher way of saying what you mean.

Sometimes an unsuccessful attempt at elevated language results in triteness. In place of the meaningful word the inept speaker uses gaudy phrases: the ocean is "the breaking waves," the new incinerator is "the long-felt need of this fair city."

The great man talking on great themes will often employ the simplest language; his speeches are made of the common words heard every day. Read such speeches. You will generally find them characterized by simplicity and restraint. Winston Churchill is a modern exemplar of the principle:

> Come then: let us to the task, to the battle, to the toil—each to our part, each to our station. Fill the armies, rule the air, pour out the munitions, strangle the U-boats, sweep the mines, plow the land, build the ships, guard the streets, succor the wounded, uplift the downcast, and honor the brave. Let us go forward together in all parts of the Empire, in all parts of the Island. There is not a week, nor a day, nor an hour to lose.[35]

Every word of this passage is in our everyday vocabulary, and of the 86 words, 71 have but a single syllable.

Slang. Whenever an expression can be used with telling effect and without offending the sensibilities of your audience, you should not hesitate to use it. Slang may serve to break the ice of formality that sometimes envelops the speaker and his hearers; a colorful phrase is sometimes a lifesaver.

But slang may be unfortunate. Sober-minded people dislike it, and even those who use it in informal speech may feel uncomfortable at hearing it in public address. Perhaps the worst feature of slang is its tendency to triteness. A colorful expression appears and sweeps the country, to be followed a few weeks later by still another. Each phrase in turn is exhausted and discarded. Furthermore, the use of a single slang expression to cover a multitude of ideas does not permit a nice discrimination. Occasionally a new expression is so vivid or so useful that it remains a part of the language, but the safest practice in public address is to use slang sparingly, if at all. You would do well to invent a fresh expression rather than take a worn phrase unimaginatively from someone else.

Colloquialism. Speaking is perhaps more colloquial than writing. The speech for a great occasion must observe the high proprieties of style; but most speeches are delivered on everyday business, and the speaker is likely to talk more directly than he would write. Although such contractions as *don't, doesn't, hasn't,* and *we're* may be frowned upon

[35] From *Blood, Sweat and Tears* by Winston S. Churchill. © 1941 by Winston S. Churchill. Reprinted by permission of G. P. Putnam's Sons. P. 225.

in formal written style, they are the standard currency of speechmakers. The fragmentary construction sometimes thought inadvisable in writing may often be employed with impunity in speeches. An inflection or a gesture completes the construction. The written text cannot always be trusted to represent what the speaker actually said, for the reporter may have tried to find word equivalents for inflections or gestures.

Grammar. The speaker's primary purpose is to communicate; bad grammar may impede communication. Even men who habitually use ungrammatical expressions may notice the bad grammar of a man in public life. To say, "I learned him," instead of "I taught him," or to declare, "He asked my friend and I," may call attention to your syntax rather than to your idea. Unconventional grammar is not likely to make the judicious think favorably of your plea. You need not be pedantic in order to be grammatical; good colloquial speech is a source of power.

Felicity

Felicity comes from the speaker's complete command of the occasion. It is the ability to say the right word in the right way at the right moment. No trace of awkwardness, no hint of constraint prevents any attribute of the speech from leading to the central impression. Felicity depends not upon language alone, but also upon the speaker's personality. Yet the finding of fresh, apt, and gracious expressions is also necessary.

Henry W. Grady was a master of oral style. His address describing the return of the Southern soldier is a fine example of felicity in speechmaking:

What does he do—this hero in gray with a heart of gold? Does he sit down in sullenness and despair? Not for a day. Surely God, who had stripped him of his prosperity, inspired him in his adversity. As ruin was never before so overwhelming, never was restoration swifter. The soldier stepped from the trenches into the furrow; horses that had charged Federal guns marched before the plow, and fields that ran red with human blood in April were green with the harvest in June.[36]

Diction

The primary end of speechmaking is effectiveness, not beauty; yet an ugly speech is likely to be ineffective. If you wish to influence your hearers, you will need to please them; and in pleasing them, you must often find words that are attractive in sense and sound as well as meaningful in context.

Sense. Some words are pleasing and others displeasing because of their association. *Cad, shyster,* and *chiseler* have an undesirable connota-

[36] Thomas B. Reed *et al.*, eds., *Modern Eloquence*, Philadelphia: John D. Morris & Co., 1900, Vol. VIII, p. 583.

tion; *hero, savior,* and *benefactor* have a desirable connotation. Know the words you choose, and distinguish every delicate shade of meaning. What distinction will you make, for example, between *courage* and *fortitude,* between *courage* and *bravery,* between *courage* and *foolhardiness?*

The English language is rich in synonyms and quasi-synonyms; yet no two words are exactly alike. There is a world of difference between *house* and *home,* between *home* and *habitation.* Words are warm or cold, friendly or unfriendly, wise or foolish. With their literal meanings they carry emotional concomitants. In a speech composition you must choose the words suited to your purpose.

Sound. Some words are pleasing and others are displeasing because of their sound. For most people, *ax, stick,* and *knack,* for example, have no innate quality of sound to recommend them; but the sounds of *oriole, symphony,* and *evening* are inherently pleasant. Seek words with enough music in them to fall agreeably on the ear; if possible, avoid such croaking syllables as "Tax schedules for the next decade must be increased by 60 per cent."

In the history of American oratory, Robert G. Ingersoll is the great exemplar of euphony. Few men would be able, as he was, to deliver effectively the eulogy from which the following selection is taken:

> Life is a narrow vale between the cold and barren peaks of two eternities. We strive in vain to look beyond the heights. We cry aloud, and the only answer is the echo of our wailing cry. From the voiceless lips of the unreplying dead there comes no word; but in the night of death hope sees a star, and listening love can hear the rustle of a wing.[37]

Language effective for solemn occasions may seem artificial in less momentous situations. Especially on everyday occasions, the speaker must avoid the obvious seeking for effect. Precise meaning must never be sacrificed to euphony.

Flexibility

Anyone who wishes to cultivate a superior oral style will be concerned with certain stylistic devices, with the speaking vocabulary, and with the preparation of the text of oral discourse. The special problems of style are perennial, but they tend to be solved by persistent effort.

Stylistic devices. The sophisticated speaker sometimes makes conscious use of such stylistic devices as the apostrophe, personification, allusion, epigram, and antithesis; and his speeches may be marked by a characteristic rhythm. The best practice for the beginning speaker is to employ the cadences of conversation and, while employing stylistic devices, to use them with discretion.

[37] Charles Morris, ed., *Famous Orators of the World and Their Best Orations,* Washington, D. C.: W. E. Scull, 1902, p. 320.

Increasing the speaking vocabulary. Everyone has four vocabularies: one for reading and one for writing, one for listening and one for speaking. The most limited is usually the speaking vocabulary, and its development is a continuing task. You must be alert to discover exact shades of meaning and to sense the emotional as well as the intellectual values of words. Concentrate not so much on learning unusual technical terms such as *dicotyledonous* or *fossiliferous* as on such problems as the difference between *fame* and *reputation* and the nuances of *crucify* and *quisling*. Learn precision in the use of simple phrases.

The student can best enrich his vocabulary by wide reading of outstanding essays, speeches, novels, and poetry. Great speakers have frequently confessed their debt to a knowledge of the Bible, Shakespeare, the orations of Demosthenes and Cicero, the public addresses of Webster, Clay, Calhoun, and Ingersoll, and to outstanding works in history and literature. To improve your vocabulary, associate with writers and speakers who use words in an expressive and original fashion; study their works for style as well as for content.

You should also be alert to the possibility of using simple words in a striking way. Nothing about *iron* or *curtain* is very startling, but in 1946 when Churchill said, "From Stettin in the Baltic to Trieste in the Adriatic, an iron curtain has descended across the continent," the whole English-speaking world caught the image, seized the phrase, and made it a part of the language. Edmund Burke was famous for uttering unusual words, but he also spoke simple words with striking effect: "I do not know the method of drawing up an indictment against a whole people"; "these facts lead to irresistible conclusions"; "none will barter away the immediate jewel of his soul." Great speakers from William Pitt and Patrick Henry to Adlai Stevenson and Winston Churchill have gained expressiveness through choice of words.

Adjusting the style to the occasion. Style should be experimental. The speech should be subject to change to meet varying circumstances. The student of speechmaking is in some danger of becoming like the centipede who traveled very well until he began to wonder which leg to move next, whereupon he fell into a state of nervous exhaustion. The multitude of details may seem bewildering; but you should be encouraged if you will remember that oral style is for listening and speaking, not for reading and writing. Take the advice of experienced men who have said, "Don't speak what you write; write what you speak." Talk out the speech; experiment with the words; change the language, the order, and the plan to fit the ear. If a manuscript is necessary, write out the spoken form that seems most acceptable.

Since some adjustment of the text to the occasion is normally required, the composition of a genuine speech includes the moment of presentation. Adjust your language to a fruitful idea that comes to you as you speak, or to an incident that offers an opportunity for orienting yourself with your audience.

Even when the speech has been delivered, the composition is not finished, for the speaker wants to know whether his discourse has met the tests of oral style. Every presentation is an opportunity to learn more about composition. Many speeches are delivered more than once, each delivery representing an adjustment to a particular group and occasion. The composition is thus progressive; the speech is always unfinished, always developing.

Part III   SPEECH DELIVERY:
Problems, Methods, and Means

I hope that your professors of rhetoric will teach you to cultivate that golden art—the steadfast use of a language in which truth can be told; a speech that is strong by natural force, and not merely effective by declamation; an utterance without trick, without affectation, without mannerism.

—John Morley

6 MEANING:
Comprehension and
Presentation

You will have carried over into your public delivery the most desirable qualities of conversational speaking when you maintain upon the platform a full realization of the content of your words as you utter them, and a lively sense of communication.
—James A. Winans

Accurate communication requires the directed mental activity of the speaker or reader and the listener. If the speaker is so distracted that his own understanding is incomplete or distorted, his hearers will be misled. If he is to convey all the overtones of thought and feeling to other people, he must have a full comprehension of his meaning at the very moment of utterance. Therefore, in reading a text or in speaking from memory, he must focus attention on each unit of thought as it is presented to the listeners. The speaker or reader must grasp the meaning with the same genuine and lively comprehension employed in answering a question or in recreating an idea in extemporaneous delivery. Mastery of the content is the first essential in any kind of oral communication. Realization of the content during presentation is the second essential in communicating with an audience.

179

ANALYSIS OF MEANING: QUESTIONING

In preparation for reading a speech to an audience, you will need to ask yourself specific questions about the ideas developed. For your analysis, there follows a section of the speech delivered by President-elect John F. Kennedy to the Massachusetts Legislature.

History will not judge our endeavors—and a government cannot be selected —merely on the basis of color or creed or even party affiliation. Neither will competence and loyalty and stature, while essential to the utmost, suffice in times such as these.

For of those to whom much is given, much is required. And when at some future date the high court of history sits in judgment on each one of us— recording whether in our brief span of service we fulfilled our responsibilities to the state—our success or failure, in whatever office we may hold, will be measured by the answers to four questions:

First, were we truly men of courage—with the courage to stand up to one's enemies—and the courage to stand up when necessary to one's own associates —the courage to resist public pressure as well as private greed?

Secondly, were we truly men of judgment—with perceptive judgment of the future as well as the past—of our own mistakes as well as the mistakes of others—with enough wisdom to know what we did not know, and enough candor to admit it?

Third, were we truly men of integrity—men who never ran out on either the principles in which they believed or the people who believed in them— men whom neither financial gain nor political ambition could ever divert from the fulfillment of our sacred trust?

Finally, were we truly men of dedication—with an honor mortgaged to no single individual or group and compromised by no private obligation or aim, but devoted solely to serving the public good and the national interest? [1]

To determine the full meaning of the quoted passage, you will ask yourself what characteristics and qualities are to be considered in the evaluation of history. How are they related to each other? You will find, on the first level of consideration, color, creed, and party affiliation; on the second level, competence, loyalty, and stature; and on the highest level, courage, judgment, integrity, and dedication. In focusing attention in the presentation of these ideas, the three levels of importance should receive increasing intensity so that a climax will be communicated.

To perceive the relations of ideas within sentences, you will need to ask yourself such questions as, Is this idea coordinate or subordinate in relation to other ideas in the sentence? The words *while essential to the utmost* will be seen as subordinate to *will . . . suffice in times such as*

[1] *The New York Times,* January 10, 1961, p. 20. Copyright by *The New York Times.* Reprinted by permission.

these. What kind of repetition is represented in the second paragraph with the words *high court of history sits in judgment* in relation to *history will not judge* in the first paragraph? Analysis will show that the repetition is not merely for coherence but also for emphasis.

ANALYSIS OF MEANING: DEFINITION OF TERMS

In making your understanding of a passage exact and thorough, you may employ a systematic analysis of the meaning. The use of a few special terms simplifies the technique of interpretation.

CENTERING

Centering is the mental process of focusing attention upon the word or words that convey the essential meaning of a phrase, so that they stand out in relief from the other words. Although this process determines how the voice indicates the meaning, it is intrinsically a mental discrimination between those ideas that should come to the forefront of attention and those that should drop into the background. Analysis of the sentence *For of those to whom much is given, much is required* reveals a parallelism between *given* and *required.* These two ideas stand out in the foreground of attention as the key ideas of the thought. The word *much* stands out as the subject of each clause, but not to the same degree as *given* and *required.* With the exception of *those,* which receives some attention, the other words in the sentence are in the background.

CENTER

A center of a phrase, therefore, is a word carrying an essential meaning of that phrase and requiring the focusing of attention upon it. A center is like a dark spot upon a light background. In the passage *And when at some future date,* the meaning will be conveyed by making *future* the key word and the single center of attention. In the passage *were we truly men of courage,* the word *courage* receives primary attention, the word *truly* secondary attention. Each word is a center. In the passage *the courage to resist public pressure as well as private greed, public pressure* and *private greed* are parallel centers receiving equal attention.

PHRASE

A phrase is a word or group of words containing at least one center of attention; it is an idea or a series of related ideas upon which the mind focuses momentarily. A phrase is thus any unit of thought, and must be

EFFECTIVE SPEAKING AND READING DEMAND SKILL IN
CONVEYING MEANING

Poet Carl Sandburg (*above*) eulogizes Abraham Lincoln before a joint session of Congress. Poet Robert Frost (*below*) recites poetry at Moscow's Library of Foreign Literature.

distinguished from the prepositional phrase of the grammarian's usage. In the first sentence of the quoted passage, phrases end with *endeavors, selected, color, creed, affiliation.* Each of these phrases contains a unit of thought with one or more centers of attention. In some instances, the thought of a speech will permit fewer or more phrases according to the judgment of the speaker.

PHRASING

Phrasing is the vocal manifestation of centering. By means of pauses and vocal changes the speaker is able to indicate phrases to his audience. The physical effect of centering and phrasing is emphasis. After each of the eight phrases in the first paragraph of the excerpt from President-elect Kennedy's speech, the speaker pauses, but only after *affiliation* and *these* does he let his voice fall to indicate that he has finished a complete assertion. Since the meaning at the end of each of the other phrases looks forward to the next phrase, it should not be cut off by a falling inflection.

PAUSE

A pause is a moment of silence required by both speaker and listener for the focusing of attention. It may come after a phrase or before or after a single word, and may be used for clearness or for emphasis. The length of a pause is determined by such factors as the length, nature, and importance of the unit of thought, the time needed by the listener to assimilate and evaluate the unit, and the time needed by the speaker to comprehend and interpret the next unit. After a question, a substantial pause permits the listener to frame the desired response.

Again, referring to the first paragraph of the excerpt from President-elect Kennedy's speech, you will note that a pause for clearness is needed after each of the eight phrases. A slight pause before each of the words *competence, loyalty,* and *stature* will lend emphasis to the three concepts.

NEW CONCEPT

A new concept is an idea appearing for the first time in a speech or passage. In the sentence *For of those to whom much is given, much is required, much* in the first phrase is a new concept because it has not previously been used in the excerpt from the speech, whereas *much* in the second phrase is an old idea because it restates the concept used in the first phrase. The old idea may or may not be the same word repeated. Although the new idea *much* is the center of attention, a new idea is not always a center of attention. The word *for* at the beginning of the first phrase is a new concept, but it is not important enough to be a center.

ECHO

An echo is an idea repeated for the purpose of clearness or coherence. Since it is merely the connective tissue of the language, it falls into the background of attention. The relation of a pronoun to its antecedent, which may be either a noun or another pronoun, is an illustration of the relation of an echo to a new concept. In the passage *recording whether in our brief span of service we fulfilled our responsibilities to the state— our success or failure, in whatever office we hold, our, we, our, our,* and *we* echo *us* in the preceding phrase. An echo may be the repetition of the same word or words, or the repetition of the same concept in synonymous language. In the first and second sentences of the second paragraph of the excerpt, the idea of what is expected of a leader is expressed first in the word *required* and second in the word *responsibilities*. The noun *responsibilities* in the second sentence echoes the verb *required* in the first sentence. An echo is never a center of attention; it is always a part of the background of a phrase.

RESTATEMENT

A restatement, in contrast to an echo, is a concept repeated for the purpose of gaining force. In the sentence *First, were we truly men of courage—with the courage to stand up to one's enemies—and the courage to stand up when necessary to one's own associates—the courage to resist public pressure as well as private greed,* the second, third, and fourth uses of courage are instances of restatement of the first *courage.* Each repetition is intended to strengthen the importance of *courage.* The restatement of *much* in the first sentence of the second paragraph illustrates a restatement which is a secondary center of attention in a phrase, receiving less attention than the primary center *required.*

A restatement, like an echo, may be expressed in the same language or in different language. An echo is never a center of attention; a restatement is always a center of attention, although it may be a secondary center rather than a primary center, as shown in the passage above. Since its function is to call special attention to a concept, it can never be in the background of thought.

AMPLIFICATION

Amplification is a development or enlargement of a concept by means of general illustration, specific instance, allusion, reference to authority, detail, or other support. In the sentence *were we truly men of integrity —men who never ran out on either the principles in which they believed or the people who believed in them—men whom neither financial gain nor political ambition could ever divert from the fulfillment of our sacred trust,* all of the language following *integrity* enlarges the thought expressed in the words *truly men of integrity* by listing the kinds of conduct of which they would never be guilty.

PARALLELISM

Parallelism refers to ideas similar or related in meaning set forth in similar structure. In the sentence *were we truly men of judgment—with perceptive judgment of the future as well as the past—of our own mistakes as well as the mistakes of others, future* and *past* are parallel, and *our own mistakes* and *the mistakes of others* are parallel. Parallel ideas receive equal attention whether they are primary or secondary centers, echoes, restatements, or new concepts.

CONTRAST

A contrast is a relationship showing the differences between two ideas. In the passage *our success or failure in whatever office we may hold, failure* is in contrast to *success.* Since ideas in contrast require special attention, they are centers. They are of equal importance.

SUBORDINATE IDEA

A subordinate idea is a thought whose level of meaning and attention is lower than that of a major idea. One thought is dependent upon another, rather than coordinate with it. In the second sentence of the first paragraph of the excerpt, *while essential to the utmost* is subordinate to the rest of the sentence and is dependent upon *competence and loyalty and stature.*

Since a subordinate thought must necessarily receive less attention than a major one, it is frequently presented on a lower pitch of the voice at a more rapid rate, and with less vocal energy, to show its dependent relationship. A parenthetical expression should be treated as a subordinate idea.

TRANSITION

A transition leads from one idea to another by means of connecting language. In the second sentence of the first paragraph, *neither* makes the transition from the first sentence. In the second paragraph, *for of those* makes the transition from *general qualities* in the first paragraph to *responsibilities of individuals* in the second. A transition ordinarily receives only passing attention from the speaker, unless the relation of one section to another is peculiarly significant.

CONCESSION

A concession, frequently subordinate in relationship, is an idea that the speaker admits. In the second sentence of the first paragraph, *while essential to the utmost,* referred to above as a subordinate idea, is also a concession.

QUALIFICATION

A qualification defines or limits an idea. In the second sentence of the second paragraph, *in whatever office we may hold* defines the area in which success or failure is to be measured. The qualification usually is subordinate to the idea to which it is related.

CLIMAX

A climax is the highest peak of attention in a passage. In the two summarizing paragraphs following the excerpt previously quoted, the speaker builds a climax as follows:

Courage—judgment—integrity—dedication—these are the historic qualities of the Bay Colony and the Bay State—the qualities which this state has consistently sent to this chamber here on Beacon Hill in Boston and to Capitol Hill back in Washington.

And these are the qualities which, with God's help, this son of Massachusetts hopes will characterize our Government's conduct in the four stormy years that lie ahead.[2]

Attention steadily rises from the summary of the historic qualities to the hope of the speaker that these qualities will characterize the federal government during his administration.

[2] *Ibid.*

STRUCTURAL EMPHASIS

Structural emphasis is the development, by appropriate changes of rate, pitch, volume, and quality, of proportion, climax, and other relationships within the larger units of the selection or the speech. In the eight paragraphs of the excerpts we have analyzed, the first two paragraphs set forth the qualities often considered adequate for officeholding and suggest their inadequacy for our times. The next four paragraphs list and describe the qualities essential for a distinguished administration. The seventh paragraph attributes these qualities to the Bay Colony and the Bay State, and the eighth paragraph expresses the hope that they will characterize the new federal administration. The structure of this excerpt therefore suggests three divisions of thought, each division becoming more significant than the preceding one for the total impression.

MOOD

Mood is the underlying and pervading mental action essential to accurate interpretation. President-elect Kennedy's address illustrates the mood of a high-minded public servant about to assume the duties and responsibilities of the highest office in the land. It is one of high seriousness, determination, and idealism. He derives his inspiration from the past and applies it to the future.

MEANING AND ATTITUDE

Meaning is not merely a logical, intellectual concept; it is also concerned with feeling—the way the speaker responds to his thought and the way he expects the audience to respond. The same sentence with the same logical meaning may convey several different attitudes. The quotation from Pericles which President-elect Kennedy used in the early part of his address to the Massachusetts Legislature—"We do not imitate, for we are a model to others"—can be presented to mean (1) this is a fact (assertive attitude), (2) this is an idea we insist upon (determined attitude), (3) the idea that we would imitate others is absurd (ridiculing attitude), (4) the idea that we would be guilty of imitation makes us indignant (contemptuous attitude), (5) the thought that we are a pattern for others to follow makes us very proud (patriotic attitude), (6) as leaders rather than followers, we are superior to others (arrogant attitude).

The final paragraph of the speech illustrates several attitudes: "Humbly I ask His help in this undertaking—but aware that on earth His will is worked by man, I ask for your help and your prayers as I embark on this new and solemn journey." In succession, the attitudes seem to be those of reverence and humility, self-reliance, earnest appeal, hope and trust, courage, zeal, and sober sense of responsibility.

THE COMMUNICATIVE PRINCIPLE

What is "communicating with the audience?" In a public or private speech, communication is more easily recognized than described. You are communicating with your hearers when everyone senses immediately, "He has his mind on what he is saying to me."

A part of the concept of communicative speaking is expressed in the popular phrase "thinking on your feet." But more is involved than intellectual awareness of an idea. You must call up the personal and emotional connotations in your speech, and you must transfer your feeling as well as your thought to your audience.

If your delivery is animated by your own full understanding of what you are saying and by a strong determination to convey your idea to other people, you are employing the communicative principle. The requirements for communication, either in public or in private, are (1) concentration on what you say as you say it, and (2) a genuine effort to gain a response from your hearers.[3]

CONCENTRATION ON MEANING AND ATTITUDE

Effective communication requires the speaker simultaneously to concentrate on his ideas and to study his hearers. The task consumes nervous energy; the speaker must work at his job.

Is the speaker actually concerned about his ideas, or is he saying one speech and thinking another? Is he dividing his mental energy between his announced topic and a host of distractions? Is he uttering words while his mind wanders far away? Or, on the contrary, is he concentrating completely on his topic in its instant relation to his audience? His hearers will know.

INTERPRETATION OF MEANING AND ATTITUDE

By his attitude and inflection the speaker distinguishes meanings. The phrase "The house will please be in order" may be spoken to communicate different ideas. The speaker's tone, manner, and bearing may be mat-

---

[3] James A. Winans was the chief modern proponent of communicative speaking. See his *Speech-Making*, New York: Appleton-Century-Crofts, 1938, pp. 11–40.

ter-of-fact, saying in effect, "The hour for convocation has now arrived. Let us begin." It may be imperious, saying, as a part of his total communication, "The noise in the back of the room will stop immediately." Or the speaker's attitude may convey the quality of beseeching, with emphasis on the *please*. The various meanings can be communicated by the speaker who knows what he means and tries to say it.

Thought and feeling must be created or renewed at the exact moment of utterance—must, in fact, be a part of the utterance. You must have prepared your speech; but your every attitude, tone, and manner should reveal to your audience, "I am saying to you what I think now," not "I am trying to find the words."

RESPONSE OF THE LISTENERS

In effective communication you make contact with your audience. While you are thinking and feeling, you stimulate your hearers to think and feel with you. You do not talk to yourself when you make a speech; you talk with other people, and you are alert to their presence. As you speak, you observe your hearers, look them in the eye, see how they respond, and adjust your presentation accordingly.

You do not really make a speech unless your hearers respond to it. Speechmaking is not mere self-expression; it is an interplay of thought and feeling. The alert speaker anticipates questions and answers them; his discourse is an interchange of responses between himself and his hearers. "Next you will want to know . . . ," he may say to them, demonstrating his realization that genuine speaking is dialogue. He adapts his speech to audience responses: applause, hissing, laughter, frowns, whispering. If he fails to get the desired response, he is stirred to greater effort; if he succeeds, he is encouraged to continue. The test of the speech is the interaction between the speaker and his listeners.

Both formal and informal speaking should be communicative. Whether you are talking to a new acquaintance, participating in a business meeting, or delivering a formal address at a convention, you should concentrate on what you are saying and endeavor to get a response from your hearers.

Customs governing both formal and informal speaking may make the beginner shy, stiff, or aggressive, and so may impede his communication. He may retreat or withdraw, or attempt to dominate his listeners. He is more likely to accomplish his purpose if he leads his listeners step by step to the conclusion he wishes them to accept. But he should speak with firmness and vigor. In conference or in assembly, everyone prefers the man who speaks with assurance.

Students must learn to interpret the responses of other people in varying circumstances. The typical conversation is clearly dialogue; the responsibility for speaking is normally shared by the participants, each having the privilege of asking questions, presenting contrary points of view, or even changing the topic altogether. Since the public speaker normally does the talking, he may be unaware of the activity of the listeners and thus lose sight of the need for communication. Although the listeners usually will not ask questions or make comments, their role is active: their smiles or frowns, applause or silence are interpreted by the experienced speaker just as if they were actually calling out to him, "That's an interesting idea; go on and develop it," or "We've lost interest in this argument; go on to something else."

Whether the audience is large or small, the problem is still communication. Large audiences generally require of the speaker simpler language, more vivid illustration, slower rate, larger volume, and greater self-assurance than do small groups. These differences should not lead the speaker into bombast addressed to no one in particular; he must remember that every audience is composed of individuals. Because of the infinite variations, no one can draw up hard and fast rules for types of speaking. A public address may be informal if you are talking to the members of your church group, or formal if you are addressing a local service club. A conversation may be informal, as with a friend; or formal, as with the governor of the state; or the governor may surprise you and put you more at ease than do any of your acquaintances.

The intelligent person adapts his presentation to the circumstances, no matter what they are. He speaks loud enough to be heard; he is as formal as the occasion requires; he prepares as well as he can.

METHODS OF PRESENTATION

The methods of presenting a speech are (1) impromptu, (2) extemporaneous, (3) from manuscript, (4) from memory. Each of these methods has its peculiar disadvantages, advantages, uses, and techniques.

IMPROMPTU SPEAKING

Many occasions may demand a speech or participation in a meeting without permitting an opportunity for formal preparation. Any citizen should be able to meet the demand to speak briefly, to respond to an introduction, or to answer an inquiry.

Two special difficulties confront the impromptu speaker: confusion and triteness. Sometimes a man called on suddenly is at a loss for ideas. In order to overcome confusion, he should decide promptly upon a theme and a plan. Impromptu speaking can then become an orderly thinking aloud. Some people find refuge from their confusion in trite phrases or hackneyed stories. Such clichés as "happy to be with you today" or "great pleasure to be called upon to say a few words" are not thoughtful responses to the opportunity.

If you are not assigned a topic, you must pick one on the instant. Frequently the theme of the occasion, the purpose of the meeting, or the remarks of a previous speaker suggest what you should say. If not, you should select a relevant topic from your own experience.

Because the time is limited, you must instantly adopt a plan; once you have a framework, your thoughts will begin to come more coherently. You may choose a single idea and support it with illustrations, preferably drawn from your own experience, or you may amplify your theme with an amusing story. When the topic is controversial, you may give your position and develop it with facts, quotations, and examples. If previous speakers have supported your opinions, you may take advantage of their assistance; if you disagree with what others have said, you may state and support your reasons. If the occasion is one in which you are talking to members of a group of which you were once a member, you may adapt your remarks to the types of members in the group making use of the interests and experiences you have shared. If there is no special aspect of the situation you can utilize, you may make use of stock divisions in relation to an appropriate topic, such as past, present, and future; who, what, when, where, and why; or the individual, the community, the state, and the nation.

EXTEMPORANEOUS SPEAKING

The impromptu talk is given on the spur of the moment. The extemporaneous speech is prepared as thoroughly as possible, but without a manuscript or complete memorization.

Adaptability and Assurance

The extemporaneous speaker has the advantages of adaptability and assurance. Being free of a manuscript, you can watch your listeners and adapt your speech to them. As you talk, they will respond, and their responses will increase your self-confidence. Your preparation will enable you to follow a channel of thought previously determined; yet you can modify your ideas as you proceed.

When the late Alfred E. Smith, governor of New York State, first began to campaign for the presidency, he read his speeches; then he suddenly announced that he would read no more. He said:

I will do the same as in my state campaigns. I made five of them and never read a speech. I never even carried a copy of it with me. Sometimes the speech prepared for the papers was more like the uncle of what was delivered, but that can't be helped.

People lose interest, Smith believed, when they see a man bending over a paper. Moreover, they may think he is afraid to say what he has in mind, and they will certainly complain if he stumbles over words. Horace Mann put the case for extemporaneous speaking succinctly:

> . . . a ready extemporaneous public speaker has an advantage over one whose eyes are riveted to his manuscript. Doubtless a coherent and logical, written discourse is far better than an unwritten, rambling one. . . . We submit to the dullness of a written discourse, rather than to the desultoriness of an extemporaneous one; but who . . . would not prefer the same solidity and copiousness of the matter, enriched by all the grace and warmth of spontaneity? [4]

Sometimes a speaker thinks he knows his material better than he actually does; as a result, he hesitates and expresses his ideas inadequately. He may underestimate the effort required to organize his material and adapt it to the audience; he rambles and omits major points. If he has never timed the speech, it may be too short or too long.

Hindrance of Notes

Beginning speakers often ask if they should use notes. For many reasons the best answer is "No." Notes hinder thinking, restrict delivery, and give the impression of amateurishness. Disraeli declared, "If I once used notes, I should lean upon them; and that would never do." [5] A wiser authority even than Disraeli is your audience; ask your listeners if they like a half-read, half-spoken delivery. Your own observation will show you that speakers who hold their listeners in close attention usually avoid notes. The speaker who frequently looks down at a note card to get his next idea seldom has good transitions leading from one thought to the next.

Beginners sometimes say, "Let me use notes just two or three times, and then I won't need them." What they mean is, "I am afraid to talk to an audience." They are merely postponing the experience of genuine communication; reading from notes is not an efficient way of learning to speak. Mastering the sequence of ideas with special attention to transitions should make notes unnecessary and ensure better continuity. Remembering key words will help to guide you through the divisions and subdivisions of your speech.

[4] *Reply to the "Remarks" of Thirty-One Boston Schoolmasters on the Seventh Annual Report of the Secretary of the Massachusetts Board of Education,* Boston: William B. Fowle & Nahum Capen, 1844, pp. 89–90.

[5] Austin Chamberlain, "How Great Speakers Prepared Their Speeches," *Living Age,* CCCXXIV, 25, January 3, 1925.

Reading Quotations

Objections to the use of notes do not extend to the reading of quoted matter. By reading a quotation, you show your listeners that you have taken special care to be accurate. In some instances, however, to choose a short quotation and give it from memory may be still more effective. Reading statistics may impress the listener with your accuracy, but you are wiser to use round numbers than to read a complex series of figures that the audience cannot keep in mind.

Unless your reading is as communicative as your speaking, it will suffer by contrast. People often stop listening when a speaker reads, and do not resume listening until he talks to them again. But they will pay attention to a quotation if the speaker is genuinely communicative.

Your obligation to the author and the audience requires you to interpret quoted matter accurately. Your understanding of the meaning of the quotation should be as clear as if you had written it yourself.

Poetry in Speeches

The reading of poetry to an audience requires the same understanding and communication necessary for the speaking or the reading of prose. In reading poetry to others, you must be thorough in your analysis of its meaning and responsive to the difficulties of your hearers. You can assist your listeners by (1) accurate centering and phrasing without distortion of rhythm, (2) good timing, (3) prolongation of sounds, and (4) special attention to run-on lines.

Both poetry and prose have principles of analysis and communication. Since poetry ordinarily has a more regular rhythm than prose, it presents a special problem. In poetry, as in prose, the smallest unit—the syllable —may be either heavily stressed or lightly stressed. The second unit in poetry is the foot, generally made up of two or three syllables. The third unit is the line, determined by the number of feet. The largest unit is the stanza, determined by the number of lines. Fortunately for the reader, the poetic structure usually reinforces the thought structure. Since poetry is ordinarily written so that stressed words are centers of attention, centering and phrasing are easily reconciled with stress, feet, and lines.

In quoting a stanza from a poem to support, illustrate, or amplify a statement in a speech, you will certainly wish to read it well. Perhaps you will conclude your speech with poetry, as Wendell Phillips concluded "The Scholar in a Republic" with the last stanza of James Russell Lowell's "The Present Crisis":

> Sit not, like the figures on our silver coin, looking ever backward.
> "New occasions teach new duties;
> Time makes ancient good uncouth;

> They must upward still, and onward,
> Who would keep abreast of Truth;
> Lo! before us gleam her camp-fires!
> We ourselves must Pilgrims be,
> Launch our Mayflower, and steer boldly
> Through the desperate winter sea,
> Nor attempt the Future's portal
> With the Past's blood-rusted key."

To read these lines with chief attention on the rhythm is to ruin their effect for a listener. On the other hand, precise centering and phrasing should overcome any tendency toward sing-song, and should make the thought significant. Centering on *occasions* and *duties* in the first line, and on *ancient* and *uncouth* in the second line, does not conflict with the trochaic rhythm. Reading the third and fourth lines as a single phrase, with *Truth* as the primary center, does not conflict with division into tetrameter lines, because a slight prolongation of the final word in the third line is sufficient for the poetic structure. Both the subordination of the *who* clause and the importance of *upward* and *onward* can be brought out without distorting the flowing rhythm.

Although poetry depends for its full effect upon the sound as well as the sense, sometimes its inverted order and compact thought make it difficult for the listener to follow. But the ease of rhythm may tempt the speaker to present it so rapidly or monotonously that his listeners do not grasp the ideas. Timing, therefore, becomes of first importance in reading poetry.

The rate should be slow enough for the listeners to comprehend the words immediately; the pauses should be long enough for the listeners to interpret the phrases. Often you should read poetry with more variety of rate and with longer pauses than you may think desirable at first.

You can increase the intelligibility and the aesthetic effect of poetry by prolonging the sounds of key words and by accelerating the rate of reading subordinate words and phrases. Let the listeners get the full effect of the sounds and combinations of sounds in the poem. Alliteration and rhyme should not be concealed. When "Lo! before us gleam her camp-fires!" is read slowly, with the sounds in *Lo, gleam,* and *camp-fires* prolonged, the line takes on added meaning and impressiveness; the image becomes sharper.

When the meaning is carried over from one line to the next, the reader must follow the meaning, not the line. You should use a falling inflection at the end of a line only when the thought unit is completed at that point. The lines "Nor attempt the Future's portal/With the Past's blood-rusted key" are one phrase, even though each line is capitalized and may look like a separate unit. The absence of punctuation after *portal* indicates the continuation of the thought. In reading the two lines together, you keep your pitch up on *portal,* prolonging the sounds; only when you come to *key* do you let your inflection fall to indicate the completion of the phrase.

SPEAKING FROM MANUSCRIPT

In some circumstances, speakers must read a manuscript. Extemporaneous or memorized delivery may be inappropriate when exact language must be used, a time limit met, or a custom observed. Statesmen speak from manuscript when they have to make a pronouncement. Accuracy of statement has the highest priority in such addresses. Although the speaker endeavors to make a favorable impression upon his hearers, he is more concerned about how the speech will look in print than he is about directness, spontaneity, and liveliness of manner.

Sometimes speakers read from manuscript when extempore presentation would be more effective, hoping to excuse themselves by such explanations as, "I wrote this out so that I wouldn't ramble." The cure for rambling is thorough preparation, not lame apology.

Disadvantages of a Manuscript

The speaker who reads a manuscript will need to consider four possible handicaps: (1) In the misconception that the writing of the speech prepares him for its delivery, he may fail to rehearse. (2) Since most people have heard enough poor reading to be prejudiced against this form of delivery, audience response may be unfavorable. (3) The speaker is likely to lose spontaneity in communicating with his hearers. (4) Some speakers cannot easily express their ideas in a formal manuscript.

Advantages of a Manuscript

For the occasions when a manuscript is necessary, reading gives the speaker four important advantages: (1) It enables him to present ideas exactly as planned, to avoid inadvertent omissions or weakening changes, to diminish the hazard of making rash pronouncements, and to prevent misinterpretations requiring embarrassing explanations. (2) It ensures the smoothness, clarity, and felicity of well-chosen language; it preserves exact statement, and guards against rambling sentences, involved constructions, incomplete assertions, inapproprate colloquialisms, and inadequate qualification. (3) It permits the speaker to choose the connotation desired. (4) It enables the speaker to observe time limits.

Self-confidence in Delivery

Fluent reading depends on a legible manuscript that permits instantaneous recognition of the words and their relations. Systematic preparation is necessary for effective delivery. Accepted practice requires the speaker to know the pronunciation of every word, to form the habits of pausing to grasp the next unit of thought and of talking with the audience, to separate by voice and action the major from the minor ideas and the key words from those of lesser import, and to indicate the precise meaning by variations in pitch, force, rate, and quality.

Constant mental alertness is a prime necessity for a meaningful reading of a manuscript. As John Dewey observed, "We get so thoroughly used to a sort of pseudo-idea, a half perception, that we are not aware how half-dead our mental action is." [6] The reader must know his manuscript well enough to grasp each thought unit at a glance. To compensate for the audience contact lost in reading, his eyes, his expression, and his bodily activity should demonstrate that he wishes to be understood. He should manage his manuscript so as to avoid distracting his audience. Often a personal observation inserted during the reading will make the reader more communicative.

SPEAKING FROM MEMORY

The problems of memorization have discouraged some speakers. As a result, they choose extemporaneous delivery almost exclusively. Yet, on occasion, complete memorization may be the best method of presentation.

Advantages of Memoriter Speaking

Memoriter speaking permits the ordering of your thoughts to the most exacting requirements, enables the speaker to choose the most felicitous expression, offers the spontaneity characteristic of the best extemporaneous delivery, and gives the speaker a confidence in himself not to be attained in any other way.

Preparation for Memoriter Speaking

Success in memorization depends on a sound procedure: creating the right conditions, maintaining physical and mental alertness, practicing at recurring intervals rather than during long periods of forced attention, learning first the large pattern of the speech before memorizing the organization and sequence of ideas, memorizing in large thought units so as to decrease the number of breaks in the thought structure, concentrating on transitions to assure smoothness in delivery, and focusing on the meaning of the text throughout the rehearsal period. The memorizer sometimes falls into a vocal pattern that carries him through the words but does not convey the full meaning. As Samuel H. Butcher said:

[6] *Democracy in Education,* New York: The Macmillan Company, 1916, p. 168.

The living voice can be at least as lifeless as the written page. Without the interchange of dialogue . . . a spoken speech may be as much devitalized as the same speech when committed to paper. One is, in fact, the mere transcript of the other.[7]

Many of the great speeches of the past were given from memory; they were learned well enough to be completely effective. Inadequate memorization, resulting in word-mindedness, stumbling, or confusion, is the danger to guard against. The alert and vigorous speaker values memorization because it facilitates communication with his audience. Edgar DeWitt Jones says of Edward Everett, the distinguished orator:

It was his habit to memorize his orations, word for word; yet it is not recorded that he ever experienced a failure of memory or gave out a faulty sentence on the platform. His speech was as perfect as is possible for a master of his art to achieve.[8]

REHEARSAL

To be fluent, you must practice your delivery. Even the ablest speakers have testified to their hours of rehearsal. You have not finally prepared your speech until you have proved it in practice. Your rehearsals are like trial flights; they may disclose faults in your presentation. You may underestimate the two great demands upon you: thinking through your topic and communicating with your audience. Practicing delivery increases confidence and fluency. Rehearsal will free you from detail and enable you to keep your mind on your ideas and your audience.

Perfunctory rehearsal results in mechanical delivery and set patterns of speech. Begin every practice with a full understanding of your ideas.

In their attempts to avoid being mechanical, some students imitate other persons. Objections to imitation are apparent. Since a speaker's superficial mannerisms are often more obvious than his substantial qualities, the imitator may merely copy the mannerisms; since the imitator keeps his mind on his model, he may neglect his topic and his audience; and since every personality is unique, imitation sometimes results in an artificial delivery readily detected by the audience.

Experience indicates the value of a systematic procedure in rehearsing. Since practice of an hour a day for five days is more effective than five hours in a single day, you should distribute your practice periods. If

---

[7] "The Written and the Spoken Word," in *Some Aspects of the Greek Genius,* London: The Macmillan Company, 1929, pp. 196–197. Copyright 1929 by Macmillan & Company.

[8] *Lords of Speech*, New York: Willett, Clark & Co., 1937, p. 54. Copyright 1937 by Willett, Clark & Co.

you can persuade a friend to listen to you, talk to him directly. If no listeners are available, speak to an imaginary audience. If possible, rehearse in the room where you are to speak. Make your rehearsal direct, vigorous, and forthright. Remember that a speech is not a speech until it is delivered; the hearer is the speech's end and object.

7 UTTERANCE:
Voice, Articulation, Pronunciation

The organs of speech can be brought by intelligent training into a complete obedience to the will and the feelings.
—Hiram Corson

Good speech requires effective use of the voice, clear articulation of sounds in words, phrases, and sentences, and acceptable pronunciation. Some speakers are fortunate enough to utilize good speech without any conscious effort, because they possess normal vocal structures and because they learned acceptable speech in their formative years. Other speakers will want to know how they can correct faults of pitch, loudness, duration, or quality. Some will need to stress work in articulation. Student speakers, particularly, will want to be assured that their pronunciation is acceptable.

THE SPEAKING VOICE

Listeners expect a speaker's voice to be reasonably clear, audible, and pleasant. They are unusually responsive if it is strong, resonant, and highly expressive of meaning and feeling. They make a judgment from the speaker's voice about the kind of person he is. Whether he is speaking from the platform, conferring with a committee, making a sale, or carrying on a conversation, his voice contributes to his general effectiveness. If the speaker finds that his effectiveness in communication is hampered by a voice that is not clear, audible, or pleasant, he will want to take steps to analyze his voice problem.

How much can a beginning student of speechmaking expect to improve his voice? Thinking of your own voice, you may ask yourself these questions: Is my pitch too high or too low? Is the quality or tone agreeable? Do I speak with the right degree of force and loudness? Should I speak more slowly or more rapidly? You may have difficulty in answering even simple questions about your own voice. You may recall occasions when you thought you were talking effectively but your listeners reported that you should have spoken with more energy. You may also recall that when you listened to your first recording, you did not recognize your own voice. Therefore, you may need expert help to answer questions about pitch, loudness, duration, and quality and to prevent your developing undesirable vocal habits. For example, you may need guidance in determining how much to lower your pitch.

Before a student undertakes to improve his speaking voice, he should consult an authority to make sure that his speech mechanism is free from serious physical deficiencies. He may need medical attention before he can wisely undertake vocal drills and exercises. Some distortions of resonance, for example, may come from adenoids or enlarged tonsils. Hoarseness can be caused by nodes on the vocal folds. Individuals with these comparatively infrequent disorders should receive the attention of a physician who specializes in laryngology and his approval before commencing to work with a teacher or a therapist.

The student working on problems of voice must be willing to study and practice diligently. Moreover, very few conditions can be overcome in a short time. With persistent effort, however, sufficient progress may be observed to stimulate you to continue your program of exercises. Experience shows that striking improvement is possible for the student who follows a sensible program. If your practice is successful, your public speaking as well as your conversation will reflect the results.

The history of speechmaking demonstrates the value of vocal activity for beginning speakers. Henry Clay practiced in the barn before the oxen and declaimed on the banks of Machump's Creek. Beecher walked up and down a large grove near his father's house, sounding the vowels with many changes of pitch and loudness. Bryan practiced in the woods with the trees as an audience and developed a voice that could be heard three blocks away. You may discover a way to develop your voice while carrying on routine activities. Expert guidance and electronic equipment not available to the speakers of the past may assist you, but you will still need to make permanent newly learned habits of speaking.

HOW VOICE IS PRODUCED

An understanding of the way in which voice is produced will give insight into the methods of voice improvement. The aspects of voice production are: (1) respiration, the generation of energy; (2) phonation, the vibration of the vocal folds; [1] (3) resonance, the modification of sound in the throat, mouth, and nasal cavities. These processes, considered separately in order to explain them, constitute sound production.

Respiration

The purpose and function of respiration are elementary topics of physiology. Through inhalation the body obtains the oxygen necessary for life; through exhalation the body rids itself of excess carbon dioxide. The cycle of inhalation followed by exhalation is repeated every three to five seconds; it is speeded up in moments of excitement or exertion, and slowed down in moments of relaxation or sleep. In speaking, respiration can be modified by voluntary effort.

In ordinary quiet respiration, inhalation is largely an active, and exhalation largely a passive, muscular process. During inhalation, (1) the raising of the ribs and sternum, or breastbone, increases the front-to-back and the side-to-side dimensions of the chest cavity, and (2) the contraction of the diaphragm, which constitutes the floor of the thorax and the roof of the abdomen, increases the vertical dimension. As the volume of the chest cavity is increased, the air flowing into the lungs equalizes the pressure inside the lungs with that outside of the body. During exhalation, a general relaxation of the muscles of inhalation allows the ribs and sternum to return to their original positions. The diaphragm also relaxes and returns to its former position. When the front-to-back, side-to-side, and vertical dimensions of the chest cavity are diminished through this general relaxation, the pressure of the air inside the lungs is increased and the greater pressure forces the air out until the pressure is equalized. Still further exhalation can be obtained by contraction of the abdominal muscles and, to a lesser extent, by certain muscles of the chest.

The whole process of breathing is a nicely balanced and coordinated muscular action. In addition to these contractions, other interactions exert a steadying and fixing influence, so that the air does not rush in and out but moves quietly, at times almost imperceptibly.

---

[1] The vocal folds are called by various writers *vocal cords, vocal bands,* and *vocal lips.* Probably no term is entirely satisfactory. The term *vocal cords,* employed by laymen and physicians, is the most commonly heard, but it gives the misleading impression that the vibrating agent is a pair of string-like cords. The term *vocal folds* is preferred by many speech scientists.

The muscles of the thorax and abdomen used in respiration also have important functions in maintaining good posture. Good posture promotes good breathing and good production of voice. The speaker should assume a comfortable, erect position on the platform, not merely for the sake of appearance, but primarily for the efficient operation of his sound-producing mechanism.

When the process of respiration is utilized for the production of sound, several important adjustments must be made. Inhalation now becomes an active process of obtaining a supply of air for voice and speech production. These changes take place: (1) The air is inhaled more quickly, usually through the mouth. In quiet breathing, the three to five seconds required for one cycle of inhalation and exhalation are divided about equally between the two operations; in speech, the air is inhaled rapidly in a second or less. (2) The normal rhythm of breathing is considerably altered. Instead of occurring at regular intervals, inhalation takes place irregularly according to the opportunities afforded by the varying length of the thought units. (3) The descent of the diaphragm is greater and more rapid. (4) Probably a person inhales more air when he is speaking than when he is silent and at rest.

Exhalation is also altered for voice and speech production. (1) It becomes an active process. Since the air being exhaled makes the vocal folds vibrate, its flow must be controlled by the muscles of the abdomen and, to a lesser extent, by those of the chest. (2) The air must be exhaled over a longer period of time. This period will vary in length according to the character of the sound produced and the length of the thought unit. Inability to control exhalation for speech is likely to result from faulty breathing, which affects the voice in specific ways. If the flow of exhaled air is not sufficiently steady and vigorous, the vocal tone may waver, or weaken, or lack fullness and resonance. If the type of breathing employed (particularly clavicular or high chest breathing) creates tensions in the muscles of the neck, the quality of the tone suffers. The various muscles of the larynx are complex in their action; they approximate and separate the vocal folds and increase or decrease their tension. Therefore an extremely high degree of coordination among them is necessary. Normal breathing is a prerequisite for their most efficient functioning. Any improvement of breathing needed to control exhalation for speech can be a modification of the method of involuntary breathing.

Phonation

Phonation, the production of sound by the vibration of the vocal folds, utilizes the energy released by controlled exhalation. As the exhaled air leaves the lungs, it passes through the bronchi into the trachea, or windpipe, and thence into the larynx. The larynx, or "voice box," houses the vocal folds. The vibration of the vocal folds produces sound.

Essentially, the larynx consists of cartilages, muscles, ligaments, and membrane. The largest cartilage, the thyroid (the term means *shield-shaped*), looks like two butterfly wings joined at the front and open at the back. The prominence caused by this cartilage is commonly known as the Adam's apple. The general size and shape of the thyroid may be felt with the finger tips. The next largest cartilage, the cricoid (the term means *ring-shaped*), is located at the lower level of the thyroid and is partly enclosed by it. The diameter of the cricoid is approximately that of a man's thumb. The signet part of the cricoid is at the rear of the larynx. On the top of the signet are mounted two small, roughly pyramidal or conical-shaped cartilages called arytenoids (the term means *ladle-shaped*). The general relation of these cartilages to one another may be seen in the accompanying figures.

The vocal folds, consisting of muscles and tendinous tissue covered by mucous membrane, are about an inch long in adult males, somewhat shorter and less massive in adult females. These characteristics account largely for the difference in pitch between male and female voices. The edges of the folds have an ivory-white appearance and are smooth and rounded. In front the folds are attached inside the thyroid cartilage just behind the point of the Adam's apple; at the back they are attached to the two arytenoids.

The action of opening and closing the glottis, the aperture between the vocal folds, is regulated by muscles which slide and rotate the arytenoids. During the production of sound, these muscular adjustments also control the length, thickness, and tension of the vocal folds as they accomplish the closure of the glottis. Air is pushed up from the lungs by the muscles used in breathing. When the pressure below the folds exceeds that above the folds, increased pressure causes the folds to open upward and sideward, producing a sound wave which moves up through the pharynx. This process is repeated again and again in speech, each time producing another vibration. The speed with which these vibrations occur helps to determine the frequency and therefore the pitch of the sound produced. Variations in length, tension, and thickness of the folds also help to control pitch, producing tones ranging from low to high. Loudness varies also according to the degree of pressure needed, determined by the adjustment of the muscles of the larynx, to close and open the glottis. The folds are made to vibrate in such a manner and at such amplitude as to assist in controlling volume.

A comparison of the use of trained and untrained voices in high-speed motion pictures demonstrates that the person with the trained voice has

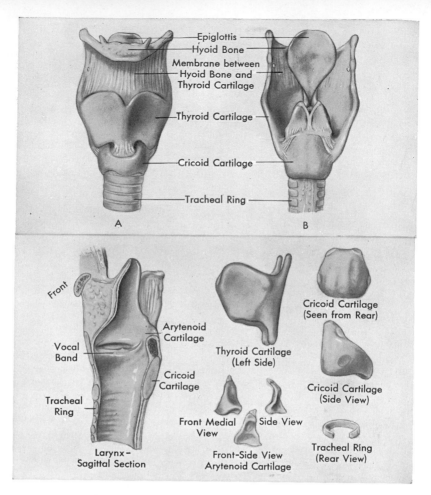

Fig. 1. Front, rear, and side views of the principal cartilages of the larynx. Reprinted with permission of the publisher from *Basic Speech: A College Text*, by Jon Eisenson. Copyright 1950 by the Macmillan Company.

learned to phonate more efficiently. Since the proper operation of the vocal folds and the optimum adjustment of the resonators require the contraction of certain muscles, the individual cannot be entirely free from tension. For the best speaking voice, however, freedom from excessive tension and the right location of tension are necessary. Exercises relaxing the whole body as well as the throat reduce tension. Voice exercises that produce better tones with economy of effort are also helpful.

Resonance

The fundamental or basic tones vary according to the vibrations of the vocal folds, but they are subjected to changes as they are modified and amplified by the cavities of the throat, mouth, and nose. This process of sound modification and amplification is termed resonance.

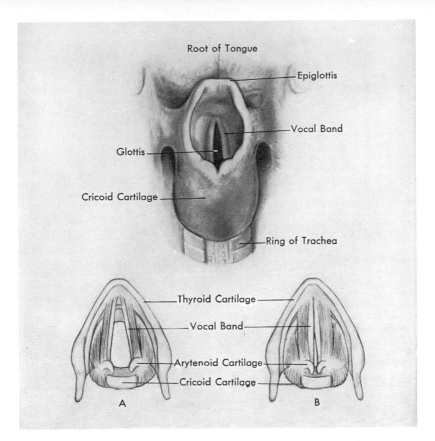

Root of Tongue

Epiglottis

Vocal Band

Glottis

Cricoid Cartilage

Ring of Trachea

Thyroid Cartilage

Vocal Band

Arytenoid Cartilage

Cricoid Cartilage

A

B

Fig. 2. Diagrammatic representations of the larynx and the vocal folds showing attachments to cartilages of the larynx. A. Shows vocal folds in position for quiet breathing. B. Shows vocal folds in position for vocalization. Reprinted with permission of the publisher from *Basic Speech: A College Text,* by Jon Eisenson. Copyright 1950 by the Macmillan Company.

The many complex problems of resonance, by no means solved, are being investigated by speech and acoustic scientists. Even a wind instrument, such as a bugle, presents a formidable problem of resonance analysis. The sound of a bugle passes through a simple tube of fixed width, length, and curvature, made of a metal of known characteristics. By contrast, the vocal-fold tone of a human voice passes through throat, mouth, and nose cavities that are uneven in size and shape, that vary in the size of their openings, that are lined with membranes of different degrees of firmness and moisture, that differ widely from individual to individual.

The vocal-fold tone is not pure, as is that of a tuning fork; it is a complex blend of a basic sound, called the fundamental, and a series of overtones of progressively higher pitch. As this complex tone passes through the cavities of the throat, mouth, and nose, some of the overtones are amplified and others are dampened or diminished. The degree of tension or relaxation of the throat, the openness of the mouth, and

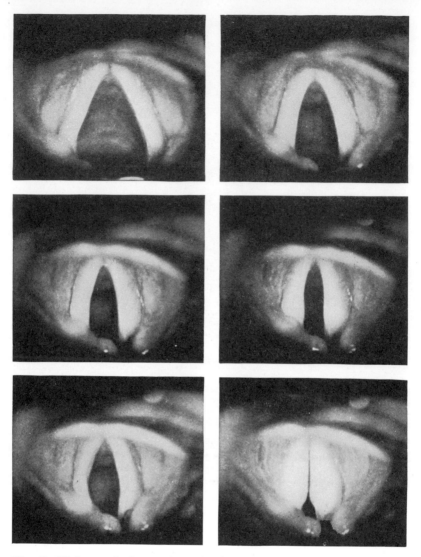

Fig. 3. High-speed photos showing changes in position of the vocal folds from quiet breathing to vocalization. Courtesy Bell Telephone Laboratories, Inc.

the operation of the soft palate to open or close the entrance to the nasal passage are among the factors that determine what overtones are amplified or diminished and how much modification they receive.

By listening to a speaker on radio, you can demonstrate that voice consists of a blend of tones. When the tone control on your radio is tuned to the treble position, the higher overtones are more prominent; the hissing of sounds like *s* and *z* is pronounced, and the voice seems somewhat thin. When the control is turned to the bass position, the hissing sounds are less audible and may vanish altogether; the voice seems fuller and deeper because the lower overtones have been made more prominent. Like the tone control, the resonance cavities of the head determine the values of overtones. These cavities can operate to make the voice somewhat thin and metallic or muffled; or they can bring out the fullest possibilities of the sound produced by the vocal folds.

Unfortunately, adjusting the resonators of the voice is not so easy as turning the control of the radio. Instead of twisting a knob, you must coordinate the groups of muscles that relax and constrict the throat, mouth, and nasal cavities and that spread, protrude, round, open, or close the lips. A good voice requires a proper balance between oral and nasal resonance. If the passageway through which the sound must travel is not obstructed—if the muscles of the throat are relaxed, except for the tension required for the production and resonation of the sound—the speaker can usually demonstrate enough control of his voice to achieve an adequate balance of resonance.

ANALYZING THE SPEAKING VOICE

In order to determine whether your voice is serving all of your needs in speaking you should consider each of its aspects. The terms *pitch, loudness, duration,* and *quality* designate these aspects.

Pitch

Pitch describes the "highness" or "lowness" of a sound. Other factors being equal, thick, long, or loosely tensed vocal folds produce low-pitched tones; thin, short, or highly tensed folds produce high-pitched tones. The muscles of the larynx make rapid, precise, and highly integrated adjustments in order to change the pitch of the voice. Some of these adjustments regulate the tension or elasticity of the folds; others alter their thickness, length, and contour. Changes in length and tension enable a speaker to produce a range of pitches. The intellectual and affective content of speech determines the pitch that is appropriate.

The individual's "optimum pitch" is dependent upon the physical structure of his larynx and resonating cavities and upon the amount of breath he uses. In the range constituting optimum pitch his voice sounds most pleasant and functions most efficiently; his voice has greatest clarity and fullness of tone. For most persons, optimum pitch level is about one-fourth to one-third above the lowest level within the range of pitch levels permitting vocalization without strain. If one's habitual pitch, that level he uses most often, is found to be more than one level below or above his optimum level, it is advisable for him to initiate voice on his optimum level.

A common problem among beginning speakers is that of monotonous pitch and inflection. A speaker may use his optimum pitch level but fail to depart from this level to convey accurately emotional and intellectual meanings. Pitch variations are termed *inflections* and are of three varieties: rising, falling, and complex or circumflex. For example: rising (curiosity), "Was it somebody I know?"—falling (certainty), "Absolutely not!" "No, Sir!"—complex or circumflex (possibility), "W-e-l-l, maybe."

No one should attempt to raise or lower the pitch of his voice without the advice of a specially trained teacher or clinician. Misguided efforts to lower pitch are sometimes accompanied by a loss of flexibility and carrying power. Hoarseness and harshness may be caused by the individual's attempt to speak in tones that are too low.

Loudness

Loudness refers to the degree of intensity. You can make a tone louder by increasing the energy supporting the breath with the use of the gross abdominal muscles and by amplifying oral resonance.

The speaker has two problems of loudness: adjustment and variation. First, he must be able to adjust the loudness of his voice to such conditions as the size of the room and the general noise level. If his listeners cannot hear him easily, he must talk louder or more distinctly, or both; but he should not shout at fifteen people as if five hundred were present. Second, the individual must be able to vary the degree of loudness; important ideas can be emphasized by variation.

Although a speaker whose voice is weak is aided by a public-address system, you must remember that it is only useful for increasing loudness. You must realize that a microphone cannot remedy vocal monotony or improve vocal quality. If you use a microphone, you will need to learn the right distance to stand from it. If you are too close, it will blast and make your speech unintelligible. If you are too far away, it will not amplify your voice.

Duration and Rate

Duration, also called quantity, is the prolonging or shortening of individual sounds. Nearly everyone has been told by some uncritical observer to speed up or slow down. An individual may utter syllables rapidly, yet the very drive and impetuosity of his speech gives it a compelling quality. His rapid rate suggests both his familiarity with his ideas and his confidence in their validity. Another speaker who utters syllables deliberately may be equally effective in suggesting knowledge and self-confidence. Accordingly, gratuitous advice about talking more slowly or more rapidly is often ill-considered. Common sense should lead you to ask, "Do I speak so rapidly that my articulation suffers; that my listeners have difficulty in keeping up with me; that I have difficulty in keeping up with myself?" Or, "Do I speak so slowly that I lose enthusiasm for my ideas; that my listeners lose interest in what I am saying?"

Rate, closely related to duration, is measured by the number of words or syllables uttered in a minute. It is affected by the duration of the sounds, but it is also affected by the number and length of the pauses. Rate varies considerably—from about 100 to 200 words a minute. Two individuals could have an identical rate—say 150 words a minute—but have different duration if one spoke his words slowly but used few or brief pauses, and the other spoke his words rapidly but used many or long pauses.

Whether you speak slowly or rapidly, your words should be distinct. You should know when and how long to pause. Effective speakers employ enough pauses of varying lengths between units of thought to convey meaning accurately; ineffective speakers use too few or too many pauses for the accurate communication of meaning. A pause should indicate to a listener that the speaker has offered a unit of thought for him to think about, or that an idea is important. To hesitate or to omit a pause may suggest to a listener that the speaker is uncertain of his meaning. Effective pauses indicate to the listeners that the speaker is genuinely communicating with them. In speaking to an audience, you should utilize the possibilities of emphasis by varying your rate. Serious matter calls for a slow rate of speaking; material that is light or gay calls for a somewhat more rapid rate. If the general tempo is slow, less important ideas will be spoken somewhat more rapidly than the more important ideas. If the predominant tempo is rapid, the more significant words or phrases should be spoken more slowly than the less significant words. In general, you should adapt your rate to the subject matter you are presenting and to the needs of your listeners.

Quality

Quality, sometimes called *timbre,* is a term often used incorrectly by the layman. It refers not to pitch, loudness, or resonance separately, but to all of these characteristics together. Pitch may be described as high or low; loudness as loud or soft; resonance as nasal or oral. Quality may be described as shrill, strident, metallic, muffled, breathy, nasal, denasal, hoarse, husky, harsh, clear, resonant, rich, or mellow. Quality distinguishes a violin from a piano when both are sounding notes of approximately equal pitch, loudness, and duration. Quality distinguishes one voice from another when both voices phonate vowels of approximately the same pitch, loudness, and duration.

In the discussion of resonance a vocal-fold tone was described as a complex blend consisting of a fundamental and a number of overtones. The physical basis of quality is the distribution of the total energy in the sound among the fundamental and the overtones. One voice may have most of its energy in the fifth and sixth overtones; another may have most of its energy in the second, third, and fourth. These differences in distribution are interpreted by the ear as different qualities of voice. Improving quality is therefore a problem of learning how to bring out the most favorable combination of overtones. It involves all the factors of breathing, phonation, and resonance. It is associated with the mood, feelings, and emotions of the speaker.

MAKING THE VOICE MORE EXPRESSIVE

A good speaking voice has variety of inflections, a wide range of pitch, differing degrees of loudness, appropriate rate with meaningful pauses, adequate duration, and a pleasant quality. The speaker who develops the skill to control his voice gives his words richer and fuller meanings, makes his ideas clearer and more emphatic, brings out contrasts in thought, expresses a variety of feeling, interprets connotations vividly and colorfully, and heightens his climaxes and total effect.

THE VOICE AND EMOTION

Emotions affect voice production. Fear has noticeable effects: the mouth becomes dry, respiration becomes irregular, gulps and swallows become frequent, and the sounds may be distorted. Unusual tensions resulting from emotional strain may produce a high-pitched or shrill voice, or a harsh or strident voice. When a person holds a positive self-concept, when he feels that he is a worthy individual, when he believes that what he has to say is important to his listeners, his voice reflects this judgment of himself and his subject. When, on the other hand, he holds a neutral or negative self-concept, when he feels unworthy, when he believes his listeners will not take account of what he has to say, his voice reflects this judgment of the inadequacies of himself and his subject. Thus the speaker who perceives himself as unable to cope with the demands of his audience may speak either too softly or too loudly, too quickly or too slowly, and with little inflection or exaggerated inflection. Without conscious control of the voice, speakers who are depressed will reveal their depression; speakers who are elated will reveal their excitement. With conscious control, speakers can convey accurately the emotional and intellectual content of their words and create the impression they want the audience to have.

VOCAL HYGIENE

Anyone who has lost his voice even for a day or two appreciates, as others cannot, its great importance in everyday living. The larynx is a delicate mechanism that can stand only a limited amount of abuse and is vulnerable to mistreatment.

Vocal strain is one of the great enemies of good voice. Shouting at ball games sometimes causes complete loss of voice and often results in hoarseness and huskiness. Speakers who overextend themselves when talking to a large audience, especially out of doors, may feel the effects of the strain for hours afterward. High-school and college debaters, speaking in long tournaments, may find themselves hoarse at the end of the sessions. Teachers, professors, lecturers, and ministers occasionally develop sore throat and voice fatigue from excessive talking. Football coaches and physical-education directors sometimes contract chronic hoarseness because of continued shouting at players in large gymnasiums and on open fields. Elevator operators, hucksters, auctioneers, newsboys, and drill sergeants often suffer from voice strain. These possibilities of misusing or abusing the voice should be a warning to anyone tempted to place excessive demands on his vocal mechanism.

Irritating substances and liquids, when brought into contact with the vocal mechanism, may be injurious. Workers who inhale dust and irritating fumes over a long period sometimes develop laryngeal infection. The immoderate intake of alcohol, by producing a congestion of the mucous membranes and a swelling and drainage, may alter both quality and pitch. The oil produced by burning tobacco apparently irritates the mucous membranes of the larynx. Some evidence exists to show that inhaling tobacco smoke tends to lower pitch and to make voice quality husky. These effects are especially noticeable in women's voices. Some professional singers not only refrain from smoking, but try to avoid singing or speaking in smoke-filled rooms.

The voice is also affected by poor health, sickness, and fatigue. Laryngologists report that what appears to be a localized vocal condition is sometimes simply a manifestation of a physically or emotionally exhausted state. To some extent, your voice reflects your way of life. A fundamental requirement of a good voice is good health. Many remedial exercises, principally those of relaxation and breathing, not only help to improve voice but also are conducive to good health.

ARTICULATION OF SPEECH SOUNDS

Those features of utterance dealing with the matters of distinctness, audibility, and intelligibility of speech sounds concern articulation or enunciation. Although articulation, taken etymologically, means *joining*, and is often applied specifically to the distinct utterance of consonants (the elements joining vowels), speech scientists and phoneticians generally prefer to use *articulation* as the broad term encompassing both consonants and vowels.

From a strictly practical point of view, the development of clear articulation is invaluable. Poor articulation may be costly: examples that come to mind are the passenger who was put on the train for Weston instead of Winston, the artillery officer who opened fire at seven hundred instead of eleven hundred meters, the quarterback whose mumbled signal "fifteen" was heard as "sixteen." Poor articulation may cause trouble: confusion among the initials *B, P, T,* and *D* in proper names: misunderstanding of telephone numbers, addresses, and names in introductions; mistakes in orders, directions, and instructions. The frequency of misunderstanding has become a part of American humor in the story of the Texas private who single-handedly brought in two battalions when the order was for two Italians. The double talk of the comedian is sometimes a burlesque of our hurried articulation.

Good articulation is essential in speechmaking. The speaker must be instantly intelligible not only to those in the front of the room, but to those in the back, to those in the alcove who cannot see the speaker's face, to those exposed to the noise from an open doorway. Not many speakers can win this comment from every listener: "I could understand every word he said."

If you have never thought about the way you utter speech sounds, you will want to make some firsthand observations. Look into a mirror while you phonate (that is, utter or speak) the *ee* in *beet,* the *a* in *father,* and *oo* in *pool.* Speak each of these three sounds as distinctly as you can. Note first the different positions of the lips: unrounded for *ee;* more open but unrounded, or only slightly rounded, for *a;* and rounded for *oo.* Note, secondly, that the tongue is higher in the mouth for *ee* and *oo* than for *a,* and that the blade of the tongue is farther forward in the mouth for *ee* than for *oo.* Note, finally, that for *a* the teeth are further apart than for *ee* and for *oo.* Phonate other vowels, and in similar fashion observe, as well as you can, the positions of the tongue and the lips. Next, observe the changes that take place when you utter various consonants. Note that the lips come together to form the *b* of *bee,* whereas the lower lip touches lightly the upper front teeth to form the *f* of *fee.* Discover the position of the tongue when you utter the *l* of *lee,* the *k* of *key,* the

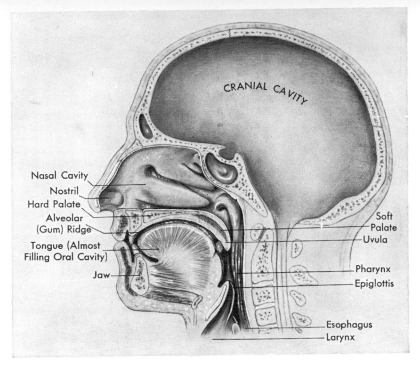

Fig. 4. The articulatory organs and principal resonators. Reprinted with permission of the publisher from *Basic Speech: A College Text*, by Jon Eisenson. Copyright 1950 by the Macmillan Company.

s of *see*, the *sh* of *she*. Clear articulation is the result of precise movement of the tongue, lips, and other parts of the speech mechanism.

THE SPEECH MECHANISM

The mechanism for producing speech sounds is not limited solely to the lips, tongue, and teeth. Figure 4 is a sagittal section (side view) of the head, showing the structures used in articulation. Note especially:

- The larynx, which houses the vocal folds—the vibrating source of sound.
- The three principal sound resonators: throat, mouth, and nasal cavities.
- The tongue.
- The velum, or soft palate, terminating in the uvula.
- The hard palate.
- The alveolar ridge, also called gum ridge.
- The upper and lower teeth.
- The lips.

Note further that the sound, as it travels up the throat and out the mouth or nasal passages, may be modified by the action of one or more of the above structures. For example, the soft palate, aided by other muscles, acts as a valve to permit the breath stream to enter the nasal cavity, the mouth, or both; or the breath may be partially or completely blocked by the back of the tongue raised against the soft palate or the tip of the tongue placed against the gum ridge.

THE SOUNDS AND THEIR SYMBOLS

The division of sounds into vowels, diphthongs, and consonants presents some difficulties. Vowels are tones free from friction or noise, emitted with relatively little, if any, obstruction of the breath. Diphthongs are blends of two vowels. In consonants, one articulatory agent acts on another; the breath stream is modified by the action of the tongue, teeth, soft palate, or lips. Consonants may be voiced or voiceless; they are voiced if the vocal folds vibrate during their production, and voiceless if the vocal folds do not vibrate. Printed letters often represent more than one sound. The letter *a* stands for the vowel and diphthong sounds in *hate, hat, what, awe, hair, ask, about, quay;* the combination *ough* is used in *through, though, enough, cough, hiccough.* With grim logic the combination *gheauxphtheighteough* has been used to represent *potato: p* by *gh* as in *hiccough, o* by *eaux* in *beaux, t* by *phth* in *phthisic, a* by *eigh* in *eight, t* by *tte* in *gazette, o* by *ough* in *though.*

Systems of diacritical marks used by dictionaries have an apparent familiarity, but are regarded by phoneticians as complex, confusing, and cumbersome. The average reader is familiar with most of the "long" and "short" markings, which do not mean long and short at all, but designate separate vowels. He loses his way in the list of dots above, dots below, circumflexes, cedillas, ligatures, and italic letters that are needed for accurate representation of all the sounds of speech.

Phonetic Symbols

The International Phonetic Alphabet, commonly called the IPA, is a set of symbols designed to represent pronunciation without respelling with conventional letters and without diacritical marks. The IPA is based upon the principle of letting one symbol represent one sound (more correctly, one sound family, or phoneme). Thus the IPA symbol [i] represents the vowel sound in each of these words: *ee* as in *seem, ea* as in *lean, eo* as in *people, ey* as in *key, ay* as in *quay, ie* as in *believe, ae* as in *Caesar, oe* as in *Phoenix, e* as in *eke, i* as in *police.* Instead of using a single printed letter to represent a variety of sounds, as the letter *a* in *hate, hat, what, awe, hair, ask, about,* and *quay,* phonetic transcription uses an appropriate IPA symbol to represent each different sound. A list of the IPA symbols and their equivalent diacritical markings follows:

PHONETIC SYMBOLS

SYMBOL	KEY WORD		DIACRITICAL MARK

Vowels

SYMBOL	KEY WORD		DIACRITICAL MARK
i	beet	[bit]	ē
ɪ	bit	[bɪt]	ĭ
e *	rebate	[ribet]	ā
ɛ	bet	[bɛt]	ĕ
æ	bat	[bæt]	ă
a **	bask	[bask]	ă, ȧ, ä
ɑ **	balm	[bɑm]	ä
ɒ	box	[bɒks]	ŏ
ɔ	ball	[bɔl]	ô
o *	obey	[obeɪ]	ō
ʊ	book	[bʊk]	ŏŏ
u	boot	[but]	ōō
ɜˑ **	burn	[bɜˑn]	ûr
ɜ **	burn	[bɜn]	ûr
ɚ	butter	[bʌtɚ]	ər, ẽr
ɔ	above	[ǝbʌv]	ǝ, ȧ, ĕ, ŏ, ẽ, ă, i
ʌ	but	[bʌt]	ŭ

Diphthongs

SYMBOL	KEY WORD		DIACRITICAL MARK
aɪ	buy	[baɪ]	ī
aʊ or ɑʊ	bough	[baʊ] *or* [bɑʊ]	ou
ɔɪ	boy	[bɔɪ]	oi
eɪ *	bay	[beɪ]	ā
oʊ *	boat	[boʊt]	ō
ɪu or ju	new	[nɪu] or [nju]	ū

Consonants

SYMBOL	KEY WORD		DIACRITICAL MARK
p	pet	[pɛt]	p
b	bet	[bɛt]	b
t	tip	[tɪp]	t
d	dim	[dɪm]	d
k	kit	[kɪt]	k
g	good	[gʊd]	g
f	fit	[fɪt]	f
v	vain	[veɪn]	v
θ	thin	[θɪn]	th
ð	then	[ðɛn]	th
s	see	[si]	s

PHONETIC SYMBOLS—Continued

SYMBOL	KEY WORD		DIACRITICAL MARK
	Consonants		
z	zoo	[zu]	z
ʃ	shoot	[ʃut]	sh
ʒ	rouge	[ruʒ]	zh
h	hat	[hæt]	h
tʃ	church	[tʃɝtʃ]	ch
dʒ	judge	[dʒʌdʒ]	j
m	mitt	[mɪt]	m
n	none	[nʌn]	n
ŋ	young	[jʌŋ]	ng
l	lull	[lʌl]	l
w	wet	[wɛt]	w
ʍ or ʰʋ	when	[ʍɛn, ʰʋɛn]	hw
j	yes	[jɛs]	y
r	red	[rɛd]	r

* As [e] and [o] are stressed and lengthened, they tend to be diph-thongized as [eɪ] and [oʊ]. Either the symbol for the vowel or the diph-thong is appropriate for recording the sound.

** For an explanation of these symbols and key words, see pages 217–218.

In the following discussion, simple respellings and key words are used to indicate specific sounds wherever practicable, but they are freely supplemented with IPA symbols. Many students will want to study the IPA symbols in order to become familiar with this more accurate and scientific method.

Vowels

Vowels are conventionally classified according to the tongue positions used in producing them. In the production of *front vowels*, the high point of the arch of the tongue is in the front part of the mouth. For *central vowels* the arch of the tongue is in the center of the mouth. For *back vowels* the arch of the tongue is in the back of the mouth.

In Figure 5 each phonetic symbol is located to correspond with the approximate position of the highest point of the tongue arch in the pro-duction of the vowel represented by that symbol. The left of the figure represents the front of the mouth. The positions indicated are conven-tional; although each vowel may be produced with slightly differing tongue positions, those given are sufficiently representative of normal pro-duction for purposes of study and comparison.

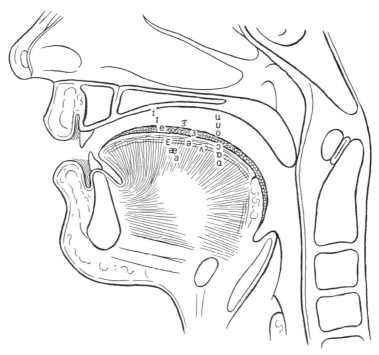

Fig. 5. Representative tongue positions for the vowels of American English speech. Reprinted with permission of the publisher from *Basic Speech: A College Text*, by Jon Eisenson. Copyright 1950 by the Macmillan Company.

The front vowels are:

[i]	"e"	as in *he*	
[ɪ]	"i"	as in *bit*	
[e]	"a"	as in *vacation*	In unstressed syllables, speakers tend less to diphthongize [e].
[ɛ]	"e"	as in *bet*	
[æ]	"a"	as in *bat*	Although most Americans use [æ] for both *bat* and *bask*, [a] is heard in regional dialects in New England and the South. It is heard regularly in the diphthongs [aɪ] and [aʊ].
[a]	"a"	as in *bask*	

If you will phonate the list of front vowels given above, beginning with the vowel of *be* [i], and will continue through the series to the vowel of *bask* [a], you will note a progressive lowering of the forward arch of the tongue as well as of the jaw. (Do not say the whole words, just the vowel sounds.) Going from *be* to *bask*, the mouth opening becomes progressively larger; the lips are somewhat retracted, or at least unrounded. The tip of the tongue is behind the lower teeth.

The central vowels are:

[ɜ] or [ɜ˞] "ur"	as in *burn*	The IPA symbol is [ɜ] if the *r* is silent, [ɜ˞] if the *r* is sounded.
[ə] or [ə˞] "er"	as in *butter*	The IPA symbol is [ə] if the *r* is silent, [ə˞] if the *r* is sounded. Similar to the preceding sounds except that the [ɜ] or [ɜ˞] of *burn* occur in stressed syllables, the [ə] or [ə˞] of *butter* occur in unstressed syllables.
[ə] "a"	as in *above*	The IPA symbol [ə] occurs only in unstressed syllables.
[ʌ] "u"	as in *bun*	The IPA symbol [ʌ] is similar to [ə] except that [ʌ] occurs in stressed syllables.

The differences among this group of sounds are subtle: some are affected by the presence or absence of the *r* sound, and some by the stress on the syllable. The arch of the tongue is in the central part of the mouth cavity. The mouth opening is relatively small for all of the sounds, and the lips are unrounded.

The back vowels are:

[u] "oo"	as in *boot*	
[ʊ] "oo"	as in *book*	Articulate the same sound in *full, could, good.*
[o] "o"	as in *obey*	In unstressed syllables, speakers tend less to diphthongize [o].
[ɔ] "a"	as in *ball*	Articulate also the vowel in *all, saw, fault.*
[ɒ] "o"	as in *box*	Articulate also the vowel in *hot, stop.* This sound is heard in American English, but many speakers will use [ɑ] or [ɔ], depending upon regional and individual customs.
[ɑ] "a"	as in *balm*	Articulate also the vowel in *farm, calm,* and *part.* Some speakers will use [ɒ].

Beginning with the [u] of *boot,* and phonating the series as listed above through [ɑ] of *balm,* you will note that the arch of the tongue becomes progressively lower in the mouth. The lips are somewhat rounded for the [u] of *boot,* but become relatively unrounded for the [ɑ] of *balm.* The tip of the tongue is low in the mouth, but somewhat farther back than for the front vowels.

You will profit from a study of the tongue and lip positions of your own speech mechanism during the production of vowel sounds. Note the differences in tongue position as you go through the series of front vowels, central vowels, and back vowels. If the differences do not seem obvious, phonate front and back vowels alternately—for example, the high front vowel [i] *ee* in *be*, followed by the high back vowel [u] *oo* in *boot*. Note also the differences in the size of the opening of the mouth and in the degree of lip rounding and lip protrusion. The following chart should help you.

Diphthongs

A diphthong is a combination of two vowels blended in the same syllable. For example, the tongue, in the production of the diphthong [ɔɪ] *oy* in *boy* glides quickly from the [ɔ] to the [ɪ] position. The first symbol [ɔ] represents the approximate initial sound and the second element [ɪ] represents the approximate final sound of the glide. Articulate each of the commonly accepted diphthongs, noting the initial sound and the final sound of each: [aʊ] *ow* in *now*, [aɪ] *ai* in *aisle*, [ɔɪ] *oi* in *boil*, [oʊ] *o* in *home*, and the [eɪ] *ei* of *rein*. There are, of course, many other diphthongs, among which are: [ɪu] or [ju], as in *new* (depending upon whether the speaker starts the combination with the vowel [ɪ] or the glide [j]); [æʊ] in *how* (a variant of [aʊ]); and those used by speakers who, because of regional variations, omit medial and final [r] from their pronunciations, as [ɛə] in *their*, [ɔə] in *fort*, [oə] in *deport*, and [ɪɔ] in *dear*.

For the most part, the beginning speaker is concerned with faulty diphthongs that result when the second vowel element is weakened or omitted, as in the use of [ɑm] *Ah'm* for *I'm*, [ɔl] *all* for *oil*, and [ɑr] *are* for *our*. Since these variations are not in common use by cultivated speakers, they are questioned by many listeners. Other variations in diphthongs include the use of [dæʊn] *daeown* for *down*. This form is commonly heard in some areas, but it is not equally prevalent throughout the country. Another questionable variation is the insertion of a third or triphthongizing element that results in the pronunciation [gɪæʊn] *giaeown* for *gown*.

Consonants

The consonants consist of both voiced and voiceless sounds. They include plosives, affricates, fricatives, nasals, glides, and the lateral.

The plosive consonants, [p], [b], [t], [d], [k], and [g], are sounds in which the breath stream is completely interrupted before the sound is made. Air pressure builds up in the mouth and is suddenly released. The soft palate is raised to prevent nasal resonance. The positions of the articulators and the presence or absence of voice determine the characteristics of the resulting sound.

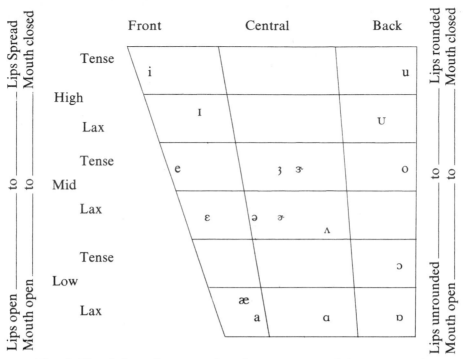

Fig. 6. Vowel chart illustrating the relative positions of the tongue and lips in the production of vowels. Adapted from Arthur Bronstein, *The Pronunciation of American English* (New York: Appleton-Century-Crofts, Inc., 1960, Fig. 31, p. 141).

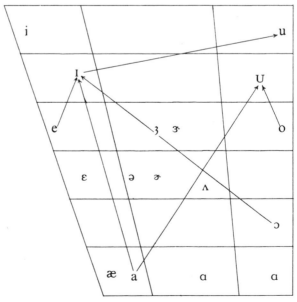

Fig. 7. Diphthong chart illustrating movement of the articulators from the first element of a diphthong to the second element.

Chart of Consonant Sounds

	Bilabial		Labiodental		Linguadental		Alveolar		Palato-Alveolar		Palatal		Velar		Glottal	
	Voice-less	*Voiced*	*Voice-less*	*Voiced*	*Voice-less*	*Voiced*	*Voice-less*	*Voiced*	*Voice-less*	*Voiced*	*Voice-less*	*Voiced*	*Voice-less*	*Voiced*	*Voice-less*	*Voiced*
Plosives	p	b					t	d					k	g		
Affricates									tʃ	dʒ						
Fricatives			f	v	θ	ð	s	z	ʃ	ʒ					h	
Nasals		m						n						ŋ		
Glides	ʍ	w								r		j				
Lateral								l								

Fig. 8. This chart indicates the classification of consonant sounds according to the character of the sounds and their place-ment.

221

DESCRIPTIVE TERM	VOICELESS	VOICED
Labial (lips)	[p]	[b]
Alveolar (gum ridge)	[t]	[d]
Velar (soft palate)	[k]	[g]

Since the voiceless [p] and the voiced [b] are formed by blocking the air stream by lightly but firmly closing the lips and then suddenly releasing them, these sounds are called labial plosives. The degree of aspiration will vary according to the position of the sound in the word; that is, if medial [p] or [b] ends a syllable, the sound tends to be somewhat weakened as compared to initial [p] and [b]. Most speakers have no difficulty in producing labial plosives.

The alveolar plosives, voiceless [t] and voiced [d], are formed by placing the tip of the tongue against the alveolar ridge, and the sides of the tongue against the inner edges of the upper teeth and gum ridge. The breath stream, blocked by this process, is suddenly released by withdrawing the tongue from the gum ridge. Distortions of these sounds arise frequently. If the tip of the tongue is allowed to touch the front teeth, dentalized [t] and [d] result. If the speaker touches the alveolar ridge with the blade of the tongue instead of the tip, the quality of the sound will be distorted. If the speaker uses too much breath, the sound may be too strongly aspirated. Because the medial [t] of words like *plenty, city, butter*, and *mountain* is articulated with less force than the initial [t], it may have some of the characteristics of [d]. Nevertheless, speakers should articulate the sound with enough force so that it can be recognized as [t].

The velar plosives, voiceless [k] and voiced [g], are formed by placing the back of the tongue against the soft palate, blocking the air stream, and then suddenly releasing the tongue. The strength of aspiration varies according to the position of the plosive sound in the word; for example, if [k] is followed by a stressed vowel, it is strongly aspirated. Medial and final [k] are usually weakened when they end syllables. Notice the articulation of [k] in *kite, packing*, and *peck*.

The affricates, voiceless [tʃ] as in *church* and voiced [dʒ] as in *judge*, are combinations of plosives and fricatives articulated in rapid succession. In producing these sounds, the tip of the tongue is placed in contact with the hard palate at a point slightly farther back than for the [t] and [d]. The air, held momentarily, as for [t] and [d], is quickly released over the blade of the tongue and is followed by the [ʃ] sound or the [ʒ] sound without any intervening aspiration which normally accompanies the [t] or [d]. The nasal passage is closed. Distortions arise when the contact of the tongue with the hard palate is not firm.

The fricative consonants, [f], [v], [θ], [ð], [s], [z], [ʃ], [ʒ], and [h], are continuants that are bursts of noise. There is a partial closure of the organs of articulation while the sound is gradually emitted. These sounds are produced with some degree of friction of the breath stream as it passes through the most constricted area of the mouth cavity, except for the [h], which is articulated in the glottal area. The nasal passage is closed for all of the sounds. The following chart should help in understanding the characteristics of these sounds:

AREA OF CONSTRICTION	VOICELESS	VOICED	STANDARD NOMENCLATURE
Upper teeth approaching lower lip	[f]	[v]	Labiodental
Edge of tongue touching upper teeth	[θ]	[ð]	Linguadental
Edge of tongue approaching gum ridge	[s]	[z]	Alveolar (blade of tongue)
Blade of tongue approaching palate	[ʃ]	[ʒ]	Palatal (blade of tongue)
Glottis narrowed	[h]		Glottal

Voiceless [f] and voiced [v] are made by placing the lower lip against the edge of the upper front teeth. The breath stream passes through this partial closure. Few Americans distort these sounds, but some foreigners may show confusion in voicing and unvoicing appropriately.

For voiceless [θ] and voiced [ð] the tip of the tongue is placed lightly against the cutting edges of the upper front teeth or against the back of the upper front teeth. The contact should be loose enough to permit the breath stream to pass through a very narrow opening. Misarticulation of these sounds occurs in the speech of those whose languages do not contain them. People who have been strongly influenced by speakers of these foreign languages may block the air stream completely, thereby substituting a [t] for [θ] and a [d] for [ð].

The voiceless [s] and voiced [z] are difficult sounds to produce acceptably. A complicating factor in the articulation of [s] and [z] is that they may be made in at least two positions. In producing them in the high-point position, the free edge of the tongue hovers near the alveolar ridge. The sides of the tongue touch the sides of the molars. The teeth meet edge to edge, and the lips are retracted slightly. A very small stream of air is directed along the center of the blade of the tongue until it passes over the cutting edge of the lower teeth. In producing [s] and [z] in the low-point position, the tip of the tongue approaches the lower gum ridge, and the blade of the tongue approaches the palate. Again the air stream is directed through a narrow groove along the center of the blade of the tongue and over the edge of the lower front teeth. Many speakers use the lower position for [s] and [z] and produce them acceptably. The high-tongue position produces sounds of higher frequency. If the required position for the formation of these sounds is not closely approximated, they may be so conspicuous that they attract attention. Any noticeable distortion is called a lisp. [s] is more likely to be noticed than [z] when these sounds are not properly articulated, because the voicing of [z] tends to cover or mask whatever error is made.

The voiceless [ʃ] and voiced [ʒ] are produced almost like [s] and [z], except that the arch of the tongue is close to the hard palate. A broader surface of the tongue is used in making these sounds than is used for [s] and [z]. The sides of the tongue firmly touch the upper back teeth. The air stream passes with a frictionlike quality through a wide, shallow passage formed between the arched tongue and the front of the hard palate. The tongue tip may point upward toward the gum ridge, or may rest behind the lower front teeth. The lips are pushed forward and rounded. These sounds are subject to some of the same faults as [s] and [z], but unless they are seriously deficient, they do not seem to attract the attention that an inadequate [s] or lisp attracts.

The voiceless fricative [h] is produced by imparting a slight amount of friction to the breath stream as it passes between the vocal folds formed into a narrow glottal opening. The articulators assume the position of the following vowel sound. Although this sound causes little difficulty for American speakers, it may present some problems for those of Spanish, Italian, Russian, or other background.

Three other continuant consonants in American English, the [m], [n], and [ŋ], are resonated in the nasal cavity as well as in the pharyngeal cavity. All other sounds depend upon resonance in the mouth and the oral and laryngeal areas of the pharynx. For all of these other sounds, the soft palate moves backward toward the pharynx and cuts off the nasal passage and the nasal pharynx. For the nasals, however, the soft palate is relaxed, and the sound is emitted through the nose. The nasals are voiced.

The sound [m] is produced by bringing together the lips as in the production of the plosive [b], but instead of being released plosively from the mouth, the sound is emitted as a continuant through the nose. The [n] is made similarly to the plosive [d] in that the tip of the tongue touches the alveolar ridge, but instead of being released plosively, the sound is resonated through the nose. The [ŋ] is formed by elevating the arch of the tongue against the soft palate, as for [g], so as to block the breath stream, but instead of being released plosively, the sound is again emitted through the nose. Whenever any obstruction blocks the nasal passage, the nasals lack resonance and sound much like their plosive counterparts. For example, *morning* becomes *bordig*.

The sound [l], also a continuant, is called a lateral. It is a vowel-like consonant because of its acoustic properties. The tip of the tongue is placed in contact with the alveolar ridge, and the sides of the tongue are lowered to permit the emission of breath over the sides of the tongue. When [l] precedes a front vowel, its position is more forward in the mouth than when it precedes a back vowel. This [l] is called a *light* or *clear* [l]. When [l] is in the medial position before an unstressed vowel, or when it precedes a back vowel, it is called a *dark* [l]. For example, contrast the sound of [l] in *lea, live, let,* and *land* with *loose, look, lone,* and *law.* The tongue position for articulating [l] varies in some words such as *billion*, in which [l] is palatalized, and in *health*, in which [l] is dentalized because it precedes [θ].

The problems connected with the articulation of [l] are numerous. Some children find it difficult to produce, and mistakenly articulate [r] or [w]. Often these defective sounds persist into adulthood. Some speakers consistently dentalize [l]; others tend to produce it with the blade of the tongue instead of the tip; some attempt to produce it with the back of the tongue against the velum; and others seem to produce a vowel instead of the dark [l].

The analysis of four sounds will complete the description of the manner of producing the consonants: the [w] as in *wait*, the [ʍ] or [hʋ] as in *white*, the [r] as in *rate*, and the [j] as in yet. They are generally called *glides*, because the speech mechanism gradually changes position during the production of the sounds.

For the voiced consonant [w] the lips are rounded and the back of the tongue is lifted toward the soft palate, as in the production of the vowel [u]. From this position of lips and tongue, the sound glides into the following vowel. In fact, the lip and tongue positions for the [w] anticipate the positions for the following vowel. For the voiceless [ʍ] or [hʋ], the positions of the articulators are similar, but a degree of aspiration normally precedes the [w]. Although some speakers make a clear distinction between such words as *ware* and *where*, *watt* and *what*, and *witch* and *which*, other speakers make no distinction between [w] and [ʍ] or [hʋ]. Some foreigners articulate [v] for [w] in such words as *why* and *wait*, and they are surprised to discover that the [w] is silent in *who, whole,* and *whose.*

In producing the consonant [r], the sides of the tongue are placed in contact with the upper teeth, and the tip of the tongue moves in an arc upward and slightly backward without actually touching the gum ridge and then reverses itself. As the vocal folds vibrate, the sound is emitted through the mouth. A second position for producing [r] is to lower the tongue tip and allow the central part of the tongue to rise toward the place where the hard palate ends and the soft palate begins. Again, the vocal folds vibrate and the sound is emitted through the mouth. If you will say such words as *red, rip,* and *rouge,* you will note the glide quality of the [r] as the tongue moves quickly from the starting position to the position of the following vowel. The [r], like the [l], may be distorted by some speakers. The sound is probably the most variable of the consonants because it is influenced by the preceding or the following vowel. In some areas of the country, a vowel is used in place of the [r] in words in which [r] appears in medial and final positions. Sometimes the [r] is articulated as a fricative, as in *tree, dream,* and *trip.* In order to articulate [r] in consonant clusters in such words as *strike, three, free, prize, breath,* and *shrew,* it is necessary to remember that the articulation of [r] is started simultaneously in the previous consonant, not sequentially.

The consonant [j] is produced by placing the tongue and the lips in approximately the position for the vowel [i]. The lips are spread, the front of the tongue is arched higher than for [i], and the glide into the following vowel is made.

Our discussion thus far has considered voice, the speech mechanism, and the articulation of individual speech sounds. Speakers must not only form each sound in a sufficiently distinct and acceptable manner; they must also utter syllables and words in a conventional way. They should, therefore, be concerned with pronunciation.

PRONUNCIATION

In its broadest sense, *pronunciation* is a term designating the utterance of any unit of language. Thus, any error in utterance could be called an error in pronunciation. As commonly used, however, pronunciation refers (1) to the selection of sounds and (2) to the location of syllabic accent. A person confronted with the word *heinous* might say "hynous" or "heenous"; both would be errors in pronunciation, because the word is uttered by educated people as "haynous." To utter "alías" for "álias" would reveal two errors of pronunciation—namely (1) selecting the wrong sounds, and (2) accenting the wrong syllable, since this word is acceptably pronounced "alias" (first syllable as in "ailing," second syllable as in "little"). A student may ask, "What difference does it make how I pronounce a word if people know what I mean? Is it a serious mistake to misplace the accent on such words as *lamentable, irreparable, formidable,* and *incomparable?*" The answer to these questions is that acceptable pronunciation is regarded by many as the sign of the educated man who reads extensively, travels widely, and confers with many people. The speaker who has a limited vocabulary and mispronounces words will be criticized. Listeners may conclude that he is uneducated. An adequate vocabulary and acceptable pronunciation do not guarantee a speaker's good sense and good judgment, but they suggest his exposure to ideas and information. A speaker who consistently mispronounces words is likely to be embarrassed in the company of people who know better. Sooner or later he finds himself avoiding words because he is not sure how to pronounce them. Men and women of talent in executive positions or in public life may be especially aware of their disabilities in pronunciation. If the speaker is a college graduate, he will be expected to sound like one.

STANDARDS OF PRONUNCIATION

The beginning student of speech is sometimes surprised to discover that no single standard of pronunciation exists—that is, that no single rule set down by some authority determines the "correctness" of pronunciation. Instead, he finds that several acceptable varieties of pronunciation are used, and that *standard pronunciation*, as used in the United States, refers to the speech patterns of the educated persons in his community. He may wonder who these educated persons are and why the patterns of speech of a majority of the people in a locality are not used to determine the standard of pronunciation. Arthur J. Bronstein answers these questions:

The student of our language must be careful to distinguish between that pattern which is commonly used and that which is considered *standard.* The commonly used forms in a given community *may* be part of the standard pattern. But "standard speech" is actually not the "average speech" of all members of the community. It is not the common denominator between the speech used by the most highly educated members of the community and that used by the least educated members of the society. It is rather the habitual, or normal, speech used by the cultivated members of our society in both formal and informal situations. Its grammatical constructions are those of the well-considered books, newspapers, and periodicals you read. Its pronunciation, melodic, articulatory, and vocal patterns are those used by the persons who read such materials and who talk about them. The standard spoken language is, therefore, neither "affected," "uneducated," nor "illiterate." [2]

With this concept of standard pronunciation in mind, the student may want to reflect on his own speech pattern and come to some conclusion as to its acceptability. He may want to know more about the factors that account for variations in pronunciation, such as sound changes that occur in fluent and connected speech, the variations due to regional and local dialects, and the changes that occur because of the formality or informality of the occasion for speaking.

Sounds in Connected Speech

The student will discover that, although he may satisfactorily articulate each of the individual sounds, he never utters sounds in isolation; he

[2] *The Pronunciation of American English,* New York: Appleton-Century-Crofts, Inc., 1960, p. 8. Copyright © 1960 by Appleton-Century-Crofts, Inc.

connects them in words, phrases, and sentences. Moreover, words, too, may be pronounced one way in isolation and another way in fluent conversation. Such changes occur because one sound often influences a neighboring sound and because of changes in stress. It is natural in American speech to economize in an effort to simplify the pronunciation of groups of sounds in fluent speech. When sound changes occur because of the influence of other sounds—that is, through the process of assimilation —the result may be acceptable or unacceptable, depending upon the degree of assimilation. If we emphatically utter the sentence "Please open the door," the word *open* would be pronounced [opən] or perhaps [opn̩]. But if we increase the assimilation, the word is likely to be pronounced [opm]. The influence of [p] changes the nasal consonant [n] to [m], a sound made similarly to [p]. This process of progressive assimilation in which one sound influences a later sound in a word, is common in connected speech. If we were to utter the sentence, "This shelf goes here," probably the [s] in *this* would be influenced by the [ʃ] in *shelf* and the [s] would be omitted [θɪʃɛlf]. When a sound influences a preceding sound, as in the example just given, the process is called regressive assimilation. In a third type of assimilation, called reciprocal assimilation, two sounds influence each other in such a way as to result in an entirely new sound. If we say, "I miss you," very slowly and deliberately, little (if any) change takes place [aɪ mɪs ju], but if we say the sentence rapidly, the [s] in *miss* and the [j] in *you* affect each other in such a way that the resulting sound change is neither [s] nor [j], but [ʃ], [aɪmɪʃə]. Reciprocal assimilation has changed the pronunciation of such words as *nature, literature, vision,* and *education.*

Assimilation normally occurs in good conversational speech; such pronunciation has long been accepted for hundreds of words. The failure to assimilate results in pedantic pronunciation; excessive assimilation results in slovenly speech.

Since acceptable pronunciation is the result of the speaker's choosing the appropriate sound and using the appropriate syllabic stress, unacceptable pronunciations occur when he fails to do either. Errors in pronunciation are often caused by excessive assimilation, faulty articulation, carelessness, or guessing at the pronunciation of a word. They may be classified as errors due to the omission of sounds, the addition of sounds, the substitution of sounds, the transposing of sounds, and inappropriate stress.

Omission of sounds.   As we have indicated previously, the spelling of a word is not a very good clue to its pronunciation. The acceptable pronunciation of such words as *hiccough, ague, blackguard, subtle, victuals, orgy,* and *awry* emphasizes this fact. Some of the sounds included in the orthographic representations have been assimilated and omitted.

In these particular words, the omissions of the sounds are not considered errors of pronunciation, because the changes have been accepted. In the word *February*, however, the first *r* is omitted by many speakers. Most dictionaries record that the *r* is pronounced, but Kenyon and Knott indicate that pronunciations with or without the *r* are acceptable.[3] Less debatable, perhaps, are the omissions of certain medial sounds in the following words: *libery* for *library*, *wonerful* for *wonderful*, *everbody* for *everybody*, and *reconize* for *recognize*. Similarly, the omission of initial and final sounds in such words as *'cross* for *across*, *'stension* for *extension*, *post'* for *posts*, *worl'* for *world*, and *mask'* for *masked* are considered mispronunciations.

Addition of sounds. Sounds have not only been dropped as pronunciations have changed; they have also been added. *Against*, formerly pronounced and spelled without the final [t], and *warmth*, occasionally pronounced *warmpth*, provide examples. The process continues, but for the most part the addition of sounds to words seems obvious, and is apparently more characteristic of uneducated speech than of cultivated usage. The addition of sounds in such pronunciations as *athalete* for *athlete*, *acrosst* for *across*, *filum* for *film*, *umberella* for *umbrella*, and *drownded* for *drowned* is not acceptable among educated speakers.

Substitution of sounds. Assimilation has brought about many sound substitutions in the pronunciation of words. For example, in the word *ink*, [ŋ] has been substituted for [n]; and the word *asked* (and numerous other words that end in *ed*) [t] has been substituted for [d]; in *Russia*, [ʃ] has been substituted for [s]. All of these changes have been accepted. A substitution that was once considered unacceptable, the substitution of the [w] for [ʌ] in such words as *when* and *where*, is now considered an acceptable variant pronunciation. Note the variety of sound substitutions in the following unacceptable pronunciations: *beuudiful* for *beautiful*, *prodestant* for *protestant*, *dese* for *these*, *dose* for *those*, *shicken* for *chicken*, *colletsh* for *college*, and *srivel* for *shrivel*.

A sound that presents special problems for some speakers is the back nasal [ŋ]. In verb forms that end in *-ing*, they may substitute [n] for [ŋ] as in *comin'* for *coming*, *goin'* for *going*, and *seein'* for *seeing*. Although this substitution is considered unacceptable by many, phoneticians report that in some dialect areas it is heard among educated speakers more frequently than is generally supposed. Some speakers, especially those whose native language did not include both [ŋ] and [ŋg], show confusion in the pronunciation of words that end in *-ng* and *-ngue*. In American English all words that end in *-ng* and *-ngue* are pronounced with [ŋ]. Instead of pronouncing words such as *tong*, *tongue*, and *ha-*

---

[3] John Samuel Kenyon and Thomas Albert Knott, *A Pronouncing Dictionary of American English*, Springfield, Mass.: G. & C. Merriam Company, Publishers, 1944.

rangue with the back nasal alone [ŋ], some speakers add to the back nasal the [g] so that [ŋ] becomes [ŋg]. When a suffix such as -*er*, -*ing*, or -*ly* is added to a word ending in -*ng* or -*ngue*, the pronunciation in American English remains [ŋ], as in *bringer, longing,* or *kingly.* Again, some speakers will probably insert [g]. The comparative and superlative adjectives and some other words are exceptions. For example, in such words as *longer, younger,* and *prolongation,* the sounds [ŋg] should be used. To omit [g] is incorrect. When the -*ng* occurs within the stem of a word, as in *finger, hunger,* and *mingle,* [ŋg] is used. To omit [g] is incorrect. Exceptions to this generalization are found in such words as *congratulate* and *congressional,* where the tendency in American English has been to retain the [n], because of the influence of the spelled form of the word. However, in some words, either the [n] or [ŋ] may be used, as in *Bengal, bronchitis, income,* and *concrete.*

Voicing and unvoicing errors also result in sound substitutions. Any voiced consonant substituting for its voiceless counterpart, or vice versa, may constitute an error in pronunciation. Again, although assimilation causes many changes in voicing and unvoicing, some of the changes have been accepted while others have not. *Absorb* and *greasy* may be pronounced with either the [s] or [z]. Sounds that cause speakers the most trouble are [s] and [z], [t] and [d], [ʃ] and [ʒ], [θ] and [ð]. Note the unacceptable substitutions that are sometimes heard in the following words: [s] for [z] in *because, queens,* and *was;* [d] for [t] in *little, butter,* and *settle,* [t] for [d] in *medal, head,* and *pedal;* [ʃ] for [ʒ] in *measure* and *leisure;* [ð] for [θ] in *bath* and *myth;* and [tʃ] for [dʒ] in *college* and *knowledge.*

Transposing of sounds. Although children are more likely than adults to transpose sounds, the reversal or transposition of sounds is a frequent occurrence. In fact Kenyon and Knott record as acceptable: *childern* for *children, hunderd* for *hundred,* and *perscription* for *prescription.* Examples of unacceptable transpositions are: *prespire* for *perspire, modren* for *modern, revelant* for *relevant, calvary* for *cavalry,* and *preform* for *perform.*

Inappropriate stress. Stress designates the relative loudness with which a syllable is uttered and its duration. The effect of these factors of loudness and duration is to give prominence to one syllable over other syllables. The speaker, therefore, is concerned with the syllabication of words and the degree of stress given each syllable, particularly the vowel in the syllable. His chief interest is in determining which syllable receives primary stress, although other degrees of stress are not unimportant. Since most dictionaries use an accent mark to show the syllable that receives primary stress, the speaker may safely assume that other syllables receive less stress and, for his purpose of determining the pronunciation of a word, are relatively unstressed syllables, unless otherwise noted. Many of our words may be pronounced in several ways, depending upon the meaning and upon the stress we give them. If we emphasize some words, we use the strong form of the vowel; if we need no emphasis, we use the weak form. Ordinarily we use the weak form of pronouns, prepositions, articles, auxiliaries, and conjunctions in conversation, except where we want to emphasize a particular word. In the following list of words the vowels are weakened in unstressed (or weak) form, and some of the consonants are lost.

WORD	STRONG FORM	WEAK FORM
a	[eɪ]	[ə]
an	[æn]	[ən], [n̩]
and	[ænd]	[ən], [n̩]
have	[hæv]	[həv], [v]
them	[ðɛm]	[ðəm], [əm], [m]
from	[frɑm]	[frəm]
must	[mʌst]	[məst], [məs]

The changes that occur in these words illustrate that vowels are lengthened or shortened when the syllable in which they are found is stressed or unstressed. Some speakers tend to overuse the weaker forms, while other speakers, particularly those unaccustomed to reading aloud, may use the stronger forms excessively. The former usage indicates careless speech; the latter, pedantic speech.

Ordinarily, speakers will have little difficulty in stressing the appropriate syllable in words that they use frequently or that they hear others about them use. However, they may need to check a reputable dictionary to accent properly the words they use infrequently or new words they add to their vocabularies. In their study of the dictionary, if they are not already aware of the fact, they will discover that some words are accented in one way when they function as nouns and another when they function as verbs. Contrast, for example, the stress on the following words when used as nouns and verbs: *subject, desert,* and *discharge.* In each word the accent shifts.

Probably no one is completely free from errors that are due to misplaced stress. From the reading books on the elementary-school level to the drill books in English composition and grammar on the high-school level, attempts are made to teach students to accent words appropriately throughout the whole process of vocabulary building. Adults who are willing to listen and to learn from the cultivated people about them and from capable radio and television speakers should be able to keep abreast of changing pronunciations.

Regional Variations

Variations in pronunciation have existed in American English from colonial times to the present. Since the colonists who settled along the Atlantic coast came, for the most part, from England, English became the established language. However, it was not a uniform English. The early settlers brought with them the patterns of speech that prevailed in their own communities in Britain. Those people who settled primarily in New England and Virginia spoke Elizabethan English as used in the south of England; those who settled in New Jersey and Pennsylvania spoke as the inhabitants of north England spoke. As the years passed, the coastal areas reflected changes brought about by the influence of later immigrants from England and from travelers who traded with the colonists. The foundations for the similarities that exist between eastern and southern speech were laid during these early years. The fact that the settlers who kept moving westward were less affected by the changes taking place along the coast probably accounts for some of the differences that exist between southern and eastern speech and the areas to the west. Of course, as the country developed, all of the influences that affect sound change played a part in creating regional variations: isolation in some communities, waves of immigration from countries other than Britain, patterns of migration as settlers moved from one area to another, the development of the means of transportation, and the growth of schools, colleges, and universities. Although American English changed throughout the years, and will continue to change, the dialectal patterns that have formed in certain areas have been firmly enough established to be designated as regional dialects.

Anyone who has traveled throughout the United States is aware that the New Englander does not speak exactly like the Southerner, nor does the Southerner speak like the Westerner. Generally, we recognize three rather broad areas of difference: Eastern American, Southern American, and the rest of the country, usually termed General American. As phoneticians and linguists continue their research in pronunciation, they are discovering that a more accurate picture of the various speech patterns reveals more than three areas. C. K. Thomas lists ten major regional speech areas: Eastern New England, New York City, Middle Atlantic, Southern, Western Pennsylvania, Southern Mountain, Central Midland, Northwest, Southwest, and North Central.[4] Some of these areas have been studied carefully; others have not. Actually, no real border line exists to indicate where one region ends and another begins. Although differ-

[4] Charles Kenneth Thomas, *An Introduction to the Phonetics of American English*, 2nd ed., New York: The Ronald Press Company, 1958, p. 232. Copyright 1958, by The Ronald Press Company.

ences in pronunciation are heard in these areas, the significant fact is that the speech of all of the regions is more alike than different. The differences that do exist revolve around the pronunciation of [r] and vowel usage.

Although any generalization about regional variations is open to exception, a few of the outstanding likenesses and differences may help the student of speech to understand the term *standards of pronunciation.*

- On a regional basis only minor differences occur in the pronunciation of consonants other than [r].
- Initial [r] is pronounced [r] in all of the regions.
- Except for a very few instances in the South, [r] is pronounced as [r] when a vowel follows immediately in the same word, as, for example, in *crow, pride, broken,* and *green.*
- When [r] comes at the end of a word or before a consonant, wide variations in pronunciation are heard. In Eastern New England, the South, and usually in New York City, the [r] is customarily omitted, and a vowel is substituted. Elsewhere [r] is pronounced.
- When [r] comes at the end of a word which is followed by another word beginning with a vowel, and there is no pause, the Eastern New England and New York City areas usually retain the [r], using the appropriate stressed or unstressed form. A similar pattern is followed in other areas, although less frequently in the South.
- Generally, in the South and East, [ɜ] is used in such words as *bird,* and *Bert,* whereas [ɝ] is used elsewhere. Similarly, in the South and East, [ɔ] is used in such words as *butter* and *hunger,* whereas [ɚ] is used elsewhere.
- There is wide variation in the use of vowels in the same words throughout the various areas. In Eastern New England, speakers tend to use the vowel [a] or [ɑ] in words where the letter *a* immediately precedes a voiceless fricative or a nasal sound, in words such as *class, grass, last, dance,* or *answer,* but [æ] may also be heard. In New York City, speakers are more likely to use [æ] although [a] and [ɑ] may also be heard. Throughout the rest of the United States, the vowel [æ] is likely to be used.

Other differences are heard: there are additional variations in the pronunciation of vowels and diphthongs; there are differences in stress; and there are differences, inconsistencies, and variations within smaller dialectical areas. Each region has a number of dialects not so generally acceptable as the regional standard. The student speaker should be aware that people pronounce words differently, but he should not draw the conclusion that the speech of one area is any better or worse than that of another area. Fewer differences are apparent in the speech of the educated throughout the country than in the speech of the uneducated. Each region has its virtues and its problems. Poor pronunciation, unclear articulation, and substandard usage are inadequate in any region. The educated person will endeavor to follow the standard of the cultivated people of his own region.

Variations Due to the Occasion

Speech must always be adapted to the audience and the occasion. In some situations, such as the formal speaking occasion, speakers are expected to be more precise in articulation than in their informal conversations. Educated audiences are quick to criticize the politician who allows his speech to deteriorate to the substandard level in his effort to be folksy. They will be equally critical of the speaker who speaks affectedly in order to impress them. The teacher may increase his popularity with his students if he assumes a very informal manner in speaking with them, but he should not forget that he is likely to be quoted as an expert not only in his field of specialization, but also in his manner of pronouncing words. The lawyer is expected to be more formal as he adapts his speech to a judge and a jury than as he talks in a community gathering, and the minister is expected to be more formal in delivering a sermon than in his conversation at a church picnic. Usage varies, but the educated man is always bound by his own standards.

THE DICTIONARY

One of the functions of a dictionary is to record language usage. As such a record, it describes cultivated usage at the particular time the dictionary is compiled. Although publishers of reputable dictionaries make an honest effort to keep up to date in listing new words and changes in pronunciation, all dictionaries suffer from infrequent revision because of the tremendous task and the expense of revising. Nevertheless, on most questions of pronunciation, next to the educated people about him, the student's best reference is a current dictionary.

The pronunciation given in a dictionary is a generalization of the way many persons say a word. If the student studies several editions, he will find differences of opinion concerning pronunciation, and he will find that although dictionaries do not record every pronunciation in common use, they frequently record more than one. In some instances, the first pronunciation is the one held to be more widely used; in others, the editor makes no attempt to indicate which pronunciation is the more prevalent. At least one dictionary, Kenyon and Knott's, shows pronunciation current in regional areas. Most do not in the body of the text. Although diacritic markings are used most often to record pronunciation, some dictionaries use phonetic symbols, and some have adopted symbols from the International Phonetic Alphabet to represent certain sounds. For example, *The American College Dictionary* and *The Thorndike-Barnhart Dictionaries* have adopted the schwa [ə] to record unstressed sounds previously represented by a variety of diacritic markings. The student will find that dictionaries vary in the level of usage represented. Some base their pronunciations on formal usage, while others use informal speech. Kenyon and Knott describe their dictionary as a "dictionary of colloquial English, of the everyday unconscious speech of the cultivated people—of those in every community who carry on the affairs and set the social and education standards of those communities." [5] The student may discover that the symbols used for representing pronunciation are inadequate accurately to represent actual pronunciation in some areas of the country—southern speech, for example. He needs also to remember that most dictionaries record words in isolation, not words in connected speech. If he followed every pronunciation rigidly, his speech would be pedantic or artificial. Finally, he should know that dictionaries record pronunciations that are heard; they never prescribe pronunciations for the cultivated and educated to follow, as does the French Academy for French usage. Keeping this information in mind, he should view the dictionary as a reference to be consulted frequently.

[5] Kenyon and Knott, *op. cit.*, p. vii.

8 ACTION:
Poise and Physical Expression

Suit the action to the word, the word to
the action; with this special observance,
that you o'erstep not the modesty of na-
ture.

—William Shakespeare

The student of speechmaking often needs to de-
velop poise. Plagued by the uncertainties of inexperience, he is afraid
of forgetting his chain of ideas, of saying something foolish, or of losing
the attention of his audience. As much as anything else, he needs to be rid
of his anxiety. He needs self-assurance.

POISE

Poise is achieved by preparing thoroughly, by knowing what to do,
by understanding stage fright, and by learning through experience. The
solid merit of a speech on an appropriate topic, developed by ideas that
are clearly organized, well adapted to the listeners, and forcefully worded,
helps to give the speaker a sense of security. Knowing how well-adjusted
speakers manage themselves relieves the beginner of the fear of doing
something wrong. Analyzing his own fears and thinking about them objectively enable a speaker to control them, to minimize them, or to live with
them successfully. Experience before an audience tends to strengthen
the speaker's confidence.

BEHAVIOR OF A POISED SPEAKER

The well-adjusted speaker does what is fitting, no more and no less. The constant exercise of tact and judgment enables him to manifest his poise.

Observing the Customs of Public Address

Through the observance of simple formalities, the speaker shows his respect for the presiding officer and the guests. He responds to his introduction by addressing the presiding officer, "Mr. Chairman" or "Mr. President." If the presiding officer is a woman, he says, "Madam Chairman," not "Mrs." or "Miss." He then calls the names of the distinguished guests or special groups, ending with a general salutation to the audience. Any of these forms is suitable: "Mr. Chairman, Professor Kovel, Fellow Alumni"; "Mr. President, Mayor Jones, Members of the City Council, Fellow Citizens"; "Mr. Chairman, Governor Jason, Fellow Americans"; "Mr. Moderator, Senator Holmes, Dr. Brett, Major Demark, Friends." To avoid making the salutation too long, he may omit naming the guests and may refer to them in his opening comments: "Mr. Chairman, Ladies and Gentlemen: I am delighted to be on this program with my college friends, Colonel Weston and Judge Maguire. The last time we met . . . ." He may acknowledge the presence of many distinguished guests by saying, "Mr. Chairman, Distinguished Guests, Ladies and Gentlemen"; or if the guests are all in one category, he may say, "Mr. Chairman, Past Presidents of Sigma Alpha, Members of the Fraternity." If no one present is to be singled out for special recognition, he says simply, "Mr. Chairman, Ladies and Gentlemen." He greets his audience cordially, not perfunctorily.

Beginning Without Stumbling or Hesitating

Knowing that the first moment is especially important, the thoughtful speaker prepares accordingly and thus avoids the faltering that betrays inexperience. He thinks out the language of his initial ideas so precisely that he does not stumble over words.

Avoiding Apologies

The speaker demonstrates confidence in himself and in his speech. He does not begin with such apologies as, "Unaccustomed as I am to public speaking. . . ." He does not obtrude into his speech explanations for inexperience, inability to prepare, or lack of information, even though he may believe such explanations warranted. Nothing marks so well a speaker's self-control as his ability to surmount obstacles without complaint or to speak without reference to them.

Referring to Personal Relationships

The well-adjusted speaker may refer to his acquaintance with other persons present as a means of creating good feeling; but he will not carry the practice so far as to create the impression of egotism, as did the toastmaster who introduced each of the seven speakers at a banquet with an irrelevant personal allusion, meaningless to the guests.

Exercising Self-Restraint

The speaker practices moderation and self-restraint. Angry words may relieve personal feelings, but they rarely win approval. The young person especially must control his emotions and subordinate his immediate impulses to the demands of his purpose and the needs of his audience.

Controlling the Use of Humor

Repartee and storytelling are popular in America, and a speaker may build a reputation upon the gift for humorous speaking. Yet the use of humor has its dangers; audiences may be offended by attempts at humor, especially when the occasion calls for dignity.

Adapting to the Size of His Audience

The competent speaker is not embarrassed if his audience turns out to be smaller than he had anticipated. Speakers who are distressed by empty chairs sometimes manifest their displeasure by complaining to their hearers, who certainly cannot be blamed for the absentees. Other speakers, perhaps inadvertently, betray a feeling that a small audience is unimportant, forgetting that the quality of a group cannot be judged by its numbers and that the approval of one or two key persons in the audience may well repay the effort of speaking. Whether the audience is large or small, the speaker should express in his every attitude the determination to do his best.

Respecting the Requirements of the Program

A speaker sometimes appears on a program with other persons. To use more than the time allotted is a grave discourtesy; the competent speaker, knowing the requirements of the program, conforms to them. Adherence to this practice is a safeguard against such embarrassment as that of the lecturer who thoughtlessly took the time of two other speakers as well as his own.

Adjusting the Length of his Speech

Last-minute adjustments in timing may be necessary. Perhaps the program started late, or someone spoke too long, or the amplifying system broke down. The competent speaker takes these irregularities in his stride.

If he has been allotted 20 minutes and now sees that he has 15, he quickly decides what to omit and prepares to meet the new situation. Or if, at the last minute, he finds that he must talk 30 minutes instead of 20, he decides what ideas to elaborate or expand. Whatever the limits set, he prefers to have his departing listeners say, "I wish he had spoken twice as long," rather than, "Why didn't he quit long ago?"

Planning His Conclusion in Advance

The knowledge that his conclusion is well prepared gives a speaker confidence throughout his speech. Sometimes, however, a hurried or inexperienced person leaves the conclusion to the inspiration of the moment of delivery. As he attempts to improvise a climax for his remarks, he may grope for thought, or he may try to capture the flagging attention of his listeners by promising to quit within a few minutes. When the promise to stop is the only hope of holding the attention of an audience, the speaker should conclude quickly without the promise.

Omitting Perfunctory Thanks

Concluding with a stilted "Thank you" merely shows that the speaker is a novice. If he feels that his listeners have been unusually attentive, he should express his thanks fully. Unless he wishes to admit having done a poor job, he is not in debt to his listeners; they are in debt to him.

Knowing When to Talk

As a speaker develops his ability and discovers how much information is needed, he will avoid two common errors: (a) that of accepting an engagement when he possesses neither special knowledge nor real authority and (b) that of speaking too often during a debate or a preliminary discussion. In a meeting with many participants he will avoid using more than his share of the time. The person who speaks too often merely compounds the discourtesy by apologizing.

The basic element in this list of suggestions is thoughtful consideration of others. The speaker avoids self-consciousness and aimless worry by graciously adapting himself to the occasion and the audience. He shows good sense and good taste when he puts himself in the place of the listener and observes what he, as a member of the audience, would appreciate from a speaker.

DIFFICULTIES IN ACQUIRING POISE

In his personal adjustment, the speaker needs the knowledge of what is acceptable in order to refrain from errors that show lack of poise. He also needs assurance that his behavior does not inadvertently reveal maladjustment.

Random Activity

Everyone has observed a speaker buttoning and unbuttoning his coat, fingering his clothing, or picking up and laying down a book. A senator automatically wiped his forehead with his handkerchief, put the handkerchief into his right rear trousers' pocket, shortly thereafter reached for it again, and repeated the procedure many times during a single speech. The action was highly visible and distracting to his audience. A minister was once observed to wind his watch chain around his finger four or five times a minute during his sermon. These random activities suggest the speaker's self-consciousness and irritate the audience. Since they occur automatically, they are not always easy to overcome. They can best be corrected by sympathetic instruction based on an understanding of the speaker's nervousness, with helpful suggestions to remove it.

Inhibition of Free Activity

Another type of maladjustment is the inhibition of free activity. The boy who says his piece looking straight ahead and holding his hands rigidly behind him suffers from restraint of the normal responses. If he has learned his words parrot-like, he may be able to utter them; but he does not communicate effectively. Older speakers also may find that their fear of the audience tends to freeze the responses normally accompanying speech. The inhibited speaker who would like to talk with his hands holds them tightly or makes abortive gestures. Again, he may be unable to move his head in a free and expressive fashion, or he may be afraid of looking directly at members of the audience. These inhibitions can and must be overcome if the speaker is to make a good adjustment.

Stage Fright

Although stage fright may manifest itself in the ways just described, it may also have a somewhat more generalized effect. Although it has no certain remedy, beginners can sometimes find comfort in the testimony of experienced speakers. In *Time Enough: Essays in Autobiography,* Frank Luther Mott relates a conversation with Leslie M. Shaw, once Governor of Iowa, Secretary of the Treasury, and a man of national reputation as a campaign speaker. Observing that Shaw was always nervous before he took the platform for Chautauqua lectures, Mott bantered him a little about his obvious tenseness:

"Governor, I should think that a seasoned stump-speaker like you would take this sort of thing in stride—just one more talk to an audience, you know. But here you are, nervous as a kitten!"

The Governor replied: "My boy, you talk like a tyro, as you are. No man ever yet made a speech that was worth hearing without getting wound up tight enough to bust a spring before he went on. Remember that." [1]

Speakers should understand the following facts about stage fright:

Stage fright is common. A degree of stage fright is the normal reaction to an audience: more people have it than do not. Furthermore, the state of tension, heightened interest, and nervous anxiety accompanying stage fright may actually be useful. The speaker who has the capacity for stage fright is likely to be effective once he has himself under control. The truly unfortunate speaker is the dull, lethargic individual who is not stimulated by the prospect of addressing an audience.

Stage fright is probably a learned reaction. Although opinions differ concerning the causes of stage fright, the most plausible theories suggest that it is behavior learned during childhood. What has been learned can be unlearned or corrected.

Stage fright can be overcome. The characteristic reactions of the dry mouth, the all-gone feeling in the pit of the stomach, the trembling of the legs, the shaking of the knees, and the rolling of the eyes can be made to disappear, and the speaker who suffers from them can be taught poise and self-control. The first step in making the adjustment is facing the problem: the fear must be confronted. Anyone who suffers more than a normal amount of stage fright should not leave the platform without completing his speech, and he should not decline opportunities to speak. The second step is the development of greater general confidence in social situations.

Stage fright can sometimes be controlled by the elimination of contributory factors. The speaker with conspicuous clothing, for example, may have difficulty in avoiding self-consciousness, whereas one properly dressed will be at ease and thus better able to control stage fright. He should direct his attention and that of his audience not to himself but to what he is saying.

Stage fright often disappears after the speaker begins. Experienced speakers say that although they are sometimes apprehensive as they begin, the fears tend to disappear as the speech gets underway. The act of speaking helps to relieve the tension caused by stage fright.

Stage fright is not peculiar to public speaking. One of the greatest living pianists, who has appeared in concerts in the leading cities of Europe and America, suffers from stage fright before each performance. Some football players say that the nervousness they feel before the game

[1] Frank Luther Mott, *Time Enough: Essays in Autobiography,* Chapel Hill, North Carolina: The University of North Carolina Press, 1962, pp. 99–100. Copyright 1962 by The University of North Carolina Press.

is relieved by the first few minutes of play. Any person who must appear in public or undertake any other serious task is likely to suffer from worries, tensions, and fears. The successful practitioners in every field have learned how to control themselves so that nervous energy otherwise dissipated in meaningless ways becomes useful in the performance of a task.

Stage fright can be reduced by a deliberate beginning. The speaker who rushes to the platform and hurriedly begins will have less self-control than the one who takes his position deliberately, throws his shoulders back, takes a deep breath, looks the audience over, and begins with a measured "Ladies and Gentlemen." When he concentrates on the importance of what he has to say, he builds up a sense of communication that gives him confidence. He must forget himself and think of his topic in relation to his hearers.

PROGRESSIVE ADJUSTMENT

All speakers, including those who suffer from stage fright, are helped materially by increasing their knowledge of speechmaking. Some stage fright can be attributed to the ignorance of what a speech is, of what a speaking occasion is like, of how a speaker goes about his task, and of what techniques he should employ. As the beginner learns to organize and adapt a speech and to hold the attention of an audience, his knowledge brings a confidence that helps in his own self-management.

OCCASIONS FOR POISE

The principles of achieving poise apply not only to speechmaking but also to conversations, interviews, and conferences. Communication is sometimes unsatisfactory because individuals stumble or hesitate at critical moments, fail to adjust to unexpected circumstances, talk too long, misjudge the listener, weaken their case by apologies, or display poor judgment in humor. Automatisms, random activity, and inhibition are found in informal as well as formal speaking. Stage fright is by no means limited to stages; the principles of achieving poise can be applied in many situations.

Poise is only one of many desirable attributes. The well-adjusted speaker cultivates fairness and tolerance; he takes criticism without indignation; he develops sympathy and perspective; he does not lose his sense of humor. Modesty, courtesy, and tact contribute to the effectiveness of speaking on all occasions. Sometimes the development of poise brings out other good personal qualities that listeners fail to observe in a self-conscious speaker.

Personal qualities desirable in speechmaking are useful also in social situations. Training in effective speaking, therefore, is training in effective living.

PHYSICAL EXPRESSION

Bodily action includes the speaker's observable behavior from the moment he becomes the center of attention until he has concluded his speech. It includes his walking to the platform, the center of the room, or the head of the conference table; his shifting of position while speaking; the action of his eyes, facial muscles, head, shoulders, arms, hands, and other parts of the body; his posture and bearing. Bodily action is the speaker's use of the body to communicate or to reinforce an idea or an emotion.

Bodily action in speaking is not new or strange. Everyone engaged in lively communication uses gesture, facial expression, or movement. The story of the man who could not describe a circular staircase with his hands tied behind his back illustrates the dependence of people upon bodily action. In fact, inexperienced speakers are perhaps the only creatures on earth who do not gesture.

Many platform gestures are almost exact duplicates of those used in conversation. If you are telling a friend the length of a five-pound trout, you hold your hands apart at the right distance. In conveying the same idea to an audience, you may use the same gesture. If you say to a friend, "Now don't forget to be there at 4:30," you may hold up a warning finger. Before an audience you may use a similar gesture to accompany a similar idea.

Bodily action may be used to convey attitudes and emotions as well as ideas. No interpreter is needed to explain the meaning of smiling, arching the eyebrows, scowling, wrinkling the forehead, or shrugging the shoulders. Sometimes a simple action is more eloquent than scores of words.

Even if a gesture only suggests an action, the audience usually has no difficulty in understanding. In suggesting that you are willing to fight for an idea, you need not go through all the motions of physical combat. Your clenched fist can give the desired impression, provided that the quality of your voice and the muscular tension of your whole body bear out the total action.

Bodily action in speaking will help you to capitalize on a great many familiar activities. It is a normal aspect of your personality; and since you cannot well avoid it, the issue is flatly whether you want to use it effectively or poorly. If you speak with little or no bodily action, the audience may conclude that you are self-conscious and inexperienced.

EFFECTIVE SPEAKERS ARE ANIMATED

Four contemporary leaders illustrate the use of gesturing in speechmaking: President Eisenhower, Secretary of the Treasury Douglas Dillon, General Lauris Norstadt, and UN Secretary-General U Thant.

USEFULNESS OF BODILY ACTION

By your bodily action as well as by your words you may show your listeners that you are eager to communicate with them. Bodily action helps (1) to relieve nervous tension, (2) to control attention, (3) to gain ease when speaking, (4) to reinforce thought and emotion.

The Control of Attention

People pay more attention to moving objects than to still life. Merchants attract the attention of passersby with mechanical gadgets or flashing signs. A speaker may not be able to arouse much interest with his preliminary statements about a slide trombone, but he very quickly catches attention when he takes the trombone from its case, adjusts the mouthpiece, and manipulates the slide. A teacher may lose the interest of his listeners by sitting at his desk and uttering a few quiet statements, but he will gain their attention if he stands up, talks earnestly, and emphasizes his ideas with appropriate action. If he can introduce still another type of action—conducting an experiment, drawing a diagram, demonstrating an object he will continue to hold attention

Action can be overdone, especially if it lacks purpose and variety. Although a speaker cannot expect to gain much emphasis from an occasional conventional gesture, spontaneous and genuine gestures can enhance the effectiveness of a speech remarkably. Somewhere between these two extremes lies the value of bodily action as a means of helping the speaker hold attention in public address.

Normal Action in Speaking

Much is said and written about "being natural" in speaking. Few individuals seem awkward when they converse; they beckon, point, describe, emphasize, and reveal attitudes. They look at the listeners, not down at the floor or out the window. They are active, because gesture is a normal part of speech. Why, therefore, should anyone stand inert, saying by his attitude, "I am no longer talking with you; I am now trying to make a speech. I am no longer my natural self; I am now trying to be a public speaker"?

Communication of Thought and Emotion

Bodily action helps to make the speaker's idea more clear, vivid, and emphatic, and his feeling more intense and convincing. Herein lie the real purpose and the greatest usefulness of bodily action. Movements of the hand indicating size and shape clarify the thought; a shake of the head or a clenching of the fist sharpens emphasis; a friendly smile adds conviction.

GESTURES HELP TO CONTROL ATTENTION
Evangelist Billy Graham crusades with vigorous gestures before a large audience in Madison Square Garden in New York City.

THE FIRST LESSON IN ACTION

The first lesson in bodily action includes such fundamentals as approaching the audience, maintaining good eye contact, and making the most of posture and appearance. The way you begin your speech can give your listeners a favorable first impression of you. Your posture and appearance should suggest self-confidence and poise; they should give dignity and authority to you as a speaker.

Approaching the Audience

You should select a good position in front of the audience. Pause long enough to catch your breath, to assume a good posture, and to look at your hearers. Do not begin your speech until you have the situation confidently in hand. Be deliberate and unhurried, yet businesslike, in addressing the chairman and the audience.

Directness

As you speak, you should look into the eyes of your hearers, just as you would in lively, animated conversation. Do not employ a quickly shifting, generalized auditorium gaze; look at groups of people in the audience long enough for them to gain a sense of communication with you. You should not ignore the listeners in the balcony or in the far corners of the room: they are there for the same purpose as those in the front row. Neither should you ignore the chairman. A good speaker will show everyone of his listeners that he wants to talk directly to him.

Two reasons underlie the necessity for eye control. The first is that listeners are most unlikely to give their complete confidence to a man who does not look at them. The second is that a speaker must be constantly alert to the responses of his listeners. Since the formalities of most speechmaking discourage members of an audience from interrupting, you must listen with your eyes. Look at that old gentleman in the sixteenth row; see how he nods his head; but look also at the young man nearby who frowns in disapproval. On the other side of the room you may observe looks of apathy or signs of weariness. Everyone of these responses is meaningful to you as a speaker; any one of them may require you to modify your speech. But you cannot hear them; you must see them.

No compromise with the principle of eye contact is possible. Sometimes the speaker is erroneously advised to talk exclusively to some member of the audience who looks friendly, or to avoid the eyes and look just over the heads of his listeners. Such advice is pernicious; it leads to the loss of eye contact and teaches the speaker the wrong mental attitude.

Posture

Good posture is essential for effective speaking. Since individuals differ widely, precise rules should not be prescribed, but the basic principles are clear: the speaker should stand comfortably erect, should feel reasonably at ease, should balance his weight about equally on both feet, and above all should show by look and action that he wants his audience to listen. Anyone who slouches, stands with all his weight on one foot, or drapes himself over a table, shows a lack of authority that may dispose the audience to inattention.

Speakers are sometimes unduly worried about what to do with their hands. The simplest and most graceful procedure is to let your hands hang at your sides. The habit of holding the hands behind the back or folding the arms increases tension, makes you look stiff and awkward, and curbs normal bodily activity. You would not try to carry on an important conversation with your hands buried in your pockets, clenched behind your back, or folded across your chest. Neither should you do so in making a speech.

Appearance

An imposing appearance is often thought to be an aid to speechmaking. Daniel Webster, William Jennings Bryan, and Franklin D. Roosevelt were impressive-looking men who bear out this theory. Yet other effective speakers have not been physically impressive. Douglas was short; Lincoln, homely; Fox, fat. Pictures of Churchill do not suggest the power of great oratory. Emerson said of John P. Hale, a famous nineteenth-century American lawyer who had astonishing effectiveness with juries, "See what an average-looking man he is. Looks just like five hundred other men. That must be where his power lies." [2] Every speaker should make the best of his physical resources. Posture is important; good judgment and good taste in dress and grooming make a favorable impression upon audiences just as they do upon individuals.

THE SECOND LESSON IN ACTION

The next step is training in the effective use of the whole body, particularly the hands, arms, and head. Gestures may be utilized for these purposes: (1) for description, (2) for attitude or emotion, and (3) for emphasis.

[2] Thomas W. Higginson, "American Audiences," *Atlantic Monthly*, XCV, 41, January, 1905.

Descriptive Gestures

The simplest kind of gesture is descriptive. "This is the proper method of holding a golf club," says a speaker, wrapping his fingers around a blackboard pointer. "A fifty-degree slant is about as steep a slope as a mountain climber can negotiate by the friction of his crepe-rubber soles," says another, slanting his forearm. "This is the correct position for starting a Christiana turn," says a third, using his whole body to describe a skiing technique.

When descriptive gestures are overdone, they lose their effect. Pointing to the sky, folding the hands over the heart, and listening with one hand behind the ear are usually in poor taste. Any pantomime that takes attention from the idea is bad. One speaker who thought that every phase of raising a crop should be fully represented by bodily action completely misunderstood the function of gestures. He demonstrated sowing the crop by broadcasting handfuls of imaginary grain and indicated the growing stalks by upward movements of his hands. When the moment came to reap the golden harvest, he bent over and sickled half the platform. Pantomime is the technique of the actor, not of the speaker. Gestures should suggest, not impersonate.

Gestures for Attitude or Emotion

Facial expression reveals attitudes and emotions. The "deadpan" look results from too little facial action; "mugging" results from too much. The right expression is a response to the changing emotional pattern of the discourse. A speech delivered with a half-frightened, worried, anxious look may fail to communicate the idea intended. Your face should be even more expressive in public speaking than it is in ordinary conversation.

The right facial action is a part of a total bodily response. A speaker cannot convincingly express determination in his face while he is expressing listlessness in his body. The grim set of the jaw and the flash of the eye are not enough to show determination. If the speaker really is determined, his voice will be altered, his hands employed, his muscular tension heightened. Good facial action results from a complete realization of an idea and a strong desire to communicate it to others.

Gestures for Emphasis

Although everybody uses gestures for emphasis, beginners find that some instruction and practice are necessary in speechmaking. The hands are often used for emphatic gestures, which are conventionally classified under five headings: the palm up, the palm down, the vertical palm, the index finger, and the clenched fist.

A common emphatic gesture is the extension of the hand with the palm up or turned slightly toward the audience. It may be used for mild emphasis or for appealing to an audience to consider an idea. It may be used to reinforce such statements as:

- I am sure you will understand that I bear you no personal grudge.
- At no time in history has your profession occupied a more conspicuous place.
- We all agree on the urgent necessity for immediate action.
- I appeal to you businessmen of the South to participate actively in the fullest development of the Nation.

The palm-up gesture is essentially friendly and appealing; the palm-down gesture is disapproving and distrustful. It is a downward or side-ward movement, indicating rejection. The following statements suggest the use of the palm-down gesture:

- America has no place for those who seek to destroy her institutions.
- We must keep from our shores the black scourge of war.
- We ought to throw away all of the books that pedagogues write.

The vertical-palm gesture suggests limitation or demarcation. The hand may be held toward the audience or to the speaker's right or left. This gesture may be used appropriately with the following assertions:

- This is as far as the party should go with its radical proposals.
- We must halt the migration from the city to the suburbs.
- We must put an immediate stop to this costly and economically foolish policy.

The index-finger (pointing) gesture suggests that an idea is especially significant. The speaker says, "Here's the point to remember," or "Your fault is this," or "This is the argument on which we differ." It is also an accusing or warning gesture. Its overuse by scolding adults has brought it into some disfavor, though it can be used with powerful effect. The following sentences are illustrative:

- I charge you to join with your friends and act now to ensure your community against the dangers of regimentation.
- Our only safety lies in knowing and understanding these fundamental principles.
- These actions will determine the fate of the nation for the next generation.

The clenched fist suggests that the speaker is prepared to fight for his idea. So forceful is the gesture that the attempt to give it additional emphasis by pounding on the table is unnecessary. It may be used to accompany strong declarations such as the following:

- These rights are the property of no one man; they are the exclusive possession of no generation.
- This tax was conceived in iniquity, has been fostered in corruption, and is maintained by the tricks and devices of politicians.
- We must be ready to defend the processes of democratic government under which men may speak their real thoughts.

GOVERNING PRINCIPLES OF EFFECTIVE GESTURING

Bodily action, particularly gestures of the hands and arms, are governed by seven fundamental principles. The gestures should be: (1) visible to the audience, (2) associated with the total bodily action, (3) purposeful, (4) timed exactly, (5) communicative, (6) varied, (7) used with restraint.

Visibility

Inexperienced speakers often make small hand movements that reveal a natural impulse to gesture. Such movements are ineffective, however, because they do not communicate the idea intended: they serve only to disclose the speaker's nervousness or timidity. Often these abortive motions toward the floor are the rudiments of serviceable gestures; improving them and bringing them into the view of the audience will facilitate good bodily action.

Use of the Whole Body

The whole body must support and reinforce every gesture made. A pitcher throws a baseball with his hand and arm, but every part of his body is involved. Hand and arm gestures require similar coordination. The elbow should be away from the trunk, not hugged against it. The impulse of the gesture is from the shoulder, not the elbow or the wrist. Ordinarily the fingers when extended should be together, not spread apart.

Purposefulness

A gesture is not a flabby waving, but a definite, purposeful movement to reinforce thought. It has three parts: the approach, the stroke, and the return. The approach is the lifting of the hand from its position at the side of the body to the point at which the gesture is to be made. This point is usually located somewhere between the speaker's waist and shoulders, a little to one side. The stroke is the gesture proper: it is a vigorous downward, upward, or outward movement. The return, which should be inconspicuous, is the movement of the hand back to its starting position. The foregoing analysis applies particularly to emphatic gestures; other types are less conventionalized. Precision in movement gives life to gesture. If a speaker points, he suggests pointing *at* something; if he uses a palm-up gesture, he suggests giving the idea *to* somebody.

Timing

The stroke should come on or before the word or syllable to be emphasized, and the approach and the return should not distract. The approach should be decisive, and the return should be a quick relaxation. The force of the gesture is lost if the speaker is slow in making it or is reluctant to let it go.

If the idea is "Never disagree with a beautiful woman," and the speaker wants to focus the attention of the audience on the word *beautiful,* the stroke of the gesture should be timed to accompany the utterance of that word. To add the gesture as an afterthought invariably creates a comic effect. If the hero says to the villain, "Leave!" he points to the door *as* he utters the word. But if he wants to burlesque the scene and get a laugh from the audience, he shouts "Leave!" *then* points to the door. It is too late to gesture after the emphatic word has been spoken.

Communicativeness

Making gestures, like forming speech sounds, should be a means to an end—the communication of meaning. Since gestures should not call attention to themselves, the speaker must not look at them. He must keep his attention focused on his audience. Looking at a gesture gives the effect of exhibiting it.

Restraint

The speaker must keep bodily action under control. Usually, you should not begin a speech with a gesture, for the audience is not prepared for it. You should not extend your arms so far forward, or so far upward, as to suggest that you are at the limit of your physical resources. You should not gesture on every word, nor labor to emphasize the obvious. Most beginners, however, use too little bodily action rather than too much.

MOVEMENT ON THE PLATFORM

Movement on the platform may indicate the major divisions of a speech or introduce variety into the speaker's position. By stepping to the right or to the left, a speaker may show that he has concluded one argument and is beginning another. A step forward suggests greater emphasis or intimacy with the audience; a step backward suggests reconsideration, summary, or review. Like all bodily action, such movements should support the idea rather than detract from it. Aimless pacing back and forth across the platform, or stiff striding from one position to another, distracts the attention of the audience. Even a single step may have a useful purpose: it may emphasize an idea or show that the speaker is about to take up a new point. The beginner who concludes a point, takes three, long, measured steps, and then resumes his argument, is emphasizing the transition beyond all reasonable proportion; his movement calls attention to itself rather than to the argument. A short step, or even a slight shift of weight, would be better. Some practice may be necessary before you feel confident of your ability to move purposefully on the platform.

IMPROVING BODILY ACTION

Gestures are not an afterthought to charm an audience; they are an organic part of speech delivery. Although bodily action used in speaking consists essentially of simple movements, the ability to relate these movements closely to the thought may require much practice.

Great speakers of the past have given considerable attention to delivery; they have used the seashore, a plowed field, an attic, or a stable as a place to rehearse without being disturbed. You may have to resort to some equally ingenious solution. Among the more effective devices is rehearsing before a mirror. This practice enables you to observe whether you are following sound principles.

After the speaker has acquired a feeling for gesture, he still has the problem of making gesturing habitual in addressing a group. His bodily action should be as much a means of communication as his utterance of speech sounds; it should be spontaneous, not forced.

Securing Coordination

Muscular exercises and drills, employed to accustom the individual to the use of the large muscles, are valuable for those who have poor coordination or who do not gesture much in everyday speech; but most students will profit from beginning immediately with the practice of sentences and short excerpts taken from the texts of speeches and short stories.

In the preliminary practice of these exercises, the speaker should use many gestures of different types. He should gesture sometimes with one hand, sometimes with the other, sometimes with both; he may even burlesque some of the lines by making sweeping gestures. A few practice periods will accustom him to the feel of speaking with the whole body and will relieve him of much awkwardness and tension.

Suiting the Action to the Word

What has been done in practice comes under the heading of experience and drill. The speaker's next task is to select gestures appropriate to the meaning he wishes to communicate. By repeated practice, while focusing on the meaning, he should make those gestures an integral part of his delivery. His ultimate goal is so to develop his gestures that they will be an integral part of the total communication that includes also language, voice, and inflection.

The problem of improving bodily action is similar in many respects to that of improving the realization of meaning. For any of several reasons, many beginners have difficulty in realizing meanings: insufficient preparation, the use of language better adapted to writing than to speaking, or the need for concentration on what is coming next rather than on what is being spoken at the instant. The causes of artificiality, constraint, and clumsiness are similar: insufficient time in preparation, the use of gestures not suited to the idea, or too much concentration on mechanics and too little on the idea.

Continuing Process

The development of bodily action, like the composition of the speech itself, should be a continuing process. As the student improves the wording by repeated rehearsals until it expresses his ideas clearly and precisely, so also does he improve gestures by repeated rehearsals until they are direct and forceful. At one moment during the rehearsal he may repeat an idea in two or three different wordings in order to select the most convincing language; at the next moment he may repeat the idea with two or three different gestures in order to select the most appropriate action. Many rehearsals should make possible the use of this wording or that gesture in any easy manner. During actual delivery, however, the influence of the audience and the occasion may cause him to change both the wording and the gestures he has planned. The impulse to gesture while speaking should produce more spontaneous, effective movements than those resulting from conscious effort.

Danger of Artificiality

Is the rehearsal of gesture likely to result in unconvincing, mechanical bodily action? It may do so if the gestures are chosen unintelligently— a shake of the head in sentence two, an index-finger gesture in sentence seven, two steps to the right in sentence fourteen. If the speaker has so drilled himself in arbitrary gestures that he is afraid to modify them, his delivery will be stilted. Finally, gesture may be unconvincing because of the inherent difficulty of learning necessary muscular coordination. A few minutes' practice is inadequate to train the speaker's nervous and muscular system so that he can speak effectively with his whole person. If he overcomes the difficulties, however, he will be able to improve bodily action.

Spontaneity

Effective speaking demands not only a native impulse to gesture, but also some skill in execution. At first, bodily action will be a matter of immediate, conscious plan; later it should become a firmly rooted habit. Once the speaker frees himself from restraint and develops a full realization of his meaning as he speaks, he will find that his gestures are as spontaneous as his inflections.

Part **IV**   SPEECH TYPES:
Opportunities, Occasions,
and Forms

*So long as you are mindful to say nothing
unworthy of yourself, nothing untrue, nothing
vulgar, you had better forget yourself altogether
and think only of the audience, how to get them
and how to hold them.*

—*James Bryce*

9 SOCIAL SPEAKING:
Entertaining

*An orator must . . . cheer his guests, and
. . . make them take pleasure, with hearing of things wittily devised, and pleasantly set forth.*

—Thomas Wilson

Speaking to inform, to impress, or to persuade is the serious business of rhetoric, but speaking to entertain contributes to the attainment of these serious purposes by recapturing flagging attention, by providing needed relief, and by making particular points stand out. Speaking to entertain may be the speaker's sole objective when he seeks to please, to divert, and to amuse his hearers, but his material and his treatment may incidentally convey information, amplify a well-known theme, or suggest a needed reform.

PRINCIPLES OF ENTERTAINING

At times a speaker is expected to hold the attention of his audience only for their pleasure and enjoyment and to treat his subject matter either for the interest and stimulation it provides or for the wit and humor he can create. The listeners assemble for good fellowship or relaxation and therefore expect to have their attention held agreeably for a period of time. Particular principles are related to the attainment of interest and stimulation that are quite different from those required for the creation of wit and humor.

INTEREST AND STIMULATION

Attention may be held agreeably when the speaker focuses upon material that is interesting in and for itself or upon material that stimulates the imagination and may produce excitement or wonderment. Ideas that are striking, antagonistic, problematic, unusual, or familiar, although they are useful in all types of speaking, have special value for interest and stimulation in entertaining.

The Striking

The striking commands immediate attention. Ideas associated in extraordinary ways and expressed in forceful and colorful language are striking. The concrete and the specific are more striking than the general and the abstract, and therefore more interesting and stimulating. The specific name of a person, place, or agent, as well as a definite amount, direction, and time, help to build a story. "I took a 707 jet to Los Angeles" is more stimulating than "I took a plane out of town." "A young family of six girls and one boy" is more striking than "a family of several children." "When I was a poor boy on the Lower East Side of New York, I knew a ward boss named Pat" is more colorful than "When I was young, there was a politician in New York." The speaker need not attempt to identify every man, dog, and village in his story, but he should make the important details precise. Pointed use of the specific contributes to the desired effect.

Specific language stimulates the listener to use his imagination. If the speaker says, "The man went across the room," the listener receives a vague and indefinite visual image. If the speaker says, "The policeman dashed across the kitchen," the mental picture is clearer and consequently more provocative. "I never seem to be able to pick a balanced menu" arouses very little interest; but "I eat Wheaties for breakfast, an ice-cream bar for lunch, and a bowl of chili for dinner" is vivid and arresting. One student, describing an unpleasant night spent sleeping on old bedsprings, threw the audience into an uproar by saying ruefully, "Next morning I felt like a waffle."

A trip to the library often helps to provide vivid details. If you want to burlesque the advertising copy used by manufacturers of beauty preparations, you should search the files of women's magazines for striking examples. If you want to familiarize yourself with the professional jargon of fire-insurance underwriters, you can get it from their trade journals. If you want to poke fun at assembly lectures, Ph.D. dissertations, or the quality of writing in the pulp magazines, obtain actual samples; they are more amusing and reliable than anything you can invent. Interesting and stimulating examples result from systematic research.

Examples of striking expressions can be found in speeches of any period. Henry Ward Beecher remarked in one of his speeches "The churches are always popular when the people hear something there that they want to hear. . . ." Will Rogers observed, concerning American diplomacy, "We never lost a war, or won a peace conference." Recently, Dr. Rozanne M. Brooks, a professor of sociology, speaking on education for women, commented ". . . the American college girl is eternally being accused of confusing the pursuit of knowledge with the pursuit of matrimony." Especially effective is the striking question such as "Do you realize that Telstar will force you to master French humor if you are to enjoy top television entertainment of the future?" or "How long will it be before taxes get so high that the government will have our houses and we'll still be paying on our mortgages?"

The bold, colorful, descriptive image has its roots deep in American life. Such expressions as "give 'em both barrels" and "flash in the pan" are characteristic of the pioneer.[1]

To achieve a striking impression, the speaker may even wish to use a paradox such as "We may yet be selling real estate on the moon." For climactic effect, the most striking device should come toward the end.

The Antagonistic

Conflict that involves activity and excitement entertains in speaking just as it does in novels, plays, and motion pictures. People like contests of wit, strength, ingenuity, endurance, and capacity. A popular lecture on deep-sea diving is effectively illustrated with a contest between a diver and a shark. A lecture on space orbits may be made interesting with an account of the tests of endurance undergone by astronauts in preparing to withstand high pressure and extreme heat. After-dinner speeches are often entertaining because the speakers boldly assail personalities and criticize actions. If the attack is vicious, the listeners may be interested, though displeased; if it is mellowed, they may be both interested and entertained.

In deciding whether to use the principle of antagonizing, you must compare the advantages and disadvantages of the direct, forthright state-

[1] Edward Everett Dale, "The Speech of the Frontier," *Quarterly Journal of Speech*, XXVII, 353–363, October, 1941. See also Lester V. Berrey and Melvin Van Den Bark, *The American Thesaurus of Slang*, New York: Thomas Y. Crowell Co., 1942. The article by Dale cites a great number of striking frontier expressions, and the latter work gives thousands of examples of American slang. Further examples may be found in the speeches of such humorists as Mark Twain, Artemus Ward, Josh Billings, Bill Nye, and Will Rogers. The wide use of slang is not generally recommended, but a certain ruggedness of speech has many possibilities in entertaining speaking when used by those to whom it is native.

ment with those of a tactful, subtle approach. If you disagree with a preceding speaker, should you say, "I enjoyed Taylor's description of big business, but I think he overlooked some essentials," or instead, "Taylor's statement that big business is altruistic is complete, utter nonsense; his idea of altruism is to keep the dividend checks large and the paychecks small"? The latter is more compelling; the issue is, Will it please? The answer depends entirely upon you, the audience, and the occasion. In some circumstances the shock technique of the antagonistic approach is necessary to capture attention and interest; in others the speaker may risk losing his audience completely.

The Problematical

The problematical is a powerful factor in entertaining. Listeners become eager to learn how the men in the coal mine were rescued, or how the European refugee managed to make a fortune from an invention he was able to patent in America, or how the gambler was able to amass several million dollars with the numbers racket. The chemist who told his audience how he discovered what made sugar lumpy used suspense skillfully. He did not solve the problem in his first sentence but let the audience work toward the solution with him. By describing amusing failures to ignite gas vapor under pressure, an engineer engrossed his audience with the story of the spark plug. A student of agriculture could see no way to make an entertaining speech on plant breeding. He was just about to abandon the topic, when he thought of the development of hybrid corn. His explanation of the difficulties and the failures of early experiments was so graphic that the listeners were eager to learn the outcome.

On many occasions you can utilize suspense or interest in the solution of a problem. If you select striking details that heighten the narrative without making it excessively long, the development of your climax will arouse the curiosity and expectation of your listeners.

The Unusual

Talking about strange people, customs, and events, about ingenious methods and devices, is a good way to entertain an audience. Margaret Mead, Lowell Thomas, and Pearl Buck have captivated thousands with their narratives of distant lands. Visitors to a world's fair often find much to talk about in the variety of exhibitions. New methods of combat catch the attention of both the civilian and the soldier. Tombs and crypts, different marriage or funeral customs, strange plants and animals, little-known manufacturing processes, novel games and sports arouse the interest of the listener.

Your own unusual experiences are often interesting and stimulating to other people. Trips to distant places, strange accidents, peculiar occupations, and odd phenomena you have observed are possibilities for entertaining.

The popularity of Ripley's "Believe It or Not" illustrates the entertaining value of unusual ideas. At an informal program, one organization invited its members to speak on "believe it or not" experiences. A botanist won the prize. While doing research in Venezuela, he captured an eight-foot green snake and put it into a large can with a tight-fitting lid, specially designed for such specimens. A few holes in the lid admitted air. The next day he discovered that the snake had disappeared. He could not explain the mystery until he noticed a few green particles on the bottom of the can. Then he realized that tropical ants had devoured his specimen.

The Familiar

People are interested in being able to identify themselves with the well-known ideas and occurrences set forth by the speaker. The most entertaining speakers in the history of public address have capitalized on the familiar experiences of their listeners by talking about the weather, babies, birthdays, operations, politics, business, and sports. Difficulties in the handling of money have a special appeal: bewilderment in listening to financial reports, the complexities of the income tax, and the struggles of living on a balanced budget. Successful after-dinner speakers have used such familiar themes as the absurd fashions of women, the misunderstandings between parents and children, the hardships of vacations intended for pleasure, the plights of the amateur sailor, and the adjustments to the shock of matrimony. The novel or the unfamiliar as a source of entertainment is limited, but the familiar is everybody's province.

If you use a commonplace idea, you should present it from a fresh point of view. For example, the familiar experience of selling a house may be developed by describing the conversations between real-estate agents and prospective buyers. Comments showing the peculiarities of individual tastes and idiosyncrasies will reveal that one caller would like the color of the house restored to its original horrendous brown, another would not want the house because it did not have enough outlets for his numerous electronic gadgets, and a third was only looking in to see how the house was furnished.

WIT AND HUMOR

The distinction between wit and humor is a subtle one. Wit is defined as more purely intellectual than humor, implying swift perception of the incongruous, and depending for its effect chiefly on ingenuity, unexpectedness of turn, or patness of application, whereas humor implies broader

Mark Twain on the Lecture Circuit   Gelli Portrait

SPEAKING IS SOMETIMES ENTERTAINING

Mark Twain's humorous lectures entertained listening audiences of his own time and reading audiences of our time.

human sympathies and a more kindly sense of the incongruous, often blended with pathos. Some of the wisest philosophers, rhetoricians, orators, and men of letters—Plato, Aristotle, Cicero, Quintilian, Campbell, Hobbes, Kant, Spencer, Schopenhauer, Hazlitt, Meredith, Bergson—have written about these concepts. Many entertaining speakers have ventured opinions about the nature of wit and humor—Mark Twain, Stephen Leacock, Robert Benchley, and James Thurber.

In Cicero's writings, for example, is much practical advice on the use of wit and humor, such as that against using jests ready prepared that do not arise out of the occasion, because they are usually frigid. In Cicero's *De Oratore*, Caesar, in response to Antonius and Crassus, analyzes humor and jesting at some length, observing in summary:

> A regard . . . to proper times, moderation and forbearance in jesting, and a limitation in the number of jokes, will distinguish the orator from the buffoon; and the circumstance, besides that we joke with an object, not that we may appear to be jesters, but that we may gain some advantage. . . .

Jokes . . . which lie in the subject and thought, are, though infinite in their varieties, reducible under a very few general heads; for it is by deceiving expectation, by satirising the tempers of others, by playing humorously on our own, by comparing a thing with something worse, by dissembling, by uttering apparent absurdities, and by reproving folly, that laughter is excited. . . .[2]

One theory of humor is that laughter arises from a perception of the incongruous: the listener is suddenly made aware of a lack of propriety, harmony, or suitability among things that should be appropriate, harmonious, or suitable. Another theory stresses the importance of the unexpected: a humorous anecdote leads the listener to expect a certain type of happening or a certain kind of response, but the expectation is suddenly altered or distorted. As Kant says, laughter is "an affection arising from a strained expectation being suddenly reduced to nothing."

These two elements, the incongruous and the unexpected, pervade most humor. If you concoct a story about a cavalry horse who went to the state university to register for a few courses under Public Law 16, you immediately put into action a dozen possibilities of the incongruous. If you devise an incident about the night you spent in an empty house, fearfully listening to various kinds of sinister noises, you set the stage for effective use of the unexpected. If you describe a veteran, impressively decorated with medals and ribbons, afraid to face the girl he has just stood up, you open up possibilities of both the incongruous and the unexpected.

Humor is not confined to jokes and anecdotes. It may be found in a well-chosen word or phrase, such as Mark Twain's "Always obey your parents—when they are present," or "You want to be more careful about lying—otherwise you are nearly sure to get caught." It may result from a sparkling description of such a commonplace event as one's first run-in with the law. It embraces understatement, overstatement, ridicule, satire, raillery, irony, burlesque, word play, and stylistic humor.

Understatement

Humor often springs from a word or phrase that is milder than the listener expects. "When I first looked at my report card and saw two D's and three F's," said a student speaker, "the fact was brought home to me that my school work was not completely satisfactory." Since the audience expected "my school work was a decided failure," the substitution of the totally inadequate description had a humorous effect. Another student made the comment, "To fall two thousand feet from a tropical mountain peak would be discouraging." The audience, expecting "fatal," "disastrous," or some other strong word, was amused by the understatement.

[2] J. S. Watson, tr. or ed., *Cicero on Oratory and Orators: With His Letters to Quintus and Brutus,* London: George Bell and Sons, 1896, pp. 292, 308.

A public official was asked by an investigating committee why he was fired from the board of directors of a large corporation. "I wasn't exactly fired," he replied. "There just wasn't any enthusiasm for me to stay."

One student vividly described the aftermath of an accident: "The car careened sharply to the right, crashed into a vegetable truck and ricocheted into a March of Dimes booth. I climbed out and surveyed the damage. A cop stepped up and said, 'Son, isn't this a bit unusual?'"

President Kennedy used understatement in an amusing introduction to his address to the National Association of Manufacturers in New York on December 6, 1961: "I have not always considered the membership of the National Association of Manufacturers as among my strongest supporters. I'm not sure you have all approached the New Frontier with the greatest possible enthusiasm. . . ."

Overstatement

The exaggeration of a detail can also make a statement humorous. Mark Twain's speech on "New England Weather" is a good example. If he had said, "The weather in New England is so changeable that the reporter has to issue ambiguous forecasts," no one would have been amused, but by exaggerating the details he entertained his hearers:

The forecaster doesn't know what the weather is going to be in New England. . . . He mulls over it, and by and by gets out something like this: Probably northeast to southwest winds, varying to the southward and westward and eastward, and points between, high and low barometer swapping around from place to place; probably areas of rain, snow, hail, and drought, succeeded or preceded by earthquakes, with thunder and lightning.[3]

"Private John" Allen of Mississippi made frequent use of overstatement. A typical instance from his speech, "A Fish Hatchery for Tupelo," is the following:

This, Mr. Chairman, is a proposition to establish there [Tupelo] a fish hatchery. We have the ideal place for a fish hatchery. Why, sir, fish will travel over land for miles to get into the water we have at Tupelo. Thousands and millions of unborn fish are clamoring to this Congress today for an opportunity to be hatched at the Tupelo hatchery. (Loud laughter.)[4]

Contrasting baseball managers, James Reston in his *New York Times* column, May 24, 1963, characterized the vigor of John McGraw with overstatement, concluding with: ". . . he would have shoved over the Washington Monument and left town in a blaze of profanity."

---

[3] Read the entire speech in *Mark Twain's Speeches,* New York: Harper & Brothers, 1923, pp. 53–57. Copyright 1923 by Harper & Brothers.

[4] *Congressional Record,* XXXVI, 3984, March 8, 1940; XXXIV, pt. 3, 2703, Feb. 20, 1901.

Ridicule

Ridicule is characterized by a degree of contempt rather than by mild jesting or bitterness. A senator ridiculed the complexity of government organization by mentioning that the Secretary of Commerce had an Under Secretary of Commerce, an Assistant Secretary, two special assistants to the Secretary, an administrative assistant, an assistant to the administrative assistant, and several other degrees and gradations of secretaries. "Think of that," he exclaimed, "a secretary to the secretary to the Assistant Secretary of the Secretary of Commerce!" (Laughter.) [5]

Addressing the Sixty-sixth Congress of American Industry shortly before Christmas in 1961, Dr. Felix Morley entertained his audience with ridicule:

Never before . . . has there been such promotion of Christmas trade. Never before, in addition to customary come-on's have there been so many secondary gimmicks, such as elaborate carnivals complete with neon lighting, Santas, and clowns. Perhaps there is something symbolic about this. Under the lurid light of radioactive fallout the patron saint of Giveaway is working overtime. And the clowns? Well, many of us are now turning compulsory somersaults.

. . . to keep out of the red, business uses every psychological aid. The advertizer feels he must tune singing commercials into wave lengths once reserved for Christmas carols. Japan, they tell me, has shown us the way in this. Not one Japanese in a thousand even professes Christianity, but the day that celebrates the birth of Christ has been ballyhooed there into the most profitable merchandising period of the pagan year. [6]

Satire

Satire lampoons eccentricities, foibles, follies, vices, and abuses. It can be either playful or insulting, making game of a person, institution, or organization either sportively and good-humoredly or unkindly and derisively. It is a verbal cartoon, utilizing mockery and caricature to expose or denounce absurd or injurious practices. Frequently it lets us see ourselves as others see us, with attention focused upon our shortcomings and weaknesses.

A speaker may satirize his own characteristics, as did the conservative Republican Senator Barry Goldwater in alluding to the 1964 presidential nomination in an address before the Alfalfa Club. He observed: ". . . I feel the White House is now ready for me since Jacqueline remodeled it in an Eighteenth century decor."

[5] *Congressional Record*, LXXXVI, 3023, February 26, 1940.
[6] From the opening paragraphs of the address entitled, "The Constitutional Design for Freedom," New York City, December 6, 1961. Text supplied by the National Association of Manufacturers. A news release.

In a television commentary David Brinkley taunted American politicians:

A student looking at American politics today finds much of it a wall-to-wall mediocrity. . . . He sees most politicians bunched together in the middle of the road, milling around, talking a lot, trying to say nothing that will offend anybody, and each one saying to the other, "I am more medium than you are." If a young, idealistic, and energetic student finds little there to engage his mind and excite his interest, it is not very surprising.[7]

Raillery

Raillery is good-humored jesting which depends upon keen and sometimes sarcastic scorn. It is pleasantry more cutting than playful banter and less flippant than persiflage. It is especially effective when used to deflate the self-important, but it can be applied generally if the speaker is sure that it will be taken in the right spirit.

Lecturing in Washington, Will Rogers poked fun at the state of the nation's preparedness, for which Woodrow Wilson, who was present, was being severely criticized:

There is some talk of getting a machine gun to capture Villa if we can borrow one. The one we have now they are using to train our Army with in Plattsburg. If we go to war we will just about have to go to the trouble of getting another gun.[8]

Malcolm Muggeridge, former editor of *Punch*, commenting on humor, used raillery:

Maybe a people living under the gathering shadow of a mushroom cloud have little taste for . . . essays in incongruity, prefer to turn their faces downward and solace themselves with the seemingly quenchless outpourings of toys and devices which our affluent societies provide. Maybe they feel that laughter might, in some mysterious way, touch off the quick alarm and atomize their motor cars and washing machines and television sets, not to mention themselves, before the payments on them have been completed.[9]

Audiences enjoy hearing a speaker banter somebody, especially when he does so in a friendly manner. The light touch is required; a stroke of sarcasm would spoil the fun. Some groups of individuals seem to be unusually tempting targets: Brooklynites, Bostonians, Texans, politicians, experts, absent-minded professors, bewildered students. The peculiarities of people provide good material. Sometimes the best target is the speaker himself. Woodrow Wilson's favorite limerick comes to mind:

[7] Edith Efron, "David of the Devastating Quip," *TV Guide,* **8,** no. 27, July 7, 1962.

[8] Max Eastman, *Enjoyment of Laughter,* New York: Simon and Schuster, 1936, p. 123. Copyright 1936 by Simon and Schuster.

[9] *The New York Times Magazine,* September 11, 1960, p. 56. Copyright by *The New York Times.* Reprinted by permission.

For beauty I am not a star:
There are others more handsome by far;
   But my face, I don't mind it
   For I am behind it:
It's the people in front that I jar.

Orson Welles, introducing himself to a small audience, had a similar opportunity to turn the banter against himself. He pointed out that he had been a director, a producer, and an actor on the legitimate stage; a writer, a producer, and an actor in motion pictures; a magician, an artist, a book publisher, a violinist, and a pianist. "Isn't it a shame," he concluded, "that there are so many of me and so few of you?"

Franklin D. Roosevelt opened his fourth-term campaign with a clever after-dinner speech to the Teamsters' Union. Especially telling was his banter in his famous reference to his dog, Fala:

These Republican leaders have not been content with attacks upon me, or my wife, or my sons—they now include my little dog, Fala. Unlike the members of my family, he resents this. Being a Scottie, as soon as he learned that the Republican fiction-writers had concocted a story that I had left him behind on an Aleutian Island and had sent a destroyer back to find him—at a cost to the taxpayers of two or three or twenty million dollars—his Scotch soul was furious. He has not been the same dog since. I am accustomed to hearing malicious falsehoods about myself—such as that old, worm-eaten chestnut that I have represented myself as indispensable. But I think I have a right to object to libelous statements about my dog.[10]

Irony

The essential feature of irony is the contradiction suggested between the literal and the intended meaning when the speaker asserts one idea and implies another. It differs from sarcasm in that it is playful instead of being harsh or cutting. In using sarcasm, the speaker may say directly what he means. The student speaker was ironical when he said: "Years from now we will all remember this beautiful classroom: the comfortable chairs, the richly-decorated walls, the thick-piled rugs. We will call to mind all the eloquent speeches we have heard, each one better than the one before."

He would have been using sarcasm had he said: "This classroom couldn't be made comfortable or attractive if you moved in the furnishings from the White House. Our dull speeches wouldn't persuade a drowning man to grab for a log."

Irony of a grim sort sometimes becomes a two-edged sword, since it invites a retort that may be more devastating than the original statement.

[10] "Keeping Political Faith," in A. Craig Baird, *Representative American Speeches: 1944–1945*, New York: The H. W. Wilson Company, 1945, p. 141.

It may seem bitter, taunting, and contemptuous even when it is not so intended. Yet the ironical touch may be used with telling effect when the speaker wishes to poke fun at such traits as inefficiency, graft, incompetence, extravagance, and pedantry.

An effective application of irony in student speaking is that of the senior who entertained his classmates with a consideration of the fate of the honor student:

The conscientious entering freshman, with habits from previous schooling making it automatic for him to do all of the assigned reading and to complete all of the written work expected, finds himself in the predicament of receiving all A's at the end of his first semester. His disease of conscientiousness grows steadily worse as he takes seriously the suggestions of his professors that he read widely from the reference lists provided. Hour after hour of his time is lost in pouring over sources that merely add to his burdensome store of information. By the end of the term he is embarrassed to find himself on the Dean's List for scholarship.

During his sophomore year, instead of doing what any sensible fellow would do—keeping up with the latest movies and popular records, and dating the most attractive girls in his classes—he tries out for the debating team and writes articles for the student literary magazine. He finds himself at the end of the semester held up to public view with the disgraceful distinction of being an honored debater and a prize-winning poet.

His malady of close application to his studies affects him more throughout his junior year as he becomes known as "The Brain" when he is elected to Phi Beta Kappa and is declared eligible to enroll in an honors program.

During his senior year his status gets entirely out of hand as he receives several scholarships for graduate study and is accepted by the graduate schools of five leading universities. Let this awful state be a warning to all entering students who have any idea of continuing their conscientious habits in their college studies.

Burlesque

Burlesque is a ludicrous characterization that distorts prominent features of the person or object held up to ridicule. Its principal distinction lies in its distortion. For the sake of laughter, it vulgarizes lofty material or treats ordinary material with mock dignity. The boy who spoke on "Women as Back-Seat Drivers" utilized good-humored burlesque. Classifying them into four types, he presented each kind as a national menace with special ways of making the driver's life miserable. The first type, the muttering worry wart, frets about making the sharp curve, passing the next car, and having enough gas to reach the next filling station. The second type, the infuriating know-it-all, is sure that the driver is on the wrong road, that the restaurant just passed would have been the best place to eat, and that the car should have been repaired at the last town.

The third type, the nagging alarmist, screams her warnings that the driver is exceeding the speed limit, that he is going through a red light, and that he is sure to collide with the on-coming moving van. The fourth type, the tense convulsive, stares at the road, stifles cries of terror, and pushes an imaginary brake through the floor board. Another speaker, deriding the attempt of some corporations to stimulate loyalty among their employees, burlesqued the song, the flag, and the motto of a fictitious box-wood firm.

At Colorado Woman's College on March 2, 1961, a professor of psychology in the United States Air Force Academy, in speaking about women, gained the effect of burlesque by quoting from several well-known writers their estimates of women:

> About a hundred years ago Schopenhauer expressed the prevailing views of his times as follows:
>
> > Women are directly fitted for acting as the nurses and teachers of our early childhood by the fact that they are themselves childish, frivolous and short-sighted; in a word, they are big children all life long. . . . It is only the man whose intellect is clouded by his sexual impulses that could give the name of the fair sex to that undersized, narrow-shouldered, broad hipped, and short-legged race. . . .
>
> To Peter the Apostle she was the "weaker vessel," to Kipling, "A rag, a bone, and a hank of hair," to Milton, "A fair defect."
>
> Ambrose Bierce, a contemporary writer, says, "Woman would be much more charming if one could fall into her arms without falling into her hands." Harry Lean Wilson in *Ruggles of Red Gap* gave his evaluation: "She'd fight a rattle-snake and give it the first two bites." [11]

Wordplay

Wordplay occurs when the listener expects a word or phrase to be used in its normal sensible manner and the speaker surprises him by using it in an entirely different way. Such turns of phrase as puns, quips, and various forms of double meaning entertain by capturing the attention with unexpected twists of meaning. In addressing an audience in Auburn, New York, the home town of Congressman John Taber, Ex-President Truman introduced a pun, "Your Congressman used a butcher knife, a saber and a meat ax on every forward-looking appropriation. I call it the Taber dance." Among famous quips is that of Adlai Stevenson: "Egg-heads of the world, unite! You have nothing to lose but your yolks." Speakers make frequent use of commonplace expressions and suggest an interpretation different from the original meaning. The passage from the

[11] Lt. Col. Gabriel D. Ofresh, "Modern Women and Modern Marriage," *Vital Speeches*, XXVII, 472, May 15, 1962.

Bible, "I was a stranger, and ye took me in," is used to berate a swindler. A contrasting use of ideas makes interesting wordplay, as in the comment by Lady Wootton of Great Britain: "Two hundred years ago we made a practice of treating lunatics as criminals. Nowadays we are more inclined to treat criminals as lunatics."

Stylistic Humor

Wit and humor may be attained by creating amusing effects or by a pervading lightness of treatment in style. The technique of parody or travesty—humorously imitating a serious interpretation, or presenting a ludicrous characterization of a serious subject—is an effective method of entertaining. Malapropisms—misapplications of words in ridiculous ways —are colorful when they heighten the effect of the humor. Deliberate misunderstanding of intended meanings may also intensify the humor. Mocking innuendos, clever thrusts, sly allusions, and unexpected shifts of imagery contribute to joviality in speaking. Several of the techniques of subtle humor are illustrated in the introduction to the commencement address by President Kennedy at Yale University in June, 1962, delivered after he had been awarded an honorary degree.

As General de Gaulle occasionally acknowledges America to be the daughter of Europe, so I am pleased to come to Yale, the daughter of Harvard.

It might be said now that I have the best of both worlds. A Harvard education and a Yale degree.

I am particularly glad to become a Yale man because, as I think about my troubles, I find that a lot of them have come from other Yale men. Among business men I have had a minor disagreement with Roger Blough of the Law School Class of 1931, and I have had some complaints too from my friend Henry Ford, of the Class of 1940. In journalism I seem to have some differences with John Hay Whitney of the Class of 1926—and sometimes I also displease Henry Luce of the Class of 1920—not to mention always—William F. Buckley Jr. of the Class of 1950.

I even have some trouble with my Yale advisers. I get along with them, but I'm not always sure how they get along with each other.

I have the warmest feelings for Chester Bowles of the Class of 1924, and for Dean Acheson of the Class of 1915, and my assistant McGeorge Bundy of the Class of 1940. But I am not 100 per cent sure that these three wise and experienced Yale men wholly agree with each other on every issue.

So this Administration, which aims at peaceful cooperation among all Americans, has been the victim of a certain natural pugnacity developed in this city among Yale men. Now that I, too, am a Yale man it is time for peace.

Last week at West Point, in the historic tradition of that academy, I availed myself of the powers of Commander in Chief to remit all sentences of offending cadets. In that same spirit, and in the historic tradition of Yale, let me now offer to smoke the clay pipe of friendship with all of my brother Elis. And I hope that they may be friends not only with me but even with each other.

In any event I am very glad to be here, and as a new member of the club I have been checking to see what earlier links existed between the institution of the Presidency and Yale. I found that a member of the Class of 1878, William Howard Taft, served one term in the White House as preparation for becoming a member of this faculty. And a graduate of 1804, John C. Calhoun, regarded the Vice Presidency, quite naturally, as too lowly a status for a Yale alumnus and became the only man in history to ever resign that office.[12]

STRENGTHENING THE WIT AND HUMOR

Much depends upon the presentation—dry, self-deprecating, bewildered, audacious, pseudobombastic, aggrieved. One speaker tells a story with a twinkle in his eye and a contagious chuckle that creates an atmosphere of amusement; another heightens the humor with a droll attitude. Only by study and experience can you determine the manner best suited to the subject, the audience, and the occasion. Dialogue, dialect, bodily action, and timing contribute to the presentation.

A university senior, returning to his speech class after an unexcused absence, was dismayed to hear that short speeches were assigned. In dialogue form he described his experience when, late in the hour, he made his speech:

I leaned over to Mr. Holmes and whispered, "What's the assignment for today?" He said, "We're to make a short speech on 'The Three Parts of a Speech.'" "And are there three parts to a speech?" I asked. "Oh, yes, indeed," replied he. "And what are they?" I pursued. "The introduction, the body, and the conclusion," responded he. "And what are we to say about them?" I inquired further. "We're to tell what they're for," continued he, burying himself in his notes, "and we're supposed to have an original introduction." So this morning I want to tell you the functions of the three parts of a speech.

The humor arises from the speaker's apparently naive inquiries about the subject of the speech, his frank confession of his predicament, and his burlesque of the assignment, but the use of dialogue is the crowning touch. A less imaginative approach would be: "When I came to class this morning, I asked Mr. Holmes what the assignment was, and he said that we were to make a short speech on the functions of the three parts of a speech," continuing in indirect style instead of using direct quotation.

The mere use of dialogue is not entertaining if the speaker's language is pedestrian. A string of colorless "he said's" and "she said's" can be extremely boring. The dialogue form is recommended because it makes possible the use of vivid and colorful language in a way that is otherwise difficult.

[12] John F. Kennedy, "The Myth and Reality In Our National Economy," *Vital Speeches*, XXVIII, 578, July 15, 1962.

To use dialect requires a good ear for sound variations, melody, and rhythm, and the ability to recapture or to reproduce them. If you have this skill, you can capitalize upon it in speechmaking, but you must realize that audiences can easily be offended by dialect that stigmatizes a particular group.

Bodily action as a means of illustrating, emphasizing, and pantomiming incidents contributes to entertaining. Psychologists have estimated that gestures and grimaces enhance the funniness of a story by 400 per cent.[13] The test of a vaudeville performer is said to be, "Do they laugh before he opens his mouth?" Mark Twain's humor was enhanced by his expressive face; and Abraham Lincoln's manner, his neighbors said, would make a cat laugh.

Humorists agree that the right timing is essential. Mark Twain thought that the real art of telling a humorous story lay in the timing. One critic described Will Rogers:

He makes a statement, then another, then a third. All together they make perfectly good sense, and are often funny, so that your mouth widens toward a smile. Then, after the briefest pause, comes a sudden final thrust of wit which explodes the whole business as if it were gunpowder.[14]

The speaker should give some thought to the way he builds up to the point of the story; he should bring out the punch line at just the right instant—not too soon, nor too late, nor with its key words muffled. He should not try to speak while the members of the audience are laughing, but should give them an instant to enjoy themselves, and then, just before the laughter has died down completely, deliver another telling statement. Pausing for effect does much to strengthen the humor presented. You must learn by experience what sort of timing is the most effective for your own delivery.

EXERCISING GOOD JUDGMENT

The methods of wit and humor can easily get out of hand. If carried too far, they can become so absurd or so tedious that they are no longer entertaining. If the barbs are too sharp or too personal, listeners will be offended instead of entertained. If jokes and anecdotes are coarse and indecent, standards of good taste are violated and the audience is embarrassed. If amusing references to individuals and groups are inappropriate, resentment will be aroused. Efforts to evoke jollity and laughter can be self-defeating.

[13] E. E. Lange, "Statistical Studies of Crowd Laughter," quoted in Eastman, *op. cit.*, p. 110.

[14] Betty Rogers, *Will Rogers*, Indianapolis: Bobbs-Merrill Company, 1941, p. 187.

SOCIAL SPEAKING

People often gather to be entertained at luncheons, dinners, banquets, and program meetings of clubs and social organizations. The principles of entertaining through the use of interest and stimulation and wit and humor apply to social speeches on such occasions.

THE AFTER-DINNER SPEECH

After-dinner speaking is an American institution. Every metropolitan newspaper carries stories about luncheon and dinner meetings featuring prominent men and women. The combination of an enjoyable dinner, the privilege of meeting people, and the opportunity of hearing a speech is an attraction of conferences, conventions, reunions, and club meetings. If the speaker meets the demands of the occasion, his own satisfaction and that of his audience are a real reward. The lack of a fixed time limit is no reason for a speaker to assume that he may talk endlessly. Toast-masters often say, "Talk as long as you like," and, if pressed, say, "Oh, about an hour." But the speaker will do well to cut the hour to a half hour or less. The best addresses are seldom the longest.

Preparation

Experienced after-dinner speakers are aware that the introduction is a critical part of the speech. If the opening remarks fall flat, the whole speech may fail; if the introduction gains a good response, the speech is likely to succeed. The speaker should prepare the best possible introduction. He may hope that the spur of the moment will provide a better one; but if inspiration does not come, he will still be prepared. He must be alert to every incident. Specific preparation is important for the entire speech, but it is essential for the introduction.

Adaptation

For most after-dinner speeches, the audience is likely to be homogeneous: all Democrats, or all mathematics teachers, or all Norwegians. The speaker thus has many opportunities for adapting his material to his listeners. Since guests at an after-dinner meeting of a professional group, a political organization, or a service club are likely to know one another, the speaker often treats a topic with an intimacy that would be out of place among strangers. He thinks of himself as holding a conversation with his friends and reminds them of their common experiences in a way that spreads good humor and good fellowship. He is not intimidated by the occasion, but he observes the limits of good taste. Above all, he is adaptable, both in his preparation and as he speaks.

Topics

For the student audience, topics related to student life and campus experiences provide opportunities for entertainment. Students have made effective social speeches using such titles as: "How to Succeed in Love Without Really Trying," "How I Live Without a Budget," "A Student's Difficult Decisions," "Keeping Up With the Joneses of the Campus," "The Fine Art of Bluffing," "Pulling the Wool Over the Dean's Eyes," "Beauty Queens and How They Got That Way," "College Registration: A Game of Monopoly," " 'I've Got It Made,' They Say Today," "Why Our Professors Disapprove of Us," and "The Social Consequences of Always Telling the Truth."

Function of the Toastmaster

The mood of the after-dinner occasion depends largely upon the toastmaster, whose chief duty is to make felicitous introductions designed to put the audience in the right frame of mind. Some toastmasters deviate considerably from perpendicular fact in adapting stories to the speakers of the evening. Introducing a speaker well known to be a Scotsman, one toastmaster told a good Scottish story, substituting the name of the speaker for that of the principal character. This procedure is effective when the toastmaster is clever, but it lacks originality. If the toastmaster knows the speakers well enough, he can often recall amusing experiences to tell about them, or he can make original observations that will be better received than warmed-over jokes. He should provide as much continuity as possible in his series of introductions.

The toastmaster is also responsible for holding the speakers, including himself, within reasonable time limits. Since talking overtime is unfortunately common, the program committee should fix definite limits in advance.

THE SOCIAL PROGRAM SPEECH

Some social occasions call for the program talk or the popular lecture. Both types have a wide variety of forms.

The program talk is designed to interest and stimulate an audience with material spiced with wit and humor. The principles of entertaining and informing may well be applied to an occasion that should neither encourage the superficial nor discourage the amusing. The success of the program talk depends upon how well the speaker understands the members of his audience and relates his illustrations to their interests and experience. The best-known program talks today are broadcast over radio and television. Those given by Leonard Bernstein on music and by David Brinkley on current affairs are good examples.

The lecture is adapted to audiences assembled to be informed and entertained on special topics related to the experiences of the speaker. Among the distinguished lecturers of our time are Norman Thomas, Margaret Mead, Lowell Thomas, and Bennett Cerf.

The popular lecturer has genuine problems of adaptation. He must select his material for the group he addresses; often he must adapt his introduction and his conclusion to local events. In order to hold attention throughout a long address, he must employ every means of gaining variety, vividness, and force. Slides or moving pictures may enable him to present his material more completely, clearly, and colorfully than he could possibly develop it in words alone.

CRITIQUES OF SOCIAL SPEAKING

The criteria for evaluating social speaking include the requirements for the choice of an appropriate topic, the finding, organizing, selecting, and adapting of pertinent material, the composition of a well-developed speech in language suited to the immediate audience, and the delivery of the speech with direct communication. In addition, effective social speaking requires the application of as many principles of entertaining as the subject, the audience, and the occasion will justify. The introduction and the conclusion demand high standards of resourcefulness and, if possible, cleverness on the part of the speaker.

Some of the particular questions that should be raised in evaluating social speaking are: Is the topic of the speech well chosen in reference to the purpose, the speaker, the audience, and the occasion? Is the title imaginative and provocative? Does the speaker's approach set the mood and gain the attention of the audience? Is his plan of developing the speech as effective as possible? Does his choice of material show resourcefulness and good judgment? Has he used enough principles of entertaining to accomplish his purpose? Are the principles used the best ones in the circumstances? Does the style give the light treatment necessary for the purpose of entertaining? Does the development of the speech rise to a climax of interest and stimulation or of wit and humor? Does the final impression make use of the basic principles of incongruity and the unexpected? Is the speaker's attitude appropriate for his purpose and for the occasion? Does his delivery apply the principles of good timing, good communication, and good bodily action?

10 CEREMONIAL SPEAKING: Impressing

The aim of those who praise and blame concerns honor and dishonor, and such speakers likewise subordinate the other considerations to these.

—*Aristotle*

If any speaking in modern times demands the qualities of eloquence, ceremonial speaking makes such a demand. Although this type of speaking serves the useful purpose of impressing an audience with the significance of an occasion, it also has certain aesthetic aspects that require special techniques of the speaker. Not only what is said but how it is said requires that the speaker observe all of the criteria of good taste as well as of good judgment. In ideas, language, and delivery the ceremonial speech should attain the highest standards of public address.

PRINCIPLES OF IMPRESSING

Seeking to impress requires the analysis of the topic in terms of motives, qualities, ends, and accomplishments approved by the audience. Since the speaker is to honor an individual or an institution, he directs attention toward high aspirations, worthy purposes, admirable characteristics, remarkable achievements, or beneficial influences. If he considers it necessary to attack an individual or an institution, he directs attention to whatever conduct or activities the audience will condemn as unworthy or detrimental.

WHAT AUDIENCES CONSIDER WORTHY

Members of a labor union may regard successful bargaining for higher wages as a triumph of justice; a group of industrialists may regard it as a serious threat to free enterprise. Yet both audiences would approve of national prosperity, individual courage, a high standard of living, and economic stability. Both groups could be impressed by a speech praising the fine personal qualities of a federal conciliator who had found a satisfactory solution to an industrial dispute.

The greatest error a speaker can make is to underestimate the standards of taste, conduct, and achievement held by his audience. He should base his speech on widely accepted ideals of civilization. In general, the larger the group, the more diverse will be the standards of its members. In order to impress his hearers, a speaker should know the material suitable for the purpose. This material may be classified as human ideals, cultural resources, and personal attributes.

Ideals

Human ideals have been handed down from the past or developed by comparison of the real world with the world as it might be. The ideals of the past are called traditions, and the goals of the future are called aspirations. Both are major sources of impressiveness in speaking.

Even in the modern age of rapid change, respect for tradition is strong. To many people the standard of perfection was attained in the past. On receiving an engraved reproduction of Magna Charta in 1940, as the newly elected president of the American Society of International Law, Cordell Hull spoke of the traditions represented by this first great Anglo-Saxon charter of individual rights. He said, in part:

This marvelous document of liberty is the heritage of the entire human race. It is a challenge to oppression and tyranny everywhere.

I have always envied those Englishmen who went out to Runnymede and secured from King John this great document of human liberty. If I could have been there and made my contribution as they made theirs to the welfare of all succeeding generations, to all civilization to come, I would not have exchanged that privilege for all the wealth of the Western Hemisphere today.

Too often the people of this recent generation are overlooking the fundamentals of popular government, of human rights, of liberty, of independence. That is the signal for oppressors to organize armies and navies and to seek to conquer the world and to destroy all that is worth while in the world.

Since the beginning of the World War in 1914 there has been a gradual lowering of all the standards of human conduct—political, economic, social, moral, religious. There is needed, as there has never been needed, an awakening among free people everywhere. There is needed a rebirth and a revival of these previous doctrines and ideas and principles written in this great Magna Charta.

I sometimes wonder, after twenty-five years of painful and patient observation of the gradual decline of the standards of individuals and governments in so many parts of the world, with preachers and teachers and parents and leaders of thought apparently powerless and helpless to check that trend, whether we will not have to await the return of some of those stern prophets of the ancient times, Amos and Isaiah, again to awaken in our minds and hearts a fear of God and a love of humanity.

I gladly reconsecrate myself to those principles of human rights and human liberties which marked the beginning of that greatest epoch in all the world's experience, the 500-year struggle for Anglo-Saxon liberty.[1]

Secretary Hull stresses the importance of the political tradition of the Anglo-Saxon heritage. He makes briefer reference to the ancient religious tradition of the Bible.

In eulogizing Chief Justice Charles Evans Hughes, Dr. Harry Emerson Fosdick alluded to family tradition: "His character was the product of that kind of family which God forbid America shall ever lose." [2]

The desire to improve present conditions and existing institutions is also strong. Just as some cling earnestly to the past, so others look hopefully to the future. Those who have benefited from their inheritance tend to preserve it; those who feel defrauded in their heritage tend to wish for a better tomorrow. Utopias and dream worlds are seldom realized, but they often lead to beneficial changes.

In an address delivered to the League to Enforce Peace, Woodrow Wilson gave expression to an ideal of reform when he declared that the peace of the world must henceforth depend upon a new and more wholesome diplomacy.[3] In an address before the Conference on World Tensions at the University of Chicago, Adlai E. Stevenson advocated new aspirations in place of those related to nuclear weapons and national prestige. He advocated aspirations related to projects "really relevant to our profoundest human needs." He elaborated:

They deal with the fundamentals of our living—with a surge of population, with an expansion of food, the mobilization of resources, the direction of science to creative ends, the opening of the doors of knowledge, the banishment from outer space of the petty rivalries of earthbound man, the expansion of beauty in our lives—through competing in excellence, not in tons of metal or kilowatt hours.[4]

[1] *Proceedings of the American Society of International Law*, XXXIV, Washington, 1940, pp. 10–11. Copyright 1940 by the American Society of International Law.
[2] *The New York Times*, September 1, 1948, p. 48.
[3] "First Commitment to the Idea of a League of Nations," in *Selected Literary and Political Papers and Addresses of Woodrow Wilson*, New York: Grosset & Dunlap, 1926, Vol. II, pp. 169–174.
[4] *The New York Times*, May 12, 1960, p. 8.

Resources

The chief resources of mankind are knowledge and experience. Knowledge may be described as the sum of information conserved by civilization, the accumulation upon which human advancement is grounded. The application of knowledge to problems results in experience which adds to the sum of knowledge available for the next problem. Both knowledge and experience give authority to those who possess them. Other resources of mankind such as health, wealth, power, and prestige are, for the most part, directly related to them.

That knowledge is power is an old axiom. The growing confidence in education and research is demonstrated by the steady increase in the number of college and university students and by the rapid development of research programs. The program of research in nuclear energy demonstrates the practical function of knowledge to the American public.

In an address before the Sixty-Sixth Congress of American Industry, Dr. Glenn T. Seaborg, Chairman of the Atomic Energy Commission, impressed the delegates of the National Association of Manufacturers with the urgent need for new knowledge:

> New scientific discoveries tend to render obsolete the very knowledge and techniques which lead to them. For example, infinitely more precise and sophisticated techniques of research and methods of education are required to probe the nucleus of the atom than were required to demonstrate that the uranium atom can undergo fission.
>
> Science plays no national favorites. Science will not wait for the United States if another "courts" her with greater skill and industry.[5]

The person who has become an expert through long experience in his field makes a deep impression on his listeners. Those who can say with conviction, "I know because I have tried it," gain ready credence. Most people respect the man who has seen for himself.

In addressing an audience of journalists, Mark Ethridge, Chairman of the Board of the Louisville, Kentucky, *Courier-Journal* and the *Louisville Times,* made good use of his five decades of newspaper experience in appraising the status of newspapers. Concerning their progress, he says:

> There has been, in my time, a great lift in the intellectual level of newspapers to which schools of journalism have certainly made their contribution. There has been, too, a change for the better, in the concept of their responsibility to the public. There is less cheapness, less tawdriness, less pandering to the baser emotions and fewer newspapers that do it than when I came along. There is more sober and generally more independent discussion of issues; there

[5] Quoted from a press release issued by the National Association of Manufacturers, Dec. 8, 1961.

is less blatant partisanship; there is better reporting: more background information, more reporting in depth, more interpretation of the news and more graphic aids for the reader. There is better packaging.[6]

From his experience he offers advice to schools of journalism: "I should like to see all of them recast so that the techniques of journalism become incidental and the emphasis is upon making the full man intellectually. . . ." [7]

Personal Attributes

Men have an abiding interest in their fellow men: their habits, ways, efforts, and accomplishments. The virtuous attributes suitable for a speech to impress may be called nobleness, genius, diligence, and achievement.

Nobleness of character has been extravagantly praised throughout history, possibly because men recognize their own shortcomings and admire others who do not have them. Whether a man is believed honest, dependable, courageous, generous, and thoughtful determines the esteem in which he is held. Capacity for leadership in any field of endeavor sets a man apart from his fellows. If fine traits also distinguish him, he is considered a noble character worthy of respect. Both what he says and what he does contribute to this appraisal. Degrees of nobleness are recognized. The man who fights for others is thought to be more noble than the one who fights merely for himself. The man whose benevolence is thoughtfully planned to benefit the greatest number of deserving people over the longest period of time is the most noble of benefactors. If he rises to the occasion in time of great need, he is especially worthy of praise. Before a joint session of the two houses of Congress, Dr. Edwin A. Alderman, President of the University of Virginia, delivered a memorial address in honor of Woodrow Wilson. He paid high tribute to Wilson's nobility of character. A typically impressive sentence is:

The direction of American affairs, as the Republic swept into the current of the World War, was in the hands of a liberal statesman, bred of democracy, firm of will, jealous of his country's honor, gifted with power to argue with cogency, capable of seeing far ahead of the movements of social progress, incapable of fear, unmoved by passion or greed of conquest, intent upon justice, dreaming of peace and the righting of immemorial wrongs.[8]

The person with extraordinary ability to create, organize, or bring a project to completion is praised as a genius. Although genius has been defined as the infinite capacity for taking pains, it usually suggests excep-

[6] *Vital Speeches,* XXVIII, 473–474, May 15, 1962.
[7] *Ibid.*
[8] *Woodrow Wilson: Memorial Address,* Washington: Government Printing Office, 1925, pp. 17–18.

tional intelligence, insight, and judgment as well. In the realm of art, the designation *genius* is usually reserved for poets, painters, sculptors, and musicians of talent and inspiration. Andrew Carnegie spoke in tribute to General George W. Goethals upon the completion of the Panama Canal. He said of the General:

At long intervals a man appears who has done something of unique importance in the world. Long has he been in training for the task, and the world knew it not; but now the world can never cease to know that your guest of tonight has proved himself a genius who has changed world conditions. France had undertaken the difficult task of uniting the Atlantic and Pacific oceans by a pass-way for ships upon the water. After years of labor the task was abandoned, and the long-cherished scheme seemed destined to fail. Nothing short of a genius for organization was needed. No man of that order seemed within reach. Geniuses are rare, but the choice fell upon our guest of tonight. . . .[9]

Upon a plane lower than nobility and genius, diligence commands respect. The man whose patience, persistence, and close application to his task have won him recognition in his field gains the admiration of his fellows, even though he may not have been brilliant. The one who combines nobleness and genius with diligence receives the highest approbation, as did Abraham Lincoln. Phillips Brooks, in the funeral address in Philadelphia, called attention to Lincoln's industry and understanding of labor:

We make too little always of the physical: certainly we make too little of it here if we lose out of sight the strength and muscular activity, the power of doing and enduring, which the backwoods boy inherited from generations of hard-living ancestors, and appropriated for his own by a long discipline of bodily toil. He brought to the solution of the question of labor in this country not merely a mind, but a body thoroughly in sympathy with labor, full of the culture of labor, bearing witness to the dignity and excellence of work in every muscle that work had toughened and every sense that work had made clear and true. He could not have brought the mind for his task so perfectly, unless he had first brought the body whose rugged and stubborn health was always contradicting to him the false theories of labor, and always asserting the true.[10]

What a man is capable of doing, or hopes to do, or even tries to do, is less important in the final reckoning than what he accomplishes. The results he achieves determine the estimate most people make of him. If his achievements are not only important but are also difficult of attain-

[9] Lewis Copeland, ed., *The World's Great Speeches,* Garden City: Garden City Publishing Co., 1942, p. 688.

[10] *Modern Eloquence,* New York: P. F. Collier & Son, 1936, Vol. IX, pp. 68–69. Copyright 1936, by P. F. Collier & Son.

ment, he is held in especially high esteem. Speaking in the House of Commons, Winston Churchill paid tribute to Franklin D. Roosevelt:

As the saying goes, he died in harness and we may well say in battle harness like his soldiers, sailors, and airmen who died side by side with ours and are carrying out their tasks to the end all over the world. What an enviable death was his.

He has brought his country through the worst of its perils and, happiest of all, its trials. Victory had cast its sure and steady beam upon him. He had broadened and stabilized in days of peace the foundations of American life and union. In war he had raised the strength, might and glory of a great republic to a height never attained by a nation in history. On her left hand she was leading the advance of our conquering Allied Armies into the heart of Germany. On her right hand, on the other side of the globe, she was irresistibly and swiftly breaking the power of Japan.

And all the time ships, munitions, food and supplies of every kind were on every side aiding on a gigantic scale her allies in the course of the struggle. But all this was no more than worldly power and grandeur had it not been that the causes of human freedom and social justice, to which so much of his life had been given, had added a luster quite of its own which will long be discernible among men.

. . . For us it remains only to say that in Franklin Roosevelt there died the greatest American friend we have ever known and the greatest champion of freedom who has ever brought help and comfort from the New World to the Old.[11]

WHAT AUDIENCES CONSIDER UNWORTHY

Audiences generally regard as unworthy the opposites of the ideals, resources, and attributes they consider worthy. The speech of blame shows that ideals have been forsaken, resources misused, or personal qualities perverted. An example of this type of impressing is found in Daniel Webster's prosecution in the Knapp-White murder case. A brief excerpt follows:

An aged man, without an enemy in the world, in his own house, and in his own bed, is made the victim of a butcherly murder, for mere pay. Truly, here is a new lesson for painters and poets. Whoever shall hereafter draw the portrait of murder, if he will show it as it has been exhibited, where such example was last to have been looked for, in the very bosom of our New England society, let him not give it the grim visage of Moloch, the brow knitted by revenge, the face black with settled hate, and the blood-shot eye emitting livid fires of malice. Let him draw, rather, a decorous, smooth-faced, bloodless demon; a picture in repose, rather than in action; not so much an example of

[11] A. Craig Baird, ed., *Representative American Speeches: 1944–1945,* New York: The H. W. Wilson Co., 1945, p. 173. Copyright 1945 by The H. W. Wilson Company.

human nature in its depravity, and in its paroxysms of crime, as an infernal being, a fiend, in the ordinary display and development of his character.[12]

Webster points to the dastardly violation of the ideals of New England society, the base and sordid use of knowledge and skill, and the fiendish character of the murderer. He shows how much worse the killer is than the demon portrayed by artists. With the addition of each detail the crime seems more and more horrible. To make it even more impressive, Webster continues with a vivid re-creation of the crime step by step.

ESTABLISHING A SETTING

An appropriate setting contributes to an impressive speech. Flags, uniforms, and stirring marches supply a fitting atmosphere for a patriotic ceremony; flowers, the singing of the *alma mater*, and academic robes for a college commencement; stained glass windows, organ music, and the cassocks of the clergy for a church service. Since any incongruity makes the role of the speaker more difficult, he should do all he can to assure a suitable background.

One year after Franklin Roosevelt's death, his admirers gathered at Hyde Park to pay him tribute. Surrounded by members of the Roosevelt Cabinet, of the Supreme Court, of the Senate and the House, and by ambassadors of many of the foreign countries Roosevelt had helped to liberate, President Truman dedicated the Roosevelt home as a national monument. Speaking from the spot where on four occasions his predecessor had received the election-night plaudits of his Hyde Park neighbors, Mr. Truman began:

We stand in reverence at this hallowed spot consecrated to the memory of a great American who has become a great citizen of the world. We stand here in solemn tribute. All over the globe, plain people join with leaders and statesmen in recognition that it was largely because of him that civilization has survived. Only history can do him full justice.[13]

In concluding her speech of presentation, Mrs. Roosevelt had said:

It is with pleasure that our children and I see this house dedicated to the people and opened to them. It was the people, all of the people of this country and of the world, whom my husband loved and kept constantly in his mind and heart. He would want them to enjoy themselves in these surroundings, and to draw from them rest and peace and strength, as he did all the days of his life.[14]

[12] *The Works of Daniel Webster,* Boston: Little, Brown, and Company, 1890, Vol. VI, pp. 52–53.
[13] *The New York Times,* April 13, 1946, p. 2. Copyright by *The New York Times.* Reprinted by permission.
[14] *Ibid.*

CREATING A UNIFIED PROGRAM

When arrangements permit, the choice of speakers, the atmosphere created, the preceding events, and even the order of speakers should create a unified impression. The laying of the cornerstone of the permanent Headquarters of the United Nations illustrates the effect possible with systematic planning. The choice of speakers and the climactic order of their speaking contributed greatly to the desired significance—the President of the Assembly, Brig. Gen. Carlos P. Romulo; United States Representative to the United Nations, Warren R. Austin, who was Chairman of the Headquarters Advisory Committee; Mayor of the host city, William O'Dwyer; Governor of the host state, Thomas E. Dewey; President of the host nation, Harry Truman; and Secretary General of the United Nations, Trygve Lie, who performed the ceremony of laying the cornerstone.

The day was the fourth anniversary of the United Nations Charter. Preceding events included President Truman's eight-mile tour of New York when he was warmly received by nearly a million people. The meeting was the 237th session of the General Assembly, held in a striking setting featuring the East River and the thirty-nine-story framework of the Secretariat Building in the background, before an audience of more than sixteen thousand spectators. A huge blue banner with the emblem of the United Nations formed the immediate background of the speakers. Below the dais, on which were seated speakers, special guests, and the seven vice presidents of the Assembly, the fifty-nine flags of the United Nations were ranged on either side of the speakers' stand. Long, tapering United Nations banners on eighteen tall staffs flanked the open-air Assembly. The ceremonies were broadcast to the nations of the world in twenty-six languages. The total impression created by both circumstances and speeches was that of unique importance for the future peace and security of the world.

AMPLIFICATION

Amplification, the basic principle of impressing, is the enlargement or extension of an idea. By various means, the speaker keeps an idea before his listeners until they fully appreciate its significance. If he wants to impress them with a remarkable exploit, he explains its various unusual aspects. He shows in detail what makes it remarkable; he builds up the accomplishment as worthy of recognition and praise. The specific methods of amplification include estimation, augmentation, similarity, inference, and cumulation.

Estimation

Amplification by estimation or appraisal offers several possibilities. In analyzing a man's character or his achievements, a speaker may use such categories as (1) the unique, (2) the first, (3) the difficult, (4) the unexpected, (5) the frequent, (6) the continuous, (7) the appropriate, (8) the beneficial, (9) the popular, (10) the honored, (11) the superlative, (12) the last. Other categories may be used for estimation or appraisal, but these are among the most serviceable.

The unique. A special mark of distinction is often granted to unique achievement. Whoever eulogizes Franklin D. Roosevelt will observe that he was the only president to be elected four times. To make the distinction more impressive, the speaker may remind the listeners that few presidents were ever elected to a second term and that none was ever elected to a third.

The first. Being first to achieve a distinction is almost as praiseworthy as being the only person to achieve it. Lieutenant Colonel John H. Glenn, Jr., was highly praised for being the first American astronaut to orbit the earth three times. Commander Walter M. Schirra, Jr., became the first American astronaut to orbit the earth six times, and Major L. Gordon Cooper, Jr., became the first to complete twenty-two orbits in thirty-four hours.

The difficult. Anyone who overcomes great difficulties wins admiration. General MacArthur, who held Bataan for many weeks against a greatly superior force, commanded such respect that the people of other nations, as well as his own, urged his appointment as supreme commander in the Pacific. Surmounting every obstacle, he won his way back to the Philippines, received the Japanese surrender, and eventually became the commander-in-chief of the occupation forces.

The unexpected. Unexpected or early success often calls forth praise. General Eisenhower, Supreme Commander of the Allied Expeditionary Forces, accomplished the tremendous task of welding the armies of several nations into a smooth-functioning military machine. Furthermore, he brought the war in Europe to an end more quickly than most Americans thought possible.

The frequent. The man who has triumphed not once, but repeatedly, merits commendation. For example, the playwright Tennessee Williams has written a successful Broadway play almost every year for more than twenty years. The late Sam Rayburn was repeatedly elected by the Fourth District of Texas to the House of Representatives and served in all congresses from the sixty-third to the eighty-seventh.

The continuous. Continuous service over a long period of time commands general respect, especially if the service is distinguished. When he died, at the age of ninety-four, Justice Oliver Wendell Holmes had been an outstanding jurist for more than fifty years. He was associate and later chief justice of the Supreme Court of Massachusetts before he was appointed to the Supreme Court of the United States. His service was distinguished by his liberal interpretation of the Constitution and by his lucid and succinct dissenting opinions.

The appropriate. The ability to take the right action at the right time is by no means common. Fortunately for the survival of civilization in Europe, Winston Churchill was the right kind of leader for the British people at the right time. In contrast to his predecessors, Churchill was farsighted, shrewd, tenacious, and dynamic. In England's crisis he held the British Empire to the stupendous task of turning back the Axis powers. When the British people were the sole bulwark against Hitler's might and defeat seemed inevitable, Churchill did not falter in his resolution to crush the Nazi forces.

The beneficial. The benefactor of humanity, who is often unappreciated while alive, sometimes becomes a hero to succeeding generations. Instead of pursuing the social life of Victorian England, Florence Nightingale interested herself in caring for the sick and making a thorough study of nursing at home and abroad. During the Crimean War she revolutionized deplorable methods in British army hospitals. Devoting herself completely to the task of caring for the wounded, she often stood for twenty hours without rest to supervise the care of patients under her charge. She forced the military authorities to make changes in sanitation, and succeeded in reducing the death rate phenomenally. Her tremendous effort brought on a dangerous illness, but she remained at her post. In our own time Dr. Albert Schweitzer and Dr. Tom Dooley have made reputations as self-sacrificing benefactors.

The popular. In a democracy a major test of a man's greatness is his popularity. Though the judgment of the people may not accord full justice, it is not to be ignored. Paderewski, the great pianist, received unprecedented popular applause all over the world; yet he also received praise of the critics for brilliance and originality. Not only was he an artist and composer of exceptional distinction; he was also a leading Polish patriot in both World Wars. He served for a time in 1919 as prime minister and minister of foreign affairs, and again in 1940 as president of the Polish parliament in exile. In the world of entertainment popularity is one of the essentials of stardom. The film actor Rock Hudson, the stage actress Helen Hayes, and the television showman Jack Paar won acclaim from the general public.

The honored. One measure of a man's achievement is the extent to which his career is recognized with honors. Fellowships, degrees, and honor societies in the academic world; prizes, commissions, and awards in literary and artistic circles; trophies, plaques, and cups in sports; citations, medals, and promotions in military life signify outstanding merit. A speaker paying tribute to Dr. Jonas A. Salk, distinguished physician and scientist, developer of the vaccine for immunizing against poliomyelitis, would observe that he has been the recipient of the Criss and the Lasker awards, that he has been honored by doctoral degrees from American and European universities, and that he holds fellowships in scientific organizations and memberships in honorary academic societies.

The superlative. Americans are fond of superlatives—the largest, the greatest, the best. Thomas A. Edison was given public acclaim because of the great number of his inventions and because of their usefulness in improving our ways of living. In his long career he received more than twelve hundred patents. His outstanding inventions included the phonograph, the incandescent electric lamp, the electric dynamo, the electric locomotive, a railway signal system, the forerunner of the motion-picture camera and photographic film, and receiving apparatus for radio sets. One of his discoveries made possible the electronic tube, essential for radio broadcasting, long distance telephony, sound pictures, television, the X-ray, high frequency surgery, and electronic musical instruments. For these many contributions to our scientific age he has been called the greatest technical genius who ever lived. He combined a phenomenal mind with tremendous energy, enthusiasm, and persistence. By thousands of experiments and long hours of tireless effort, he demonstrated his own definition of genius as 2 per cent inspiration and 98 per cent perspiration.

The last. The last survivor, the last representative of a group, or the last example of a class receives respect that sometimes approaches reverence. As a link with a past that cannot be restored, the last survivor captures the imagination of those who honor him. The last member of the Union Army, Albert Woolson, who died in 1956, was honored with a bronze statue on the battlefield of Gettysburg.

Augmentation

Augmentation is a means of amplification by heightening the consequence of an act or adding dignity to what might otherwise be treated as commonplace. By gradation the speaker may show the unsuspected significance of the thought, the event, or the deed. Quintilian explains the device:

. . . *augmentation* is most impressive when it lends grandeur even to comparative insignificance. This may be effected either by one step or by several, and may be carried not merely to the highest degree, but sometimes even beyond it. A single example from Cicero will suffice to illustrate all these points.

"It is a sin to bind a Roman Citizen, a crime to scourge him, little short of the most unnatural murder to put him to death; what then shall I call his crucifixion?" If he had merely been scourged, we should have had but one step, indicated by the description even of the lesser offence as a *sin,* while if he had merely been killed, we should have had several more steps; but after saying that it was "little short of the most unnatural murder to put him to death," and mentioning the worst of crimes, he adds, "What then shall I call his crucifixion?" Consequently since he had already exhausted his vocabulary of crime, words must necessarily fail him to describe something still worse.[15]

Henry Cabot Lodge used augmentation in eulogizing Theodore Roosevelt:

At the beginning, moreover, he had physical difficulties not lightly to be overcome. He was a delicate child, suffering from attacks of asthma. He was not a strong boy, was retiring, fond of books, and with an intense but solitary devotion to natural history. As his health gradually improved he became possessed by the belief, although he perhaps did not then formulate it, that in the fields of active life a man could do that which he willed to do; and this faith was with him to the end. It became very evident when he went to Harvard. He made himself an athlete by sheer hard work. Hampered by extreme nearsightedness, he became none the less a formidable boxer and an excellent shot. He stood high in scholarship, but as he worked hard, so he played hard, and was popular in the university and beloved by his friends. For a shy and delicate boy all this meant solid achievement, as well as unusual determination and force of will.[16]

A few appropriate lines from a poem or a hymn will often make a thought more impressive. President James Bryant Conant, in a baccalaureate address at Harvard University, reminded the graduates of the change in the nation. Dwelling upon the increasing indifference of Americans to the sacrifices of the grim war years, he called for a re-evaluation of American philosophy:

You gentlemen, a great majority of whom are veterans, hardly need to be reminded of the days of war. Many of you know from personal experience the uncertainties of battle; you know the terrible history of the war years and how fortunate are the people of the United States as compared with the inhabitants of countries which were once the scenes of action. You know how many "might have beens" on many fronts could have prolonged the war for years. To you the fourth stanza of the traditional Harvard Hymn may have a special meaning:

Let children learn the mighty deeds
Which God performed of old.

[15] Quintilian, *Institutio Oratoria,* with an English translation by H. E. Butler, New York: G. P. Putnam's Sons, 1921, Vol. III, p. 265. Copyright 1921 by Harvard University Press.

[16] *Modern Eloquence,* New York: P. F. Collier & Son, 1936, Vol. IX, p. 322. Copyright 1936 by P. F. Collier & Son.

Which in our younger years we saw
And which our fathers told.[17]

Historical allusion is another method of augmentation. President Conant used both allusion and quotation when he said:

"How shall we behave ourselves after such mercies?" wrote Oliver Cromwell to an Overseer of Harvard College, describing his military triumphs in Scotland. Without necessarily subscribing to seventeenth-century Puritan theology, we must feel the force of this question. In modern secular terms, we may say our responsibilities as a nation are commensurate with our good fortune; shall we prove worthy of the opportunity presented to us by the hand of fate?[18]

Augmentation may be attained in many different ways: by expanding a statement with details; by enumerating instances; by giving the testimony of those whose competence the audience recognizes; by citing apt references; by developing a striking illustration; by drawing parallels from Biblical, legal, and literary sources; by putting an idea or an act in the best or the worst possible light; by associating the theme with people or institutions approved by the listeners; by making literal or figurative comparisons.

Similarity

Similarity or dissimilarity is a common method of amplification. The speaker makes his character or institution appear to advantage by comparing or contrasting it with another that is highly regarded. Rufus Choate used this method well in eulogizing Daniel Webster. After recounting some of Webster's forensic triumphs, Choate builds up a composite impression of Webster with the implication that he combines the talents of several great men of the past:

And now, if this transcendent professional reputation were all of Mr. Webster, it might be practicable, though not easy, to find its parallel elsewhere, in our own, or in European or classical biography.

But, when you consider that, side by side with this, there was growing up that other reputation—that of the first American statesman; that, for thirty-three years, and those embracing his most herculean works at the Bar, he was engaged as a member of either House, or in the highest of the executive departments, in the conduct of the largest national affairs, in the treatment of the largest national questions, in debate with the highest abilities of American public life, conducting diplomatic intercourse in delicate relations with all manner of foreign powers, investigating whole classes of truths totally unlike the truths of the law, and resting on principles totally distinct—and that here,

[17] *Vital Speeches* XIV, 642, August 15, 1948. Copyright 1948 by City News Publishing Company.
[18] *Ibid.*

too, he was wise, safe, controlling, trusted, the foremost man; that Europe had come to see in his life a guaranty for justice, for peace, for the best hope of civilization, and America to feel surer of her glory and her safety as his great arm enfolded her—you see how rare, how solitary, almost, was the actual greatness! Who, anywhere, has won, as he had, the double fame, and worn the double wreath of Murray and Chatham, of Dunning and Fox, of Erskine and Pitt, of William Pinkney and Rufus King, in one blended and transcendent superiority? [19]

Inference

Logical sequence of ideas may be used to amplify as well as to prove. Archibald MacLeish used the method of inference in praising Wendell Willkie:

The mystery, if you wish to find a mystery, is this: that the people know this man is lost to *them;* not to his hopes or to his future or his friends but *them.* It is not of Wendell Willkie we must think but of the people if we wish to understand this.

How do the people know that he is lost to them? For this: because he trusted them and they remember. Because he trusted the people. Because he trusted the people not in a form of words, or for the length of a campaign tour, or as a part of a political strategy, but trusted them.

Because he believed literally, and word by word, and intending the meaning of each word, the great American Proposition that the people—not the American people only, but *the people*—that the people can govern themselves, and of right ought to.

Because he believed, believed literally, believed in sober earnest without reserve, that if the great American Proposition is true for part of the world it is true for all of the world. . . .[20]

S. Parkes Cadman used the method of inference in reference to Robert E. Lee:

When he died, there was an outpouring of appreciation and even of awe which few of us are permitted to receive. Since then those who had resisted him in battle were among the first to see in his symmetrical personality, and transfigured by his unselfish career, some of the noblest elements which human nature can possess. . . .[21]

Cadman implies that a man who is respected by his enemies must be an admirable character. To receive the tribute of friends is high honor, but to receive the tribute of opponents is even higher.

[19] *Modern Eloquence,* New York: P. F. Collier & Son, 1936, Vol. IX, pp. 104–105. Copyright 1936 by Little, Brown & Company.

[20] A. Craig Baird, ed., *Representative American Speeches: 1944–1945,* New York: The H. W. Wilson Co., 1945, p. 188. Copyright 1945 by The H. W. Wilson Company.

[21] *Modern Eloquence,* New York: P. F. Collier & Son, 1936, Vol. IX, p. 81. Copyright 1936 by P. F. Collier & Son.

Cumulation

Cumulation depends chiefly upon language. The speaker repeats an idea in different words and builds steadily to a climax that rises to a high point of intensity. Showing that a gift purchased by school children with their pennies means more than a gift of a wealthy benefactor, a speaker may heighten the effect by picturing the individual sacrifices of the children, in contrast to the luxury enjoyed by the benefactor. In his tribute to Charles Evans Hughes, Elihu Root makes effective use of cumulation:

> But it is not merely what Mr. Hughes has done that has shed honor upon us all, upon all of his countrymen. It is what he has stood for. He never sought an office; he never administered an office with a view to keeping it longer, or with a view to getting another. (Applause.) He never attempted to build up a personal political machine for his own aggrandizement. He never abandoned or suppressed an opinion which he thought ought to be expressed, in order to please anybody. He never hated or abused or imputed sinister motives to an adversary who differed from him. He always argued his case and never argued the merits or demerits of his adversary. . . . (Applause.) [22]

MINIMIZING

Minimizing is the opposite of amplifying. Instead of stressing the significance of achievements, it belittles them. Although this device is sometimes used in sermons and ceremonial addresses, it is employed most frequently in courts and legislatures. The methods of minimizing parallel those of amplifying, but have the opposite effect. Dr. Eliphalet Nott used the device in denouncing dueling:

> You need not be informed that it originated in a dark and barbarous age. The polished Greek knew nothing of it—the noble Roman was above it. Rome held in equal detestation the man who exposed his life unnecessarily, and him, who refused to expose it when public good required it. Her heroes were superior to private contests. They indulged no vengeance except against the enemies of their country. Their swords were not drawn unless her honor was in danger. Which honor they defended with their swords not only, but shielded with their bosoms also, and were then prodigal of their blood. [23]

TYPES OF CEREMONIAL SPEECHES

The ceremonial speaker is concerned chiefly with expressing the courtesies appropriate to an occasion and impressing the audience with the

---

[22] Willard Hayes Yeager, *Effective Speaking for Every Occasion*, New York: Prentice-Hall, Inc., 1940, p. 120.

[23] *A Discourse on the Death of General Alexander Hamilton: Delivered in the North Dutch Church of Albany, July 29, 1804*, 4th ed., Boston: 1805, pp. 6–7.

significance of certain ideas. His language should be dignified and gracious, but brief and simple. Since the major purposes of ceremonial speaking are to promote good will and to cultivate the appreciation of people, institutions, and events, ceremonial speeches may be classified into two groups: felicitative and commemorative.

FELICITATIVE ADDRESSES

Felicitative speeches may be classified into ten major groups—the introduction or installation, the welcome, the response, the farewell, the congratulation, the stimulation, the presentation, the acceptance, the commencement address, and the dedication. Each has distinctive attributes.

The Introduction or Installation

The speech of introduction should arouse the interest of the audience in the speaker and his subject and motivate the speaker to do his best. By impressing the hearers with the speaker's ability, the introducer can heighten their anticipation; by welcoming the speaker, the introducer can put him at ease. The introducer will thus need information about the speaker, the topic, the audience, and the occasion.

Since an introduction may be concerned exclusively with the speaker of the day, the first task is to find out about him. The introducer may obtain information from friends of the speaker or from the usual reference sources; or he may ask the speaker himself which of his accomplishments should be mentioned. The introduction should be so worded as to honor the speaker without embarrassing him. A thoughtful person is displeased by excessive public adulation, but he may be gratified by discerning praise. The introducer must be accurate. He must pronounce names correctly and state titles and positions exactly. He must be sure to associate names with the right places and events. He should avoid embarrassing the speaker to follow by attributing to him accomplishments and honors that belong to others.

The introducer should inform himself about the topic. He should know enough about it to avoid distortion and confusion in making a short statement. His reference should be complete, so that the speaker will not have to make corrections, and succinct, so that the speaker will not be robbed of ideas he had hoped to present.

If the occasion is the first of its kind, the introducer may dwell briefly on this fact or other outstanding features. He may point out the relation of the speaker to the occasion—the relative of a founder to the institution named in his honor, a labor leader to Labor Day, a class president to a university commencement.

A novel introduction that does not distract attention from the speaker and his subject is usually well received. An audience is pleased when the speaker finds some way to avoid the trite, "We are happy to have with us today. . . ." Introducing Roosevelt to a Los Angeles audience during the 1932 presidential campaign, Will Rogers used a novel introduction: "If this introduction lacks enthusiasm or floweriness, you must remember you're only a candidate yet. Come back as President and I'll do right by you. I'm wasting no oratory on a prospect."[24]

Sometimes the introducer installs the speaker in office. He tactfully impresses upon the newly elected officer the importance of his responsibility, and upon the organization the competence of the officer. When the speech of installation is a part of a formal ceremony, its content is prescribed by ritual or custom; otherwise it affords an opportunity for reviewing the history and traditions of the organization.

The Welcome

The address of welcome presents a visiting speaker in the best possible light. It also makes the audience eager to hear him and identifies him with the welcoming group. On behalf of the listeners, the welcomer extends hospitality to the guest. He may tell the audience and the guest interesting facts about each other; he may allude to the mutual interests of the groups concerned.

A representative from another campus, a visitor from another organization, or an official from another government is entitled to a welcome that goes beyond generalized expressions of good will. The welcome should describe the accomplishments of the visitor or of those whom he represents. Yet it should not be a mere catalogue, but rather a judicious mixture of praise and cordiality.

The Response

The response may be a prelude to another speech or the major part of a ceremonial program; but it should be well adapted to the occasion. The speaker should reply with suitable cordiality and dignity to the welcome given. An excellent speech was delivered by Lord Lothian before the Legislature of Virginia in response to a welcome by the Governor. Lord Lothian referred to many ties between himself, an Englishman, and the Virginians in his audience—that the first permanent English settlement was established only a few miles away; that the fine buildings of the nearby College of William and Mary were designed by Sir Christopher Wren; that Lady Astor, a native of Virginia, was one of his best friends. He praised the Virginians of a hundred and fifty years ago who led the Revolution, drew up the Constitution, and wrote the Federalist papers.[25]

[24] Betty Rogers, *Will Rogers*, Indianapolis: Bobbs-Merrill Company, 1941, pp. 172, 179. Copyright 1941 by the Bobbs-Merrill Company.

[25] The speech may be found in *The American Speeches of Lord Lothian*, July, 1939, to December, 1941, New York: Oxford University Press, 1941, pp. vii–ix, 64–69.

The Farewell

The speech of farewell may express appreciation for courtesies, honors, and friendships. The speaker should make his hearers regret that he is leaving and hope for his early return. If he is going as a representative, he may express appreciation for the confidence shown in him. If he is retiring from office, he may thank the audience for the help he has received and bespeak good will for his successor. When a citizen is elected to high office, he may have to leave his home; when a businessman accepts a position in a distant city, he may have to bid goodbye to his friends. Whatever the occasion, the speaker should express himself in the most felicitous language. When General of the Army Douglas MacArthur addressed the cadets of the Military Academy of West Point upon his acceptance of the Sylvanus Thayer Award for service to his nation, he closed with a sentimental farewell to his *alma mater:*

. . . the soldier above all other people prays for peace, for he must suffer and bear the deepest wounds and scars of war. But always in our ears ring the ominous words of Plato, that wisest of all philosophers: "Only the dead have seen the end of war."

The shadows are lengthening for me. The twilight is here. My days of old have vanished—tone and tint. They have gone glimmering through the dreams of things that were. Their memory is one of wondrous beauty, watered by tears and coaxed and caressed by the smiles of yesterday. I listen vainly, but with thirsty ear, for the witching melody of faint bugles blowing reveille, of far drums beating the long roll.

In my dreams I hear again the crash of guns, the rattle of musketry, the strange, mournful mutter of the battlefield. But in the evening of my memory always I come back to West Point. Always there echoes and re-echoes: Duty, honor, country.

Today marks my final roll call with you. But I want you to know that when I cross the river, my last conscious thoughts will be of the corps, and the corps, and the corps.

I bid you farewell.[26]

The Congratulation

When anyone distinguishes himself, his friends wish to honor him. A representative may be chosen to present the congratulations. The speech of congratulation should review the exploits of the guest of honor, express appreciation of his accomplishments, and praise the qualities of character that made them possible. In 1962, Lieutenant Colonel John H. Glenn, Jr., was congratulated at a joint session of Congress for his achievements in space exploration. Also in 1962, Richard Rodgers was congratu-

[26] *Vital Speeches*, XXVIII, 520–521, June 15, 1962.

lated on his sixtieth birthday for his distinguished musical productions, among the best known of which are *Oklahoma, Carousel, The King and I, South Pacific,* and *The Sound of Music.* Inventors are congratulated upon the success of their efforts; teachers upon the conclusion of a period of service; politicians upon their election to office.

The Stimulation

When an occasion requires that the speaker dwell upon the rewarding experiences of the past and the pressing needs of the future as the inspiration for continued or greater service and achievement, he delivers a speech of stimulation. As a leader with a sense of urgency and high purpose he pays tribute to his audience with full appreciation for all that has been accomplished but expresses unwillingness to believe that those who have a fine record of achievement will be content to rest on their laurels. Even greater triumphs than those of the past will be expected in the future, and those who have already demonstrated their ability and courage must be counted upon to produce even greater results for the cause they serve. This type of address may be given at a baccalaureate ceremony to stimulate graduates to exert themselves to the utmost in their chosen professions for the benefit of society: their academic distinction and specialized preparation place new responsibilities upon them for contributions to humanity. The speech of stimulation may also be given at a rally for any cause, when the speaker is chosen to give official approval for what has already been done with sincere praise for hard work, and to impress upon the audience the immediate need for further sacrifice and more devoted effort to reach the goal. The chairman of a committee of a university alumni association charged with the responsibility of raising funds for scholarships gives a speech of stimulation at a rally of his classmates.

The Presentation

In making a presentation, the speaker should bear in mind that a gift is a symbol of esteem. Whether the gift be a watch presented to an officer leaving for a new post, a family heirloom to a historical society, or an endowment for a charitable organization, the speaker may so review the accomplishments of the recipient that all concerned will renew their pride of achievement. The speaker should devote part of his address to the gift itself. He can elaborate its special worth or the unusual significance of its associations. He enhances its intrinsic value by demonstrating how highly the donors regard it. Yet the speaker should not dwell unduly upon the importance of the gift. Although he may point out appropriately what it can be expected to do for those receiving it, he should assume that they will use it to best advantage. Every presentation is unique; the speaker should magnify it. Nothing is more likely to give offense than treating the occasion perfunctorily. Its distinctive features should be pointed out—the largest group ever assembled in the community to honor a distinguished explorer, or the first convocation of the school ever to honor a student winning a scholarship to the state university. Avoiding sentimentality, flippancy, and triteness, the presentation should fit the recipient. Each year the leading scientific and professional organizations present awards for distinguished achievement. In 1961, Dr. Harold C. Urey, distinguished scientist, was one of eight Nobel Prize winners honored with a Hamilton Medal at the Alexander Hamilton Award Dinner at Columbia University.

The Acceptance

An acceptance requires of the speaker a genuine feeling of good will toward those who present the gift, as well as the skill to express his feeling graciously. One who receives a gift may praise the fine spirit of those who have presented it. By assuring them of the propriety of the gift, he will confirm their pleasure in what they have done. The speaker may dwell on the merits of the gift. If it is a symbol, he should devote a part of his speech to its symbolism. By praising the occasion, the speaker can make everyone feel its importance. He can demonstrate that the gift represents more than its intrinsic value, great though that may be. He can explain how much the occasion means now and how much more it will mean in retrospect. In accepting the first four volumes of *The Adams Papers* from Thomas Wilson, Director of the Harvard Press, President Kennedy stressed the significance of the gift and paid tribute to the Adams family for their devotion to the public interest. He complimented Thomas B. Adams, the President of the Massachusetts Historical Association and the great-great-great-grandson of John Adams, and the editor, Lyman H. Butterfield. He observed, "Four volumes out, and only eighty or a hundred more to go. Obviously, the worst is over." He concluded with praise of the Adams family:

. . . we can consider that they have bequeathed to us two extraordinary and important qualities: conscience, Puritan conscience, and courage—the courage of those who look to other days and other times.

A few days before John Adams . . . died, his fellow-townsmen of Quincy asked him to send them a toast for the Fourth of July. His response was brief but comprehensive. His toast stands both for the Adamses and for America. He recommended that the patriots of Quincy drink to a simple sentiment: independence forever.[27]

[27] *The New York Times,* October 4, 1961, p. 29. Copyright by *The New York Times.* Reprinted by permission.

The Commencement Address

The commencement address is a principal feature of graduation exercises at most schools and colleges. Usually it is partly ceremonial, in that the speaker congratulates the graduates, their parents, and their friends, and partly deliberative, in that he counsels them. Since the candidates for graduation have come to the climax of a long period of study, the speaker should make them feel the importance of their achievement. Since they are undertaking new responsibilities, he should encourage them to do their best. The speaker faces a difficult problem in adapting his remarks both to the graduates and to their well-wishers and in avoiding the clichés characteristic of these addresses. The best solution is to center the address on the graduates, to recognize their academic maturity, and to relate the subject matter to their plans. Since the members of the audience will be interested in overhearing the advice given to the graduates, a skillful speaker can adapt his ideas to include everybody present.[28]

The Dedication

The address of dedication requires gracious dignity. It should be closely related to the object of the dedication—its history, present status, and possible future. The speaker should impress his hearers with the planning, labor, or generosity required to create what is being dedicated; he should dwell on its immediate value and its future worth. His function is often to arouse his hearers. Among the best-known speeches of dedication are Webster's *Bunker Hill Oration* and Booker T. Washington's *Address at the Opening of the Atlanta Exposition.* A recent dedication of international significance occurred when President Dwight D. Eisenhower joined President Prasad of India in dedicating the first World Agricultural Fair in New Delhi.

COMMEMORATIVE SPEECHES

Commemorative speeches may be classified into two major groups: the anniversary speech and the eulogy. The former may relate to an institution or an individual, living or deceased, whereas the latter is generally devoted to a tribute to a deceased person.

Anniversary Address

The anniversary speech usually marks the founding of an institution or the birthday of an individual. Although it emphasizes a particular

---

[28] A good commencement address is that of T. F. Patton, President, Republic Steel Corporation, delivered at Ohio State University, Columbus, Ohio, December 15, 1961. *Vital Speeches*, XXVIII, 226–229, February 1, 1962.

SPEAKING IS FREQUENTLY CEREMONIAL

Dr. Ralph Bunche speaks in honor of Count Bernadotte at the Memorial Library at St. Peter, Minnesota.

time in the past, it offers the speaker an opportunity to present suggestions for the future. By praising the listeners or dwelling upon the significance of the event they are observing, he may encourage them to emulate past accomplishments. Significant anniversary addresses were given by General of the Army Douglas MacArthur in Manila, July 4, 1961, marking the fifteenth anniversary of Philippine independence from the United States; by Csanad Toth, Chairman of the Hungarian Students Association of America, at the fifth-anniversary celebration of the Hungarian Revolution in New York City, October 22, 1961; by Henry Ford II, Chairman of the Board of the Ford Motor Company, at the twentieth-anniversary dinner of the Advertising Council in New York City, January 17, 1962, on "New Directions in World Trade."

The Eulogy

In precise and felicitous language, the eulogy formally commemorates the character and services of some person, usually deceased. The speaker may give simple illustrations showing the fine qualities of the person eulogized, or dwell upon his services to others, or repeat what other people have said about him. Often the speaker reminds his hearers, in language of suitable impressiveness and appropriate style, of what they already know. In 1924, Edwin A. Alderman spoke in high praise of Woodrow Wilson before a distinguished audience at the Capitol in Washington. On February 12, 1959, Carl Sandburg, speaking before a joint session of Congress, delivered a memorable eulogy on Abraham Lincoln. On October 26, 1963, at Amherst College, President Kennedy, addressing an academic convocation paying tribute to Robert Frost, eulogized the eminent poet for his insight, his candidness, and his fidelity as an artist and as an American.

CRITIQUES FOR CEREMONIAL SPEAKING

Ceremonial speaking makes exceptional demands of the speaker, because audiences attending ceremonies expect him to use excellent judgment in what he says, distinguished style in the way he says it, and discriminating taste in his presentation. The specific occasion often determines the character of the ceremonial speech to a greater degree than it does for any other type, because every ceremonial occasion has its own traditional aspects. When the speaker finishes a ceremonial speech, his audience should feel that he has paid tribute to the individual, the organization, or the institution that the occasion honors with a treatment that is complete, appropriate, dignified, and impressive.

Some of the questions that should be raised in evaluating ceremonial speaking are: Does the speaker's approach set the mood and gain the attention of the audience? Is his plan of developing the speech directed toward making his subject as worthy of praise as possible? Does the material he uses amplify the central idea of tribute? Has he used the principle of impressing that is best suited for his purpose? Does he make use of striking imagery, appropriate allusions, fitting quotations and references, and vivid illustrations? Does his style attain simplicity, grace, dignity, variety, and power? Has he avoided the trite, the perfunctory, the insincere, the ostentatious in his composition? Has he kept in mind the tastes and sensibilities of his listeners in his presentation?

11 PROFESSIONAL SPEAKING:
Specializing and Popularizing

True eloquence does not consist in speech.
Words and phrases may be marshalled in
every way, but they cannot compass it. It
must consist in the man, in the subject, and
in the occasion.

—*Daniel Webster*

Public address is often the means of meeting responsibilities in business and the professions. Professional men and women are called upon to make speeches to their colleagues and to laymen. Although the fundamental principles of speechmaking apply to professional addresses, each occasion imposes special requirements upon the speaker. The standards for professional speaking must be high, because both the professional man's colleagues and the lay public would be pleased not only to receive his expert knowledge but also to observe unusual skill in its presentation.

CHARACTERISTICS OF PROFESSIONAL SPEAKING

Much of the time and energy of any professional man is devoted to the communication of his ideas, in large part orally, to his colleagues and to the people with whom his profession brings him into direct contact. How well he makes himself understood and how well he is able to adapt himself to the needs of his listeners determine much of his success in professional life. The professional man who cannot or who does not communicate well has a severe handicap to overcome, or to offset, in his career.

NECESSITY

If we observe any professional man in his daily activities, we must be impressed by the talking required of him—to those to whom he is responsible, to those who work with him, to those who work for him, and to those to whom his work is applied. In carrying out the responsibilities of his profession, the lawyer must talk with judges; in developing the details of his cases, he must talk with other lawyers, both in and out of the courtroom; in managing his legal affairs, he must communicate with his legal, clerical, and secretarial assistants; in serving the needs of his clients, he must talk with them to get the facts and, in court cases, to prepare them for participation in the trial. In carrying out his responsibilities, the physician talks with administrators of hospitals, officers of medical associations, and officials of the government; in diagnosis and consultation, he talks with other doctors; in carrying out the treatment of his patients, he talks with interns, nurses, clinical assistants, and secretaries; in serving his patients, he discusses their symptoms and directs their therapy. The talk of lawyers and physicians is typical of the professions.

PRACTICALITY

Society depends upon the smooth functioning of professional people. If oral communication among them, or between them and members of the community, breaks down, disorder results. If the minister fails to communicate effectively with his congregation, he may suffer personal consequences, and the members of his congregation may lose the benefit of religious guidance and the assurance of their faith. If the teacher fails to communicate, he loses status in his profession, and his students may not only be deprived of a mastery of their subject but may also be penalized in their education. If the space engineer fails to explain and to justify his expensive projects, he may lack public support for his program. The practical result of incompetence in oral communication is harm both to the professional man and to the people he serves.

SIGNIFICANCE

Progress in civilization from generation to generation and from country to country is completely dependent upon clear communication of the leaders of each profession with their fellows and with the general public. Some mechanical and agricultural skills known in ancient times have been lost because of a breakdown in communication from one generation to another. In Israel the farmer of today has been attempting to re-establish the technique of irrigation that made areas of the Middle East fertile. In order to increase their crops, the Russians have been seeking to transfer to their own country the expertness of the Iowa farmer. As the world accumulates more and more professional knowledge and skill, communication has increasing significance for the rapid development of mankind.

INHERENT QUALITY

As professions have developed, communication has become increasingly difficult. In ancient Greece every citizen placed on trial was expected to speak in his own defense. If he could not construct a good speech, he employed a speech writer to prepare one. As society has grown more complex, an expert has become necessary to plead cases in court. From the beginnings of religion, the minister has been called upon to interpret orally the teachings of his faith. And today, preaching from the pulpit is a major responsibility of his pastorate. Each profession inherently depends in some measure upon oral communication for the execution of its functions.

INDIVIDUALITY

Professional speaking presents special problems because every profession and the individuals within it speak for specific professional purposes. The civil engineer tells a city council what kind of water supply will meet its needs; the mechanical engineer tells the weapons expert what mechanism will increase the firepower of his guns; the electrical engineer tells the broadcaster what electronic device will reduce the size of the receiver; the chemical engineer tells the toy manufacturer what process he should use to produce the right plastic. Each expert must talk about his own problems to other experts and laymen in ways and in language that will accomplish his immediate purpose.

DIVERSITY

There are as many different kinds of professional speaking as there are professions, and as many applications of speaking as there are specialities within a profession. In the field of science there are physical scientists and biological scientists, and among the biological scientists there are botanists and zoologists. Among the botanists there are plant physiologists and plant pathologists. The more limited the scientist's province of knowledge, the more technical his vocabulary becomes. The proliferation of the sciences increases the diversity of professional speaking.

THREEFOLD NATURE

Professional speaking serves three major needs in our society. It enables the expert to talk directly to his fellow specialists; it enables the expert of one profession to talk to the experts of another profession; it enables the expert to talk to laymen about his professional knowledge. A psychologist reporting the results of his research to his colleagues at a professional meeting is an expert talking to his fellow specialists. In some instances the research is of interest only to a very limited professional group—for example, the clinical psychologists. A psychologist presenting the results of his investigations to a conference of semanticists is an expert of one profession talking to the experts of another profession. The psychologist interpreting his theories of mental disturbance to mothers considering the problems of their children is an expert talking to laymen. The kind of speaking required in one instance is different from that required in each of the other instances. What the expert can say to other specialists in his field is very different from what he can say to the specialists in another profession, and different from what he can say to laymen who have only a vague knowledge of his specialty and who are familiar with few, if any, of its terms. The responsibility of the professional speaker in the first instance is to add to the knowledge of his colleagues, in the second instance to apply his expert knowledge to the needs of another profession, and in the third instance to make his specialized information useful to laymen.

ADAPTABILITY

In his professional capacity, a person will find a variety of occasions for speaking to audiences of his colleagues, of laymen, or of both. To adapt his subject matter to various occasions, he should be able to select the right purpose or combination of purposes. For example, to interpret the news adequately, the newscaster must narrate and describe as he informs. Since he is expected to be objective, he should attempt persuasion only on special assignment. At a convention of broadcasters, the news commentator may be asked to speak at a business meeting during which he proposes a change of policy. This occasion calls for a persuasive speech supported by evidence. At the same convention he may be asked to speak at a dinner during which he will entertain his colleagues. At the dedication of a new broadcasting station, he may wish to impress his audience with the achievements of the leaders of the industry. On each of the occasions suggested, a professional man is speaking in his professional capacity to his colleagues, to laymen, or to both for a single purpose or a combination of purposes. Hence he must be able to adapt the subject matter of his profession as the occasion demands, to inform, to persuade, to entertain, or to impress his listeners. Adaptability is an essential characteristic of professional speaking.

DEMANDING REQUIREMENTS

The necessity for good professional speaking, its practical usefulness, its individuality, and its diversity make great demands upon the expert in communicating his information and his proposals to his colleagues and to laymen. What the speaker says, what means he employs to adapt his ideas to his listeners, what language he uses to convey his meaning, and what method of presentation he follows to hold the attention of his listeners require exact and specific application of principles. The information conveyed by the nuclear scientist to the ordnance officers of the army must make the listeners competent to deal completely with the nuclear weapons in their assignments—one to transport them, another to store them, a third to assemble them, and a fourth to fire them. In selecting the means to adapt the specialized knowledge to each of the kinds of officers with different responsibilities, the scientist will need to decide what aspects of his information are appropriate. In choosing language to convey his precise meaning, he will need to translate the terms familiar to him into those that the officers will comprehend. In developing a method of presentation that will hold the attention of his listeners, he will want to keep in mind the rate at which the officers can absorb the technical information he gives them and the variety of voice and action essential to maintain their interest. The principles of preparation and delivery for professional speaking are the same as for other kinds of discourse, but the special problems of professional men call for special treatment.

PRINCIPLES OF PROFESSIONAL SPEAKING

The specific principles of professional speaking differ from the principles of speechmaking in general, with reference to the function of the speaker and the kind of audience. A member of a profession must speak in his capacity as an expert with whatever function is appropriate for his immediate audience.

RELATION OF SPEAKER TO AUDIENCE

The expert addressing experts must function in his professional capacity and must meet the particular needs of a professional audience in the same or in a related profession. In a speech delivered to the Sales Executive Club of New York on September 11, 1962, Arthur K. Watson, President of the I.B.M. World Trade Corporation, spoke in his professional capacity and showed his understanding of the interests of a closely related group of specialists when he said:

> Today, as I have already said, these American consumer products are only moderately successful in Europe. I don't believe this, in most cases, is a question of our manufacturing costs. It's rather a question of design. Dollar for Deutschemark, feature for feature, we can build vacuum cleaners, washers and television sets that will compete with anything made in Europe. But we won't sell them probably in Europe because we're offering in some cases too many features that Europeans don't think they really need and, at this stage of their development, can't really afford. We are rarely priced out of the market, and if we lose a market, I submit that for the most part we're designed out of that market.[1]

The principles applied by the professional speaker in his analysis of the needs of an audience in a related area are illustrated in a speech delivered by Deborah Partridge Wolfe, Education Chief of the United States House of Representatives, at the Annual Leadership Conference of the Prince Hall Masons and the Order of the Eastern Star, Dillard University, New Orleans, on August 2, 1962. She declared:

> We must urge, therefore, that in our high schools greater stress be given to vocational and personal guidance which leads to diversity of occupational choice based upon the opportunity to explore a wide variety of vocations during the high school career. Our high schools would likewise need to realize that if we are to start where the learner is, we will start with young Negroes who have lived in segregated communities, attended segregated schools, segregated churches, segregated barber shops and beauty parlors, segregated movies and other places of amusement—who have not had a rich cultural experience in what we consider our western heritage and plan a curriculum which will begin with him as a learner where he is; moving him as rapidly as possible to an understanding of his role in a larger society.[2]

The professional man engaged in speaking needs to analyze himself as his audience will receive him in his capacity as an expert. He also needs to analyze his audience of fellow specialists as a group of individuals with patterns of thought and behavior conditioned by their par-

[1] *Vital Speeches,* XXIX, 16, October 15, 1962.
[2] *Vital Speeches,* XXIX, 25, October 15, 1962.

ticular experiences in their profession. Jacques Barzun, Provost and Dean of Faculties at Columbia University, addressed a Convocation of the Graduate School of Cornell University, December, 1958, on the topic "The Place and Price of Excellence." As a former dean of a graduate school, he showed his awareness of the problems and difficulties facing graduate students preparing for future careers when he began:

Although there are many subjects in which I am sure you take an interest comparable to mine, I have chosen one which (as I hope) is particularly suited to your present concerns and also to the times. You are students, presumably engaged in studying; you are graduate students, who may soon become teachers; you are parents or shortly to become parents; you are citizens, whose votes and whose taxes are being, or are going to be, solicited in the name of education. I am accordingly going to talk to you about education—or so it would seem. But as I have often said, talk about education bores me, so under guise of education I am going to talk to you about Intellect, and Intellect of the kind that is rarest and most excellent. I am going to use the facts and follies of education to talk to you about intellectual excellence.[3]

After developing the inadequacies of existing educational practices and attitudes and showing the need for paying the price of intellectual excellence, he concluded:

It is therefore not for the sake of turning out more engineers than Russia, not to manufacture as many linguists as the State Department wants, not to provide the colleges with enough teachers, it is not even to enable the du Pont Company to hire more chemists and produce the ultimate plastic which shall be food, clothing, and shelter all in one—it is not for these imperative or alluring prospects that this country must radically change its attitude toward scholastic excellence: it is simply and solely to put an end to the cruel injustice of letting rot, through protracted cowardice masquerading as kindness, the unimaginable endowments of youth and the tradition of Intellect which is their birthright.[4]

The professional man as a speaker needs to analyze an audience of laymen as a group of individuals relatively uninformed about the profession with which he is very familiar. In a speech delivered to the National Convention of the American Legion in Las Vegas, Nevada, on October 9, 1962, J. Edgar Hoover, Director of the Federal Bureau of Investigation, challenged his audience of laymen to realize their responsibility for assisting law-enforcement officers in the control of crime:

We are an idealistic Nation—a Nation ruled by laws, not by men. Yet, each year shows new record peaks of crime and lawlessness.

[3] Carroll C. Arnold, Douglas Ehninger, and John C. Gerber, *The Speaker's Resource Book*, Chicago: Scott, Foresman Company, 1961, p. 26.
[4] *Ibid.*, p. 32.

Nearly 200 years ago, Edmund Burke warned, "The only thing necessary for the triumph of evil is for good men to do nothing." How meaningful these words are today.

We have failed to meet the postwar goals which America had established for herself because the "good men" to whom Burke referred—the forces for decency in our country—have failed in many respects to live up to their duties and responsibilities. . . .

Crime and subversion are formidable problems in the United States today because, and only because, there is a dangerous flaw in our Nation's moral armor. Self-indulgence—the principle of pleasure before duty—is practiced across the length and breadth of the land. It is undermining those attributes of personal responsibility and self-discipline which are essential to our national survival. It is creating citizens who reach maturity with a warped sense of values and an undeveloped conscience.

Crime is a parasite, feeding upon public disinterest and moral lethargy. This day, more than 5,200 felonies—4 serious crimes every minute—will be committed across the United States. They will include 430 crimes of violence —murders, forcible rapes, and assaults to kill. At least 250 robberies, 10 an hour, will be recorded, as will 4,500 burglaries, major larcenies, and automobile thefts.[5]

EXPECTATIONS OF THE PROFESSIONAL AUDIENCE

An audience of his fellow experts will expect the professional man to show that he is aware of recent developments in their profession, to give them credit for being aware of these developments, to relate his findings to these new ideas wherever possible, to make significant contributions to the area he represents, to support his theory with sufficient data or demonstrations to meet their standards of research, and to clarify his conclusions in terminology common to the profession. W. B. Murphy, President of the Campbell Soup Company, in addressing the Twentieth Annual Newspaper Food Editors' Conference, shows his awareness of recent developments of interest to food editors. He contrasts the difficulties experienced by the Communists in the raising, processing, and distributing of food with the achievements of America's food industry. He points out that under our way of life the farmer, the processor, the distributor, and the food editor are seeking to serve the consumer and, in doing so, serve themselves. He supports his theme by demonstrating the contributions made by the three principal segments of the food industry; he cites statistics to show the farmer's staggering investment in specialized farm equipment and vehicles, the processor's tremendous expenditure for agricultural research, and the distributor's outstanding contribution in providing new stores and values to attract consumer buying. President

[5] *Vital Speeches,* XXIX, 98–99, December 1, 1962.

Murphy attempts to clarify his conclusions in terms familiar to his audience by referring to the complexities of the industry and the superiority of American private enterprise over Marxist centralized control.[6]

PATTERNS OF THOUGHT AND BEHAVIOR OF THE PROFESSIONAL AUDIENCE

The professional man as a speaker should recognize the peculiar characteristics of the audience of specialists. They are individuals more difficult to unify than the people in a general audience, because each has status resulting from his achievements in his field and in varying degrees each has become somewhat isolated from some of his fellow experts by the very intensity of his specialization. The status of each expert makes him highly critical and sensitive in evaluating the ideas he is asked to accept. Because specialization has been carried to such a high degree in contemporary society, no one can be sufficiently erudite in other areas of knowledge to see all of the implications and relations of new thought without systematic identification of the speaker's views with the preconceived ideas of his listeners. The vested interests of specialists frequently dominate their analysis of new proposals, and, sometimes becoming obsessed with the furthering of their own interests, they have difficulty in recognizing the goals of the profession as a whole. In seeking to retain their rights and privileges, they become partisans instead of objective listeners. At times their behavior is not at the level to be expected from highly educated and broad-minded members of a profession. The college professor addressing his colleagues on proposed reforms in the curriculum finds it necessary to keep in mind that each listener tends to react to the proposed changes in the light of the effect they may have on his subject and his department. Henry A. Murray was aware of this restrictive outlook of specialists when he addressed the Phi Beta Kappa Chapter at Harvard University in June, 1959:

I suppose that most of you, just-honored intellectuals, will necessarily be occupied for the next years in thinking in a differentiated way, thinking as specialists—as lawyers, businessmen, doctors, scientists, historians, educators. There is vigor and ample creativity involved in all of these professions. But later, if not sooner, you will be pressured from within or from without to think seriously once more about yourself and your relations with women and with men, to think personally and then impersonally, to ask yourself embarrassing questions—knowledge for what? freedom for what? existence for what?—to think, in other words, as a free-lance philosopher, or generalist, about matters of profound and superordinate concern. . . .[7]

[6] *Vital Speeches*, XXIX, 20–23, October 15, 1962.
[7] Henry A. Murray, "Beyond Yesterday's Idealisms," in William T. Hastings, ed.,

NEEDS OF THE LAY AUDIENCE

Although the expert enjoys a high degree of personal proof because of his reputation in his field, he can easily disappoint a lay audience if he does not have the dignity, the patience, the warmth, and the sympathy to appeal to his listeners. He may fail to meet the requirements of his audience if he takes too much for granted on the one hand, or if he makes his explanation too elementary on the other hand. He may leave an audience bewildered if he does not supply illustrations and applications that enable his listeners to solve their specific problems. He may cause them to be confused rather than enlightened if he fails to translate his advice from the specialized jargon of his profession into terms they can readily understand. The pediatrician who is called upon for advice to expectant mothers will be of maximum service to them if he creates a favorable personal impression with the right attitudes, if he adapts his language to their understanding, if he deals with specific problems they will face before and after childbirth. Professor Francis O. Schmitt of the Massachusetts Institute of Technology, speaking to the graduating students and their parents and friends in June, 1961, recognized the needs of the lay members of his audience when he interpreted the development of the sciences:

As a biologist I should like to consider the changes and the potentialities for change in the field of the life sciences and to attempt to give a realistic notion of the dynamics of change and its impact on man and his affairs. The last hundred years are regarded as "the Century of Physics"; the next may well be called "the Century of the Life Sciences."

The present era may be but the flowering of what history will call the 20th Century Classical Period of the life sciences. Will this be followed by revolutionary conceptual advances comparable with those of the three decades from 1895 to 1925 that shook the foundations of physics? . . .

Biologists of my generation have dealt effectively with two major problems: 1) the search for physical and mental health and the conquest of disease and aging; 2) the search for an understanding of the biochemical foundations of life. We are now beginning a third: the search for the physical basis of mind.[8]

Although not all of his terminology is familiar to the lay members of his audience, he makes his basic question concerning the future contribution of biological science clear:

To communicate with his fellows, man now transduces his thoughts to spoken or written symbols. These are reasonably satisfactory for simple mes-

Man Thinking: Representative Phi Beta Kappa Orations, 1915–1959, Ithaca, New York: Cornell University Press, 1962, p. 381. Copyright 1962 by The United Chapters of Phi Beta Kappa.

[8] *Vital Speeches,* XXVII, 726, September 15, 1961.

sages, but inadequate for conveying complex conceptual ideas, human emotion, and spirit. Will biophysical research on mind pave the way for bypassing sensory mechanisms? . . .[9]

He states very simply the benefits and the dangers of the application of scientific knowledge:

With knowledge through science comes the ability to control and conquer. The assault on malnutrition, disease, and the degenerative processes of aging has increased the life span, but resultantly is creating a population explosion that will present ethical problems of the first magnitude.

Knowledge of atomic physics leads to the possibility of liberation and control of enormous energy for peaceful purposes, but stockpiling threatens the use of weapons by men to control and conquer other men.

Knowledge of mental biophysics and biochemistry may be expected to lead to new understanding of the mechanisms underlying man's conscious, cognitive processes of learning and may lead to a new hierarchy of intelligence. Such knowledge could be used by men for the conquest and control of other men's minds. This could be the most frightful prospect of all, a living hell far worse than annihilation.[10]

In unmistakable language he presents the challenge of materialism to the status of idealism:

We can no longer be apathetic to the problem of materialism which has widely proclaimed its militant program: the conquest of men's minds. Mere shrugging off the crass aspects of materialism as contrary to an ill-defined attitude—"the democratic way of life"—will not suffice. In view of the global dangers created by science and the heightened responsibilities thereby incurred, a middle, neutral course is not possible. Needed is a positive affirmation of the world view on which we propose to meet the problem and chart our course.[11]

Dwelling on the importance of the control of ends as well as the command of means, Professor Schmitt concludes:

Our genius for efficient production of means, though dedicated to no profound end, compounds the problem and fails to offer the ingredient that will ensure true freedom.

More deep-seated than is commonly realized is the concern for security—economic, military, and most of all ideological—as a necessary guarantee of freedom. . . .

To achieve true freedom, we should be willing to subject to critical scrutiny our deepest inner aims, to refine and distill them until their essence is so clear that we can with surety bespeak them to others, and, most importantly, install them as precepts along with other values that integrate and actuate our being.

[9] *Ibid.*, 727.
[10] *Ibid.*, 727–728.
[11] *Ibid.*, 728.

To each of us as individuals comes the call for deep commitment to what we believe, to live at the level of the truth we know. May each of us be granted the needful wisdom to choose that better part that man cannot take away and that can give inner fulfillment and true freedom—freedom to mount the altar stairs of human destiny.[12]

This speech exemplifies the technique of the expert in suggesting to his lay hearers what may be the consequences and the dangers of the practical applications of research in his special field.

TYPES OF PROFESSIONAL SPEECHES

Every profession creates needs and opportunities for many types of professional speeches. So varied are these types that only the outstanding ones can be identified and discussed in a brief treatment of professional speaking, but the ones considered will be representative.

SPEECHES RELATED TO THE LAW

The practice of law requires many types of speeches. In the courtroom the lawyer speaks when he examines a witness or pleads to a jury, and the judge speaks when he charges the jury or hands down a decision. Both the lawyer and the judge carry out professional obligations when they address a meeting of a bar association. Outside the professional legal environment, the lawyer is in demand by a variety of audiences. He interprets the standards of his profession to lay groups, and speaks *pro* or *con* on the need for legal reforms. When a lawyer discusses a public policy, he combines his functions as a professional man and as a citizen relating his professional knowledge to the problems of his community, his country, and the world. The legal aspects of many public questions account in some measure for the number of lawyers in public life. Such a lawyer in public life is Charles S. Rhyne, Past President of the American Bar Association, who addressed the Conference on World Peace through the Rule of Law of the Lawyers of Asia, held in Tokyo. He spoke on "The People's Choice: World Law or World Holocaust." [13]

SPEECHES RELATED TO THE MEDICAL PROFESSION

The practice of medicine creates obligations calling for several kinds of speeches. In his office and in the hospital the physician delivers more or less informal remarks to his colleagues and to his patients. The phy-

[12] *Ibid.*, 729.
[13] *Vital Speeches*, XXVIII, 28, October 15, 1961.

sician often prepares reports on unusual cases, special research projects, or recommended practices, and presents them as papers before his medical society. He may be called upon to address the graduating class of a medical school, as was Dr. Lowell T. Coggeshall, a physician and vice president of the University of Chicago, who delivered a commencement address to the Chicago Medical School on "Government Interest in Medicine and Health: The Impact of Social Change." [14] In his community the physician may address the lay public on problems of public health and medical care. And when legislation respecting the medical profession is proposed, he may wish to express his judgment on the desirability of the proposed laws. On broad public questions, such as the dangers of nuclear fallout, the general public will expect him to employ his professional knowledge in recommending the course of action to be taken.

SPEECHES RELATED TO THE MINISTRY

The ministry requires many kinds of speeches. In the pulpit the minister conducts the ritual of the service, gives the formal prayer, and delivers his sermon. Preaching is a highly developed type of speechmaking with a long tradition. At religious conferences the minister advises his colleagues in matters of faith and of practice. In many communities he is invited to speak before lay audiences. Because of his special preparation, he is expected to be proficient in giving baccalaureate sermons, prayers at ceremonial and social occasions, and eulogies at funerals. In determining policy on such public questions as birth control, divorce, and the adoption of children, the lay public seeks the point of view of the minister. Rabbi Julius J. Nodel was invited to express his views on public problems to the 1961 Women's Forum on National Security in Washington, D.C. He spoke on "Freedom's Holy Light: Understanding America." [15]

SPEECHES RELATED TO TEACHING

In discharging the responsibilities of his profession, the teacher uses explanation, narration, and persuasion. In the classroom, from the kindergarten to the graduate seminar, he demonstrates principles, methods, and skills. He tells students the story of past civilizations, and he stimulates them to greater achievement. At academic conventions, institutes, and workshops he offers the conclusions of his research for the criticism of his colleagues. He may have an opportunity to offer advice to an audience of experts in a related field. Dr. T. Earle Johnson, a professor of speech,

[14] *Ibid.*, XXVIII, 629, August 1, 1962.
[15] *Ibid.*, XXVII, 290, March 1, 1961.

addressed The Alabama Broadcasters Association on "Excellence in Our Lives: We Must Overcome the Cult of Mediocrity." [16] Outside the classroom the teacher addresses civic groups concerning the problems of education. Citizens often expect the teacher to advise them on measures for the common good.

SPEECHES RELATED TO BUSINESS AND INDUSTRY

Speechmaking has wide scope in modern business and industry. In making decisions on policy, boards of directors listen to the speeches of their members. Foremen hear executives discuss the functioning of the plants they operate. Employees depend upon the directions of their supervisors in the performance of their daily tasks. Lines of oral communication throughout a business or an industry are essential to the efficiency and the morale of the personnel. Conferences of business and industry schedule informative and persuasive speeches concerning policies, practices, plans, and techniques affecting growth and development. A businessman may be called upon to propose a policy to an audience of experts in a specialized area of his field. Harry R. Hall, Executive Vice President of the Michigan State Chamber of Commerce, proposed a policy to the Management Conference sponsored by the Bureau of Industrial Relations of the School of Business Administration of the University of Michigan. He spoke on "The Need for Politically Sophisticated Managers: We Cannot Afford Indifference to Public Affairs." [17] The prosperity of business and industry is, in large measure, determined by contact with the general public. Since neither labor nor management can be indifferent to the public interest, their public relations have become vital. Hence the leaders of labor and industry frequently address audiences in an effort to maintain a favorable impression with the public. In modern business the man who can explain a process or persuade a group toward a course of action finds many obligations to speak in public meetings or on radio and television. Citizens expect representatives of labor and management to speak out on public policy.

SPEECHES RELATED TO AGRICULTURE

As a major aspect of the life of the country, agriculture requires many types of speeches. In some of its ramifications, agriculture requires speeches similar to those of business and industry. Farm bureaus, granges, and rural youth organizations, such as The Future Farmers of America and 4-H Clubs, devote meetings to ways and means of improving pro-

[16] *Ibid.*, XXVIII, 183, January 1, 1962.
[17] *Ibid.*, XXVIII, 51, November 1, 1961.

SPEAKING IS OFTEN PROFESSIONAL

(*Above*) Cardinal Spellman, Roman Catholic Archbishop of New York, delivers the sermon at Good Friday devotions at the Pentagon. Members of the Army chorus are in the foreground. (*Below*) Shown in this photo, taken at a meeting in Detroit, are four corporation presidents engaged in discussion: Harlow Curtice of General Motors, George Romney of American Motors, Henry Ford of the Ford Motor Company, and L. L. Colbert of the Chrysler Corporation.

duction, distribution, and income. Extension leaders, officers of organizations, and representatives of government departments address farmers on their problems. An agricultural journalist may be asked to speak to executives of other professions, as was Richard J. Babcock, President of *The Farm Journal, Inc.*, when he addressed the Niagara-Mohawk Executive Conference on "What's Really Happening in the Nation's Biggest Business: Who Will Control Farming?" [18] Leaders in agriculture accept opportunities to make known their difficulties to the general public through community discussions and radio and television broadcasts. Since the prosperity of the farmer concerns the nation, and since farmers exercise political influence out of proportion to their numbers, their views are respected in discussion and debate on public issues.

SPEECHES RELATED TO ENGINEERING

Public speaking has long been considered an essential part of the professional education of the engineer. Surveys indicate that engineers today must meet higher standards of communication than their predecessors. As engineering has developed more and more specialties—civil, mining, mechanical, electrical, chemical, aeronautical, and administrative, for example—engineers must talk to their colleagues in related fields in order to correlate their technical services. To enable industries and governmental bodies to understand engineering installations needed in their operations, engineers must explain the technical advantages of their equipment. Each branch of engineering holds conventions for reporting research. An engineer in his capacity as head of a corporation concerned with manufacturing, engineering, marketing, and finance may find occasion to address experts from business and industry on general public problems of interest to them all, as did Robert Paxton, President of the General Electric Company, an electrical engineer. He spoke to the Los Angeles Chamber of Commerce on "Toward a Better Business Climate: Lift the Level of Economic and Political Understanding of the Community." [19] Since engineering contributes to the technological advancement enjoyed by the public as new products increase the efficiency and convenience of living, public relations is a major interest of the engineer. By addressing community groups and broadcasting talks and demonstrations, he may take advantage of opportunities to keep the public informed. As the stake of the engineer in public affairs has become more important, his voice has become steadily more influential.

[18] *Ibid.*, XXVIII, 665, August 15, 1962.
[19] *Ibid.*, XXV, 307, March 1, 1959.

SPEECHES RELATED TO SCIENCE AND TECHNOLOGY

Science advances so rapidly today that concepts and terminology of a few years ago have become obsolete. Hence clear communication becomes imperative. In carrying out industrial research, scientists hold conferences to discuss needs, plans, and methods. Each separate branch of science holds its own convention to hear scientists describe new discoveries. The scientist may bring his professionalized knowledge to other professional groups, as did Dr. Glenn T. Seaborg, Chairman of the Atomic Energy Commission, who addressed the Sixty-Sixth Annual Congress of American Industry, sponsored by the National Association of Manufacturers, on the work of the Atomic Energy Commission.[20] Recent research in nuclear energy and the development of missiles has emphasized the need for scientists to popularize their knowledge. The lay public needs to hear scientists talk about their specialties in terms that the ordinary person can understand. International policy, even the likelihood of peace or war, depend on decisions grounded in scientific research and communicated to government officials and to the people who choose these officials.

SPEECHES RELATED TO NATIONAL DEFENSE

On June 6, 1962, President Kennedy, speaking as Commander-in-Chief of the Armed Forces, told the commencement audience of the United States Military Academy that "The graduates of West Point, the Naval Academy, and the Air Academy in the next ten years will have the greatest opportunity for the defense of freedom—risking their lives not as combatants but as instructors, or advisers, or as symbols of our nation's commitments." [21] He warned them that nonmilitary problems—diplomatic, political, and economic—will demand their greatest talent, training, and skill. His warning points up the need for officers of the armed services to address the men under their command, and for the personnel of specialized schools to confer, instruct, and discuss future plans for improving the efficiency of their units. Since the armed services have been greatly expanded in the last decades, their relationship to the public is much closer than it used to be. Leaders of national defense assure the citizens that their funds are being wisely spent, that their training programs are adequate and efficient, and that the defense posture is being improved. Since no public policy can be divorced from national defense, representatives of the armed services must be ready at all times to speak

[20] Press Release, December 8, 1961.
[21] *Vital Speeches*, XXVIII, 546, July 1, 1962.

on behalf of the nation. General Maxwell D. Taylor, Military Representative of President Kennedy, spoke at the Printing Week Dinner in New York City on "Our Changing Military Policy: Greater Flexibility." [22]

SPEECHES RELATED TO THE MASS MEDIA

In the history of mankind, the concept of mass media has been revolutionized several times. With the introduction of new means of communication, radio and television have transformed our ways of living. They share with the press the responsibility of disseminating news and of making known the activities of the day. Executives in journalism and broadcasting experience a need for close communication among the divisions of their media, and therefore hold frequent conferences to discuss their mutual problems and to coordinate their plans. Press associations and organizations of broadcasters hold conventions at which they hear addresses from their leaders, panel discussions on their activities, and speeches in recognition of achievements. In the practice of their profession, they inform the public in newscasts, in commentaries, in interviews, and in discussions. An editor may have an opportunity to address fellow journalists on a topic of interest to the profession. Alan Barth, editorial writer for the *Washington Post*, was invited to be the first lecturer for the Nieman Series sponsored by the Marquette University College of Journalism. His subject was "The Press as Censor of Government: Atrophy of the Editorial Page." [23] Since the business of the mass media is to keep the public informed, the journalists and broadcasters maintain close contact with the responses of the public and with any changes that occur. As they interpret their media, they correct false impressions and create favorable opinion in talks before service clubs, student assemblies, and civic groups. Legislators, statesmen, and diplomats depend upon the mass media to help the citizens understand public affairs and to gain support for their policies. The mass media thus occupy a critical position in public communication.

PROCEDURES IN PROFESSIONAL SPEAKING

The basic principles of speech preparation and delivery apply to professional speaking of expert to colleague and expert to laymen. In speeches of inquiry or advocacy, the speaker employs the principles of discussion and debate. Each kind of professional speaking involves special problems.

[22] *Ibid.*, XXVIII, 347, March 15, 1962.
[23] *Ibid.*, XXVIII, 340, March 15, 1962.

SYSTEMATIZING WHAT TO SAY

Although all professional speeches require skill in investigation, selection and organization of subject matter, some professions stress this aspect of speech preparation. Courtroom requirements place special obligations upon the legal advocate. He must carry on extensive research to find precedents and to construct a brief of argument and documented evidence presenting a solid case for his client. He needs to be competent in the testing of evidence, the analysis of argument, and the detection of fallacies. Even the attorney who does not appear in court finds the rhetorical methods of discovering and evaluating facts and opinions to be of the greatest usefulness. The minister makes a particular study of homiletics with emphasis upon the interpretation and illustration of theological texts. The businessman or the industrialist needs skill in bringing the best available statistics to the support of his thesis. Such data must not only be valid; they must also be meaningful in the speech he has to give. Speakers in other professions will discover techniques peculiar to their needs in gathering and systematizing their material.

ADAPTING MATERIAL TO THE AUDIENCE

Whenever a special set of circumstances occurs, as it does in professional speechmaking, adaptation to the audience takes on added significance. When the lawyer cross-examines, he must be able to draw from the witness the required response. In order to adapt materials to students of varying abilities, the teacher makes a special study of individual differences. In order to adapt his talk to his prospective customers, the salesman studies their habits and latent desires. When the professional man addresses a variety of groups, he must be flexible enough to adjust his subject matter to divergent audiences and occasions. To accomplish this end he must be able to analyze these audiences and occasions, to identify their interests, motives, and feelings, to establish his authority with his listeners, to suit his proofs to them, and to communicate with them.

CHOOSING LANGUAGE THAT COMMUNICATES

The difficulty sometimes experienced by the professional man is that he has much to say but does not say it in language that his listeners can follow. The engineer who explains *stress* as "mutual force or action between contiguous surfaces of bodies, due to external force, or the cohesive force or molecular resistance in a body opposing such action" will find his listeners bewildered. He must use less involved language if he is to make his concept clear to the layman. The physician who refers to a disorder of the blood as "a haemic condition" may confuse the layman. The philosopher who attempts to explain *existential* by quoting G. F. Stout, "in the *existential* proposition, 'A exists' or 'there is an A,' 'Is' or 'exists' cannot be legitimately regarded as a predicate of A," will find his audience still asking, "What does it mean?" Each profession has its own language, meaningful within the profession but obscure to laymen.

PRESENTING THE SPEECH

The standard of good delivery, requiring a full realization of meaning and a lively sense of communication with the audience, applies as completely to professional speaking as to any other kind. Some professions have developed unfortunate peculiarities of delivery to be avoided. The ministerial tune, more common a few decades ago than it is today, is still heard in some areas. The ill-trained minister substitutes a solemn sing-song for the full realization of meaning that produces good centering and phrasing. The pretentious teacher, eager to be a model of correctness for his students, accents every syllable in pronouncing his words. The overaggressive business executive, inflated with his success, delivers his words with patronizing pomposity. The ill-prepared industrial leader, called upon to address a conference, comes with a manuscript that his secretary has prepared for him and stumbles through a perfunctory reading of it. The academic scientist, enamored of his newly discovered ideas, assumes that his audience must be interested in his findings and makes no attempt to command attention. The fully competent professional man ought to know that an audience is unlikely to accommodate itself to his lack of preparation. He should be willing to present his ideas with good projection, clear articulation, a variety of tone, and animated force. He should think through his ideas with the hearers and communicate directly with them.

CRITIQUES OF PROFESSIONAL SPEAKING

Somewhat different standards will be required in evaluating professional speeches given by experts to their colleagues (who are also experts) and professional speeches given by experts to lay audiences. In both types the basic considerations will apply: How well did the speaker communicate his thoughts? How effectively did he adapt them to his listeners? To what extent did he accomplish his purpose? With reference to the first group, however, personal proof presents an important category of criticism. It raises such questions as: Did the speaker live up to his reputation as an expert? Did he contribute new ideas to his colleagues? Did he add to his prestige? With reference to the second group, one of the most important categories for criticism concerns adaptation to the audience. It raises such questions as: Did the speaker analyze his audience accurately with reference to intelligence, information, and interests? Did he choose illustrations suited to the experience of his audience? Did he express himself in language familiar to his hearers?

The professional person speaking for different purposes on different kinds of occasions will be expected to meet higher standards than some other speakers. When he delivers an after-dinner speech to his colleagues, to laymen, or to both, he will be expected to show good judgment in his use of wit and humor, good sense in satirizing aspects of his profession, and good taste in his illustrations and his language. When he presents a ceremonial address to an audience of his colleagues, or laymen, or both, he will be expected to show a fine appreciation of the mood of the occasion, distinction in thought and style, and insight in his adaptation of material to his listeners. When he participates in deliberative situations calling for public address, discussion, or debate, he will be expected to show a full understanding of the problem being considered with a clear analysis of the issues, a ready use of cogent reasoning and supporting evidence, and a dignified, self-assured, modest attitude toward his fellow participants. He will be expected to contribute intelligently to the solution of a problem or the defense of a proposal without imposing his ideas in an arrogant, condescending way.

12 DELIBERATIVE SPEAKING:
Inquiry and Advocacy

Every man who says frankly and fully what he thinks is so far doing a public service. We should be grateful to him for attacking most unsparingly our most cherished opinions.

Leslie Stephen

Americans have developed the habits of discussion and debate. In rural communities and in the great cities, people gather to discuss and to debate in person questions and propositions of common interest. In Wisconsin, dairy farmers meet to inquire, "What can we do to help ourselves decrease the cost of producing milk?" In Missouri villages, groups of citizens debate a proposition for school districting. In Los Angeles, Dallas, St. Louis, and other cities, housewives form groups to discuss the problems of the family. In every state in the union innumerable study clubs carry on organized discussion concerning such varied topics as nuclear testing, the plays of Tennessee Williams, the life of Dag Hammarskjold, and the planning for the expansion of urban communities. In legislative bodies representatives debate proposed bills after thorough discussion in committee hearings.

As everyone should know, the American habit of discussing public questions is of long standing. The New England town meeting is justly famous as an example of public discussion; but in other parts of America, albeit in somewhat different forms, discussion has been just as full, free, and vigorous as in New England. Anyone who has had occasion to consult newspapers of former days knows of countless examples.

323

Time after time—so clearly repeated in our history that it forms a pattern of activity—the American way of meeting problems has been demonstrated by the following means: (1) call a discussion group, (2) announce a public meeting, (3) appoint a committee or committees, (4) act or subside. Sometimes the problems considered have been of purely local concern—obtaining donations of books for a town library, or protesting the action of the school board in proposing a bond issue for new buildings. Sometimes the discussions have concerned matters of domestic or foreign policy—slavery, free silver, the League of Nations, or foreign aid to communist countries. Characteristically they have been initiated by the people; they have not been managed or imposed by a governmental or other outside agency. That is why an acute observer noted that public matters, undertaken in France by the government or in England by a noble lord, are undertaken in America by a committee.

The great principles of present-day life in America were once problems for inquiry by discussion and for advocacy by debate. In country store and city park, in village church and town meeting, our forefathers settled for themselves and for us whether church and state should be separate, whether a laboring man should have the right to join a union, whether public schools should be established free to all children. After discussion came debate; after debate came law; and after law came administration. We accept the institutions today with perhaps too little thought about the process that created them.

CHARACTERISTICS, TYPES, PROCEDURES, AND CRITIQUES OF INQUIRY

Discussion may be defined as "the free and unhampered consideration of a problem or problems by a cooperative group of persons talking together under the direction of one of its members." "Free and unhampered consideration" means that the group deliberates seriously, with only such self-imposed restraints as may be necessary for the conduct of the meeting. The group is not constrained, as in debate, to uphold a stand already determined, nor required, as in conference or committee, to reach a decision in a given form or at a certain time. "Problem or problems" suggests one or more questions of actual or potential concern to the group, and possibly to others. "Cooperative group of persons" does not mean a body in agreement; the members may agree to disagree. It does mean a body composed of individuals having in common the willingness to seek the answers to questions. "Talking together" implies a face-to-face meeting, with the opportunity for everyone to take a thinking and a speaking part. "Under the direction of one of its members" means that the group

DISCUSSION HELPS TO SOLVE WORLD PROBLEMS
The techniques of discussion are used by the Security Council to consider world problems.

will not be without leadership. If the leader comes from the outside, he will so orient himself with the group that the discussion can take place.

Discussion reveals, propaganda conceals, means and motive. Discussion is relatively objective and free; propaganda is owned and controlled. Discussion should aid inquiry; propaganda is designed to induce action without inquiry. Although both may be organized and both may be influential, and although they employ common media of communication, they stand at opposite ends of a line drawn to represent the possibilities of discourse.

So far as they can be measured, the results of propaganda may well be in the public interest—inducing drivers to obey traffic regulations, producing funds for a cancer hospital, or winning a war. Yet to say that propaganda is neutral, that all depends on whether the end is good or bad, is not correct. The end is tainted with the means; and the means is bad, particularly in a free society, because people grown accustomed to responding to propaganda tend to lose the habit of critical inquiry. The remedy for propaganda is discussion.

This definition of discussion is intended to exclude informal conversation, public address, debate, and conference or committee sessions, and to include such forms as the group discussion, the panel, the symposium, and the lecture forum. Whereas the primary purpose of the debater is advocacy and that of the conferee is decision, the primary purpose of the participant in discussion is inquiry. At times advocacy may accompany and decisions may follow discussion, but the distinctive central tendency and purpose remain. An observation of practice will clarify the definition:

In an American town some citizens conceive the idea that a community building for civic enterprises and public functions would be an asset. They ask the postmaster, a popular citizen, to bring together a group of men and women for a discussion. The members of the group approve the idea and wish to have it considered by the entire community. They call a public meeting, where they discover that constructing the building would require raising the local tax rate. Loud objections are heard in some quarters. The consensus of the public meeting is that the whole question should be referred to a conference committee instructed to study the question and to report to a second public meeting. The committee reports in favor of constructing the building and of holding an election to raise the tax levy, but the opposition is unconvinced. An election is scheduled; public addresses are made for and against the proposal; debates take place, with some citizens taking the affirmative and others the negative.

CHARACTERISTICS OF INQUIRY

The habit of public discussion is one of the most important facts about America. In a free society the right practice of discussion unifies rather than divides a people. The spirit of confidence engendered by the freedom to talk things over, as well as the lessons learned in the process, accounts in part for the tremendous productive capacity of the American people and for their ability, in time of stress, to meet the attack of other nations supposed to be better organized.

Freedom

To deny that discussion in America is free is merely to quibble. Limits, differently construed and exercised by public opinion in various parts of the country, restrict its practice; but no society has ever accepted discussion more widely and freely as a part of the life of the whole people. In America, discussion is not managed by a Bureau of Public Enlightenment. It is not tolerated by a benevolent dictator. It is taken for granted. Citizens are assured of the right, perhaps the obligation, to consider on their own initiative any matter touching their own or the public interest. Ignorance, prejudice, ugly passions, and vested interest obstruct the stream of public discussion, but the basic right to assemble peaceably together, without the interference or the questionable assistance of government, is so much a part of American life that Americans have no real understanding of existence in the modern tyrannies.

For Americans, the truth about a specific issue, however firmly based on fixed principles, is a conclusion reached by groups talking together; for the subjects of a dictator, the truth is an official decree. For Americans, the truth is the survivor of many candidates for the public favor, and another candidate may be elected if need requires; for the subjects of a dictator, the truth is a policeman in uniform, and only the color of his shirt is subject to change. One way to describe democracy, as Lyman Bryson wisely observed, is to call it a system providing for the management of public business by public discussion. And discussion is also the determiner of the public business; it prepares the agenda. The great social issues of our time have arisen from the persistent talk of men and women in groups.

Function

The primary *purpose* of discussion is inquiry; the primary *function* of discussion is learning. The member of a well-conducted group has the opportunity to learn about the question, the group, the method, and himself.

The exchange of information among the informed members of a discussion group has a value proportionate to the qualified experience of the participants. Each member may learn from every other. Facts are good servants but poor masters. Facts are not useful until they are fitted together. At least as important as facts, therefore, are ideas about the question. From speculation, conjecture, and hypothesis, compounded with common sense and subjected to the critical examination of a group, value judgments are made and policies formed. Obtaining them is perhaps the major reward of discussion.

The participant in a group discussion has an opportunity—in some ways unparalleled—to learn more about other people. How do they respond to questioning? How do they react to criticism? What do they profess to believe? How do they get from premise to conclusion? What do they assume to be true? What happens to a group when problems of consequence are discussed? The answers to these questions, invaluable to the active citizen, cannot be had entirely from textbooks, from lectures, or from reflection. They can be learned only by observing people, and probably they can be learned best in group discussion. Many a public speaker would do well to stop making speeches for a while and observe discussion groups. He would learn much about the people who sit in his audiences—what they know, what they do not know, what they believe, what they like, what they dislike, what they think about strikebreakers, policemen, college professors, and public speakers.

The ability to discuss is not innate; it must be acquired, and it can be learned effectively only by participation. One of the functions of discussion, therefore, is the continued maintenance, as well as the transmission from generation to generation, of the knowledge and skills required. The techniques, apparently simple when employed by a qualified person, really demand experience and judgment. The unskilled leader, for example, is bewildered by such problems as these: How do you manage cross-talk? What do you do when members of the group engage in personalities? How do you move a discussion off dead center? When do you stop? Only experience in discussion, coupled with the desire for competence, will improve method.

Participation in discussion can be most valuable to the individual. Especially if a good critic is at hand, the benefits may include for the timid, overcoming stage fright; for the sensitive, willingness to accept criticism; for the prejudiced, a stimulation to straight thinking; for the scatterbrained, an incentive to listen intelligently and to organize thought.

The emphasis attached to different functions varies with different groups. Self-improvement may be important to students; the subject matter of discussion may be of first interest to mature men and women. Moreover, the by-products should not be overlooked—new attitudes, revised beliefs, released tensions, changed opinions, and minds opened to the searching doubts that are the beginnings of education.

Purpose

The pedant observes that the members of a discussion group are often ignorant and uninformed. Their general education is defective; their understanding is limited; their collective intelligence is low. The catchiest statement of the pedant's objection, more likely to be spoken than written, is heard now and again, "If you get a lot of ignoramuses together and let them talk, what you get is pooled ignorance." This statement flatters those who assume a superior culture. In spite of superficial cleverness, it is without merit, because it supposes participants in discussion to come largely or even exclusively from the intellectually underprivileged—whereas, in fact, discussion is practiced at all levels—and because it begs the question, "What is discussion for?" The function of discussion is learning—that is, the remedying of the state to which the pedant objects. Group discussion is a stimulant to, rather than a substi-

tute for, private study. To object to discussion because it pools ignorance
is no more reasonable than to object to hospitals because they pool sickness.

Goal

The specialist's objection is directed typically not so much to the participants as to the goal and method. "You can't make new facts," he is
likely to say, "by sitting around a table." Or again, "Such questions should
be left to the experts who have the facts." In a complex civilization the
need for the specialist becomes obvious; and the function of the ordinary citizen, who may be a specialist in shirt sleeves, unfortunately
becomes obscure. Yet no matter how complex the social order, the citizen has his obligations and the specialist his limitations. A part of the
misunderstanding lies in the assumption that the citizen and the specialist are in competition; they are not. No one who understands discussion
would employ it to get facts ascertainable by other means. Rightly conducted, it occurs on the highest level of information available, on the
basis of facts already ascertained by specialists. One way to describe
discussion is to say that it projects the spirit of science into places where
science cannot, or will not, go—into the realm of ethics, judgments, and
conscience.

Questions arising outside the realm of science cannot be ignored.
As a scientist declared, "The most important event in all natural history
was the birth of conscience in man." The plain citizen is often assigned
the disagreeable and perplexing tasks that the specialist has the opportunity to decline. The tasks are not always academic or merely specula-
tive. To that combination of discussion group, committee meeting, and
debating society called the jury in Anglo-American countries is put one
of the most fateful questions that human beings have to consider: Should
the man sitting now before us be found guilty or not guilty? Doubtless
many faults can be found with the jury; but no better institution has yet
been devised for the consideration of complicated problems of value,
fact, and conscience that must somehow be resolved, not in the abstract,
but in a living society.

The conclusion of the matter is that the specialist's objection should
inspire caution; it appears to be invalid because he mistakes the purpose
and field of discussion, and because he assumes a competence in areas
where no special knowledge exists.

Discursiveness

The authoritarian objects that discussion is inefficient. It wastes time
and effort. The directive or the decree, he says, gets things done without
waste motion. Apparently, in certain short-term circumstances, the

authoritarian objection is valid. Issuing an order is quicker than holding a council of war; promulgating an edict is simpler than forming a policy. Even believers in the democratic doctrine are sometimes exasperated by its tedious processes. The great value of discussion, however, is not for the short run but for the long run. Benito Mussolini was more complimentary, as well as more factual, than he knew when he disparaged the democracies as *talking* governments. In the short-run task of keeping the trains on time, the decree may sometimes be effective, but in the long-run project of making better railroads, more productive workmen, and more competent citizens, the decree is less efficient than the discussion. The growth of conference and discussion in American industry does not result from sentimentalism. Managers have discovered that organized discussion is a better producer than executive order alone. Cooperation and participation bring more efficient production, higher wages, and greater dividends. The reasons are manifest. The man who understands his job is not just a tool; he is an intelligence. The man who believes himself to be cooperating in a larger task is not merely an intelligence; he is a force. The authoritarian objection to discussion is invalid, because it is based on too narrow a concept of efficiency.

Discipline

Those who practice discussion must be patient. Gifted persons in an average group must especially discipline themselves. Time is required to orient the group, to exchange information, to discover and comprehend points of view, and to resolve possible conflict.

Problem Solving

Some people who have been trained by debating and public speaking to look for logical analysis and close reasoning are unsympathetic to discussion because it sometimes appears to have no plan. That discussion groups react in the way most people do when faced with a problem is fairly clear—by fits and starts, illuminated with occasional flashes of insight. The thinking is problem solving rather than syllogistic.

Unpredictability

Even the most experienced leader is never sure how a given discussion will turn out. Statements concerning *discussions* are fairly safe; but a prediction about the outcomes of any single discussion is liable to error. Sometimes the most promising group performs poorly; and a less able group may respond amazingly well. Nor can group attitudes toward a question be assumed. Those who work with discussions deal in surprises.

Limitations

Enthusiasts who believe that group discussion will work miracles are mistaken. The forms of discussion are tools—ancient, tried, and trusty. In the hands of competent and honest workmen they are useful; in the hands of the incompetent or the dishonest they are useless or worse. Discussion is circumscribed by its dependence on people of varying levels of ability, by the occasional mischance that everybody leaves preparation to everybody else, by the unhappy choice of ill-advised or vaguely worded questions, and by the misconception current that it is merely a diversion for dilettantes.

Imperfection

Unscrupulous persons can bar full and free discussion, or they can twist it to their own advantage. The best insurance against fraudulent practices is the knowledge that they can be employed.

Another abuse is perhaps more common. Sometimes participants in a discussion, particularly in questions of personal concern or in matters where tensions are high, skirt the edges of a question without actually dealing with it. The participant conceals his opinions, hides his attitudes, and suppresses his judgments for fear of offending the group or making himself unpopular. Whatever the motive, the result is defeating.

TYPES OF INQUIRY

An accurate description of the types of discussion must be prefaced with the observation that variations can be created at will. In recent decades industry, government, education, and radio and television have experimented widely with forms and procedures. The types outlined here simply represent the more common molds into which practice has fallen. The most obvious division is twofold: public and private. Each of the types can be held before an open or a closed group. In practice, informal group discussion is limited to private meetings, usually with only the participants present. The panel, the symposium, and other types in which the audience may participate are necessarily public.

The Group Discussion

In the informal group discussion or round table there are, in addition to the leader, enough discussants to provide for adequate contributions. With too few members, a good interaction of ideas is impossible; with too many, confusion results. The preferred number of participants would range from four to seven, but good informal discussions may be held with as many as fifteen or as few as three. In the informal group, attempts are made to follow the problem-solving method. The discussants should cooperate courteously in reaching a solution. A member need not be formally recognized by the leader; when he has something worthwhile to say, he should contribute it. The outstanding characteristic of this type of discussion is its informality.

The Panel

The panel, an adaptation of group discussion, may be held before a closed group, such as a class or shop committee, or before a meeting open to the public. Frequently it provides for the participation of other persons after the panel members have concluded the period reserved for them. The optimum number for a panel varies from four to eight, but the number depends chiefly on whether the meeting is public or private. In a closed meeting of thirty members, for example, as many as fifteen have been used on a panel. This arrangement amounts to dividing a discussion group, with one part of the group participating, the other part observing. If the group wishes, the persons observing during the first part of the meeting may be brought into the discussion at the close. One variation is to have the observers and the panel change places during the discussion. For public meetings, especially when an audience of two hundred or more is anticipated, the panel should probably include not more than six members, who should be seated in front of the audience.

Usually members of a panel are given the opportunity to ask each other questions before the audience is invited to participate. The cross-questioning enables the members to correct their misconceptions, to verify evidence and authorities, and to pinpoint their differences in interpretation and judgment.

Inexperienced members of a panel may want to rehearse before a public meeting. Although each member of the group should be encouraged to make preparation, rehearsal is inadvisable. It robs the final presentation of its greatest asset: spontaneous, free, and challenging thought in process.

The Symposium

Each member of the symposium, usually composed of three to five participants, is an expert who presents a prepared talk on his phase of the question. In a symposium on discussion methods, for example, one speaker discussed the panel, another spoke on group discussion, and another discussed the lecture forum. In a symposium on labor legislation, speakers were selected to represent labor, management, and the public. The symposium becomes a symposium forum if it is opened to the audience after the speakers have concluded. The symposium panel, in which a panel discussion follows the symposium, is an interesting variation; and the panel discussion may be followed in turn by an open forum.

The symposium and its various derivatives are likely to encourage thoughtful preparation. An outstanding weakness of other forms of discussion is the disposition of each member to rely on the others to prepare. The symposium does not guarantee speaker preparation, but the responsibility of each participant to present the facts for his special area in the discussion induces him to do the necessary research.

The Lecture Forum

The combination of lecture and forum is now used frequently as a means of presenting information to large groups. This method is usually more successful in giving information than in gaining responses. The values of the lecture forum probably lie first in some adaptation on the part of the lecturer in anticipation of the forum to follow, and second in somewhat better listening by members of the audience in expectation of the right to participate after the lecture. Since the lecturer is not necessarily a good discussion leader, the best practice is to have the forum conducted by a leader skilled in eliciting responses from an audience. A variation of the lecture forum is the lecture panel, or the lecture panel forum. If the lecture and the panel speeches can all be kept within an hour's time, this arrangement may be more satisfactory than the lecture alone.

The Debate Forum

Strictly speaking, the debate forum is not a type of discussion, since it includes formal advocacy as well as inquiry. Yet the combination has proved stimulating when used in favorable circumstances. A debate is arranged on a question amenable both to advocacy and to inquiry. It is followed by two or three speeches presented by members of the audience. The speakers are free to say anything they wish, but a careful selection of men to be invited assures representative points of view. Following the speeches, additional members of the audience are recognized by the chairman. A simple *yes* or *no* ballot is taken on the question, "Are you in favor of the proposition before the house?" Since members of the audience merely vote their opinions on the question, the ballot is not construed as a decision on the merits of the debate forum.

In some circumstances the debate forum is an excellent device because it elicits lively and extensive audience responses. Moreover, it allows experts on a controversial question to speak freely as advocates. It tends to make delivery in debate communicative, and sets standards for argument and evidence.

Other Types

Other types of discussion are employed to meet the needs of various groups. The colloquium, an enlarged and only mildly directed conversation, is used at meetings, particularly of learned and scientific societies. The dialogue frequently is presented on the radio or on television as an interview. Public hearings, particularly those of the committees of the House and Senate, are now beginning to assume a set form and may have still greater influence on discussion in the future.

The type of discussion chosen for a program should be selected freely from all those available or, if necessary, adapted to meet the specific need. No merit inheres in any type apart from its usefulness to the immediate group concerned.

THE PROCEDURE OF INQUIRY

In one way or another all activities of the American public depend upon discussions. Past failures often have been associated either with the breakdown of discussion or with the appearance of a problem too difficult to be solved by the forms then available. The alternative to discussion apparently is decree. As John Dewey observed, the essential need of the day "is the improvement of the methods and conditions of debate, discussion, and persuasion." [1] The effective practice of discussion involves a number of considerations. The most important are the question, the leader, and the members of the group.

The Question

Good discussion begins with the selection of a good question. Choosing an excellent question depends upon seven principles that have stood the test of experience:

It should be truly interrogatory. The term *question* is sometimes used loosely to refer to a topic or a proposition, but good discussion is inquiry. "Federal World Government" is not a discussion question, nor is "Resolved: That Federal World Government Should Be Established." "What kind of international political union should be established?" is a properly worded question.

It should be either timely or timeless. Some questions are hardy perennials; they never cease to be challenging. Others must be picked up while interest is high, or else let alone. Many come from the headlines of today's newspaper.

---

[1] *The Public and Its Problems,* New York: Henry Holt & Company, Inc., 1927, p. 208.

It should be stimulating. It should provoke thought and arouse enthusiasm.

It should be discussable. If everyone has the same point of view or a full understanding of the problem, the essential reason for discussion is lacking.

It should be stated simply, fairly, and clearly. The statement should not operate against any opinions in the group.

It should be manageable. For some types of discussion, the question must be susceptible of ready division into parts. For any type, it should be important enough to encourage consideration, yet not so weighty as to discourage treatment by the group.

It should be suited to the level of the discussants. Beginners should avoid topics too abstruse for initial efforts.

Discussion questions concern fact, value, or policy. Distinguishing the characteristics of each kind requires a specific knowledge of their nature.

Questions of fact are not usually chosen for discussion: they should be submitted to objective evidence. "Is the Dow-Jones average higher today then a year ago?" "Has Indianapolis gained in population during the past decade?" "Is overweight related to longevity?" These questions cannot be discussed profitably, since available sources readily provide the answer. Sometimes, however, a question of fact involves interpretation or prediction: "What is the meaning of the election returns?" "What are the aims of the Russian government?" Such questions as these are suitable for discussion, because the answers, however involved in facts, must still be largely conjectural.

Questions of value are suitable for discussion: "Are our public schools worth what they cost?" "Is tragedy more intellectual than comedy?" "Is Rome more beautiful than Paris?" These questions bring out differences in personal preference or in standards of taste.

Questions of policy related to a course of action are generally considered to be the best questions for discussion. Questions are best worded to bring out an evaluation of alternative policies. "What should be the policy of the United States toward the European Common Market?" "What should be the policy of the United States toward nuclear testing?" "How can the liberal-arts curriculum be improved?" Questions of policy often have the merit of including questions of fact and value, and of putting them to the test of action.

As a rule, provocative issues lead to good discussion provided always that a qualified leader is in charge. If the question can be reported in the newspapers, it can safely be taken up in a public meeting. A well-conducted discussion is more likely to produce adjustment than conflict.

The Leader

The effectiveness of organized discussion depends to a great extent on the ability of the leader. He assumes the major responsibility for the meeting, but he succeeds only insofar as he is able to get others to co-operate. The leader who tries to run a one-man show does not know his job.

The qualifications for leadership vary greatly, but one general qualification seems to permit no exception: the leader must be able, by one means or another, to command respect or liking and to obtain cooperation. He will be judged on his knowledge and his personality.

The leader should understand the method of discussion, the special matter of the question, and the ways of people. His mastery of techniques, including those of speech, facilitates the processes and gives him confidence in himself. Knowing the subject matter enables him to test the accuracy of information presented and to keep the discussion moving. Understanding the ways of people permits him to create group spirit and to adjust himself to it.

The leader's understanding of the question should be lively rather than academic. The tendency to departmentalize knowledge, however useful in some circles, is not healthy for discussion. Certainly, a judicious leader will not say, "but that is an economic theory and our question is sociological, therefore we shall pass on. . . ." The leader should have had his knowledge long enough for the labels and price tags to be removed.

The understanding of people cannot be stereotyped into a frame of "how people are supposed to act" according to the laws of psychology. The proper study of the discussion leader is the activity of flesh-and-blood folk who may or may not read books on psychology, but who believe they know what they like.

The leader is alert. He makes up his mind and, when necessary, acts quickly. Yet he exercises self-restraint at all times. He evinces not mere tolerance, but genuine respect for the personality and opinions of other people. His sense of humor is available to save a situation endangered by bad feeling. The warmth of his personality tends to make him liked. His comments on contributions are put tactfully; his suggestions for the conduct of individuals are given without asperity. He commands respect because he is objective in his judgments and impartial in his leadership. His personal integrity is above question. He is neither aggressive nor timid. The total effect of his personality inspires confidence, creates a spirit of cooperation, and stimulates open-minded inquiry.

Outstanding ability in leadership is developed by knowledge and experience. The truly excellent leader must have a liberal education of books and of life.

Successful discussions do not just happen. They are planned, and the leader is primarily responsible for the planning. The question itself should be selected by the group, but the leader must see that it is well worded and announced in ample time for study. An enterprising leader will supply a reading list, and he may distribute clippings, pamphlets, or other relevant material.

For a public discussion, the leader should be consulted about the selection of the participants. For informal group discussions, especially those conducted regularly by a class or a club, the problem is not likely to arise, since everyone will take part by arrangement.

Current practice in the making of plans for discussion is neither uniform nor consistent. An experienced discussion leader may be able to carry a well-developed pattern in mind without putting it on paper. The best practice for beginners, however, is to work out a plan in writing. It may be kept entirely for the leader's use, or presented to the group as a means of opening the discussion; but it should not be used as a blueprint to which the group must conform.

A useful plan for discussion is likely to indicate the leader's acquaintance with John Dewey's analysis of reflective thought.[2] The leader, in consultation with the discussants, should choose a method of preparation suited to the particular discussion, but the following steps in systematizing thinking are generally useful.

State the proposal clearly. In a well-conducted discussion, the chairman will present the problem or proposal at the outset. If he does not, the participants should seek it out. Thinking about an undefined proposal is inefficient.

Define the terms. "How may you and I help to improve our community?" seems fairly clear at first. Yet, in one group "you and I" was variously defined to include from two to 130 million people, and "community" was defined both as "town" and "nation."

Analyze the problem fully. What are the issues? What effects can be observed? What are the causes? The individual participant can aid the group by determining the aspects of the problem.

Evolve possible solutions. Finding the cause is not enough. Remedies should be considered.

Test the suggestions. After all the solutions have been developed, each must be tested. Some problems may have only one solution; others may have many. Before beginning to test the ideas, however, the individual should determine his standards of evaluation. He should weigh the advantages and disadvantages of each proposed solution.

2 *How We Think,* Boston: D. C. Heath and Company, 1910, p. 72.

Arrive at a conclusion. The discussant should reach a conclusion he can defend, but he should realize that evidence presented by other discussants may require him to modify his conclusion.

Consider the means of putting the conclusion into operation. Most discussants will be interested in knowing the practical applications of any plan proposed.

Review the probable consequences of putting the proposal into effect. Practical people will want to know the probable effect of a proposal. Specifically, they may inquire whether it is likely to initiate new benefits or unsuspected evils.

The use of these steps should help to insure a comprehensive discussion. Improperly used, any plan tends to create artificiality and to discourage genuine interchange of ideas.

The responsibility of the leader extends to the details of the hall or meeting room, to the seating and equipment, and to the time limits. In large gatherings or in regularly established forums, the leader delegates responsibility to qualified persons. In smaller, less organized groups he may need to make sure that details are well managed. If the discussion does not go well, the leader is blamed.

Before the meeting opens, the leader should welcome the members of the group and introduce them to one another. He should start promptly. His duties thereafter depend upon the type of discussion, the kind of audience, and the purpose of the group. In a public meeting he will present the members of the panel or symposium to the audience, setting an example of tact and brevity with his introduction. In an informal group discussion, the leader may begin by a short analysis of the question or a thought-provoking statement. He may conclude his introduction with a question or comment likely to evoke an immediate response from one or more members of the group. From time to time, the leader should provide running summaries that make transitions from point to point, integrate contributions by the members, remind the group of the question originally undertaken, or assess the progress made toward a conclusion. Although the goal of group discussion is often a common understanding of points of view rather than unanimity, most groups like to have running summaries indicating consensus or variations therefrom. The responsibilities of a leader during the progress of a discussion, like those of a fire chief at a conflagration, are many and varied. His task is to do whatever is necessary to keep the discussion moving intelligently in the direction of problem solving or group understanding of the difficulty. Observation indicates that successful discussions are most likely to occur when the members lose themselves almost completely in the question without looking too much backward or forward, while at the same time the leader constantly remembers what has occurred and keeps in mind alternative possibilities of what may yet happen. The leader's responsibility differs from that of the other members of the group in this respect: he must always keep in view the whole movement of the discussion.

Moment-by-moment direction, the most obvious of the leader's duties, requires constant attention. He must subordinate his own point of view without abdicating his position as leader. Given a choice between contributing a salient fact himself or drawing it from a member of the group, he tries always to get it from the member. Only as a last resort, if no member of the group will do it, should the leader contribute to the body of the discussion. Yet he may talk a great deal more than he or the group realizes, provided the talk is stimulating or provocative. He will not withhold useful information out of undue respect to rule. In presenting a necessary fact, he should associate it, if possible, with a previous contribution—for example, "But wouldn't Henry's conclusion be modified by the data from *The Congressional Record?*"

In the moment-by-moment direction the leader is neither dictator nor servant. He has the status of friend and guide, not unlike that of the woodsman who conducts hunters through the forests. On occasion he draws out the timid or controls the aggressive. He maintains a balance in contributions from members, repeats varying points of view, and endeavors to give everyone a hearing.

Opinions differ about pacing. Public discussions, especially those broadcast, must maintain a lively movement to hold their audience, but private discussions may have some liberty. In intimate groups the moment of silence is understood as a period of reflection; it may occur after the statement of a paradox or the discovery of a striking inconsistency. No one wishes to talk until he has reoriented himself. To one learning to lead discussion, such silence may be distressing, but a moment's waiting will usually relieve it.

The leader must sometimes intervene to prevent cross-talk—that is, a more or less private interchange between two members who threaten to monopolize the discussion. "That's an interesting difference of opinion," he may say, "but Harvey seems to have another point of view. How about it, Harvey?" Sometimes he must rescue the discussion from a single talkative member who tends to make it a monologue. Breaking in while the talkative one catches a breath, the leader says, for example, "You have a point there, but now we would like to hear what Helen thinks about it."

During the discussion a responsible leader is constantly on guard to check the validity of the evidence. If questionable evidence is introduced, he should wait for it to be challenged by some member of the group. If no member responds, the leader may say, for example, "Robert, do those figures on total tonnage check with the annual report?"

The leader should decide when to quit; a discussion should be completed, but never allowed to die a lingering death. The group should leave thinking, "I'm sorry it's over so soon," rather than saying, "I thought it would never end." While the discussion is still vigorous, the leader should offer a final summary and close the meeting.

The conclusion may be a brief review of the discussion, a critical analysis of differences of opinion, or a restatement of the basic points of view. Some discussions conclude with a vote, but a vote is not necessary.

Everyone experienced in discussion has observed certain personality types. Almost any meeting open to the public is liable to be visited by an individual with a fixed idea. The idea varies, but the individual appears always to be the same. Another recurrent type is the person who wants to use a discussion group as an audience for his own speech. Permitted to ask a question, he launches into what threatens to be a twenty-minute talk. Still another type is the simplifier: he would solve every problem by a mandate. A discussion may be frustrated by the peremptory type: with Olympian majesty he declares that the problem cannot be solved.

Sometimes the leader has to deal with bad manners or bad feeling between members of the group. No amount of advice in handling such questions can substitute for good common sense supplemented by observation and experience. All types of personality problems must be met with tact, firmness, dignity, and patience.

Following a lively discussion, the group may break up into smaller units and continue to discuss the matter at issue. The leader may join one of these groups to learn what elements of the discussion were most interesting.

A current practice is the recording of the discussion, with possibly an immediate playback before the group. This practice sometimes has a chastening effect on overconfident members. Objective listening following active participation is one of the best ways to study the discussion process.

Some groups designate one of their number as an official listener. He does not take part, but observes all that goes on. The purpose is to give the chosen member an opportunity to study the discussion in action. He may be called upon later to report what he has seen and heard.

The enterprising leader is wise to make a checklist for self-questioning. The list should be derived from his qualifications and duties.

The Member

The qualifications of a leader are desirable for every member of the group. The difference in duties and responsibilities of leader and member, however, suggest somewhat different emphasis and application.

The member should know both the general method and the spirit of discussion, as well as the customs acceptable to the group in which he is participating. Procedure varies in different types of discussion, but certain basic attitudes and practices are observed in every type.

Avoid digressing from the main line in order to tell a story or make a remark amusing to you but possibly distracting to the group. Ask yourself how you can contribute to the central idea.

Discussion is not merely an intellectual exercise in which emotion is entirely sublimated. For most Americans a question unworthy of feeling is unworthy of discussion. Emotional attitudes toward a question or toward another member of the group, however, should be under control. Restrained emotion is a powerful factor in motivating and maintaining discussion, but emotional tensions used unwisely harm the individual, the group, and the ideas presented. The foregoing observation is by no means a suggestion that emotion is to be avoided. Discussion is often involved in conflict that is better exposed than concealed. A forceful statement of a position with direct and accurate description of a contrary point of view is certainly legitimate and often helpful; it clears the air. The problem is not so much of words as of manner. Given the right inflection, almost any term may suggest liking or respect. "When you call me that, smile," said Owen Wister's Virginian.

Different groups approve different traits. The quickness of decision that might appeal to a sales conference would be offensive in a group discussion. Such traits as courage, geniality, self-control, and respect for others, however, are generally appealing. The initial estimate of an individual is often formed from his posture, walk, or handshake. Dress and manners should be appropriate to the occasion.

Comprehensive knowledge of the subject is just as necessary for the members of a discussion as for the leader. The give and take of questions and comments exposes superficiality, guesswork, and bluffing. On the other hand, the discussant should not make a display of his knowledge. The group may prefer conciseness to a lengthy statement of proof. Knowledge is well used in answering questions, in alluding to timely examples, in quoting authorities, and in asking intelligent questions. Knowledge is especially well used in recalling significant aspects of the subject that have been overlooked or in citing facts and figures when the group requests them. If the discussion reaches the point that other persons ask you for information and opinions, you begin to be influential if you can give the answers.

"I do not know" is better than bluffing, even though it may weaken a discussant's influence; an apologetic "I had a reference on that point, but I lost it" is better omitted entirely. Inaccuracy and falsehood are even more disastrous; understatement makes a better impression than overstatement. Frankness will usually command the respect it deserves.

Some men know the facts but fail to organize them well. The man who explains clearly and gives pertinent illustrations is respected more than the one who presents his ideas incoherently. The respect accorded him is just, for he has mastered knowledge as well as accumulated it.

The participant who has nothing to say and the one who talks at every opportunity fail to cooperate in a discussion as they should. The garrulous one incurs so much resistance that his ideas are discounted. The participant who is too glib arouses the suspicion of the group because he has an answer for everything.

The outstanding discussant makes contributions characterized by quality, not quantity. He thinks before speaking; his contributions are concise and to the point. His well-considered and penetrating observations influence the thinking of the other participants. He judges rightly when to offer extended remarks and when to limit himself to brief and informal comment.

Discussants form opinions early. They decide that one member is dull and uninteresting; that another is tedious and scatterbrained; that still another is tricky and impetuous. On the other hand, they discover that one of their number is clearheaded and discriminating and that another is seriously trying to focus the thinking of the group on a practical solution. Such impressions are more easily created than changed.

Discussants respond favorably to humor when it is appropriate and in good taste. The right sort of humor is helpful, particularly in resolving conflict. Benjamin Franklin, one of the most successful conferees in the history of diplomacy, was a master of humor.

Dogmatism reduces personal effectiveness. The discussant must listen to learn, not to refute; he must endeavor to show what his proposal has in common with the proposals of others; he must try to make friends, not antagonists. If his suggestions are criticized, he must exercise self-control and react intelligently. He must know when to stop pressing a point. Dropping an idea too soon may suggest weakness, but maintaining a position too long may brand him as stubborn and unreasonable. A fair interpretation of other points of view helps to win respect.

The proposal of a possible solution indicates constructive thinking. Willingness to admit error is generally accepted as a sign of fair-mindedness. "In the light of these facts, I concede that I am wrong" is usually interpreted as showing strength. Concessions may gain larger objectives beneficial to the group.

Too obvious attempts to please, however, react adversely. The individual may be regarded as unctuous or ingratiating. The group may be polite to such a person and yet hold him in low esteem.

The best contributions are timely, apt, and pertinent. They are timely, because they are made when they are needed. Early in a discussion a group might appreciate knowing how many women are enrolled in schools and colleges. Thirty minutes later the same information might be irrelevant or bothersome. The members' response must meet the current need.

The contribution should be pertinent to the discussion. Its relation to what has just been said should be either obvious or clarified. Egotistic contributors, moving away from the main line of the discussion, ignore what has been going on; sometimes they are brilliant, but more often they are merely disturbing.

Each contributor's thinking must be supported by clear exposition, striking examples, and evidence suitable to the occasion. He may need documents, charts, slides, pictures, and samples. Demonstrations clarify explanations.

Participants should study their fellow discussants. What are their interests, known and secret? What are their pet ideas? Who will be friendly, disinterested, neutral, antagonistic? What motives control their thinking? Governments often brief their diplomats with information concerning the habits, prejudices, and peculiarities of the men they will meet. Age, sex, race, political affiliation, occupation, geographic background, religion, education, and income level are among the factors that influence thinking. Advance knowledge concerning the participants aids in predicting their habits of thought.

Some members are active only when they are talking. At other times, obviously bored, they relapse into absorbed or fidgety idleness. Their attitude disturbs the group and, since it is contagious, worries the leader. In discussion, most of the group is silent most of the time. If the silence of the participants is merely a vacuum, then the discussion is defeated at the outset. Every member should be an active listener, alert to the group and to the person responding at the moment.

Some good people are deterred from taking part in discussion because, as they say, "I'm not good enough" or "I'm afraid I'll show my ignorance." This attitude is encouraged by the formidable list of requirements set up in some of the manuals. If only those who have good speech, good voice, and a college education are to be permitted to take part, then the art of discussion will no longer be an instrument of the people. Habitually good speech, for example, is certainly a desirable quality for everyone; but useful discussion groups can be carried on by people who speak imperfect English. The only positive requirements for the participants in discussion are, first, intelligibility; second, ideas worth considering; and, third, willingness to cooperate.

Not only significant assertions, but also judicious questioning, is needed in a good discussion. If a discussant enables the members of a group to reach a conclusion for themselves, he makes them more confident of the policy approved; they have discovered it. Unless the question is phrased clearly, concisely, and directly, it may throw the discussion into confusion. The questioner should seek information useful to the group; he should be patient with those who disagree. He can suggest ideas to other people by using such an inquiry as "Isn't it true that the Chicago milkshed extends well into Wisconsin?"

Intelligent questioning shows respect for the opinions of others. When used in good faith, it contributes much to keeping a discussion on a high plane.

All of the efforts of discussants can be set in the right perspective if each participant shows genuine respect for himself and for others. Instead of a domineering, conceited, or patronizing attitude, the useful participant will endeavor to be modest, tolerant, and imaginative.

If the members of the group are on an equal social or professional level, and particularly if they have known each other well for a long time, formality may be out of place. The error, however, is frequently in not being formal enough. Even though the occasion may not establish precedence, young people are wise to defer to age and experience. Young and old discussants alike should remember that bluntness may offset cogent reasoning and that tactlessness may defeat a pointed illustration. They should avoid private conversation and should include the entire group in replying to a question. The ordinary courtesies expressed in the consideration of others are nowhere more persuasive than in group discussions.

Language of Inquiry

The use of effective language aids the discussant. A desirable style has clarity, conciseness, and concreteness—clarity to avoid misunderstanding, conciseness to prevent waste of time, and concreteness to make the contribution vivid.

Barbarisms, slang, and errors in grammar may suggest ignorance and incompetence; affectation, pedantry, and priggishness may suggest condescension and self-importance. The use of good colloquial speech is the mark of the effective discussant. Timely illustrations, appropriate epigrams, meaningful comparisons, and a ready vocabulary—in short, desirable qualities of style—increase the individual's usefulness in discussion.

Good discussion style has many of the characteristics of good speech composition, but it differs in one important respect: restatement and amplification, so vital to effective public address, are unnecessary and even tedious in discussion. If members desire the proof, repetition, or illustration of a point, they will ask the necessary questions. The discussant may well delete the formal introductions customary in public speaking; he must proceed without delay.

If the discussants have a similar background, vocabulary should not be a difficult problem. Colleges of agriculture, however, have advised county farm agents to choose language and illustrations familiar to rural people. Such advice is sound because the county agents are familiar with the practical aspects of farming. On the other hand, a business executive or a college president attempting to employ the vernacular of a country audience would appear condescending or ridiculous. Language should be neither bookish nor provincial.

Oral Presentation

The delivery of men accustomed to addressing large audiences needs to be modified in discussion. They should adapt themselves to the size of the room and the proximity of the group. They should not talk to ten people in a small room as if they were trying to reach five hundred in a large auditorium. Discussants should enunciate clearly enough to be easily heard. Sometimes they mumble so that their colleagues either cannot understand them or lose the force of their remarks.

Pausing between units to permit the listener to assimilate the idea is just as necessary in discussion as in other types of speaking. Continuous speech with little vocal variety is fatiguing to the hearer and therefore inefficient.

The principles of communication are indispensable to the effective discussant. Like other speakers, he must realize completely the significance of his ideas and make an earnest effort to transmit them to his group. He must also be immediately responsive to the ideas expressed by his fellows.

CRITIQUES FOR INQUIRY

The problem of evaluating discussion has two parts: (1) Do the various forms of discussion have value for society? (2) Has a specific discussion measured up to a reasonable standard of excellence?

Value of Discussion Forms

Whatever its limitations, discussion is a necessary component of a free and responsible society. The specific values of discussion, however, need not rest entirely upon assumption or even on unchecked judgment. Well-conducted researches indicate:

- that discussion does influence opinion.
- that uninfluenced judgment of a given group in matters which can be checked is better than that of the judgment of most individuals in a group.

- that right answers on questions which can be checked are more influential than wrong answers in forming a group judgment.
- that some individual members of a group will respond more accurately than the group as a whole.
- that right answers are usually more firmly held than wrong answers.
- that discussion is more effective than individual effort in exploring a field and in offering criticisms of a plan.

The evaluation of a discussion is best accomplished by a separate consideration of its phases. One method takes up four factors: location, information, cooperation, and communication:

- How well did the group locate and define the problem?
- What was the extent and usefulness of the combined information?
- How well did the group work together?
- At what level did the group employ the skills of speech and other methods of communication?

When a formal evaluation is required, it is usually made by a critic outside the group. Every member of a group, however, especially one composed of learners, should review the discussion in order to determine how well it met standards of excellence and how the problems that arose might have been better handled. The following practice, employed by some learning groups, is recommended. After concluding the discussion of the day, the group should undertake a discussion of the question, How well did our group succeed? The evaluation of the discussion should be conducted by a new leader. If well conducted as a critical analysis, it is an excellent means of improving leadership and participation, particularly when a transcription of what has just taken place is available for reference. Experience suggests that analysis by the group is markedly more effective than criticism by a judge or an instructor. It is particularly helpful in effecting behavior changes of individual members.

Plan for Evaluation

The critical analysis of a discussion may utilize the following systematic plan:

1. How well did the leader succeed in:
   a. putting the group at ease?
   b. stating the problem?
   c. initiating the discussion?
   d. eliciting responses?
   e. keeping friendly control?
   f. offering running summaries?
   g. approving responses?

    h. handling conflict?
    i. appraising the discussion?
    j. summarizing and concluding?
2. How well did individuals in the group:
    a. understand the problem?
    b. contribute information?
    c. react to criticism?
    d. give attention to others?
    e. manage ideas?
    f. show a willingness to cooperate?
3. How well did the group taken as a unit:
    a. understand the issues in the problem?
    b. possess the necessary facts?
    c. attain a group spirit?
    d. evaluate proposed solutions?
    e. achieve a conclusion of value?

The analytic process may be carried to the "why" stage in an attempt to discover reasons for certain responses by the leader, by specific individuals, or by the group. Even though he may have some difficulty in doing so, especially after a particularly lively discussion, the leader of the critical analysis must keep a line drawn between the discussion of the *original question* on the one hand, and the discussion of the *discussion* on the other.

The procedure of discussion followed by systematic evaluation should have attained three ends in the learning process: some mastery of the technique of group discussion, some increase in the understanding of a problem needing inquiry for a solution, and some ability to apply standards of evaluation in appraising the value of the discussion.

CHARACTERISTICS, TYPES, PROCEDURES, AND CRITIQUES OF ADVOCACY

To parties in conflict, advocacy offers a procedure for submitting to an audience qualified to reach a conclusion the evidence, arguments, and appeals bearing on a proposition. "Parties in conflict" refers to the individuals or groups representing two or more opinions. "A procedure" implies the following of rules established by long usage or agreement of the parties. "Audience qualified to reach a conclusion" means one or more persons to whom the evidence, argument, and appeals are addressed for the purpose of obtaining commitment. "Evidence, arguments, and appeals" includes substantive material designed to induce acceptance of beliefs by hearers. "Proposition" suggests that a previous conference will

DEMOCRATIC GOVERNMENT REQUIRES DEBATE ON PUBLIC ISSUES
The televised political debates between Kennedy and Nixon became the outstanding feature of their ardent campaign for the presidency. Future candidates will be required to meet their opponents before millions of viewers.

have formulated the indictment, resolution, motion, or bill concerning the differences admitted to exist. This definition of advocacy is intended to exclude contentiousness and mere differences of opinion.

CHARACTERISTICS

The primary purpose of advocacy is the settlement of differences or the reaching of a decision. Although its characteristics vary with the requirements of the institutions employing it, they are essential to its purpose and function. Three characteristics are common: (1) In formal debate the parties in conflict appear before each other and before the' same audience, but in other types of controversy, confrontation may or may not occur. (2) When limited, as in formal debate, time is allotted in substantially the same measure to all parties at interest. (3) The proposition, in the form of an indictment, a resolution, a proposal, a motion, or a bill, is available to all parties concerned.

Whether a speech of advocacy is a part of a formal debate or a separate public address, it is concerned with a matter of fact, a judgment of value, or a decision on a policy or a course of action. The greatest number of speeches of advocacy are concerned with propositions of policy.

Since the primary purpose of the speech of policy is to show why one proposal is superior to any other, the deliberative speaker employs assumption, inference, interpretation, and prediction. When he makes a judgment about the future, he is dealing in probabilities. "If Roosevelt is elected," said Hoover in 1932, "grass will grow in the city streets." It did not. "The German army," said Goebbels in 1941, "will spend this Christmas in Moscow." It did not. On the other hand, speakers have successfully urged their hearers to separate from the mother country, to unite under a constitution, to preserve the union, to open up the western lands, to tax incomes, and to insure security for the unemployed and the aged.

Although the speech of policy deals with probabilities, it must be grounded upon a strong foundation of fact. The speaker often has three audiences: the group in front of him, those following his address over the air, and the readers of the newspapers. Errors of fact, quickly detected by the informed members of these audiences, will be exploited by the opposition. In important campaigns, candidates engage a research staff to gather speech materials, to assist in the preparation of addresses, and to analyze the opponents' speeches.

The policy-forming speaker is an adviser who proposes a course of action. If he is running for office, he issues a platform; if he is speaking on the floor of an assembly, he predicts the results of proposed legislation. He collects testimony, statistics, and historical precedents.

The policy-forming address may censure as well as offer a constructive proposal. Speeches of censure may criticize fashion or taste, or denounce evil in an individual or a group. Only an occasion of high seriousness justifies public attack on a person or an institution, and no one should deliver such a speech unless he has thought through the issues involved and considered the probable outcome.

Three major problems confront anyone who undertakes a denunciation. He should avoid personalities, except as they can be stated within proper parliamentary form, and he must be correct in language and behavior, especially if he castigates an opponent severely. He should be certain of his facts, and he must be willing and able to document his charges. Even if no slander is involved, other people may see the matter differently. He should not overstate his case; he must not extend his charges beyond his proof.

TYPES OF ADVOCACY

In practice, institutions have modified the forms of advocacy. The four kinds of debate in current use can be designated as joint, legislative, forensic, and educational. The eight kinds of policy-forming speech-making are the nomination, the acceptance or declination, the campaign address, the inaugural, the legislative message, the keynote address, the legislative address, and the speech of public policy.

Kinds of Debate

Debating occurs in election campaigns, in lawmaking bodies, in law courts, and in educational institutions.

Joint debating. The joint debate is the argument of a proposition of interest to the public, often with a view to soliciting votes in a coming election. The evidence, arguments, and appeals of the opposing speakers are in juxtaposition. The special rules are usually agreed upon for each occasion, but they generally accord with long-established practices. In 1858 Abraham Lincoln and Stephen A. Douglas engaged in a memorable series of debates on the preservation of the Union. In 1860 Thomas Huxley engaged in a notable joint debate with Bishop Wilberforce on the question of evolution. In 1960 Richard Nixon and John F. Kennedy participated in televised debates on national policy for the sixties.

Legislative debating. A free people differ from the subjects of a dictator in their means of creating law. In ancient tyrannies, law was merely the sovereign's wishes promulgated as decrees. The modern tyrant makes a pretense of consulting the popular will, but he permits no genuine deliberation among the people or their representatives. In a free and responsible society, however, both the election of legislators and their right to debate are protected by law, by precedent, and by the public will. In the Congress, in the legislatures, and in municipal councils, debate is the American method of presenting formally to the body concerned, and often to the public as well, the evidence, the reasoning, and the appeals necessary for reaching conclusions. The ancient rules of debate are guarded in their exercise by parliamentarians. Although even the best friends of representative government are sometimes vexed at delay or abuses of privilege, Americans believe that in the long run a legislative agency, chosen by the people and free to debate proposed legislation, is the most effective guarantee against tyranny and the best way to resolve differences concerning public policy.

Forensic debating. When laws are passed, the means of dealing with violations must be established. The subjects of a tyrant may be accused of violating a law and be given summary "justice" by a bureaucrat or a member of the secret police. In a free country, charges made by the government against any citizen must be submitted to judicial process. The agent of the government comes into court like any other person and presents the indictment. The accused has the right to debate on equal terms with the agent of the government. In civil trials, a judge or jury hears debate between a plaintiff and a defendant about a disagreement they have been unable to settle out of court. The verdict rendered closes the case, subject to legal process covering error, new trial, or appeal. The judgment of the court is enforceable by the authorized agency—bailiff, constable, sheriff, or marshal.

Conflicts in society have multiplied the agencies competent to make rulings in the public interest, convenience, and necessity. The Interstate Commerce Commission and the Federal Communications Commission, as well as many other federal, state, and municipal bodies, have established practices governing counsel who appear for or against a proposed order or ruling. Groups sponsoring television quiz shows, for example, may have to prove that the public is not being deceived by "rigged programs." Counsel for telephone companies and attorneys for the opposition appear before state boards to debate an increase in rates. In administrative law, as well as in the civil and criminal codes, provision is made for the debating of substantive issues.

Moreover, private agencies in business, the professions, and public life constantly debate their own legislation under parliamentary procedure. The House of Delegates of the American Medical Association, for example, passes laws governing the affairs of the Association.

Educational debating. Throughout the western world, debate has been used from the earliest days as a method of teaching the principles of advocacy and of presenting differences of opinion. Education in the United States has followed this tradition. Beginning in the eighteenth century, students in colonial universities were required to take part in debates or disputations. Many distinguished political figures gained valuable experience as collegiate debaters, and two presidents, John Quincy Adams and Woodrow Wilson, advised debate groups on the campuses of Harvard and Princeton.

College and university debating today is largely extracurricular and intercollegiate. Representative teams hold intercollegiate debates throughout the country and occasionally abroad. During the last quarter of a century, debate tournaments have become an outstanding feature of intercollegiate debating. Many more students take part in them than could participate in single engagements; but since the tournament debate is often delivered with the judge as sole listener, it is not the equivalent of speaking before an audience. Perhaps the well-conducted tournament should be regarded as a learning exercise in certain phases of argumentation rather than as practice in genuine debating.

Modern debating in the schools takes many forms. The congress, the moot court, the cross-examination, the direct clash, and the problem-solving type are all variants of the conventional procedures.

The debaters' congress, modeled on the legislative session, permits debaters to gain experience in parliamentary debate through serving in a deliberative body. Like the tournament, the congress enables many students to take part, but the debaters in the congress form their own audience. Some observers believe, however, that the participant in the congress is insufficiently motivated to make preparation, and that, consequently, time that should be devoted to debating is spent in parliamentary management.

Speaking in moot courts modeled after the courts of law has become an important means for students in many schools and colleges of law to gain experience. Students serve as plaintiffs, defendants, attorneys, members of the jury, and functionaries of the court. Usually a member of the faculty or a practicing attorney acts as judge at the moot session.

The cross-examination debate was devised as a means of approximating more closely than does conventional collegiate debating the problems met in life outside college. The special feature of the plan is the sequence of searching questions with which the debaters test their opponents. The form of the debate has been modified in many ways, one of which is to assign twelve minutes each to the first affirmative and first negative to present their entire cases, ten minutes each to the second negative and the second affirmative for cross-examining the members who have spoken, and eight minutes each to the third negative and third affirmative for summaries.

The direct-clash debate, designed to prevent quibbling resulting from the failure of teams to agree on the meaning of a proposition, has as its special feature an initial period in which a member of each team defines and analyzes the proposition. Thereafter the debate proceeds issue by issue, each side presenting evidence and argument.

The problem-solving debate in some respects resembles the conference and the discussion. Using a question rather than a proposition, the debaters spend a major part of their time searching for points of agreement. The problem-solving debate is best adapted to the three-man team, with each man having a special task: the first speakers of each team are assigned ten minutes each for analysis; the second speakers of each team are given twelve minutes each for presentation; the third speakers of each team are permitted eight minutes each for evaluation. Questioning may occur under fixed rules at any point, and a debater may modify his position whenever, in his opinion, a change is warranted by the evidence and the argument.

The conventional pattern of debating predominates in the great majority of colleges and universities: a meeting of two teams, usually of two speakers on a side, to argue a proposition previously announced. Usually each debater has a constructive speech and a rebuttal, and follows a time schedule agreed upon, such as ten minutes each for the first affirmative speaker and first negative speaker and for the second affirmative speaker and second negative speaker to present their constructive speeches, five minutes each for the first negative speaker and the second affirmative speaker to give the first rebuttal speeches, and five minutes each for the second negative speaker and the first affirmative speaker to deliver their rebuttal speeches. In this arrangement the affirmative opens and closes the debate.

Educational debating is not limited to the colleges. It is carried on in the high schools throughout the nation. Among adults, debate is undertaken for the analysis of issues and the training of speakers. Professional organizations sponsor systematic programs of debate as a means of teaching analysis of public questions and the principles of advocacy.

Kinds of Policy-Forming Speeches

Policy-forming speeches occur in political conventions, on the campaign platform, in meetings of organizations, in legislative bodies, and in public gatherings.

The nomination. Since the nominating speech is concerned with the choice of a person to fill an office, the issues are, What are the requirements of the position, and who is best qualified to meet them? The nominator should keep in mind both his immediate hearers and the audience outside the meeting. He should remember also that in small organizations the first person nominated is often elected without opposition.

The nominator should demonstrate his candidate's fitness for the position. If the office requires skill in financial administration, for example, the speaker should show that the nominee has this qualification. The past performance of the candidate offers the most acceptable proof of what he can do.

The nominator should show that the candidate has more than the minimum qualifications for filling the office. If he can demonstrate that the candidate's personality enables him to get along well with people, that his discretion leads him to choose associates wisely, and that his judgment constrains him to act carefully but promptly, the audience should be impressed with the fitness of the man for the office. Specific examples, not mere assertions, are persuasive.

The nominee's term of service in the organization, his part in formulating past policies, and his capacity for teamwork, as well as his reputation, his known accomplishments, and his popularity, have a bearing on his candidacy.

The nominating speech should be designed to advance the interests of the person nominated. In order to make people see the candidate's possibilities, the speaker should associate him with outstanding men. He should avoid derogatory comments about rivals for the office. In demonstrating the superiority of his candidate, the nominator should use indirect generalizations rather than invidious comparisons. For example,

Franklin D. Roosevelt, in nominating Alfred E. Smith for the presidency, did not say that Smith would be the opposite of anyone else in honesty. He said:

I speak of that honesty that lets a man sleep of nights well, fearing no Senatorial investigation, that honesty that demands faithfulness to the public trust in every public servant, that honesty which takes immediate action to correct abuse.[3]

The speaker should seek the striking phrase that will make his nominee the man of the hour. Franklin D. Roosevelt applied this principle in designating Alfred E. Smith "the happy warrior."

The acceptance or declination of a nomination. The speech of Franklin D. Roosevelt accepting the nomination for the presidency in 1932 illustrates the twofold function of the speech of acceptance: it expressed appreciation of the honor and outlined the policies Roosevelt proposed to follow during the campaign. It disclosed his views on such problems as the depression, taxes, unemployment, agriculture, and relief. The conclusion, in which he pledged himself to a "new deal" for the American people, supplied his party with a slogan for several years.[4]

The declination of a nomination should express the nominee's appreciation of the honor and explain why he cannot become a candidate. In some organizations an incumbent officer is renominated and re-elected in spite of his protests. In such a predicament he may combine his declination with a speech nominating somebody else, and give substantial reasons why his nominee should be elected.

The campaign. The campaign speech is a common type in democratic countries. Its essential purpose is to set forth proposals persuasively.

A comprehensive view of political campaign speeches, whether on national, state, local, or campus issues, discloses two tendencies. One is the back-slapping, guitar-playing, slogan-making type of campaign oratory which indeed has often been successful. A speaker may win by showmanship, and a candidate may gain office by chicanery. The preponderance of evidence, however, points to the long-range effectiveness of taking a definite point of view, of presenting it clearly, and of advocating it forthrightly.

The campaigner must reach three groups of people. Some are reason-

[3] James M. O'Neill and Floyd K. Riley, eds., *Contemporary Speeches*, New York: Century Co., 1930, pp. 497–503.

[4] The complete address may be read in *The Public Papers and Addresses of Franklin D. Roosevelt*, I, New York, 1938, 647–659. The address deserves study. See also the study by Professor Robert T. Oliver entitled, "The Speech that Established Roosevelt's Reputation," *The Quarterly Journal of Speech*, XXXI, October, 1945, pp. 274–282.

ably sure to vote for the candidate, but the campaigner cannot neglect them; they need to be encouraged to go to the polls, and their enthusiasm may help to win others. A second group includes those who will almost surely vote for someone else. They are nearly, but perhaps not quite, beyond persuasion. As Edmund Burke wrote, many good partisans will not follow a leader to the extreme, and on these a good speech will have some influence.[5] Other voters are in neither camp. They listen to speeches with some hope of arriving at an honest conclusion; they really want to do what is best. Prime Minister Stanley Baldwin declared, "[Audiences] are not amused by mere abuse of a speaker's opponents, by sarcasm, by special pleading, and the tricks of the old school. Vast numbers of our electorate are not attached to a party, and in great mass meetings you get men and women of all parties and of none; and the quiet hearing you get is remarkable." [6]

The campaigner must be accurate. Any mistake of fact may be used by the opposition to suggest that the speaker is not trustworthy.

Errors of syntax, grammar, or pronunciation may be magnified to demonstrate that the offending speaker is incompetent. Even the unimportant lapses of Al Smith in 1928 and Wendell Willkie in 1940 were spread throughout the land.

The fundamental issues of a campaign may be highly complicated. The campaigner must simplify them. "How can we accelerate our economic growth?" "Has internal wrangling made the present administration inefficient?" "Does the Congress deserve censure?"

Sometimes personalities so intrigue the public interest that the issues become secondary. In the opinion of seasoned political observers, Reynolds of North Carolina gained a seat in the Senate by dramatizing his opponent as a caviar-eating occupant of a high-priced Washington hotel. Brookhart of Iowa lost his seat because his opponent continually referred to the number of Brookhart relatives on the public payroll. "Private John" Allen won a congressional election in Mississippi by pinning the label of *general* on his opponent while presenting himself as an ordinary, hard-working *private*.

An issue may sometimes be characterized by a slogan: "Tippecanoe and Tyler too," "Don't swap horses in the middle of the stream," "the New Deal," and "the New Frontier." But slogans sometimes backfire: the term "New Frontier" has been used by its opponents to symbolize the errors of the Kennedy administration.[7]

[5] James Prior, *A Life of Edmund Burke,* London: Geo. Bell and Sons, 1911, p. 166.
[6] "Ideals of Democracy," *School and Society,* I, 271, August 26, 1939.
[7] For an interesting article on campaign slogans and other verbalisms, see Robert Oliver, "The Influence of Verbalisms in American Political Campaign Speaking," *Papers in Rhetoric,* Donald C. Bryant, ed., St. Louis, 1940, pp. 46–55.

The campaigner attempts to find common ground with every audience. He identifies himself with the immediate environment of his listeners. If he solicits votes from people living over a large area, he has the problem of selecting questions of immediate interest to the members of every audience: power development in the northwest, unemployment in the coal regions, labor legislation in the industrial areas.

The campaigner should establish his physical, intellectual, and moral competence. The voters must have faith in his understanding of their problems and his sympathy for their burdens. Many citizens will vote for a candidate in whom they have confidence, even though they do not understand the issues.

The campaigner should identify himself with stated principles and policies. In 1952 Eisenhower promised to go to Korea and to bring the war to a successful conclusion. In 1960 Kennedy assured the people that he would stimulate the forces of economic growth and aid the depressed areas of the country.

The principles of campaign speaking are applicable to class, campus, and local organizations, as well as to state and national politics. The candidate for class treasurer or county commissioner has many of the problems of the presidential nominee. The issues vary: a candidate for class treasurer may discuss fairness in collecting dues; a candidate for county commissioner may promise better roads. The basic principles of campaigning are the same for offices high and low.

The inaugural.   The inaugural address, both ceremonial and policy-forming in character, has four major functions. It expresses appreciation, attempts to unite the group, announces the official's intention to discharge his duties, and presents a broad outline of the official's program for the coming term. The most famous examples are those of the presidents of the United States.

The legislative message.   Through the legislative message the executive officer of an organization advises the policy-making group—a committee, a board of directors, a city council, a state legislature, or a national congress. The legislative message usually has little or no ceremonial aspect: it deals with one or more specific issues rather than with a broad program, and it proposes a definite course of action. Recommendations are usually presented in general terms.

The keynote address.   At the opening of a convention a distinguished member may present a keynote address. Since the speaker sets the tone for the convention, he has an exceptional opportunity for leadership. The keynote address has two important functions: to pay tribute to the organization and to present major problems confronting it. It is both a speech of stimulation and a speech of policy. The keynote addresses at the national nominating conventions of political parties are noteworthy.

The legislative address. The legislative address, a common speech of policy in organized bodies, is an attempt to win support for or against a specific ordinance, bill, or course of action. The speaker must be prepared to adapt himself to the parliamentary practices of the group and to deal tactfully with interruptions, questions, contradictions, and requests for additional information.

In recent years, appearances before committees, boards, and administrative agencies have assumed unusual importance. Statements made in the hearings conducted by such bodies assume some of the aspects of courtroom address while retaining most of the characteristics of the speech of policy. Issues of the highest importance, particularly in matters affected by public opinion, have been dealt with by committees of the House and the Senate.

Speech of public policy. The speech of public policy is often delivered before groups having no official connection with the branches of government. Its function is to influence opinion concerning the wisdom or expediency of proposals for action. A citizen endeavoring to improve health, sanitation, or safety in his community needs to deliver speeches proposing a change and appealing for action. The professional man who speaks well on civic questions renders a public service as he advances his career.

THE PROCEDURES OF ADVOCACY

The procedures of advocacy are similar in both debate and policy-forming public address. Accepting debate as the major means used in learning the principles of advocacy, the student of speechmaking can well afford to learn the practices of the conventional two-team debate now most widely used. Success in debating, as in most other endeavors, depends largely on effective preparation according to systematic plan.

Proposition

The first phase in preparation for a formal debate is the phrasing of a proposition to meet certain conditions. To be most useful, (1) it should be stated clearly, concisely, and affirmatively, (2) it should embody one, and only one, essential idea, (3) it should give the affirmative the burden of proof, and (4) it should be susceptible of proof, yet not obviously true or false. Propositions usually arise out of socio-economic problems; frequently they concern policy. The rules for constructing a statement in a sentence analysis serve as a guide to wording a proposition.

A proposition should be so balanced that the arguments can be developed *pro* and *con*. Other things being equal, the best proposition is one that is currently deliberated in the legislature, in the city council, or in the press. Good debate propositions are often phrased from topics in the headlines. Especially for first practice, a fairly simple and interesting topic should be chosen. Does the city need a new charter? Should the railroads in the United States be nationalized? Should the federal government provide funds for the public schools? From each of the foregoing questions a debatable proposition can be framed:

Resolved: That the city should adopt a new charter.
Resolved: That the railroads in the United States should be nationalized.
Resolved: That the federal government should provide funds for public-school construction.

In recent years the following propositions have served intercollegiate debating in the colleges and universities:

Resolved: That the noncommunist nations of the world should establish an economic community.
Resolved: That the basic American concept of the philosophy of states' rights is outmoded.
Resolved: That Congress should have the power to overrule Supreme Court decisions.

Each of these propositions is so phrased as to require the affirmative to move the resolution.

Often the most interesting, as well as the most effective, debating takes place when the speakers are directly identified with the proposition. In 1947, teams representing the University of Hawaii spoke with unusual effectiveness, both in Hawaii and on the mainland, in advocating the proposition, "*Resolved:* That Hawaii should be granted statehood."

Debate propositions are usually based on serious topics, but humorous or quasi-philosophic debates have been popular. Abraham Lincoln, for example, participated in them. The Oxford Union sometimes has its largest meetings and most engaging speeches on such propositions as, "*Resolved:* That this house pities its grandchildren," or "*Resolved:* That the policeman's lot is not a happy one." College and university teams in the United States have recently debated the following propositions of the lighter vein: "*Resolved:* That life begins at forty" and "*Resolved:* That man's place is in the home." Debates on humorous, literary, or philosophic propositions are more in the vein of after-dinner speaking than of conventional debating, but they may offer excellent practice in delivery and in repartee. They do not usually afford the opportunity for the thorough preparation generally characteristic of American intercollegiate debating.

Analysis

Having the proposition before him, the debater must begin by analyzing it (1) to discover what brings it up, (2) to learn something of its
origin and history, (3) to define its terms, (4) to admit, waive, or declare
irrelevant any matters that may be confusing, (5) to find the major
points of difference between the proponents and opponents of the measure, and (6) to discover the basic issues.

Immediate cause of controversy.   The first step in analysis is to discover what circumstances suggest or require the debating of the proposition. Serious debate ordinarily arises from a genuine difference of
opinion.

Background of the question.   The second step is the historical background of the proposition. In a series of debates on compulsory arbitration of labor disputes, for example, students soon found that compulsory
arbitration had been practiced in Kansas, Australia, and New Zealand.
Although past experience is not a final determinant, the debater who
does not know the historical background of his proposition is unlikely
to do it justice.

Definitions.   An absolute prerequisite for meaningful debating is the
accurate definition of terms. Although dictionary definitions are useful as
a beginning, they are seldom adequate for a proposition, because the
debater commonly employs a more specialized meaning than the best
dictionary affords. The problem of definition is, first, that of the debater's
own full comprehension and, second, that of statement in precise terms.
In such an apparently simple proposition as "*Resolved:* That a federal
world government should be established," many debaters found that every
one of the apparently simple terms needed study. Here are some questions that arose in squad meetings: What is *federal* government, and
precisely how does it differ from any other? What are the minimum
essentials for justifying the use of the term *federal* with reference to any
government? What precisely is meant by *world* in this connection? Does
the term mean literally *all* of the world or does it mean *most* of the
world? Specifically, would a government of all countries except Russia
deserve the name *world* government? What is meant by *government?*
What powers must be secured to the central body before it can become a
government? Does this term *should* involve any of the meaning of "will"?
Specifically, does the term require the affirmative to show that the proposed government is going to be established? Some debates revolve
unsuccessfully around the meaning of the word *should.* One side maintains that since the action could not be taken, it should not be. The
other maintains that since the action is necessary, it must be possible.
Such debates become problems in metaphysics. They are not fruitful,

because they avoid the substantive issues involved and disappoint speakers and audiences alike. The remedy is for all concerned to agree upon any necessary definitions in advance of the debate.

Infrequently a debate team resorts to the unfortunate practice of trying to win a debate by definition. Attempting to twist the terms to meet their own predilections, the team leaves no room for argument.

A satisfactory definition will attempt to discover a precise use of each term under the following rules:

- The definition should include all that belongs and should exclude all that does not belong to the term.
- The definition should be phrased in simpler language than the proposition itself.
- The definition should not employ any terms or derivatives of the terms in the proposition.

Irrelevant, admitted, and waived matter. After the proposition has been well defined, the debater restates it and discards matter that should be admitted, waived, or declared irrelevant.

To know what bears upon a proposition is difficult, because good propositions change from day to day. Yet the discovery of the issues depends upon distinguishing the relevant from the irrelevant material. The effort spent in exploring bypaths defeats debating because it wastes time and leaves the real issues undiscovered. The test for irrelevance is definition; debaters who have defined their terms well are less likely to be confused.

Every debater should decide what can and what cannot be admitted within the logic of his case. Both in preparation and in delivery, debaters should take care not to admit inadvertently any point critical to the defense of the case. Admissions should not be made in an apologetic manner damaging to the reception of the argument. They should be stated so explicitly that misinterpretation is impossible.

By custom or by agreement some matters are waived from intercollegiate debate. By universal practice, for example, the constitutionality of a proposition is waived. No one can be certain what the Supreme Court will decide; and even if a measure should be declared unconstitutional, presumably it could be made constitutional by amendment. Therefore the debate should be limited to the substantive issues of the proposition.

The major points of contention. Once the terms are clear and the elements likely to create confusion are eliminated, the remaining matters presumably present real differences of opinion. Contrasted, these differences reveal both the affirmative and the negative contentions concerning the proposition.

The issues. The issues of a proposition are questions arising from directly opposing contentions of the affirmative and the negative. To each of the issues the affirmative replies "Yes," the negative "No." In a given debate proposition the range of issues is almost illimitable; by exercise of judgment, however, the debaters determine which are basic to the structure of the argument. Certain stock issues recur in the arguing of propositions of policy: Is there need for a change? Is the proposal the best change to make? Are there evils in the proposal greater than any probable benefits?

In the theory of debating, an affirmative team must be able to show a need for a change commensurate with the action proposed. Furthermore, the affirmative must defend the proposal against any alternative and against the charge that new evils are likely to arise from it, and therefore must carry the burden of proof.

In the theory of debating the negative responsibility is somewhat different. A negative team, for example, may admit that present conditions demand a change. The negative may in theory even go beyond the affirmative in establishing the evils of the present system or in deploring present practices. The negative team, however, then assumes joint responsibility with the affirmative in proposing a remedy. The debate thus becomes an argument not between the affirmative proposition and the *status quo,* but rather between the affirmative and the negative remedies for an admitted evil.

Besides the so-called stock issues, every debate is subject to special issues arising from the varying circumstances or from an unusual statement of one or more of the stock issues.

The brief. The brief surveys the field of thought covered by a proposition. It has five characteristics:

- The brief is both affirmative and negative; it is objective. It combines an intellectual diary, a catalogue of ideas, and a topographical map of an area of controversy.
- The brief is complete. Since it is not a set of notes for a single speech, but a survey of the whole area from which many speeches may be drawn, it should not be fragmentary.
- The brief has three parts: introduction, body, and conclusion. The introduction embodies the analysis of the proposition. The body sets forth the affirmative and negative proof derived from the analysis with necessary support. The conclusion summarizes the points made about the issues and relates them to the proposition as restated.
- The items in the brief should conform in design and arrangement to accepted practice. Indentations, symbols, and divisions should be uniform.
- Each item following a symbol should consist of a single, descriptive statement. Fragmentary and ambiguous wording should be eliminated.

The *introduction* to the brief is a systematic statement in prescribed form of the material discovered in the analysis. Since the problem of the analysis is to arrive at the issues, inspection of the introduction should not reveal whether the brief was prepared by the affirmative or by the negative. The introduction should be clear, orderly, and impartial. In sequence, the parts designated with Roman numerals should be:

    I. The Immediate Cause for Discussion.
   II. The Background of the Question.
  III. The Terms to be Defined.
  IV. The Irrelevant Matter.
   V. The Admitted Matter.
  VI. The Waived Matter.
 VII. The Affirmative and Negative Contentions Contrasted.
VIII. The Main Issues.
  IX. The Enumeration of Points to be Established to Prove or Disprove the Proposition.

The *body* of the brief sets forth the argument. The points set for proof should derive from the issues. If the introduction indicates that three issues are immediately relevant, then a point must be set for proof on each of the three. Every statement in the body should offer proof for the statement immediately superior to it. The relationship can be tested by the use of the word *because* following the proposition itself and the items of support thereafter.

Proofs of the same order should be parallel and should be designated with like symbols. The major contentions are designated with Roman numerals, and the supporting statements with capital letters. The next order of support should be indicated with Arabic numerals, and the supporting statements with small letters. Wherever there is a division, at least two supporting subdivisions will follow. Both the evidence and the sources should be set forth in the body of the brief.

The *conclusion* of the brief is an ordered restatement of the points that were set for proof, each point being preceded by the word *since*, and the whole followed by the proposition as restated. The conclusion of the affirmative brief on federal world government could be:

CONCLUSION

  I. Since prevention of war is necessary,
 II. Since federal world government would prevent war,
III. Since no other method except federal world government would prevent war,
THEREFORE, Federal world government should be established.

The *case* is a plan for the management of the various parts of the field. The members of the team must decide what elements of the brief are to be used in the forthcoming debate and how much attention is to be given to each, what general line of attack should be followed, and what basic differences should be maintained.

Although the patterns for building a case are not so conventional as are those for constructing a brief, some rules are necessary: (1) the members of the team must be in agreement; (2) the case should be unified and organized into a logical whole; (3) the case should be illustrated; (4) the case should not go beyond the point necessary to establish the proposition; (5) the case should be built on few points rather than many; (6) the case should be built to resist attack. The constructive-debate speech is an application of the principles of informing and persuading within the framework of forensic customs. The debate speech requires close adherence to time limits, but adherence to these limits does not justify crowding the speech or rushing the delivery. Every factor in the debate speech emphasizes the need for an orderly arrangement and presentation of ideas. The debater should know what he proposes to prove and should deliver the proof promised. He should show the relation of his proof to the proposition and to his opponents' contentions, and he should summarize quickly and accurately.

Debating has special terminology, and students sometimes allow themselves to lapse into jargon. The opposing team may understand the phrase "the burden of proof is on the affirmative," but the members of the audience may not. The best debate speech avoids technical terms relating either to the substance of the proposition or to the technique of debate.

The debater has a threefold problem of adjustment: he must meet the opposition; he must satisfy the audience; and he must serve his own purpose. This process of adjusting is frustrating to the slow-witted, but to most debaters the constant testing of ideas, the meeting of attacks, and the holding of positions are the exhilarating features of debate.

The speech should be addressed to the audience, small or large. A mature speaker refrains from talking to a single defenseless judge as though he were a thousand people in an amphitheater. The debater adapts himself to the size of the room and to the existing conditions. His primary purpose is to obtain adherents for his cause. Working within the rules of the debate, he advocates a proposition not simply to entertain or to inform, but to change the opinions and perhaps to win the votes of his audience. A good debate speech, therefore, is prepared not as a somewhat perfunctory exercise, but as a means of influencing or preventing action.

The *rebuttal* is devoted exclusively to refutation and the summation of the case. It represents about a third of the time of each side in the debate. Both the affirmative and the negative cases are laid down for the examination of debaters and audience alike before the rebuttal begins. New evidence, but no new lines of proof, may be presented in the rebuttal. A debater who has systematically studied, analyzed, and briefed the area of the proposition should be able to refute his opponents. Since rebuttal deals with assumptions, evidence, and reasoning, the debater should be able to use without hesitation the necessary principles of persuading, especially as they apply to refutation. Rebuttal requires selection based on sound principles. Refutation, based on points vital to the case of the opposition, should be directed toward the essential elements of the opposing argument.

In some instances a keen debater who has worked systematically during a long period of preparation may be disappointed in the final outcome because his intelligence and knowledge appear unavailing in gaining the decision of the audience and the judges. His strong points are sometimes offset by faults growing out of ignorance of right attitudes, customs, and practices in debating. For example, questions for debate are not susceptible of proof "beyond the shadow of a doubt." The debater seeks to show strong probability. The personalities of the opposition should be disregarded, but their arguments should be handled vigorously. Whether the hearers be many or few, the debater should gain and hold their interest with an attitude of modest self-assurance and concern for their favorable attention. The total impression of debaters depends not alone upon their speaking, but also upon their general manners and their behavior.

CRITIQUES FOR ADVOCACY

Advocacy can be evaluated in reference to the effectiveness in the use of the kind of proof, of its style, and of its delivery, and it may also be evaluated in its relation to the speaker, the occasion, and the audience. General criteria may be applied to both formal debating and to policy-forming speechmaking, but each has special criteria.

Critiques for Debate

Each of the four major types of debate—joint, legislative, forensic, and educational—has its own methods of evaluation. Change of opinion sometimes registered at the polls measures the effect of joint debate. The votes of members on roll call provide a decision in legislative sessions. The ruling of the court or the verdict of the jury may show the effects of the attorneys' pleas. Since at least one function of educational debate is training for effective participation in the other types, the practices in judging intercollegiate debates are not uniform. They vary from section to section and from institution to institution according to the concept held of debating and to the requirements of the specific debate.

Whenever a debate occurs, some kind of decision results. The term *non-decision* is a misnomer. Research has disclosed, for example, that although neither Lincoln nor Douglas was declared the winner of their series by a debate judge or by audience vote, their debating resulted in personal decisions.[8]

One practice in intercollegiate debating is to leave the decision concerning both the ability of the debaters and the validity of the proposition to the judgment of everyone concerned. The personal decision is now in common use in intercollegiate debates frequently held before service clubs or similar groups more interested in the substance of a proposition than in the contest element in debating. In some universities the practice prevails for on-campus debates as well. The personal decision has much to recommend it where these favorable conditions appear: (a) mature speakers who are willing to accept the challenge of a proposition and an audience as sufficient reason to prepare, (b) audiences interested in public questions, (c) the use of a number of timely debate propositions, (d) a director of debate willing to serve as critic and to advise students about their weaknesses and strong points, and (e) an energetic forensic program based on the tradition of debate as a public forum.

On the assumption that a given debate is comparable to a legislative session, the decision may be based on a vote by members of the audience. In a debaters' assembly or congress, when the passing or rejection of resolutions is the business of the group, the legislative vote is sound procedure. Even here, however, conclusions about the merits of the debating based solely on the results of the balloting are of dubious value. A poor team may lose votes for a popular measure without losing enough to prevent its passage; a good team may gain votes for an unpopular measure without gaining enough to overcome the feeling against it. Three types of decision based on audience vote have been used in intercollegiate debating: the judgment on the merits of the debate, the audience vote for or against the proposition, and a measure of the shift of opinion.

An audience judgment on the question, "Which team did the more effective debating?" has little to recommend it. What constitutes effective debating is a technical question involving standards of judgment. Unless the audience happens to be composed exclusively of qualified persons, therefore, an audience judgment on the merits of the debate is no more sound than an audience judgment on any other technical matter.

A ballot taken on the question, "Do we favor the proposition before the house?" is a means of maintaining speaker enthusiasm and listener interest and is sometimes useful as an informal poll of public opinion. Since many factors other than the debate affect the result of such a vote,

[8] See the study by Forest L. Whan, *History and Criticism of American Public Address,* W. Norwood Brigance, ed., New York: McGraw-Hill Book Company, 1943, Vol. II, p. 823.

it cannot properly be construed as a decision on the effectiveness of the debaters.

One method of decision common in intercollegiate debating resembles a jury verdict. A group, usually of three or five qualified, experienced, and impartial persons, renders a verdict on the question, "Which team did the more effective debating?" The jury method is preferable to the general audience vote on the same question, both because the jury members can be carefully selected and because they are likely to take their duties more seriously than would a general audience. Even so, the method leaves much to be desired.

In recent years, the common practice in contest debating has been to appoint an expert judge, who renders an oral decision analyzing the debate and giving the reasons for his award. If proper discretion has been employed in appointing the judge, a valid decision is likely, and the debaters will benefit by his expert analysis and criticism. The audience may learn much about the debate they have heard and about the principles of advocacy. A qualified judge holds and reveals certain standards of debating, and criticizes a debate by those standards. Although their decisions may vary in a given debate, qualified judges are likely to agree on the importance of understanding the proposition, discovering the issues, supporting affirmative or negative contentions with valid evidence and cogent reasoning, adapting to the opposition, exhibiting a communicative attitude, and conducting an effective refutation.

Decisions are important. More is at stake than the question of winning or losing the debate. Decisions tend to fix standards of debating and therefore to teach students and audiences what merits praise and dispraise. A wrong decision is harmful because it tends to inculcate error and to perpetuate bad practice. For the debater the significant fact about the decision is not whether he won or lost, but how well he debated. Sometimes the losers get more value from a debate than the winners— knowledge of method, improvement in technique, intelligent analysis of the problem, and the determination to succeed. As an educational procedure, debating is, after all, merely a tested means for teaching young men and women how to advocate a proposition. The decision is useful only in so far as it accomplishes this purpose.

Critiques for Policy-Forming Speeches

On the basis of what criteria does a listener make a decision on the proposition presented by a policy-forming speaker? Each type of policy-forming speech will have some criteria peculiar to the type, but all types will have some criteria in common.

A speech of nomination should satisfy the listener that the nominee meets the requirements for the position and that he is the best-qualified person to serve. He should be convinced that the candidate has all of the particular qualifications for the office to be filled, and that the past performance of the candidate indicates that he will be a competent official. The listener should be persuaded that the candidate has the personality, the judgment, the experience, and the qualities to get the necessary work done with efficiency and with distinction.

A speech of acceptance should assure the listeners that the nominee appreciates the honor and responsibility conferred upon him and that the policies he favors will be appropriate. A speech of declination should enable the listener to understand why the nominee cannot undertake the responsibilities of the office to which he is nominated even though he appreciates the honor of being nominated.

A campaign speech should make the listener aware of the issues and of the position taken by the speaker. It should convince the listeners that the speaker is the man to deal with the issues if elected, and that he is physically, intellectually, and morally competent to fulfill his obligations if the listener votes for him.

The inaugural should meet the ceremonial requirements. At a high level of aspiration it should set forth a program for action.

The legislative message should inform the legislators of the need for a course of action, with the reasons for a particular proposal for meeting the need. The recommendations should be made clear and as specific as the circumstances permit.

The keynote address should set the tone for the convention, should compliment the group, and should present the major problems upon which the convention should deliberate. The speaker should relate these problems to past experience and future needs.

The legislative address should establish a specific policy to be adopted and should offer supporting evidence, reasoning, and appeals to persuade the members of the assembly to vote affirmatively on the policy. An opponent of the policy should convince the members of the assembly, with evidence and reasoning, that the adoption of the policy would not serve the best interests of those to be affected by it.

The speech of public policy should be adapted to the interests, experience, and other particular characteristics of the audience. It should relate the proposal to the expectations of the listeners, and should show that it meets their needs. It should be presented in a form that will enable the listener to take the specific action that will further the cause.

All policy-forming speeches should be evaluated for their selection and organization of material, their effective use of the kinds of proof, their oral style, and their communicative delivery. All factors in the speech should contribute to a total persuasive effect—the acceptance of the proposition.

Part **V** KNOWLEDGE
AND SKILL:
Principles and Application

*. . . there is no institution devised by man
which the power of speech has not helped us to
establish.*

—Isocrates

13 EVALUATION AND CRITICISM: Understanding and Judgment

A speech is effective . . . if it achieves an end or response consistent with the speaker's purpose—provided that the purpose is, in turn, consistent with the dictates of responsible judgment in solicitous regard for the positive good of an enlightened society.
—*Lester Thonssen* and *A. Craig Baird*

Like the other arts, speechmaking has its own criteria for appraisal and evaluation. These criteria are derived from two major sources: the techniques developed by speakers throughout the history of speechmaking, and the idealistic standards set forth by students and teachers of the art of speechmaking. In evaluating any speech, at least two different points of view are possible: that of the individual who is analyzing, and the point of view (so far as it can be determined) of the audience that actually heard the speech. The first point of view will give a subjective judgment, and the second, to some extent, an objective judgment. If the purpose of evaluation is to improve your own speechmaking, the first point of view will have some importance. If the purpose of the evaluation is historical perspective, the second point of view becomes more important.

The term used for the evaluation of speeches is *rhetorical criticism.* The concept is parallel to that used for other art forms, such as literary criticism for literature. An essential difference between rhetorical criti-

371

cism and literary criticism is that speechmaking is essentially a useful art and literature is essentially a fine art. Speechmaking, for the most part, is directed toward practical results, and literature, particularly poetry, is directed toward aesthetic enjoyment. Whereas literary criticism, derived from the principles of poetics, is concerned with universal and permanent values, rhetorical criticism, derived from the principles of rhetoric, is concerned with current and immediate issues. The poet's audience may be mankind of the present and the future, but the speaker's audience is the particular group he faces with the possibilities of a more remote audience. Just as poetics sets forth the nature and laws of poetry, so rhetoric sets forth the nature and principles of speechmaking. Literary criticism utilizes the principles and practice of poetics; rhetorical criticism utilizes the principles and practice of rhetoric. The practice of poetics produces the forms of literature; the practice of rhetoric produces the forms of public address.

CATEGORIES OF RHETORICAL CRITICISM

The categories of rhetorical criticism—the topics which enable the evaluator to appraise speechmaking—are related to the occasion, the audience, the speaker, and the speech. A speech cannot be judged fairly if the critic does not know the occasion and the audience, since every genuine speech is planned for a specific occasion and a particular audience. Furthermore, to understand the speech, the critic should know the speaker as well as the speech.

THE OCCASION

The critic should view the occasion broadly, to include not only the immediate circumstances but also the relevant background. He should be interested in the events giving rise to the discussion of which the speech is a part. Although this kind of background is useful in understanding a ceremonial speech, a social speech, or a professional speech, it is most important for understanding a speech of policy, as is the consideration of the present state of the discussion. Such a consideration would include opponents, colleagues, previous speeches and writings, contentions of each faction, and the exact position taken by the speaker, by his colleagues, and by his opponents. The critic should also estimate the status of public opinion—considering factions, institutions, means, leadership, the public, and the issues. Facts about the immediate circumstances should include time, place, purpose of assembly, size and nature of the room, the position of the speaker, the proximity of the audience, and the program of the occasion.

SPEAKING IS SOMETIMES ELOQUENT

Winston Churchill's fame as a great orator has been established for all time.
Here he is shown campaigning in one of his last elections, delivering the kind
of speech that helped him rise to world leadership.

In order to understand Winston Churchill's famous legislative address
in the House of Commons on June 18, 1940, referred to as "This Was
Their Finest Hour," the critic should know the preceding events which
led to the delivery of the speech. He should know as much as possible
about the progress of World War II as it affected England, and particularly of the time between the British evacuation of Dunkirk and the
date of the speech. Several of Churchill's previous speeches are of particular interest for background, but the speech of June 4, in which he
reported to Parliament and the world the successful retreat of the British
forces from France, has a close relation to the speech of June 18. Both
the friends and the foes of Britain were wondering whether Britain, too,
would surrender, and therefore Churchill had the responsibility of restor-
ing the confidence of his own people and reassuring other countries that
Britain would fight on. Americans in particular need to know how the
House of Commons differs from the House of Representatives in physical
arrangements in order to visualize the relationship of the speaker to
his audience. For an understanding of the problems Churchill had in
adapting his delivery to his listeners, his position, surrounded by members on all sides, becomes essential.

In order to understand Franklin D. Roosevelt's first inaugural address on March 4, 1933, the critic should know the preceding events leading up both to the election of Roosevelt and to the delivery of the
inaugural. He should know as much as possible about what had happened
since the stock-market crash of 1929. He should be familiar with the
issues of the campaign, based on the platforms of the Republican and
Democratic parties, and with the contrasting positions taken by Herbert
Hoover and Franklin Roosevelt. His outstanding addresses, from his
acceptance speech at the Democratic Convention to his final address in
the campaign, help the critic to understand the content of his inaugural.
He should know that the voters were greatly disturbed by the critical
economic conditions and had lost confidence in the previous administration with respect to the banking crisis and the rise in unemployment.
The critic should take into account that the inaugural ceremony was
held in front of the national Capitol in the rain.

In order to understand Clarence Darrow's defense of Henry Sweet,
accused of manslaughter in a murder trial in Detroit on May 19, 1926,
the critic needs to know that the Negro quarters in the city were so
overcrowded that some Negroes were forced to move into white districts,
and that when whites attacked Negroes who moved into their neighbor-
hood, Dr. Ossian Sweet armed his fellow Negroes and fought back, with
the result that his brother Henry, who allegedly fired the shot that
killed a white man, was on trial for his life. The critic should be aware
of the extent of the tension and bitter feelings of both whites and Negroes

and of the treatment of the problem in the local press. The critic should inform himself about the size and nature of the courtroom in which the trial was held in order to understand the conditions in which Clarence Darrow spoke.

THE AUDIENCE

Frequently a speaker has both an immediate and a remote audience—the audience he sees before him, and the audience that sees him on television, hears him on radio, or reads his speech in the press. Sometimes the speaker addresses both the immediate and the remote audience, and sometimes the remote audience merely overhears an address directed to the immediate audience. Considering each audience separately, the critic must determine as well as he can the size, the sex and age groups, and such characteristics as intelligence, education, experience, information on the subject, and attitudes toward speaker and subject. He will need to judge the relation of the speaker to his audience by estimating the extent to which the speaker establishes common ground of information, interests, beliefs, feelings, and patterns of action. He will need to take into account the differences in the audience with reference to such aspects as race, sex, family, health, age, nationality, region, community, religion, politics, profession, occupation, economic status, social position, and personal prestige. He will also want to know the function of the audience, its knowledge of and part in the discussion, and the factions, opinions, prejudices, desires, tensions, and moods it represents. He should try to find out how the audience received the speaker, how well it could hear and understand him, and the attention it gave to his speech.

The critic will need to know that Churchill was addressing both an immediate audience and a remote audience when he delivered his speech on June 18, 1940—the immediate audience, the House of Commons before him, and the remote audience, the radio listeners in his own country and in other countries and the people who read his speech later in the press. He will need to determine the character of both of these groups, particularly their information on the status of Great Britain and their attitudes toward Churchill and the progress of the war. He will need to consider how well Churchill established common ground, particularly of beliefs and feelings, and how well he recognized the differences, particularly those of nationality and politics, in the groups. He will also want to find out what function the audience was expected to perform and what factions, opinions, prejudices, and tensions existed. He should try to find out how the audience received Churchill and what attention it gave to his speech.

The critic will need to know that Roosevelt was addressing both an immediate audience and a remote audience when he delivered his inaugural address on March 4, 1933—the immediate audience, the people gathered in front of the Capitol, and the remote audience, the radio listeners throughout the United States, Western Europe, and Australia and the people who read his speech in the newspapers the next day. He should know that the size of the immediate audience was over a hundred thousand people, and that the remote audience numbered millions. He should evaluate the attitudes of the immediate and remote audience toward Roosevelt and the policies he set forth, considering the common ground of information, interests, beliefs, feelings, and the differences in region, politics, occupation, and economic status. He should take into account the wide variety of functions represented—from congressmen who were to be asked to vote on emergency legislation, to the people in other countries looking for leadership from the United States. He should realize that the depression had created factions, prejudices, tensions, and despondent moods, and that the election had raised hopes for constructive action. He should understand that the audience response to the clear and confident presentation was unusual in the enthusiasm aroused and the anticipations created.

The critic will need to know that Darrow was addressing an immediate audience of twelve jurors and excited spectators in a crowded courtroom, and that his speech was read with great interest as it was reported in the press. He should give special weight to the character of the all-white jury, with particular attention to their intelligence, education, experience with race relations, information on the existing feuds, and attitudes toward Darrow and the race problem. He will need to analyze the common ground Darrow established, especially with reference to beliefs and feelings and the differences he recognized—particularly those concerned with race, community occupation, economic status, and social position. He should note that the functions of the audience varied—from that of the jury, required to bring in a verdict, and that of the judge, required to advise the jury and pronounce sentence, if any, to the people who were expected to reach their own decisions on the justice of Darrow's plea. He will need to appraise the factions, opinions, prejudices, desires, tensions, and moods of all the groups involved. He should estimate the importance of the silent attention given to Darrow over a period of several hours and of the shift from antagonism to respect shown to him.

THE SPEAKER

Concerning the speaker himself, the critic should know all that is pertinent to the interpretation and evaluation of the speech. Such biographical facts as childhood environment, education, experience, and associates may contribute to the appraisal. The critic will do well to know the physical characteristics, such as personal appearance, health, bearing, voice, gesture, and mannerisms. He will also want to consider the importance of intellectual habits, moral traits, and temperament. The speaker's personal and professional reputation, as well as his reputation as a speaker and his reputation with his audience, will be of interest. The critic should try to determine the principles and beliefs held by the speaker, his authority on his subject, his prejudices, attitudes, and personal interest in the outcome, as well as his function in the discussion and any special advantages or disadvantages he holds. He should know how well acquainted the speaker is with the members of his audience and what attitude he has toward them. Any information he can find on the speaker's methods of preparation will be especially interesting.

The critic will be interested in such biographical facts as Churchill's education for leadership, his experience in public affairs, and his relations with associates, particularly with reference to his checkered career in public life. He will need to assess the importance of Churchill's physical characteristics, especially his personal appearance, voice, and mannerisms. He will want to know how his intellectual habits, moral traits, and temperament bore upon his speechmaking. He will be concerned with Churchill's personal and professional reputation, his reputation as a speaker, and his reputation with his audience. He will need to evaluate the significance of Churchill's principles and beliefs, his patriotic loyalty to the British cause, and the prestige of his position as Prime Minister in the discussion of the future of British policy. He should consider how thoroughly Churchill knew the British people and how eager he was to serve them. He will have an incidental interest in knowing what methods Churchill employed in the preparation of this speeches.

The critic will find that the biographical facts concerning Roosevelt's struggle to overcome a serious physical handicap are related to his success in politics and speechmaking. He should know that Roosevelt was much influenced by his environment and his associates. He will not find it difficult to assess the contribution to Roosevelt's personal proof made by his appearance, health, bearing, voice, gesture, and mannerisms. He will observe that Roosevelt's intellectual habits, moral traits, and temperament met the needs of the times. He will see that Roosevelt's personal and professional reputation were based on a successful career as a state senator, an assistant secretary of the navy, a candidate for vice president, and governor of New York, and that his reputation as a speaker and a person well known to his audience was already established, particularly by his acceptance speech and his campaign addresses. He should study Roosevelt's principles and beliefs and the experiences that established his authority on the subject of national policy, as well as his prejudices, attitudes, and personal interest in achieving a successful administration.

He will need to stress the high position of leadership Roosevelt held as the result of winning the election by a landslide, and the advantage he held as a president who was expected to re-establish the prosperity of the country. He should recognize the extensive acquaintance Roosevelt had with the people of the United States and the sympathetic understanding he had of people in foreign lands. He should point out that although Roosevelt benefited from the research of his staff, he infused his own personality into his speaking style.

The critic should relate Clarence Darrow's independent and self-reliant life to his devotion to the defense of the underdog. He should evaluate Darrow's serious interest in books, his unusual experiences with all kinds of people, and his strange environment of opposition in relation to his later successes as a trial lawyer. He should inform himself about Darrow's physical characteristics that had a bearing upon his speech-making. He will want to consider his penetrating mind, which enabled him to analyze human needs and emotions; his moral traits, based on a deep sympathy for the oppressed; and his temperament, developed from his unwillingness to submit to ordinary rules and restraints. He will need to estimate the strength of his personal reputation as a formidable, courageous, and devoted opponent of injustice, his professional reputation as an attorney who successfully pleaded for the accused in over a hundred murder trials, and his reputation with his audience as an unrelenting "propagandist for humanity." He should give adequate attention to Darrow's social philosophy and interest in economic problems, his intimate knowledge of the difficulties of the laboring class and of minority racial groups, his prejudice in favor of the underprivileged, and his irrepressible drive to vindicate his belief in those who had been unfairly attacked. He should indicate the advantage Darrow held as an effective attorney for the defense in relation to his function as the attorney for the accused in the trial of Henry Sweet. He should know that Darrow was famous for obtaining jurors favorable to his cases, toward whom he had the attitude of expecting complete agreement. He should attempt to appraise the adequacy of Darrow's informal methods of preparation.

THE SPEECH

The heart of the criticism will be the evaluation of the speech itself. Even though the critic hears the speech as a member of the immediate or the remote audience, he will need an authentic text of the speech for close study. If he is dealing with a speech of the past, he will need to investigate the reliability of his text as well as the existence of recordings. It will be important for him to know whether the speech was delivered impromptu, extemporaneously, from manuscript, or from memory. In studying the speech, he will wish to set forth the general and the specific purposes, the classification of the address as ceremonial, social, professional, or policy forming, and the type of speech within that classification. He will want to formulate the proposition or the statement of the central idea and the supporting divisions and subdivisions of the thought structure. He will seek to identify the plan of adaptation to the occasion and the audience, with attention to the introduction, the body, and the conclusion. He will be interested in the sources of the speaker's ideas, both general and specific, and in the mood or tone of the speech.

The speaker's use of the modes of persuasion, both nontechnical and technical, is a major concern of the critic. He will analyze the speech to discover the use of nontechnical logical proof, such as laws, witnesses or authorities, contracts, and evidence extracted by force or based on the taking of an oath; of nontechnical pathetic proof, such as concrete objects submitted to stir the feelings of the audience; and of nontechnical ethical proof, such as the speaker's reputation before giving the speech. He will proceed to find the artistic or technical proof—proof based upon the rhetorical skill of the speaker in reasoning, disposing, and accrediting. He will examine the logical proof, both constructive and refutative, considering the basic assumptions, the adequacy and validity of the evidence, and the soundness of the methods of reasoning. He will interpret and evaluate the psychological proof, noting the appeals to feelings, motives, interests, beliefs, and habits. He will observe the speaker's skill in establishing personal proof, revealing qualities and qualifications that give the audience confidence in the speaker, such as experience, judgment, integrity, and loyalty.

Since the effectiveness of a speech depends a great deal upon the language the speaker chooses, the critic must turn his attention to the style, keeping in mind that good communication with the audience is the standard of excellence. He will need to remember that the style of a persuasive speech differs from the style of a familiar essay; that a speech, as Professor James A. Winans said, is not "an essay standing on its hind legs." He will look for the characteristics of style that reveal the personality, the informality, and the communicativeness of the speaker. He will recognize directness in the use of questions, imperatives, hortatory expressions, direct address, and the first and second personal pronouns. He will determine the forcefulness of the language by the extent to which it exemplifies the use of strong verbs, striking imagery, perceptive adjectives, colorful illustrations, realistic contrasts and comparisons, insistent restatements, compelling formulas, stirring exclamations, and powerful climaxes.

If the critic attends the speech, he can observe the delivery and decide whether the presentation is an asset or a liability. If he cannot see the speaker in action, he must depend upon the impressions of those who report the speech in attempting to judge the quality of the delivery. In either case he will be interested in such basic principles as realization of meaning at the moment of speaking and the sense of communication with the listeners, and with such technical adequacies as audibility, distinctness, range and flexibility of voice, acceptable pronunciation, poise and appropriate bodily activity, and the observance of platform etiquette. Peculiarities of dress, manner, and speech are relevant.

The rhetorical effectiveness of the speech may be very difficult to estimate. So far as the critic is able, he should endeavor to judge the immediate effects and the ultimate effects of the speech. He would like to know the effects upon the immediate audience as a whole as indicated by the attention given the speaker, the applause, hecklings and interruptions, laughter, changes of attitude and belief, and actions taken. He would also like to know the reactions of members of the immediate audience as revealed in comments of reporters, letters or notes referring to the speech, incidental comments in editorials or elsewhere, and subsequent speeches expressing approval or disapproval. Similarly, he would be interested in learning the effects upon the remote audience from whatever sources are available. To judge the ultimate effects of the speech, the critic may require historical knowledge and perspective, basing his own appraisal in part upon the interpretations of historians and contemporary rhetorical critics. If the speech is recent, ultimate effects can only be the subject of speculation. The effects of favorable or unfavorable reactions upon the speaker himself may be worthy of consideration, such as honor or scorn, promotion or demotion, increase or decrease of prestige, appointment to or removal from office, election or defeat at the polls, and encouragement or discouragement in his career. Reasons for the success or failure of the speech may be political, personal, or rhetorical. In making his final appraisal, the critic may wish to make comparisons and contrasts with speeches of the same or different speakers, with speeches of the same type or different types, with speeches of the same period or different periods, and with speeches of the same movement or different movements.

The critic will need to subject whichever speech he is studying to the systematic analysis and evaluation to be developed from the application of the criteria set forth. For example, he will find that the Churchill speech is a policy-forming speech, that the Roosevelt speech is partially ceremonial but largely policy forming, and that the Darrow speech is professional; that the Churchill and Roosevelt speeches were delivered from manuscript, and that the Darrow speech was extemporaneous. For each speech he will need to discover the statement, the divisions, the subdivisions, and the plan of adaptation. He will proceed to apply all categories related to the modes of persuasion, the language, and the delivery. He will attempt to reach a sound judgment on the rhetorical effectiveness of the speech with both the immediate and remote audiences. For example, he will discover that the Churchill speech received much praise from both friends and opponents, and that it exerted a tremendous influence on the morale of the allies; that the Roosevelt speech set the tone for a vigorous program of emergency actions resulting in the passage by Congress of much remedial legislation, and brought Roosevelt to the attention of the world as a new leader; that the Darrow speech won the acquittal of Henry Sweet and reinforced Darrow's reputation as an outstanding lawyer of his day. The critic will do well to make comparisons and contrasts of Churchill's June 18 speech with his other speeches concerned with World War II and with his speeches of other periods, with the speeches of other world leaders, and with the speeches concerning other wars. He will do well to make comparisons and contrasts of Roosevelt's March 4, 1933 inaugural with other speeches concerned with national policy, with his speeches of earlier and later periods, with the inaugurals of other presidents, with the speeches of other world leaders, and with the speeches concerned with other crises in national affairs. He will do well to make comparisons and contrasts of Darrow's May 19, 1926, speech with his other speeches in defense of clients accused of murder, with speeches earlier and later in his career, with the speeches of other successful trial lawyers, and with the speeches concerning other types of cases.

THE SCOPE OF RHETORICAL CRITICISM

The rhetorical critic has a twofold task in appraising a speech: first, he must analyze it and understand it for itself and in relation to the occasion, the audience, and the speaker; and second, he must apply criteria of achievement and excellence derived from the philosophy and the principles of rhetoric. To reach a sound judgment, a critic must utilize all of his scholarship. At times extensive research will be necessary to obtain the facts for a complete interpretation. Rhetorical criticism may proceed on a modest scale, or it may demand elaborate investigation.

CATEGORIES FOR STUDYING AN ADDRESS OF IMPORTANCE

The following categories should serve as a basis for a critical appraisal of a speech of historical significance. Specific items in the divisions of these categories may or may not be applicable to the study of a particular speech.

THE OCCASION

1. What were the events and circumstances giving rise to the discussion of which the speech is a part?
     opponents
     colleagues
     previous speeches and writings
     contentions of each faction
     position taken by the speaker
     position taken by his colleagues
     position taken by his opponents
2. What was the status of public opinion at the time of the speech?

factions	leadership
institutions	the public
means	the issues

3. What were the immediate circumstances?
     time of day
     place of assembly
     purpose of assembly
     size and nature of the room
     position of the speaker
     proximity of the audience
     program of the occasion

THE AUDIENCE

1. Did the speaker have both an immediate and a remote audience? If so, did the speaker address both audiences, or did the remote audience merely overhear or read the address?
2. Considering each audience separately, what were important aspects?

size	intelligence
sex	education
age groups	experience

3. In each audience, what was the effect of the following?
     information on the subject
     attitude toward the speaker
     attitude toward the subject
4. Did the speaker establish common ground?

of information	of beliefs
of experience	of feelings
of interests	of patterns of action

5. Did the speaker take any of the following differences into account?

age	health
sex	religion

race
nationality
country
region
community
family

politics
profession
occupation
economic status
social position
personal prestige

6. What was the function of the audience?
7. What was the audience's knowledge of and part in the discussion?
8. What factions, opinions, prejudices, desires, tensions, and moods does the audience represent?
9. How did the audience receive the speaker?
10. How well could the audience hear the speaker?
11. How well could the audience understand what the speaker said?
12. How attentive was the audience to the speaker and his speech?

THE SPEAKER

1. What biographical facts concerning the speaker are pertinent to the interpretation and evaluation of the speech?

childhood   experience
education   associates

2. What were the outstanding physical characteristics of the speaker?

appearance   voice
health   gestures
bearing   mannerisms

3. What were the speaker's intellectual habits, moral traits, and temperament?
4. What was the speaker's reputation?

personal   as a speaker
professional   with the audience

5. What were the principles and beliefs held by the speaker?
6. What was the speaker's authority on his subject?
7. What were the speaker's prejudices, attitudes, and personal interests in the outcome?
8. What was the speaker's function in the discussion?
9. What special advantages did the speaker hold?
10. How well acquainted was the speaker with the members of his audience, and what attitude did he have toward them?
11. What methods did the speaker use in preparing his speech?

THE SPEECH

1. Is there a verified text of the speech?
2. Are there recordings of the speech?
3. How was the speech delivered (impromptu, extemporaneously, from memory, from manuscript)?

4. What was the general purpose of the speech?
5. What was the specific purpose?
6. Was the purpose worthy or unworthy?
7. If the purpose was unworthy, was it intentionally to exploit or unintentionally evil?
8. How should the speech be classified (ceremonial, social, professional, or policy forming)?
9. What type of speech within this classification does it exemplify?
10. What is the proposition or statement of the central idea?
11. What are the supporting divisions?
12. What are the supporting subdivisions of each division?
13. What is the plan of adaptation?
14. With what kind of introduction does the speech begin?
15. With what methods is the body developed?
16. With what kind of conclusion does the speech end?
17. What are the sources of ideas used in the speech?
18. What is the mood or tone of the speech?
19. What nontechnical means of persuasion are used?

   laws   sworn oaths
   authorities   contracts
   evidence by force
20. Are concrete objects used to stir the feelings?
21. Does the speaker's reputation enhance the speech?
22. What technical logical proof is used?

   basic assumptions   constructive reasoning
   kinds of evidence   refutative reasoning
23. What technical psychological appeals are used?

   to feelings   to interests
   to desires   to beliefs
   to motives   to habits
24. What technical personal proof is used?

   experience   integrity
   judgment   loyalty
25. To what extent is the language communicative?

   choice of words   means for directness
   kinds of sentences   devices for force
26. Are unworthy techniques employed?

   distortion of facts
   unsupported assertions
   withholding of evidence
   witticisms substituted for evidence
   slogans substituted for reasoning
   sweeping generalizations

careless exaggerations
strawmen and red herrings
appeals to the baser emotions and prejudices
emotionally charged language
27. What were the characteristics of delivery?
realization of meaning (centering and phrasing)
communication with the audience
voice, articulation, poise, and bodily activity
28. What was the immediate effect of the speech?
29. What was the ultimate effect of the speech?
30. In your judgment, what is the value of the speech?
31. How does the speech compare with other speeches?
32. Why does this speech have historical significance?
33. Does the speech have literary as well as rhetorical merit?
34. Were the results of the speech socially desirable?

14 CONCLUSION:
Uses and Abuses

Words can more than convey a policy.
They can also convey and create a mood,
an attitude, an atmosphere—or an awaken-
ing.

—John F. Kennedy

Excellence in speechmaking comes only with directed effort. The lives of such men as Chatham, Burke, Fox, Clay, Webster, Lincoln, and Churchill reveal that their abilities in speaking resulted largely from wide reading, study, and conference; from intensive practice in writing and rewriting; from rehearsal of speeches in empty rooms, in fields, and in groves; from speaking in debating and literary societies and in clubs; from formal classroom training by teachers of rhetoric and public speaking; from critical reading and listening to speeches; from thoughtful preparation and continued practice in speechmaking. Many outstanding speakers had deficiencies of voice and articulation, limitations of formal education, or fear of audiences; but by close application, they surmounted their handicaps and eventually achieved their high competence.

The accomplishment of students today is sometimes equally noteworthy. Many of those about us have learned, through organized instruction, to present their ideas with tremendously improved effectiveness. Many college and university alumni testify to the value of their undergraduate course in speechmaking.

ACHIEVEMENT FROM THE PRACTICE
OF SPEECHMAKING

As a speaker, you will be judged largely by the reliability of your statements, by the quality of the advice you have to offer, by the clarity of your explanations, and by the wisdom of your counsel. To make your subject interesting and illuminating, you must draw upon a wide range of experiences and ideas. Therefore, extensive reading and study are an important part of learning to speak more effectively. Your study and practice up to this point should have resulted in some definite achievement.

ACQUISITION OF POISE AND CONFIDENCE

Students often say that courses in speechmaking give them poise and self-assurance, not only before their classroom audience, but also before other groups. Perhaps you will never altogether lose your tension in speaking, and perhaps you should not; but you have doubtless learned to manage preliminary feelings of anxiety and apprehension.

DEVELOPMENT OF INTELLECTUAL ALERTNESS

Since speechmaking is concerned with the capture and pursuit of ideas and their organization and management in motion, it requires the speaker to grow intellectually. You have learned the necessity of being alert and well informed. Moreover, you have been exposed to the thinking of students of different backgrounds and interests. Perhaps you have influenced some of their attitudes; they may have modified yours.

ACQUAINTANCE WITH DIFFERENT KINDS OF SPEAKING

A speaker has not matured until he has gained experience in making many different types of addresses. You have had the opportunity to inform, to persuade, to impress, and to entertain. You have made short and long speeches on different kinds of topics.

AWARENESS OF GOOD CRITICISM

Mere repetition does not make a good speaker; some of the poorest speakers have had the most experience. Your listeners have helped you to survey both your strong points and your weak points; they have taught you how to tell a good speech from a poor one; and they have encouraged you to correct your faults and to build on your strength.

KNOWLEDGE OF BASIC PRINCIPLES

You have surveyed the basic principles of speaking—choosing a topic, finding ideas, organizing and adapting material, wording the speech, improving the management of the voice and body, achieving the speech purpose, understanding audiences, and appraising the requirements of the occasion. These basic principles are of first importance to you, because, taken as a whole, they provide you with a concept and a theory of speechmaking; and in speechmaking nothing is more practical than a sound theory. You have heard speakers who, by long practice based on misconception, have become habituated to error. The man whose theory of speechmaking is mistaken or inadequate may regard a public address as a monologue, or as an opportunity for exhibition of personal prowess, or to the shouting of sounds and the waving of arms. He does not understand the function of public address in forming policy or motivating action. Thirty or forty years of practice based on an unsound theory may have made him a public nuisance or worse.

High competence in speechmaking is not easily achieved, but you have laid a sound basis for progress by gaining an understanding of principles tested by speakers in generations past. Your future effort should therefore perfect you in right practice.

THE RESPONSIBILITIES OF SPEECHMAKING

Speechmaking has responsibilities as well as rewards. As a citizen and a speaker, you should accept these responsibilities.

You should know when to speak, when to confer, and when to be silent. No one should speak unless he has something to contribute. Better speaking, not more speaking, should be your aim. "Think before you speak" is a wise motto. Yet, although some people speak too frequently and at too great length, others form the equally bad habit of speaking cryptically or not speaking at all. A group that has met to solve a problem may be bored by a long-winded speaker, but it also suffers if helpful ideas remain unexpressed. In a free society the right to make and to listen to speeches is the privilege of every citizen, not the prerequisite of a favored few.

You should know that problems cannot be solved solely by speeches. The action and interaction involved in speechmaking is necessary in a free society, but other forms of action should not be minimized. The greatest speakers have often been active in many enterprises; the most satisfying speeches are those that are a part of a full life.

WOMEN PLAY AN INCREASING ROLE IN PUBLIC AFFAIRS
Mrs. Franklin D. Roosevelt realized the power of the spoken word. Her effectiveness, both at home and abroad, earned for her the title First Lady of The World.

You should know that the gifted speaker has a special obligation to be intellectually honest. The ancient principle that only a good man can become a truly great speaker still retains its validity. The speaker should possess and demonstrate good judgment, good character, and good will toward his audience. He should weigh his purposes; he should measure his words.

A well-presented speech, filled with sturdy argument and solid sense, increases influence, enhances reputation, and augments prestige as it advances its cause. A single effective and timely speech may accomplish more than a whole year of unimaginative plodding at the daily job. A single poor speech may display more ignorance, shallowness, and ineptitude than the public might otherwise discover in a long time. The opportunity to speak should be used in the interest of one's group. No speaker who talks effectively for his fellows is likely to suffer in their esteem, but one who refuses to speak or who speaks ineffectively may do his cause and his compatriots a grave disservice.

The responsible citizen realizes that public address is an instrumental art that can be used for good ends or bad. A Lincoln will use public address to promote the brotherhood of man; a Hitler will use it to incite race prejudice. The responsible speaker and listener will not be satisfied with emotional appeals for contributing money to a cause; he will want to know the facts about its purposes, its management, and its usefulness. He will analyze the case for a change in policy to make sure that the assumptions are sound, that the facts are accurate, relevant, and adequate, that the authorities are appropriate and competent, that the reasoning is valid, that the appeals are worthy, and that the conclusion is justified.

When a new playground is needed, when a code of ethics in his profession is suggested, or when a rehabilitation program requires funds from his organization, he should know how to make the best use of his knowledge and skill to establish the proof that will get results. By showing other citizens sound principles of evaluation and of advocacy of public policies and programs, he can help to raise the standards of judgment in his community and in his profession. He has at his command the means to be an influential citizen.

A responsible government in a free society, now as always, must depend upon the making and judging of arguments and appeals in speeches. Now, as was true when Plato first made the observation, "the punishment suffered by the wise, who refuse to take part in the government, is to live under the government of bad men."

APPENDICES

APPENDIX I:
A Speech for Study

"DAVY CROCKETT'S TONGUE-TIED ADMIRERS"

TRAINING FOR AN ARTICULATE DEMOCRACY

By ROBERT G. GUNDERSON
*Chairman, Department of Speech, Oberlin College, Oberlin, Ohio
Delivered before the University of Virginia Institute for Teachers of
English, Speech and Drama, Charlottesville, Va., August 8, 1955* *

A lecturer, says the bitter lexicographer, Ambrose Bierce, is one who has "his hand in your pocket, his tongue in your ear, and his faith in your patience." The process of lecturing is, in fact, designed to induce that heroic euphoria which psychiatrists now call, with appropriate apologies to James Thurber, the Walter Mitty syndrome. "No one can imagine what dreadful hard work it is to keep awake and listen to what's said," confessed the restless Coonskin Congressman, Davy Crockett, after a term in Congress. "Splitting gum logs in August is nothing beside it." Over one-hundred years have passed since the King of the Wild Frontier uttered these immortal words, and during that time Americans have distinguished themselves as genuinely lazy listeners. Indeed, public opinion polls prove that people resist serious talk, as Davy would say, just as a coon dog fights fleas. So determined are they to be amused that Dr. George Gallup, in all seriousness, worries publicly for fear that they may die laughing.

According to the best evidence of our pollsters, we devote but little time to serious reading and listening. An analysis of 131 television programs last Sunday reveals that twelve programs, less than ten percent, were devoted to subjects which might, with some stretch of the imagination, be called informative or educational. Twelve were religious broadcasts, and the remaining seventy-two percent strained manfully to keep listeners amused. Sunday, of course, is a day of rest and relaxation. But

* *Vital Speeches*, Sept. 1, 1955, pp. 1462–1466. Reprinted by permission of Professor Gunderson, now Professor of Speech, Indiana University, Bloomington, Indiana.

393

on Monday, a week ago today, there was even greater opportunity for amusement. Ninety-one percent of the broadcast time went for hot-weather entertainment fare—or handy-dandy know-how and uplift. In a total of 149 listings, there were eleven short news broadcasts and only two manifestly significant programs. Well, it's August, you may say, and the educational Sahara of last week end is atypical. This, however, is unhappily not the case. During all of 1953, Americans devoted more man hours to "I Love Lucy" and "Show of Shows" than to all the educational programs broadcast.

It would be comforting to discover that those not listening to Lucy were busy reading *Harper's* or the New York *Times*—or perhaps some recent best seller. Again, public opinion surveys demonstrate that Americans look at the printed page primarily for amusement. Many adults don't even have a kinesthetic appreciation of books. "Despite the fact that we have the highest level of formal education in the world," says Dr. Gallup, "fewer people buy and read books in this nation than in any other modern democracy." The average American—and when pollsters use the term *average* they evidently mean what they say—spends less than four minutes a day reading about national or international news. A survey of metropolitan newspaper readers reveals that more people read the most popular comic than read the most important news item.[1]

These reading and listening habits might logically lead one to suspect that Americans run a good chance of being ignorant. Several polls do indeed confirm this suspicion. In his presidential address at the Seventh Annual Convention of the American Association for Public Opinion Research, Bernard Berelson concluded that from twenty to forty percent of the public is "totally uninformed" about specific issues of the day.[2] On tests of simple information results are appalling. After the biggest radio, television, and news coverage of the nominating conventions in history, one citizen in four was still unable to name the two vice-presidential candidates. Lest you think this is an even greater reflection on the vice-presidency, let me add hurriedly that one in ten had never heard of the atomic bomb, two in every ten were unable to identify the United Nations, and only one in four had a "reasonably accurate" idea of what the Bill of Rights was about. Three out of every four were unable to identify Nehru or Molotov.[3]

[1] George Gallup, "Mass Information or Mass Entertainment," *Vital Speeches*, May 15, 1953, 473–4.

[2] Bernard Berelson, "Democratic Theory and Public Opinion," *The Public Opinion Quarterly*, XVI (Fall, 1952), 318.

[3] Gallup, *op. cit.*, 473–4; Rensis Likert quoted in Quincy Wright (ed.), *The World Community* (Chicago, 1948), 282; Bernard Berelson and Morris Janowitz (eds.), *Reader in Public Opinion and Communication* (Glencoe, Illinois), 487; Ralph O. Nafziger, Warren C. Engstrom, and Malcolm S. Maclean, Jr., "The Mass Media and an Informed Public," *The Public Opinion Quarterly*, XV (Spring, 1951), 106.

If citizens know little about current affairs, they know even less about the history of their country. In a widely heralded New York *Times* survey of 7,000 students in thirty-six colleges during World War II, eighty-four percent were unable to cite two of the many contributions made by Thomas Jefferson. Twenty-five "scholars"—though certainly no Virginians —managed to get to college with the erroneous idea that George Washington was president during the Civil War. Only two in a hundred could identify Alexander H. Stephens. A third of them thought Alexander Hamilton distinguished himself as president; some—and these were college folks, remember—thought he was famous because of his watches. In a more recent survey, high-school students demonstrated that they knew more about current events than did most adults; but both groups, to quote the New York *Times*, were "shockingly ignorant." Last month, the Gallup poll proclaimed that the "average college graduate has a knowledge of geography unworthy of an eight-year-old." [4] More people than ever before are graduated but not educated.

Worse still, we are scared as well as ignorant. *Time* calls this the "silent generation"; a survivor of the Korean War calls it the "beat generation"; and President Eisenhower worries because we are becoming a nation of spectators in sports, too timid, apparently, to take the field— even at play. Projected into the more unfamiliar realm of ideas we feel our way timorously like a barefoot boy on a cinder path. At a Madison, Wisconsin, Fourth-of-July celebration several years ago, only one stalwart patriot out of 112 was brave enough to affix his signature to the Declaration of Independence. A leading Protestant clergyman testifies that ministers today avoid basic social and moral issues in sermons which are studiously "inoffensive." [5] Robert M. Hutchins, one of the boldest of our educational leaders, and certainly not one to be easily intimidated, is quoted as saying that it's dangerous to join any organization, "even one whose sole objective is merely to preserve and perpetuate Mother's Day in America." After bewailing this sorry kind of "hostility to eccentricity and controversy," Governor Adlai Stevenson begged the girls at Smith to be more "ornery," while noting that our century needs more "idiosyncratic, unpredictable" characters. [6]

Wallowing thus in a morass of intellectual timidity, those of us yet free enough to lift a finger point it quite appropriately at demagogues, witch-hunters, and other cowardly neurotics who are, in fact, the most frightened folks of all, for they are afraid to let us decide things for ourselves. In our dismay over these antediluvians, however, we forget that

[4] New York *Times*, April 4, 1943; March 22, 1953; *Time*, July 4, 1955.

[5] Roy A. Burkhart, "Action from the Pulpit," *The Annals* of the American Academy of Political and Social Science, Vol. 250 (March, 1947), 80.

[6] New York *Times*, June 7, 1955.

we are, after all, the ones who educated those who support them. Aren't we in some measure, at least, to blame for the prevailing fear of deviationism? By preachment and assiduous practice we prepare an intellectual atmosphere in which it is more comfortable to be docile. Who among us can say in candor that he has not taken a kick-at-the-cat of eccentricity lately? Oh, to be sure, the less vigorous among us may perhaps have only clucked our tongues to advertise the horrors of being different; but, in general, we pay a studied obeisance to sacred cows of fashion in art, architecture, dress, grammar, literature, pronunciation, and parlor games. Preoccupied with the tattle-tale gray of social irregularity, we find little time for new ideas. From nursery school to graduate seminar our favorite expression is, "We don't do that." The massive disapproval of society is thus marshalled against even the most incipient tendency to stray from tribal mores or ritual.

Ignorance and intellectual timidity look bad on a Rorschach ink-blot test of democratic society. There is, as Delbert Clark has warned, "danger in what we don't know." Scared, uninformed people inevitably inspire cynicism and demagoguery in others, who, as Ambrose Bierce says, find it convenient to exploit "the conduct of public affairs for private advantage." Annoyed by the remote, impersonal operation of government, the uninformed citizen all too easily loses his faith in democratic processes. When I tell students to write their Congressman, for example, they laugh with the same cynical laugh of the G-I when told to "go see the chaplain."

Unfortunately, this kind of cynicism is subtle, pervasive, and fashionable. Brisk young advertising men in charcoal-gray suits on Madison Avenue, tired no doubt of recommending the proper taste in toothpaste, now talk knowingly about "the engineering of consent." [7] Viewing the uninformed mass mind as merely a goose-like vacuum for them to stuff, they feed it capsulated wisdom predigested in the capacious gizzards of the great public-relations agencies. A better educated public can successfully resist this forced feeding, but we should start educating fast for as Alistair Cooke has pointed out, "We can keep hydramatic drive and still lose our democracy." [8] Our liberties are safe, said the founder of this University in a far less complicated day, only in the hands of people with a certain "degree of instruction." "If once they become inattentive to public affairs," Mr. Jefferson warned, ". . . Congress and Assemblies, Judges and Governors, shall all become wolves."

Pioneer Americans provide a refreshing contrast to the "beat" generation of today. They admired vigor in speech, bombast in oratory, hyperbole in humor, and no-holds-barred in politics. "I'm David Crockett, fresh from the backwoods, half horse, half alligator, a little touched with

[7] Edward L. Bernays, "The Engineering of Consent," *The Annals, op. cit.,* 113–20.
[8] Alistair Cooke, *Vital Speeches,* November 15, 1951.

snapping turtle," proclaimed the newly-elected Congressman on his first trip to Washington. "I can wade the Mississippi, leap the Ohio, ride a streak of lightning, slip without a scratch down a honey locust, whip my weight in wildcats, hug a bear too close for comfort and eat any man opposed to Jackson." The irrepressible Representative from West Tennessee hardly needed to add, "I'll wear no man's collar." Like many Westerners, our hero was suspicious of the kind of pussyfooting now popular with many who today sing his praises. "Always suspect a man," he said, "who affects great softness of manner, or unruffled evenness of temper, or an enunciation studied and slow. These things are unnatural. . . . The most successful knaves are usually of this description, as smooth as razors dipt in oil, and as sharp. They affect the softness of the dove, which they have not, in order to hide the cunning of the serpent which they have." When a White House functionary cried, "Make way for Colonel Crockett," Davy responded with a vigorous independence now alas out of fashion: "Colonel Crockett can make way for himself."

Foreign travelers invariably testified that nineteenth-century citizens were bold, articulate champions of democracy—convinced of their own stake in the American experiment—and of their own important role in it. Charles Dickens was dismayed because politics was the "national amusement." Count Adam Gurowski noted that "the thirst for knowledge" was a major "characteristic of the American mind." Though admittedly most citizens lacked formal education, de Tocqueville found "hardly a pioneer's hut" which did not "contain a few odd volumes of Shakespeare." Philip Hone, onetime mayor of New York, observed that an American blacksmith "would think meanly of himself if he could not argue a point of law with the village lawyer." James Bryce reported a kindly sense of "human fellowship" in which citizens valued the integrity of others and felt that citizenship itself constituted "a certain ground" for respect.

Though respecting each other as individuals, our ancestors did their own thinking. Since they enjoyed controversial talk, they spoke frankly—and often at great length—even when sometimes they had little to say. So eager were they for speechmaking that they preferred it even to drama. "Lectures," complained the aristocratic Philip Hone in 1841, "are all the vogue, and the theaters are flat on their backs." Speakers displayed a remarkable laryngeal stamina, and listeners rewarded them with an even more remarkable patience, if not to say interest. A commentary of thirty minutes or an hour was hardly worthy of being called a speech. During the famous hard-cider canvass of 1840, for example, William C. Rives of Albemarle County made many speeches, some of which were over four hours' duration. A detailed analysis of these verbal marathons proves that they were informative as well as lengthy; a few, in fact, were outstanding. The solid intellectual content and the frequent classical allusions testify to the respect which speakers once accorded their listeners. As always, of course, there were those who said a lot about nothing. "Their tongues," said Congressman Crockett, "go like windmills whether they have grist to grind or not."

With the passing of the Frontier, Americans evidently lost something of their independence, something of their bold coonskin self-assurance, their articulate capacity for talk, and their willingness to listen. In the present age of mass production and specialization, individuals speak collectively through pressure groups. We hire a public-relations mouthpiece to do our talking for us; and most debate takes place at the Summit, if one can call it that, between special-interest-group spokesmen. Where once politics was truly the national pastime, the engrossing subject for conversation around every village pump and cracker barrel, it now finds itself far subordinate to baseball, and way out in the deep left field of national interest. According to a recent survey, fully half of our adult population rarely if ever talk politics—and then only when activated by dramatic events. Twenty-five to thirty percent do not engage in political discussion at all.[9] The old-fashioned general store is gone; and in the jostle of the super-market, there is no room for the pot-bellied stove which once fostered an articulate democracy.

Mass production has spread from industry to art and communication. Industrial workers, bored by their routine operations, quite understandably seek escape in passive entertainment. Frustrated after eight hours with spot welder or soldering iron, they crave to be amused—thus a passionate preoccupation with the frivolities piped out of New York and Hollywood—amusing spectaculars requiring no mental effort, only a bovine capacity to endure commercials. The political programs that do find their way into our communications channels are usually concerned either with the carnival aspects of politics or with clichés—comforting verbal massage carefully designed to ease intellectual labor pains.

Yet never before have we been so well equipped to develop an enlightened electorate. In a land completely wired for sound and picture, the discouraging revelations of the pollsters are hardly credible. Our means of communicating enlightenment are unexcelled. "You are," as the Bell Telephone advertisement confidently says, "now in touch with more people and more people are in touch with you than ever before." Last year, fifty million homes had radio; the knobs of thirty-three million television sets dialed feverishly for Sullivan, Gobel, Godfrey and the rest. Meanwhile, a Ford Foundation study at the University of Toronto demonstrated that instruction by television was "as effective in teaching as classroom lectures." [10] At last, we have the technical capacity to bring

[9] Berelson, *Public Opinion Quarterly*, XVI, 323.
[10] *World Almanac*, 1955, 789–90.

enlightenment into every home—to achieve the kind of responsible and responsive democracy heretofore possible only in the small Greek state, the Swiss canton, and the New England town meeting. If we would insist, our public officials could be forced to thrash out current issues in our living rooms; but instead we apparently prefer the saturnalia of national conventions and the fanfaronade of investigations, rituals certainly more designed to debase than to enlighten.

The commercial-minded executives of our mass media will of course continue the present imbalance in favor of the frivolous and the spectacular only so long as we continue to show a taste for it. Thus it's not so much a question of will our politicians talk sense to the American people as it is a question of will we listen if and when they do. Obviously this is our problem and not one for UNIVAC.

There of course are those who say why bother. In a genuinely provocative book, *The Lonely Crowd*, David Riesman musters his brilliant Freudian mumbo jumbo to ridicule "indignants" who are so Draconian as to demand that mass media project "civic affairs and other serious matters" into the already crowded airwaves. Though Riesman hints darkly that such "inner-directed" middle-class moralists are motivated by "a Puritanical dislike for leisure," I nevertheless should like to suggest that our mass media might well devote more than one hour out of every ten to educational broadcasting. If this informational hair shirt is too uncomfortable for a civilized citizenry, I'll purge myself of that "neo-Puritanic hygienic feeling" by scrawling "I Love Lucy" five hundred times on a *Variety* billboard, while recalling Alistair Cooke's heartening assurance that "the piety" of Queen Victoria "depressed the English sinner for sixty hopeless years." [11]

Teachers, as Henri Peyre of Yale has said, should be bold intellectual leaders, not "retiring recluses." We should lead, not follow, public opinion. Our freedom to criticize is not a privilege granted magnanimously by a tolerant public; it is a duty and a responsibility. The Riesman doctrine of relax and enjoy TV is merely a hedonistic determinism which in practice gives the country over to the hucksters of imbecility.

More specifically, what can we do to train a better informed and more articulate democracy? Professor Harold Lasswell says we need "a new way to talk." Public discussions need a new functionary, Mr. Lasswell says, a "clarifier" who abruptly interrupts the continuous drone of sound in order to force intelligibility into talk.[12] He would operate as a kind of Mr. Quiz, not too unlike the amiable but skeptical professor on Herb

[11] David Riesman, *The Lonely Crowd* (New Haven, 1950), 210–24; Alistair Cooke, *Vital Speeches*, November 15, 1951.

[12] Harold D. Lasswell, "Democracy through Public Opinion," in Berelson and Janowitz (eds.), *Public Opinion*, 469–83.

Schreiner's program, who speaks up when there's a communications failure. By calling the speaker back to order, the clarifier might also rouse
listeners from their chair-bound Walter Mitty exploits and reveries. In
practice, this means less old-fashioned oratory and more face-to-face discussion, more cross-examination, more meet-the-press kind of interroga-
tion. It also means a more active, if not to say aggressive, role for listeners.
Our students should be encouraged to ask why and when—and the rest
of the stock questions required of all good reporters. Public officials need
the vigorous give-and-take of cross-examination. In a free country, they
are our servants, as Davy Crockett and his contemporaries frequently
reminded themselves. They are not our masters, nor are they our in-
quisitors. We are the ones who should be asking the questions. Students
should discover, as a colleague of mine once said, that they are free—not
just at large.

In training a more articulate democracy, we should worry less about
adjustment and more about what can be done to improve the body
politic. Democratic living of course requires adjustment and compromise,
but it also demands the mastery of troublesome human problems—
problems to which we should not become adjusted. In the past, we have
talked too much about adapting the individual to his surroundings and
not enough about adapting the surroundings to the individual. If a member of the current silent generation were perchance to find himself trans-
ported across the Stygian creek to Hades, he would hurriedly recall our
advice, toss a bone to Cerberus, shake hands with the Prince of Darkness,
and try to acclimate himself as best he could to his uncongenial surroundings. This is not, as we have often kept repeating, training for democratic
living; it's the softening-up process for George Orwell's *1984.*

In an articulate democracy there should be more ideological warfare,
a kind of conflict which needs our vigorous encouragement. The whisper
in the Voice of America overseas is in part caused by an acute aphonia
around the domestic cracker barrel. We can't export a clear conception
of our way of life unless our citizens are capable of phrasing their con-
victions. If students learn by doing, as of course we all believe, then there
should be more training in discussion and debate, the essential tools in
a democratic society. Here, as Professors Henry L. Ewbank and J. Jeffery
Auer point out in *The Bulletin* of Secondary School Principals, we have
the ideal laboratory method for training in the solution of "social, political, and economic problems." [13]

Mere talk, of course, is not enough. Students must have something
to say. Part of the prevailing cynicism about politics arises from a popular

[13] Henry L. Ewbank and J. Jeffrey Auer, "Decision Making: Discussion and
Debate," *The Bulletin* of the National Association of Secondary-School Principals,
XXXII (January, 1948), 34–50.

feeling that speechmaking consists largely of saying nothing well. Max Eastman writes of "the lost art of oratory," and Professor William G. Carleton of the University of Florida bemoans the "deterioration" in the "intellectual content" and "literary style" of even those leaders who "by reputation stand in the first rank." [14] The stockpile of quotations ("commonplaces" Aristotle called them) which American leaders glean from their schooling is so inadequate that of course they must rely upon ghost writers. Recognizing this, the Harvard Committee on *General Education in a Free Society* urges more memorization of "poems and passages of lasting significance." The British debaters who tour our campuses each year have given American debaters a profound sense of inferiority for they clearly demonstrate that they are at home with ideas; they have wit, and a classical culture to draw upon for their illustrations. In short, they are articulate, and we, for all our file boxes of information, are tongue-tied. A part of this Oxford erudition comes from a regimen of memorization, a practice abandoned here as unrealistic; yet the same generation which rejected this as too artificial, now accepts the inherent dishonesty of the ghost writer without blush or embarrassment.

An articulate citizenry must know both facts and logic. Facts are what people think with; consequently, it's impossible to teach thinking in a factual wasteland. The most pointless, yet often the most acrimonious, arguments develop over questions which might be settled quickly by shuffling a few pages in the *World Almanac*. Arguments arising from faulty logic, however, are less easily settled because most of us are unable to find the right page in Aristotle's handbook. More time can well be spent specifically on the labyrinthian mysteries of the reasoning process itself. As Professor Arleigh B. Williamson suggests, we might well add a "T" to the three "R's," reading, writing, arithmetic, and *thinking*.[15]

By emphasizing facts and logic we can perhaps encourage a corresponding lack of respect for successful sophistry. When leading rabble-rousers pay eloquent tribute to their academic training in public speaking, we all cringe in collective embarrassment for obviously an ethical X-factor has been neglected, even though a success-mad society is no doubt more blameworthy than the educational system which reflects it.

Finally, students in an articulate democracy must have more respect for ideas—particularly for the ideas of others. Lord Bryce listed this as an American characteristic of the 'eighties, and isn't it indeed a basic ingredient of true democracy? Despite their self-canonization as apostles

[14] Max Eastman, "The Lost Art of Oratory," *Saturday Review,* XXXVI (March 6, 1954), 11–12, 36; William G. Carleton, "Effective Speech in a Democracy," *Vital Speeches,* June 15, 1951, 541.

[15] Arleigh B. Williamson, "Safeguarding Channels of Communication," *The Annals, op. cit.,* 10.

of Americanism, those who would silence us by inquisitorial stratagems are Archenemies from an Underworld of Authoritarianism. "In America," wrote two distinguished foreign observers a century ago, "the spirit of progress is bold, and often encroaching . . . new ideas easily get a fair chance of being practically tried; the public at large does not shrink from testing . . . different solutions of a political problem, and the Sovereignty of the States affords great opportunity for it." The University of Virginia was established in this bold spirit as a testing ground for ideas. "This institution," said Mr. Jefferson of the newly-founded University, "will be based on the illimitable freedom of the human mind. For here we are not afraid to follow truth wherever it may lead, nor to tolerate any error so long as reason is left free to combat it."

Training for an articulate democracy, as John W. Studebaker, former Commissioner of Education said of teaching, is not "a task for timorous or feeble souls; nor for the complacent and uncertain. It requires Americans whose faith in democracy does not waver or falter because they know whereof they speak and are convinced that the values they defend are eternally right and true." [16]

[16] *Congressional Record,* 80th Congress, 2d Session, Vol. 94, Pt. 10, 2205–06.

APPENDIX II:
A Speech for Criticism

CUSTODIANS OF HISTORY

DEVOTION TO PEACE AND JUSTICE

By ADLAI E. STEVENSON
United States Representative to the United Nations
Delivered in General Session, United Nations, New York City
September 20, 1962 *

. . .

I

I should like to begin by re-affirming, as emphatically as I can the high significance which the Government of the United States attaches to the work of the United Nations. My Government is more than ever convinced that the success or failure of this Organization could well mean the difference between world order and world anarchy. We believe that the work that lies before this 17th General Assembly is serious—and that it is also urgent.

First let me, on behalf of my Government and the City of New York welcome the delegates to this historic Assembly. We congratulate you Mr. President, on your election as President of the 17th General Assembly. You assume a place of honor among the world leaders who have been chosen to preside over the forum of the world in a time of peril and promise—a place which your talents and attainments can only further exalt.

And I also warmly welcome the addition to our membership of Trinidad-Tobago, Jamaica, Rwanda and Burundi—four new nations from sunny lands blessed with tropic beauty that I have had the good fortune to visit and admire.

But I welcome most of all the opportunity this session gives us to

* *Vital Speeches*, Oct. 15, 1962, pp. 10–14. Reprinted by permission of Ambassador Stevenson.

consider as a body the direction in which our affairs are moving and the action needed to bring us closer to the world we seek—a world of justice, freedom and peace.

II

A year ago we met at a time of doubt and danger. In the twelve months since, much has taken place to justify a measure of fresh hope for the future.

—A long, bitter war in Algeria has come to a close.

—A threatened conflict between two of our members in the Southwest Pacific has yielded to peaceful settlement—through statesmanship on their part and skillful conciliation by the United Nations;

—In Laos, civil war, abetted by foreign intervention, has been replaced by a cease-fire and an independent government under international guarantees;

—In the Congo—where the UN has played such a decisive part—war and threat of war seem to be yielding to new hopes for the peaceful reintegration of Katanga into the new Congo state, and to the Secretary General's vigorous efforts, with our support and that of the great majority of the members, to get early implementation of the United Nations reconciliation plan;

—Disarmament negotiations, with the encouragement of the General Assembly, have resumed in a new forum with non-nuclear powers playing a useful and constructive role;

—We have begun, under United Nations auspices, a search for cooperation in the development of outer space in the interests, not of any one nation, but of humanity;

—We have begun, too, an intensification of the drive against poverty under the United Nations Decade of Development.

These are all legitimate sources of gratification and there are others. But we would be deceiving ourselves if we looked on the bright side alone. We still—all of us—continue to live in a dark and precarious world.

—The crisis in Berlin has not exploded into war; but the pressures and harassments against West Berlin continue to rank as a most ominous threat to the peace of the world;

—The government of Cuba, with moral and material support from outside, carries on a campaign of subversion and vituperation against its neighbors in the Western Hemisphere.

—Unprovoked aggression from North Viet-Nam continues to threaten the freedom and independence of the Republic of Viet-Nam and to menace the peace in Southeast Asia;

—The Chinese Communists continue their policy of provocation, their acts of force and subversion.

—The threat of conflict still smolders in the Middle East, damped down but not quenched by the peace-keeping machinery of the United Nations;

—Disputes involving members of our organization continue unresolved on every continent;

—The continued repression of the people of Eastern Europe remains an underlying danger to peace;

—The concluding stage of the worldwide movement toward national independence elsewhere is complicated by issues, which though transient and manageable, could become explosive if cool heads do not prevail over hot tempers;

—The prevalence of poverty in great areas of the world remains a source of moral frustration and political danger;

—And, most ominous of all, the suicidal arms race continues unabated.

These situations raise serious dangers to the peace of the world.

It was to deal with such dangers to the peace that half the states in this Assembly Hall established the United Nations 17 years ago—and that the other half have adhered to the Charter in the years since.

The Charter issued a lofty challenge to mankind. It cannot be claimed that in these 17 years the United Nations has established a reign of peace on earth. But the record of our organization in meeting specific challenges to the peace is nonetheless impressive. In these years the United Nations, whether through the Security Council or the General Assembly through conciliation of cease-fire, through peace observation or truce supervision or direct military action, has helped avert or end hostilities in Iran, in Greece, in the Middle East, in Kashmir, in Indonesia, in Korea, at Suez, in Lebanon, in the Congo, and now in West New Guinea.

If the United Nations has not succeeded in bringing the great powers together, it has often succeeded in keeping them apart—in places where face-to-face confrontation might have changed difficult situations into impossible situations.

If the United Nations has not succeeded in settling all international disputes, it has prepared the way for the peaceful evolution of an international order. In that process, the UN has not made the fatal error of trying to freeze the movement of history. It has not sought peace at the expense of needed change. And we must be equally sure that in a world as volatile as our own change is not sought at the expense of peace, which is needed above all.

III

The record of accomplishment is formidable; but the movement of history is more peremptory than ever, and today's challenges of peace and of progress are therefore more urgent than ever. To meet these challenges, we need not just a strong but a still stronger United Nations. The most important general issue before this Assembly is to get on with the business of steadily improving our organization so that it can deal ever more energetically, efficiently and promptly with the dangers to peace and the obstacles to progress.

This is the essence—this is the heart—this is the day-to-day stuff of our duty in this Assembly as we see it: to build mightier mansions, to keep strengthening the United Nations. The worth and the loyalty of the members will be tested by this standard: do their actions—do their proposals strengthen or weaken our organization?

Strengthening the United Nations involves questions both of structure and of strategy.

So far as structure is concerned, a first necessity is to set the UN on a sound financial basis. Our organization has today a deficit of more than $150 million—brought about largely by defaults or delays in payments for peace-keeping operations which have proved as expensive as they were necessary.

The emergency plan to meet this deficit through the sale of bonds is good as a stopgap. As a result of action by our Congress, the United States Government will be in a position to lend the UN half of what it will borrow under this plan. Other nations already have pledged $73 million. We hope—and that's a mild word for it!—that these states, along with nations still unpledged, will bring the total pledge to $100 million. My government can then use its full authority to match that sum.

But this is only a palliative, it is not a solution. The current deficit is a symptom of a deeper problem—a problem created by the inaction of too many of the governments in this Assembly Hall. One can understand past reasons for reluctance to accept collective financial responsibility for UN actions. Some states, for example, doubted whether the General Assembly could legally make a binding assessment for the UN's peace-keeping expenses. But any legal uncertainties have now been cleared up by the recent opinion of the International Court of Justice.

This Assembly now faces the compelling obligation of affirming a policy of collective financial responsibility for actions of the United Nations. I believe that this session of the Assembly should accept and act upon the Advisory Opinion of the International Court of Justice as past Assemblies invariably have accepted and acted upon other advisory opinions. The financial integrity and independence of the UN are at stake. But something even more important is at stake—the rule of law. The Court has ruled on the law; it remains to this Assembly to manifest at once its respect and its compliance by converting the law into policy.

I believe that this Assembly must also devise a financing plan for future peace-keeping operations to take effect when the proceeds from the bond issue are exhausted. The details of such a plan are open to discussion. But whatever the character of the plan, it should require that every member meet its obligations when an assessment is duly voted.

We hope this Assembly will work out a program which will finance operations authorized by itself or by the Security Council. Otherwise we doom our organization to impotence. We cannot expect the United Nations to survive from day to day by passing a cup like a beggar in the street.

There are other problems of structure, in addition to finance. No one knows better than we in this Hall the need to streamline the procedures of this greatly expanded organization, so it can deal efficiently with the complex business which crowds our long agenda.

We must enlarge the Security Council and the Economic and Social Council to assure fair representation to every region of the earth.

We must review the rules and practices of our international civil service, particularly in the relation of Member States to the Secretariat, so the staff of the UN remains "exclusively international"—as the Charter stipulates.

We also must elect unconditionally a Secretary General for a full term of office. After the tragic death of Dag Hammarskjold last year, the Assembly went through a protracted but instructive constitutional crisis. We resolved this crisis by vindicating—overwhelmingly and I trust permanently—the integrity of the office of Secretary General as established by the Charter. We then selected unanimously as Acting Secretary General a diplomat of extraordinary personal qualities, who has served this Organization well in a time of transition and uncertainty.

Our responsibility in this Assembly is to make sure that this important office is as well filled in the next five years as it has been in the past—and that he who holds the office retains the full freedom and authority provided under the Charter.

IV

But the solution of all the problems of organization would still leave unsolved the question of how we use the machinery we have devised. I take it that our essential purpose is to find practical means of fulfilling the intentions of the Charter. But I sometimes wonder whether the means adopted are always the best way to achieve the ends desired.

I am well aware of the frustration, temptations and conflicts in any parliamentary democracy, but it happens to be the best system ever invented to protect and reconcile all interests in the conduct of public affairs. Given the inherent complexities of this form of organization— given the gravity of the matters with which we deal—given the youth of the United Nations—given its extremely rapid growth—it must be said that the General Assembly, with few exceptions, has conducted itself with surprising responsibility and maturity.

Our plain duty now is to perform our business in such a way as to make this Assembly even more responsible, more mature—and therefore more effective.

It is clear that the business of this Assembly cannot be conducted effectively in the manner of a protest demonstration in a public square. It is clear that the influence of this Assembly cannot grow if the quality of its debate is debased by propaganda or by speeches designed, not to further the business before the house but to gratify emotions back home.

Indignation and outrage have been powerful enemies of injustice since the beginning of history. It would be surprising if they had no place in the proceedings of the United Nations. But the test of resolutions presented to this Assembly must surely be whether they promise to bring us closer to rational solutions or real problems and thereby closer to justice.

For example I think we must all beware of the resolution which invokes high principle in support of unrealistic action and does nothing to advance a practical solution. If this becomes common practice, we would risk destroying the influence of our organization—for the value of its recommendations would depreciate like inflated currency.

In the United Nations, all members, large and small, are juridically equal. That is why it is so often called the hope of the world. That is why it is the great guardian of the interests of smaller states. And that is also why, as the Assembly grows in numbers, we must match its size by its sense of relevance and its sense of responsibility.

We must also recognize, I think, that open debate under the TV cameras is not always conducive to the moderation and restraint essential when proud and sovereign states are in dispute. Nor is the Assembly the only means through which our organization achieves its purposes. We saw a year ago that this Assembly could not agree on how to settle the dispute over West New Guinea. We know today how much the UN has been able to accomplish in composing this dispute by entering it as a quiet third partner.

I believe that there will be many opportunities for the UN to serve as a "third man" in world affairs: as the objective fact-finder—the impartial "presence"—the policeman on the beat—the instrument of quiet diplomacy. On some issues before us even today, for example, the UN might appoint a *rapporteur* to ascertain the facts and analyze the problems and thereby facilitate sound decisions by the General Assembly.

Nothing is more important to all of us than a sustained and systematic attack on the conflicts which threaten the peace. Our world is now a crowded house. Our planet a single powder keg. We believe that all nations must stay their hands in pursuit of national ambitions involving conflict with others until the world community has had a chance to find solutions through patient and quiet diplomatic effort.

The point here is not to oppose or to postpone desirable change; the point is not to stall or to evade needed action. On the contrary, the point is precisely to select the most effective technique—to search out the most relevant formula—to insure that change can in fact take place, that action can in fact be taken to secure the peace of the world and strengthen the United Nations.

There is work enough to do—and tools enough to do it. Let us resolve to set about it in an orderly fashion; let us use and combine our tools and techniques for a period of active inventive diplomacy; let us—in this 17th General Assembly—aspire to the highest forms of political art and usher in a time of peaceful solutions of conflict—of peaceful passage, through the vast transformations which contemporary history demands.

V

The path to peace lies through thickets of conflict. And the biggest obstacle in the path, the most overwhelming danger of all, is the onrushing arms race. Every day it gathers momentum as the nuclear powers and others, large and small, enlarge their arsenals. Some of us continue to invent and test frightful new weapons. We feel obliged to do this for the sake of our separate national interests—at a time in history when the national interest of all nations, those with nuclear weapons and those without, demands not the expansion but the abolition of the power to wage war.

Let me be as clear and simple as I can: this prodigal arms race is dangerous and deadly folly. Here in the United States we want to save, not destroy our fellow man. We want to devote the resources now swallowed up by this insatiable monster to the unfinished tasks of our own society. And we want to devote these resources to giving every soul on this earth a chance for a better life.

Yet the arms race goes on. It goes on because no nation, confronted by hostile nations, can neglect its defenses. No great power can risk unilateral disarmament. There is one way—and one way only—out of this intolerable dilemma; that is a system of complete and general disarmament under which all nations progressively tear down—in plain view of the international community and with suitable safeguards—their own capacity to wage war.

A great achievement of our last session was to endorse an agreement on a set of principles for general and complete disarmament in a peaceful world. But while we have made some progress, we have not made enough progress toward translating these agreed principles into an agreed plan—to move by mutual actions in rapid stages toward total disarmament and effective international peacekeeping.

The United States has proposed such a plan. It has submitted its proposals to this Assembly and to the 18-Nation Disarmament Conference at Geneva.

But, just as it takes at least two to make an arms race, it takes at least two to stop an arms race. No one in his senses would expect one side to abandon the means of self-defense unless it knew for sure that the other side was giving up its arms as well. This means that practical verification is the essence of any workable agreement on general disarmament.

It need not be total verification. We have demonstrated again and again during long negotiations that we are prepared to take certain risks to lessen the chance of an intensified arms race. But we are not prepared to risk our survival. If other nations permit—as we have agreed to do— the degree of international inspection technically required for mutual security, we can end the arms race. But we cannot stake our national existence on blind trust—especially on blind trust in a great and powerful nation which repeatedly declares its fundamental hostility to the basic values of our free society.

The issue is plain. The price of general disarmament is mutual security within the framework of the United Nations. Because such security would be by international inspection, it could have no conceivable connection with espionage. Is inspection by a United Nations agency too high a price to pay for the safety, perhaps survival, of mankind? Can any society value its secrecy more than everyone's safety—especially a society which avows itself the model toward which all other societies must irresistibly evolve?

Mr. President, I put this issue in all gravity. I ask the members of this Assembly to join the peoples of the world in demanding a program of general disarmament which stands a chance of ending the arms race.

Once again, the answer to this issue is not to be found in exhortation or emotionalism. It is not to be found by passing virtuous resolutions which proclaim noble ends without realistic means. It is to be found only in remorseless effort to solve the infinitely complicated problems of disarmament. We believe that serious negotiations in Geneva will bring us closer to our goal, and I hope the discussions there will continue to have the prayerful and wholehearted support of this Assembly.

Here in New York, the Assembly can insist on the indispensable condition of world disarmament: assurance that agreements made are agreements kept.

But there is a situation even more immediate and more hopeful than general disarmament. I refer to the testing of nuclear weapons. If we see in this a more acute problem, let me suggest that it is also more manageable—and therefore offers brighter hopes for early progress.

For nearly four years the nuclear powers, including my country, have been locked in negotiation for a reliable and permanent ban on the testing of nuclear weapons. From such a ban would come a barrier to the spread of such weapons; and there would come an end to this new source of radiation in the human environment; and a great step toward the comprehensive disarmament treaty we so earnestly seek.

As is plain from the draft treaties tabled in Geneva, the United States Government is prepared to stop the testing of all nuclear weapons, provided only that others are prepared to assume the obligation to do the same. Testing in the atmosphere, in the oceans and in space causes radiation. Testing underground does not. We are prepared to stop testing even without any international verification in the atmosphere, in the oceans and in space, because we have national means of detecting testing by others. And we are prepared to stop testing underground—where we don't have our own means of verification—provided an international system is created to assure that others are doing the same.

It may be interesting to you to know that since 1945, when it began, the United States has exploded nuclear devices with a total yield of about 140 megatons.

Since 1949, when it began, the USSR, so far as we can tell by distant instrumentation, has exploded devices with a total yield of approximately 250 megatons.

Since the USSR broke the moratorium last fall, its explosions have yielded 200 megatons—those which the United States was then compelled to undertake, only 25 megatons.

I repeat, we want to cease testing nuclear weapons. If other nuclear powers are also willing to make an agreement to cease, the testing will cease. But let there be no doubt about it—the United States prefers a comprehensive treaty banning all tests in all environments for all time. On this transcendent issue, we in the United States are in dead earnest. And I conclude with the thanks of my government to the eight non-aligned nations for their helpful and constructive efforts to bring about agreement at Geneva.

VI

The objective of peace is inseparably intertwined with the objective of progress. As we improve our organization's capacity to keep the peace, we also strengthen the United Nations for its other essential tasks: to help build nations in dignity and freedom—to help liberate humanity from century-old bonds of want and squalor. And, as we build healthy modern societies, we knit stronger the fabric of peace; we reduce the chance that misery and failure will explode into conflict. Thus are peace-keeping and nation-building two sides of the UN coin.

We who have attended these General Assemblies of the United Nations have been witnesses of a great historic transformation. In the years since 1945—and with the support of this Assembly—we have seen the age of classical colonialism move toward an end. In these years 46 nations— nearly half the present membership of this organization—have gained their independence. This has represented a revolutionary change in the structure of international relations and international power.

It has been a change, I need hardly say, which has been enthusiastically welcomed in the United States. As the first modern state to win freedom from colonialism, we have been proud to help other states begin that most precious and difficult of adventures—the adventure in self-government. We count no task more important than assisting those everywhere, in the older colonial areas and elsewhere, to self-determination.

This task will engage this Assembly in grave and determined deliberations in the months ahead. In no part of the world has the movement toward national independence attained more spectacular results in the last three years than in Africa. In no part of the world is it more important to make further progress in solving the remaining issues of classical colonialism on the basis of genuine self-determination. For many months, the Special Committee of 17 on colonialism has addressed itself to these issues. We hope that the Committee will be able to conduct its work in the future in an atmosphere undistracted by the emotions of the cold war which affected its work this year—in an atomsphere where states old and new can work together to help bring into existence in lands not yet free the conditions essential for successful nationhood.

For a nation is not created by a stroke of a pen. A declaration of political independence is a beginning not a conclusion. Nothing more discredits the great historic transformation of our epoch than for newly independent states to fall into chaos and become an international problem or an international danger. The long labor of nationhood requires the reality as well as the rhetoric of independence: it requires an emerging national will capable of the political wisdom, the administrative vigor, the economic energy and the moral discipline necessary to convert the promise of national independence into a free and productive life for its people. The interest of my government and of the world lies not in the mere multiplication of nations—but in the multiplication of nations where peoples are free and have the strength to survive, and to grow and to contribute to the vitality of the international order in the world community.

VII

Nation-building thus has its political dimension—but national independence has its social and economic and moral dimensions as well. That is why I hope that this Assembly will devote its attention to the next great item on the agenda of nation-building—that is, helping the new nations fashion the tools to carry out their tasks of self-development.

Never has a time been more propitious for the successful discharge of these tasks. If the miracles of science have given mankind new power to destroy, they have also given mankind new power to create. The challenge which confronts us is to turn the miracles of science to the service of man —and of man the laborer on this earth, as well as man the explorer of the universe beyond.

We have a right, I think, to congratulate the Committee on Peaceful Uses of Outer Space on its progress toward international scientific and technical cooperation, progress which holds high promise for both peace and the advancement of knowledge. But what does it profit if a few men orbit the earth while below them millions are starving? What is the point of our technological prowess if it can launch men into space but cannot lift them from the swamps of poverty?

To set out consciously to abolish poverty as the prevailing condition of humanity is as formidable a task as man ever set himself, and I would ask you not to underestimate its difficulties.

But if the task is enormously complex, it can also be deeply fulfilling. I am proud that my own country pioneered in offering a helping hand to nations prepared to start along the road toward self-sustaining growth. I am gratified too that so many of the other industrially developed nations have followed suit. It is heartening that groups of nations are beginning to work out their economic destinies in common through regional organizations, and coordinating their assistance to the emerging nations.

Over the years, the UN itself has established an impressive range of technical institutions geared to the job of helping the less developed nations to modernize their economies. The United Nations family of agencies is the source of new and exciting projects: A World Food Program is just getting under way. The Board of Governors of the World Bank is calling right now for recommendations on the expansion of capital for the International Development Association. An unprecedented conference on the application of science and technology to the problems of development will be held in Geneva early next year.

Other projects and programs attest to the growing maturity, the expanding scope, and the rising operational capacity of the UN family of agencies. This is all to the good.

The challenge before us now is to make our UN agencies better with each passing year—to endow them with sound procedures and adequate resources—to staff them with disinterested and expert talent—to improve their planning and programming and administration and coordination—to see that they meet the needs of realistic development in the new nations —to integrate them with the other forms of development assistance, national, regional and international, presently going to the emerging nations —and thereby to insure that development aid will be be applied everywhere on a cooperative rather than a competitive basis.

We need to produce a closer harmony from the orchestra of aid instruments already available to us.

The full promise of development cannot be achieved within national boundaries. To stimulate general prosperity, we must remove the barriers which block the free flow of men, money and goods across national frontiers.

We have seen the extraordinary burst of economic activity which has attended the evolution of the European Common Market—one of the great adventures in creative statesmanship of our age. Groups of countries in other parts of the world are also seeking ways to build regional economies which in turn can further thrive on expanded world trade.

It is essential of course, that such groupings should offer to non-members the fullest possible advantage of the larger market. We know now that one nation cannot buy its prosperity by limiting the prosperity of others.

An expanding world trade, built on the scaffolding of the General Agreement on Tariffs and Trade, rests in turn on that further social progress, that larger freedom, that broader structure of international peace which it is the purpose of the United Nations to secure. That is why the United States was pleased to join with its fellow members of the Economic and Social Council in the unanimous call for a United Nations Conference on Trade and Development. We will do everything we can to help this conference succeed.

We need to move—under the challenge of the Decade of Development —toward a clearer strategy of development—toward a better sense of priorities—toward a sharper division of labor among the various aid institutions—and toward a keener appreciation that the economic and social development of a country is not the result only of outside capital and assistance, but of political leadership, institutional growth, economic and social reform, and national will.

VIII

Here, then, are our twin tasks: to replace strident politics with quiet but determined diplomacy—and to replace the arms race, as the President said last year, with a peace race—with a creative race in the production and exchange of goods and the elevation of living standards.

These tasks are not new—nor will they be finished before we adjourn. But before we adjourn I trust that the 17th General Assembly will energetically get on with the job of peaceful settlement, of non-violent change, and of war against human want.

As the custodians of the history of our times, we can do no less. To the discharge of these responsibilities, my own government pledges its firm and unswerving support. Animated by the ideals of the Charter and by our obligations to our fellow men we, the members of this Assembly, cannot adjourn our deliberations without providing the world tangible evidence of our devotion to peace and justice. This tangible evidence, Mr. President, can lie only in our decisions and deeds in the months ahead.

APPENDIX III:
Parliamentary Procedure

The following glossary of parliamentary terms provides essential information concerning motions, functions of officers, and concepts and methods for participation in a parliamentary assembly.

GLOSSARY OF PARLIAMENTARY TERMS

Adjourn.   A motion—usually privileged—used to close a meeting.

Agenda.   The official items of business to be considered at a meeting arranged in a predetermined order.

Amend.   A subsidiary motion used to change the wording of another motion. Parliamentary usage recognizes two degrees of the motion to amend. The primary amendment is applied to the main motion; the secondary amendment is applied to the primary amendment. The motion to amend is classified as to form: (1) to insert, (2) to add, (3) to strike out, (4) to strike out and insert, (5) to substitute an entire motion. Only one primary and one secondary amendment may be considered at a time. The amendment must also be germane to the motion or amendment being discussed. It is out of order to amend a motion by inserting the word *not* in the motion, first, because this procedure violates the principle that motions should be stated affirmatively, and second, because the same objective (defeat of the proposal) should be achieved by voting negatively on the motion.

Amendability.   Whether or not the wording of a motion may be changed.

Appeal.   An incidental motion used to compel the chairman to submit a disputed decision to a vote of the assembly.

Basic tenets.   Some of the basic assumptions of parliamentary procedure are: (1) Only one main motion can be considered at a time. (2) Every argument has at least two sides. (3) Everyone has a right to express his opinions. (4) Every member of the group has the right to vote. (5) All members have equal rights and privileges, but also equal duties and re-

416

sponsibilities. (6) The majority rules. (7) The presiding officer is expected to exercise his authority with fairness, judgment, and responsibility. (8) Motions have a prescribed and logical order of precedence. (9) Proceedings are a matter of record so that everyone may know what business has been transacted. (10) Both majority and minority rights are safeguarded.

Bylaws. Part of the rules governing an organization. The bylaws contain more details of the articles that appear in the constitution, qualifications and privileges of different types of membership, dues, duties of officers, methods of election, names and duties of committees, the provision for parliamentary authority, a definition of a quorum, and a method of amending the bylaws.

Call for orders of the day. A privileged motion used to direct the chairman's attention to an order of the day about to be overlooked.

Chairman. The presiding officer. The chairman holds a position of authority and responsibility. His job is to get business transacted; his obligation is to act with honesty and judgment. He should be tactful and diplomatic, but he should also be vigorous and definite. He should guard against unauthorized monopoly of the floor by recognizing each speaker by name and by following the rules of parliamentary procedure. If he wishes to speak on a motion, he must yield the chair to the vice chairman or to some other member, and then speak from the floor. He does not assume the chair again until action on that particular motion is completed. The chairman must master the verbal formulas of parliamentary procedure. Such routine phrases as the following are used frequently: "Is there any further business?" "It has been moved and seconded that . . . ." "Is there any discussion?" "Those in favor signify by saying *aye;* (pause) those opposed, *no.*" "A division has been called for."

Closing nominations. An incidental motion used to stop further nominations.

Commit. See *Refer to a Committee.*

Constitution. The rules governing an organization. A constitution includes five basic articles: (1) the name and purpose of the group, (2) membership, (3) the names of officers and the time of their election, (4) the time of meetings, and (5) a method of amending the constitution. See *Bylaws.*

Debatability. Whether or not a motion may be discussed.

Division of the assembly. An incidental motion used to compel the chairman to recount a doubtful vote. Not to be confused with *Division of the question.*

Division of the question. An incidental motion used to divide a motion concerned with more than one topic into separate propositions or resolutions which can then be discussed and voted upon separately. Not to be confused with *Division of the assembly.*

Fix the time to which to adjourn. The highest-ranking privileged motion. Used to set the time of the next meeting; has nothing to do with time of adjournment of the present meeting.

General Consent. Unanimous approval by the group. The chairman says, "If there is no objection," and then states the proposed motion or action. If no member objects, the proposed action is adopted. If a single member says, "I object," the proposed motion must be formally voted upon.

Incidental motions. Motions that arise out of another question and must be disposed of before any other business is taken up. Some of the most useful are: (1) Appeal, (2) Close Nominations, (3) Division of the Assembly, (4) Division of the Question, (5) Leave to Withdraw or Modify a Motion, (6) Object to the Consideration of a Question, (7) Parliamentary Inquiry, (8) Question of Order, (9) Suspension of the Rules, and (10) Motions Relating to Voting. These motions have precedence only over the motion out of which they arise.

Lay on the Table. A subsidiary motion used to defer action temporarily. The motion that is laid on the table (that is, placed in charge of the secretary) cannot be brought before the house until there has been some intervening discussion. See *Take from the table.*

Leave to withdraw (or to modify) a motion. Incidental motions used to withdraw a motion, or to change the wording of a motion, before it is stated by the chair.

Limit (or extend) debate. Subsidiary motions used to fix a time limit on individual speeches (for example, "I move that debate be limited to five minutes per member") or to fix the time at which debate shall cease (for example, "I move that the debate end at 2:30 P.M.).

Majority. More than half of the votes (for example, 6 out of 10, 7 out of 13). Unless stated otherwise, a majority vote refers to a majority of those present and voting (a quorum being present), not of the entire membership.

Minutes. The secretary's record of the meeting. The record of each meeting should tell (1) the kind of meeting, regular or special; (2) the name of the organization; (3) the date and hour of meeting and, unless it is always the same, the place; (4) the presence of the presiding officer and the secretary, or the names of those who act in their places; (5) the number of members present and the names of absentees; (6) the action taken on the minutes of the previous meeting; (7) all main motions except those withdrawn, with the names of the members who introduced them and the actions taken; (8) points of order and appeals, whether sustained or lost, and all other motions not out of order or withdrawn; (9) the program, if any; and (10) the time of adjournment. For an example, see the sample set of minutes in this Appendix.

Motion. A formal statement of a proposal to be acted on by a group, or of some action to be taken with reference to a proposal before the house; or a formal request for information; or a question regarding a point of order or of privilege. Motions are classified as Main motions, Incidental motions, Privileged motions, Renewal motions, and Subsidiary motions. Since motions are the essence of parliamentary procedure, the student should master the information concerning each motion in order to answer for himself the following questions: (1) What kind of motion is it? (2) What is its purpose? (3) Does it require a second? (4) Is it debatable? (5) Is it amendable? (6) What vote is required? (7) What is its precedence—that is, its priority for consideration?

Motions relating to voting. Incidental motions used to order the vote to be counted; to be taken by *ayes* and *noes*, by show of hands, by standing, by ballot, or by roll call.

Objection to the consideration of a question. An incidental motion used to prevent a main motion from being considered by the house.

Order of business. The fixed order in which the business of the assembly is taken up. See the sample in this Appendix.

Orders of the day. Motions or business scheduled to be taken up at a definite time.

Parliamentary inquiry. An incidental motion used by a member who seeks information on some point of parliamentary procedure. He may say, "Mr. Chairman, I rise to a parliamentary inquiry." The chairman says: "State your inquiry," and the member does so. "Would it be in order to move the previous question on the motion under discussion?" The chairman gives the information requested or calls upon the parliamentarian.

Plurality. A vote indicating that one candidate receives more than any other (there must be at least three candidates) but not a majority of the votes cast.

Points of order. See *Questions of order.*

Postpone indefinitely. A subsidiary motion used not only to postpone but also to kill the main motion. If adopted, the main motion cannot be brought up again unless it is introduced as a new motion at a later session.

Postpone to a definite time. A subsidiary motion used to set a time, not later than the next session, at which discussion of the motion will be resumed.

Precedence. The ranking of motions. The privileged and subsidiary motions must be learned in order of their rank. When any one of the twelve privileged and subsidiary motions is pending, those of higher rank are in order, and those of lower rank are not in order. See Table I in this Appendix.

Previous question. A subsidiary motion used to close debate and bring about a vote on the immediately pending question, or on all pending questions, if worded, "I move the previous question on all motions before the house."

Privileged motions. A group of five motions of highest precedence requiring immediate consideration by the assembly. In order of precedence they are: (1) *Fix the time to which to adjourn,* (2) *Adjourn,* (3) *Take a recess,* (4) *Question of privilege,* and (5) *Call for the orders of the day.*

Put the question. The chairman's call for the vote.

Questions of order. Incidental motions used by a member who seeks to correct a ruling made by the chair. The member says, "Mr. Chairman, I rise to a point of order." The chairman says, "State your point of order," and the member may say, "The amendment offered by Mr. Jackson is out of order because a secondary amendment is already before the house." The chairman may reply, "Your point is well taken. Mr. Jackson's motion is out of order." On a question of order, any member who believes that the ruling of the chairman is wrong may appeal from the decision of the chair.

Questions of privilege. Motions relating to the privileges of the individual or the assembly, such as heating, lighting, ventilation of the room, or the conduct of members. Not to be confused with *Privileged motions.*

Quorum. The number of members necessary to transact business. Usually a quorum is somewhat less than a majority of the membership.

Reconsider. A renewal motion introduced by a member who voted with the prevailing side for the purpose of setting aside a vote previously made and bringing that motion again before the assembly. Cannot be made except on the day of the taking of the vote that is to be reconsidered or the day following it. After this time has elapsed, the motion to reconsider is not in order, but the motion to *rescind* may be made.

Reconsider and enter on the minutes. A renewal motion used by a temporary minority to suspend action upon a vote taken at a meeting at which only a small percentage of the membership is present.

Refer to a committee. A subsidiary motion used to authorize a committee to transact specified business. In order to save the time of the group, the maker of the motion should be very specific in wording the motion. "Mr. Chairman, I move to refer this motion to a committee of three, appointed by the chair, who will report to the club at the next meeting."

Renewal motions. A certain group of motions used to bring motions again before the assembly. They are commonly called "miscellaneous," "unclassified," or "motions with rank of main motions." Examples: (1) *Reconsider,* (2) *Reconsider and enter on the minutes,* (3) *Rescind,* and (4) *Take from the table.*

Reopening nominations. An incidental motion used to allow further nominations to be made.

Rescind. A renewal motion used for the purpose of nullifying a previous vote. Can be made when it is too late to move to reconsider—that is, can be made after the day following the vote or action which it is moved to rescind.

Second. A parliamentary device used to indicate to the chairman that the member wishes the motion just proposed acted on by the group. A member wishing to second a motion need not stand or be recognized; he calls out, "Second the motion" or simply "Second." His second does not indicate that he favors the motion, but only that he wishes it brought before the group.

Secretary. The secretary holds a responsible position in any organization. As the recording officer, custodian of the records, and member in charge of correspondence and official papers, he is responsible for the prompt performance of numerous duties. He must be thoroughly trustworthy, accurate, dependable, and loyal. One of the secretary's most important duties is to record the minutes of the business meetings without comment or criticism. The minutes are signed by the secretary and sometimes by the president; the date of approval is added. Usually the minutes of the preceding meeting are read at the beginning of the next session. See the sample set of minutes in this Appendix.

State the question. The formal statement by the chairman of the motion before the house—for example, "It has been moved and seconded that the Speech Guild go on record as approving the proposed increase in the sales tax."

Subsidiary motions. A group of seven motions which have to do with the disposition of another motion, usually the main motion. The subsidiary motions must be learned in order of precedence: (6) *Lay on the table*, (7) *Previous question*, (8) *Limit (or extend) debate*, (9) *Postpone to a definite time*, (10) *Refer to a committee*, (11) *Amend*, and (12) *Postpone indefinitely*.

Suspension of the rules. An incidental motion used to suspend certain standing rules that interfere with some proposed action.

Table. See *Lay on the table*.

Take a recess. A privileged motion used to give the assembly a brief intermission.

Take from the table. A renewal motion used to bring before the assembly a motion previously laid on the table.

Voice vote. A vote by *ayes* and *noes* (called *viva voce*, "by the living voice").

TABLE I

A TABLE OF COMMONLY USED PARLIAMENTARY MOTIONS

The following summary of motions is designed for those just beginning to study parliamentary procedure. To participate effectively in a parliamentary body, the student must learn thoroughly the information provided in this table. The numbering of the motions is significant in that certain motions take precedence over others; motion number 1 takes precedence over all others. Motion number 10 takes precedence over number 11, number 12, and number 13, but is itself outranked by motions numbered from 1 through 9.

PRIVILEGED MOTIONS

1. **Fix the time to which to adjourn**
   A second required; amendable; not debatable; majority vote required.

2. **Adjourn**
   A second required; not amendable; not debatable; majority vote required.

3. **Take a recess**
   A second required; amendable; not debatable; majority vote required.

4. **Question of privilege**
   No second required; not amendable; not debatable; no vote required.

5. **Call for orders of the day**
   No second required; not amendable; not debatable; no vote required.

SUBSIDIARY MOTIONS

6. **Lay on the table**
   A second required; not amendable; not debatable; majority vote required.

7. **Previous question**
   A second required; not amendable; not debatable; a two-thirds majority required.

8. **Limit (or extend) debate**
   A second required; amendable; not debatable; a two-thirds majority required.

9. **Postpone to a definite time**
   A second required; amendable; debatable; majority vote required.

10. **Refer to a committee**
    A second required; amendable; debatable; majority vote required.

11. **Amend**
    A second required; amendable; debatable; majority vote required.

12. **Postpone indefinitely**
    A second required; not amendable; debatable; majority vote required.

ALL OF THE FOREGOING TAKE PRECEDENCE OVER

13. **The main motion**
    A second required; amendable; debatable; majority vote required.

TABLE II

TABLE OF PARLIAMENTARY MOTIONS *
(Arranged in Alphabetical Order)

Type of motion	Preced- ence of motion	Motion	In order when another has floor?	Requires a second?	Debat- able?	Amend- able?	Vote re- quired	Can it be con- sidered
P	2	Adjourn (when privileged)	No	Yes	No	No	Maj.	No
S	11	Amend	No	Yes	Yes [3]	Yes	Maj.	Yes
I		Appeal	Yes [1]	Yes	Yes	No	Maj.	Yes
P	5	Call for orders of the day	Yes	No	No	No	None	No
I		Closing nominations	No	Yes	No	Yes	⅔	No
I		Division of assembly	Yes [1]	No	No	No	None	No
I		Division of question	Yes [2]	No [2]	No	Yes	None [2]	No
P	1	Fix time to which to adjourn	No	Yes	No [4]	Yes	Maj.	Yes
S	6	Lay on table	No	Yes	No	No	Maj.	No
S	8	Limit or extend debate	No	Yes	No	Yes	⅔	Yes
M	13	Main motion	No	Yes	Yes	Yes	Maj.	Yes
I		Objection to consideration	Yes	No	No	No	⅔	Yes [8]
I		Parliamentary inquiry	Yes	No	No	No	None	No
S	9	Postpone to definite time	No	Yes	Yes	Yes	Maj.	Yes
S	12	Postpone indefinitely	No	Yes	Yes	No	Maj.	Yes [8]
S	7	Previous question	No	Yes	No	No	⅔	Yes [9]
I		Questions of order	Yes	No	No	No	None	No
P	4	Questions of privilege	Yes	No	No	No	None	No
R		Reconsider	Yes	Yes	Yes [5]	No	Maj.	No
R		Reconsider and enter on minutes	Yes	Yes	No	No	None	No
S	10	Refer to a committee	No	Yes	Yes	Yes	Maj.	Yes [10]
I		Reopening nominations	No	Yes	No	Yes	Maj.	Yes [11]
R		Rescind	No	Yes	Yes	Yes	⅔ [6]	Yes [11]
I		Suspension of the rules	No	Yes	No	No	⅔ [7]	No
P	3	Take a recess (when privileged)	No	Yes	No [4]	Yes	Maj.	No
R		Take from the table	No	Yes	No	No	Maj.	No
I		Voting, motions relating to	No	Yes	No	Yes	Maj.	Yes
I		Withdraw a motion, leave to	No	No	No	No	Maj.	Yes [11]

* Explanation of abbreviations in column 1: P—privileged; S—Subsidiary; I—incidental; R—renewal; M—main motion. The numbers in column 2 indicate that motions have different degrees of precedence. Highest precedence is indicated by 1, next highest by 2, etc. Motions for which no number is given have no precedence established.

[1] Cannot, however, interrupt speaker.

[2] If motion relates to different subjects which are independent of each other.

[3] Not debatable when motion being amended is not debatable.

[4] Not debatable when another question is before the assembly.

[5] Not debatable when motion being reconsidered is not debatable.

[6] If previous notice has been given to all members, a majority vote suffices. A majority vote of the entire membership may rescind without previous notice.

[7] Except certain standing rules, such as those governing time and place of meeting, which may be suspended by majority vote.

[8] Negative vote cannot be reconsidered.

[9] Cannot be reconsidered after it has been voted upon.

[10] Cannot be reconsidered after committee has taken up the subject. But a ⅔ vote will discharge committee.

[11] Affirmative vote cannot be reconsidered.

TABLE III

TABLE OF PARLIAMENTARY MOTIONS

(Classified According to Types and Showing Order of Precedence)

Rank	Name and type of motion	In order when another has floor?	Requires a second?	Debat-able?	Amend-able?	Vote Re-quired?	Can it be re-con-sidered?
	Privileged Motions						
1	Fix time to which to adjourn	No	Yes	No [4]	Yes	Maj.	Yes
2	Adjourn (when privileged)	No	Yes	No	No	Maj.	No
3	Take a recess (when privileged)	No	Yes	No [4]	Yes	Maj.	No
4	Questions of privilege	Yes	No	No	No	None	No
5	Call for orders of the day	Yes	No	No	No	None	No
	Incidental Motions (Have no rank among themselves, but grow out of other motions.)						
	Appeal	Yes [1]	Yes	Yes	No	Maj.	Yes
	Closing nominations	No	Yes	No	Yes	2/3	No
	Division of assembly	Yes [1]	No	No	No	None	No
	Division of question	Yes [2]	No [2]	No	Yes	None [2]	No
	Objection to consideration	Yes	No	No	No	2/3	Yes [8]
	Parliamentary inquiry	Yes	No	No	No	None	No
	Questions of order	Yes	No	No	No	None	No
	Reopening nominations	No	Yes	No	Yes	Maj.	Yes [11]
	Suspension of the rules	No	Yes	No	No	2/3 [7]	No
	Voting, motions relating to	No	Yes	No	Yes	Maj.	Yes
	Withdraw a motion, leave to	No	No	No	No	Maj.	Yes [11]
	Subsidiary Motions						
6	Lay on table	No	Yes	No	No	Maj.	No
7	Previous question	No	Yes	No	No	2/3	Yes [9]
8	Limit or extend debate	No	Yes	No	Yes	2/3	Yes
9	Postpone to definite time	No	Yes	Yes	Yes	Maj.	Yes
10	Refer to a committee	No	Yes	Yes	Yes	Maj.	Yes [10]
11	Amend	No	Yes	Yes [3]	Yes	Maj.	Yes
12	Postpone indefinitely	No	Yes	Yes	No	Maj.	Yes [8]
	Renewal Motions						
	Reconsider	Yes	Yes	Yes [5]	No	Maj.	No
	Reconsider and enter on minutes	Yes	Yes	No	No	None	No
	Rescind	No	Yes	Yes	Yes	2/3 [6]	Yes [11]
	Take from the table	No	Yes	No	No	Maj.	No
13	Main motion	No	Yes	Yes	Yes	Maj.	Yes

[1] Cannot, however, interrupt speaker.
[2] If motion relates to different subjects which are independent of each other.
[3] Not debatable when motion being amended is not debatable.
[4] Not debatable when another question is before the assembly.
[5] Not debatable when motion being reconsidered is not debatable.
[6] If previous notice has been given to all members, a majority vote suffices. A majority vote of the entire membership may rescind without previous notice.
[7] Except certain standing rules, such as those governing time and place of meeting, which may be suspended by majority vote.
[8] Negative vote cannot be reconsidered.
[9] Cannot be reconsidered after it has been voted upon.
[10] Cannot be reconsidered after committee has taken up the subject. But a 2/3 vote will discharge committee.
[11] Affirmative vote cannot be reconsidered.

PROCEDURES AND FORMS FOR A PARLIAMENTARY ORGANIZATION

To set up an organization and make it function smoothly, the following procedures and forms are essential.

The Steps in Forming an Organization.

Since social, educational, business, and political clubs are founded frequently, an approved method of organizing a typical group will be illustrated. An efficient procedure in forming an organization requires six steps:

Making the initial plans. Assume that a small group of men and women, observing their need for practice in speechmaking, decide to organize a club for the discussion of public affairs. They make a list of others who might be interested, and invite them to attend a preliminary meeting the following week. In order that the meeting may begin without confusion, they agree among themselves that Thomas Bentley will call the meeting to order and move that Leland Jones be temporary chairman.

Electing a temporary chairman. At the preliminary meeting, after fifteen or twenty people have gathered, Thomas Bentley walks to the front of the room, calls the meeting to order, and moves that Leland Jones be elected temporary chairman. After the motion is seconded, Mr. Bentley then puts the motion to a vote, saying, "It has been moved and seconded that Mr. Jones act as chairman. Those in favor say *aye.*" After the affirmative vote is taken, he says, "Those opposed will say *no.*" If the majority is affirmative, as it usually is, he will say, "The ayes have it, and the motion is carried." If the motion is defeated, he will say, "The noes have it, and the motion is lost. Another motion is in order." The procedure continues until a chairman is elected.

Electing a temporary secretary. The first action of the temporary chairman is to call for the election of a temporary secretary. Usually, a member of the original group will rise and say, "Mr. Chairman." The chairman grants him the floor by saying, "Mr. Murphy." Mr. Murphy continues, "I move that Sara Stern be elected temporary secretary." Someone else seconds the motion. The chairman then puts the motion to a vote; if the vote is favorable, he says, "The ayes have it, and the motion is carried. Miss Stern is elected temporary secretary." If the motion is defeated, the chairman says, "The noes have it, and the motion is lost. Another motion is now in order." This procedure continues until a secretary is elected.

Stating the purpose of the meeting. The chairman next calls upon Mary Rinehart, one of the original group, to state the purpose of the meeting. She addresses the chairman and is recognized. She then states the reasons for calling the meeting, enumerating the advantages of the proposed organization. Some discussion may follow her remarks.

Introducing a resolution of purpose. After discussion of the purposes for forming an organization, the chairman should entertain a resolution to form a club. Mr. Blake obtains the floor and moves the adoption of a motion similar to the following: "Resolved: That this group should form a public affairs club in order to provide opportunities for training in speaking, for practice in parliamentary procedure, and for the discussion of public affairs." After the resolution is seconded, the chairman restates it or has the secretary read it from the minutes. Discussion by the group is in order. After everyone has had an opportunity to state his views or to offer amendments, the chairman takes a vote on the resolution.

Appointing a committee to draft a constitution and bylaws. Because the constitution and bylaws cannot be formulated efficiently by the whole group, the task ordinarily is assigned to a committee. Miss Rinehart offers the following motion: "I move that the chairman appoint a committee of three to draft a constitution and a set of bylaws for this organization, the committee to report at a later meeting of the club." The motion is seconded. After it is discussed and passed, the chairman appoints three people to serve on the committee. Since he does not designate a chairman of the committee, Miss Rinehart, the first-named member, becomes the chairman. Other business may be discussed, but before the group adjourns, a time must be set for the next meeting.

An Example of a Constitution and Bylaws.

CONSTITUTION OF THE SPEECH GUILD

ARTICLE I. NAME AND PURPOSE

Section 1. The name of this organization shall be The Speech Guild.

Section 2. The purpose of this organization shall be to increase the opportunities of its members for training in public speaking, for practice in parliamentary procedure, and for the discussion of public affairs.

ARTICLE II. MEMBERSHIP

Section 1. This club shall be limited to twenty-five active members.

Section 2. Vacancies shall be filled by nominations from the Membership Committee, approved by a majority vote of the members of the organization.

ARTICLE III. OFFICERS

Section 1. The officers of the organization shall be a president, a vice president, a secretary, and a treasurer.

Section 2. Officers shall be elected twice during the year: at the first meeting in September, and at the first meeting in February.

ARTICLE IV. MEETINGS

Section 1. The organization shall have weekly meetings.

Section 2. By a vote of two-thirds of those present at a regular meeting, special meetings may be called.

ARTICLE V. AMENDMENTS

This constitution may be amended at any regular meeting of the club by a two-thirds vote of the members present and voting, provided the amendment has been submitted in writing at a previous meeting.

BYLAWS OF THE SPEECH GUILD

ARTICLE I. MEMBERSHIP

Section 1. Members in good standing shall be defined as those who have paid the dues and who have met the standards of attendance set by the Executive Committee and approved by a majority vote of the club.

Section 2. The dues shall be ten dollars a year, payable in advance by every member in good standing.

Section 3. Nominations for honorary membership may be made by the Membership Committee at a regular meeting previous to the meeting at which members are elected.

Section 4. Honorary members may have all the privileges of regular members except that of voting.

ARTICLE II. OFFICERS

Section 1. A nominating committee consisting of three members shall be elected. The duty of this committee shall be to nominate one or more candidates for each office to be filled.

Section 2. Officers shall be elected by ballot. A majority vote shall be necessary to elect. If, on the second ballot, no candidate is elected, on the third ballot the names of all candidates except the two receiving the highest number of votes shall be dropped.

Section 3. The duties of the president, the vice president, the secretary, and the treasurer shall be those which usually devolve upon such officers as set forth in Robert's *Rules of Order*.

ARTICLE III. COMMITTEES

Section 1. The Executive Committee shall consist of the officers of the club and shall perform such duties as the club may assign to it.

Section 2. The president, at the beginning of his term of office, shall appoint the following standing committees:

 a. A program committee of three members
 b. A social committee of three members
 c. A membership committee of five members

ARTICLE IV. PARLIAMENTARY AUTHORITY

The rules contained in Robert's *Rules of Order* shall govern the club in all cases to which they are applicable and in which they are not inconsistent with the constitution and the bylaws of the club.

ARTICLE V. QUORUM

Seven members of the club shall constitute a quorum.

ARTICLE VI. AMENDMENTS

These bylaws may be amended at any regular meeting of the club by a majority vote of the members present and voting, provided the amendment has been submitted in writing at a previous meeting.

An Example of a Typical Order of Business

 Meeting called to order by the presiding officer
 Roll call by the secretary
 Minutes of the last meeting read, corrected, and approved
 Reports of officers
 Announcements
 Reports of standing and special committees
 Unfinished business
 New business
 Program
 Adjournment

An Example of a Set of Minutes for a Club

MINUTES OF THE SPEECH GUILD

The Speech Guild held its regular meeting Friday, January 3. President Martin called the meeting to order at 7:30 P.M. Eighteen members were present; Mr. Watkins and Miss Myers were absent. The Minutes of the previous meeting were read and approved as corrected.

The Committee on Membership reported favorably on Paul Bowers for membership in the club. On the motion of the chairman of the committee, Miss Laskey, the report of the committee was adopted, and Mr. Bowers was declared elected to membership.

Mr. Evans moved to substitute for the next Friday meeting a joint meeting with the History Club to be held on Thursday, January 11, at 8 P.M. Mr. Horn moved to amend the motion to substitute January 18 for January 11. The amendment was seconded and carried. The motion, as amended, carried.

The president appointed Mr. Archer as program chairman for the meeting, and the following speeches were given:

"The Missiles Race"—Mr. Tracey

"The Bermuda Conference"—Miss Walker

"The New Isolationists"—Mr. Richards

"Russia's Reversal"—Miss Ewald

The meeting adjourned at 10:30 P.M.

Approved:

January 18, 1964   Mary Cantel, Secretary

INDEX

Abelard, Pierre, 18, 147
Accent, syllabic, 226
Acceptance, speech of, 298, 354
Accrediting, 379
Achievement from the practice of speechmaking, 387
Acquaintance with different kinds of speaking, 387
Action, 236 ff.
  improving, 253
  usefulness, 245
  first lesson in, 247
  second lesson in, 248
Adams, John, 19, 298
Adams, John Quincy, 20, 351
Adams, Samuel, 19
Adams, Thomas B., 298
Adaptability, 191
Adaptation, 109, 320
  choice of plan, 136
  kinds of, 128
  plans of, 127
  to professional audiences, 320
Address of welcome, 295
Adjourn, 416, 422 ff.
Adoption of constitution and bylaws, 426
Advocacy, 323, 347 ff.
  analysis, 359
  audience judgment, 365
  background of the question, 359
  ballot, 365
  brief, 361
  burden of proof, 361
  critiques of, 364 ff.
  definition, 347, 348
  definition of terms in, 359
  expert judge, 366
  immediate cause of controversy, 359
  irrelevant, admitted, and waived matter, 360
  issues in, 361
  kinds of debate, 350
  kinds of policy-forming speeches, 353
  major points of contention, 360
  personal decision, 363
  policy-forming speeches, 366
  procedures, 357
  purpose, 348
  roll call vote, 364
  speech of, 348, 349

speech of censure, 349
speech of denunciation, 349
speech of policy, 349
types, 349
see also Debate
Affricates, 222 ff.
After-dinner speech, 263, 275
  adaptation of, 275
  preparation, 275
  toastmaster's function, 276
  topics, 276
Agenda, 416
Agreement, the method of, 94
Alcuin, 18
Alderman, Edwin A., 301
  quoted, 282
Allen, "Private" John, quoted, 266, 355
Alliteration, 194
Allusion, 291, 292
  historical, 291
  sly, in humor, 272
Alveolar ridge, 213
Amend, 416, 422 ff.
Amendability, 416
American College Dictionary, 235
Amiability, 108
Amplification, 185, 286
  augmentation, 286
  cumulation, 293
  estimation, 287
  inference, 292
  similarity, 291
Analogy, 92, 167
  tests of, 93
Analysis, 50 ff., 181, 337, 359
  a continuing process, 50
  definition of terms used in oral reading, 181
  for debate, 359
  for discussion, 337
  informative, 56, 57
  methods of, 56
  minimum essentials of, 60
  of meaning in oral reading, 180, 181
  persuasive, 59
  preliminary, 51
  questioning in, 180
  statements for, 52 ff., 56, 59, 86
  systematic sentence, 52
  uses, 61
Anniversary address, 299

Announcement, in introduction, 134
Antagonistic, the, 261
  conflict, 261
Appeal, 131, 416
  from the decision of the chair, 416
  in conclusions, 131
Appearance, 248
Appraisal, 286
  of a speech of historical importance, 381
Aquinas, Thomas, 18
Argument, 93, 96, 362
  a fortiori, 93
  ad hominem, 96
Argument and appeal, plan of, 141
Aristotelian theory, 15, 16
Aristotle, 15, 16, 17, 83, 264
  quoted, 278
Arnold, Carroll C., 308n
Articulation, 199, 212 ff.
Artificiality in delivery, 254
Arytenoids, 203 ff.
Aspirations, 278
Assertion, in introductions, 134
Asseveration, 156
Assimilation, 228
  progressive, 228
  reciprocal, 228
  regressive, 228
Assumptions, 12
  attacking, 97
  errors in, 96
Assurance, 191
Attention, 100, 179, 260
  appeals to fundamental interests, 102
  approach to audience, 101
  arousing curiosity, 101
  dominant idea, 101
  use of concrete and specific, 101
  use of illustration, 102
  use of novel and familiar, 102
  use of personality, 103
Attic oratory, 21
Attitude, 187
Attraction, 107
Audience, 110 ff., 189, 279, 284, 309 ff., 382
  analyzing the, 110
  approaching the, 110

Audience (*cont'd.*)
  expectations of, 124, 309 ff.
  holding attention of, 100
  homogeneity and heterogeneity of, 127
  moods of, 124
  needs of, 311 ff.
  patterns of thought and behavior of, 112, 310
  questions, 160
  relating topic to, in introduction, 133
  relation to occasion, 126
  relation to preparation, 122
  relation to purpose, 124
  relation to speaker, 123
  relation to topic, 125
  response, 18
  what the audience considers worthy, 279
  what the audience considers unworthy, 284
Audiences, recognizing differences in, 114 ff.
  age, 114
  communities, 118
  economic status, 119
  education, 120
  intelligence, 120
  nationality, 118
  occupation, 119
  opinions, attitudes, and desires, 121
  political beliefs, 120
  race, 118
  region, 120
  sex, 119
  social position, 119
  tensions, 122
Auer, J. Jefferey, quoted, 400
Augmentation, 289
Austin, Warren R., 286
Authority, 12, 71, 89
  tests of a witness, 89

Babcock, Richard J., 317
Baccalaureate ceremony, 297
Bacon, Francis, 18
Baird, A. Craig, 49n, 78n, 98n, 104n, 132n, 141n, 154n, 157n, 163n, 166n, 167n
  quoted, 371
Baker, George Pierce, 21
Baldwin, Charles Sears, 21
Baldwin, Stanley, quoted, 355
Barnard, Raymond H., 27n
Barth, Alan, 319
Barzun, Jacques, quoted, 308
Basic tenets of parliamentary procedure, 416, 417
Beecher, Henry Ward, 39, 135, 200
  quoted, 166, 261
Benchley, Robert, 264
Benton, Thomas Hart, 20

Berelson, Bernard, 394, 398
Bergson, Henri, 264
Bernard of Clairvaux, 18, 147
Bernays, Edward L., 396n
Bernstein, Leonard, 277
Beveridge, Albert J., 20
Bibliographies, 43 ff.
  annotating, 48
  form for, 47
  illustration of, 48
  preparing, 47
Bierce, Ambrose, quoted, 72, 271, 396
Biographies, 44
Blair, Hugh, 18
  quoted, 62, 78
Blame, speech of, 284
Bodily action, 243 ff.
  appearance, 248
  approaching the audience, 247
  communication of thought and emotion, 245
  continuing process, 254
  danger of artificiality, 255
  directness, 247
  first lesson in, 247
  improving, 254
  in controlling attention, 245
  in presenting humor, 274
  movement on the platform, 252
  normal action, 245
  posture, 248
  second lesson in, 248
  securing coordination, 253
  spontaneity, 255
  suiting the action to the word, 254
  usefulness of, 245
Body of a speech, 128
  a brief, 362
  principles of development, 129
  types of development, 129
Bohman, George, 19n
Bok, Edward William, quoted, 75
Books and periodicals, 41 ff.
  as aids in speaking, 41
  as references, 43
  for quotations, 45
  used efficiently, 45
Boredom, 9
Boswell, James, 74
Boucher, Jonathan, 19
Bowers, Claude G., quoted, 166
Breathing, 202
Brewer, David J., 157n
Bridge of persuasion, 86
Brief, the, 361
  body for, 362
  conclusion for, 362
  introduction for, 359, 362

rules for constructing, 363
Bright, John, 18
  quoted, 165
Brinkley, David, 277
  quoted, 268
Bronstein, Arthur J., 220
  quoted, 227
Brookhart, Smith W., 355
Brooks, Phillips, quoted, 283
Brooks, Rozanne M., quoted, 261
Brougham, Lord, 18
Bryan, William Jennings, 20, 200
  quoted, 76, 168
Bryce, James, 397, 401
  quoted, 257
Bryson, Lyman, 327
Buck, Pearl, 262
Bunche, Ralph, 300
Burden of proof, 361, 363
Burke, Edmund, 18, 355
  quoted, 175, 309
Burkhart, Roy A., 395n
Burlesque, 270
Butcher, Samuel H., quoted, 196
Butler, H. E., 290n
Butterfield, Lyman H., 298
Bylaws, 417
  example of, 427
Byrnes, James F., quoted, 66

Cadman, S. Parkes, quoted, 292
Calhoun, John C., 20, 175
Call for orders of the day, 417
Campaign speech, 354
Campbell, George, 19, 264
  quoted, 109
Canons of rhetoric, 16
Captiousness, 9
Card catalogue, 42
Carleton, William G., 401
  quoted, 165
Carnegie, Andrew, quoted, 283
Case, in debating, 363, 364
Causation, 93 ff.
  tested by method of agreement, 94
  tested by method of agreement and difference, 95
  tested by method of concomitant variations, 95
  tested by method of difference, 95
  tested by method of residues, 95
Censure, the occasion for, 349
Center, 181
Centering, 181
Ceremonial speaking, 278 ff.
  commemorative addresses, 299

Ceremonial speaking (*cont'd.*)
  creating a unified program,
    286
  critiques for, 301
  felicitative addresses, 294
  types of, 293
Cerf, Bennett, 277
Chairman, 417
  electing a temporary, 425
  of a group discussion, 338
Chamberlain, Austin, 192n
Chatham, Lord, 18, 270
  quoted, 169, 170
Choate, Rufus, quoted, 291,
    292
Choosing a topic, 26
Churchill, Winston, 288, 373,
    374, 375, 377, 380, 381
  quoted, 18, 131, 135, 169,
    170, 172, 284, 301
Cicero, Marcus Tullius, 16,
    17, 78, 175, 289
  quoted, 25, 264, 265
Clarity of style, 162 ff.
  analogy, 167
  comparison, 166
  concreteness, 162
  illustration, 167
  parallelism, 167
  periodicity, 168
  precision, 166
  specificity, 163
Clark, Champ, 20
Clark, Delbert, 396
Classical arrangement, plan of,
    145
Classified file of ideas, 38
Clay, Henry, 20, 175, 200
Climax, 170, 186
Closing nominations, 417
Cobden, Richard, 18
Cogency in logical persuasion,
    90
  analogy, 92
  causation, 93
  deduction, 90
  generalization, 91
Coggeshall, Dr. Lowell T., 314
Coherence, 151 ff.
  continuity, 153
  reference, 155
  transition, 154
Colbert, L. L., 316
Colloquialism, 172
Colloquium, 334
Commemorative speeches, 299
  anniversary address, 299
  eulogy, 300
Commencement address, 299
Commit, 417
Common feeling, 159
Common ground, 110
  discovering, 110
  in introductions, 133
  of beliefs, 112

  of information, 110
  of interests, 111
  of patterns of action, 112
Communication, 7, 21, 146,
    179
  by use of bodily action, 245
Communicative principle, 188
  concentration on meaning
    and attitude, 188
  interpretation of meaning
    and attitude, 188
  response of listeners, 188
Communicativeness, in deliv-
    ery, 252
Comparison, 166
Completeness, 152
Composition, speech, 146 ff.,
    151
Comprehension, 179 ff.
Compton, Arthur, quoted, 78
Conant, James Bryant, quoted,
    290, 291
Concentration, 188
Concept, new, 183
Concession, 186
Conclusion, 96, 97, 130, 386
  appeal, 131
  illustration, 131
  in arguments, 96, 97
  of a speech, 130
  of the brief, 362
  planning in advance, 239
  principles of development,
    130
  quotation, 132
  refuting a, in arguments, 97
  summary, 132
  types of, 131
Concomitant variations,
    method of, 95
Concrete, the, 101
Concreteness, 162
Confidence, acquisition of, 195,
    236, 387
Congratulation, speech of, 296
Congressional Record, 41
Connotations, 188, 195
Consonants, 214 ff., 219
  affricates, 222
  chart of, 221
  continuants, 223, 224
  explanation of, 221 ff.
  fricatives, 222
  glides, 224
  lateral, 224
  nasals, 224
  plosives, 219
Constituents, plan of, 138
Constitution and bylaws, 417
  example of, 426 ff.
Constructive speeches, in de-
    bate, 363
Content, 179
  mastery of, 179
  realization of, 179

Contentions of affirmative and
    the negative, 360
Continuity, 153
Contrast, 185
Conventional debating, 352,
    357 ff.
Conversation, 39
Conversational quality, 188
Cooke, Alistair, quoted, 396,
    399
Cooper, L. Gordon, Jr., 287
Cooper, Lane, 21
  quoted, 72
Coordination, in delivery, 253
Corax, 15
Corson, Hiram, quoted, 199
Courthope, William J., quoted,
    76
Cox, Leonard, 18
Credit, giving, in speeches, 49
Cricoid cartilage, 203 ff.
Criticism, 78
  awareness of good, 387
  categories, 372
  rhetorical, 371
Critiques, 277, 301, 321, 345,
    364, 366
  for advocacy, 364
  for ceremonial speaking, 301
  for inquiry, 345
  for policy-forming speeches,
    366
  of professional speaking, 321
  of social speaking, 277
Crockett, Davy, 393 ff.
Cromwell, Oliver, 291
Cross-examination debating,
    351, 352
Cumulation, 293
Curiosity, 101
Curtice, Harlow, 316
Curtis, George William, quoted,
    158
Custodians of History, 403
Cutten, George Barton, quoted,
    157

Dale, Edward Everett, quoted,
    261
Darrow, Clarence, 374, 375,
    376, 377, 380, 381
Davis, Elmer, quoted, 131, 132
*Davy Crockett's Tongue-Tied
    Admirers,* 393
De Oratore, 16
Debatability of motions, 417
Debate, 347
  analysis for, 359
  brief, 361
  characteristics of, 347
  congress, 351, 352
  conventional procedures in,
    352, 357
  critiques for, 364
  cross-examination, 351, 352

Debate (*cont'd.*)
  direct clash, 351, 352
  educational, 351, 353
  evaluation of, 364
  forensic, 350
  forum, 333
  function of, 348
  intercollegiate, 351, 352
  joint, 350
  kinds of, 350
  legislative, 350
  moot court, 351, 352
  problem-solving, 351, 352
  purpose of, 348
  two-sided propositions for, 348, 349, 357
  see also Advocacy
Decisions in debating, 364, 365, 366
  audience judgment, 365
  ballot, 365
  expert judge, 366
  group verdict, 366
  legislative vote, 365
  personal, 365
Dedication, speech of, 299
Deduction, 90
Definitions, 71, 72
  in debate, 359
  of terms in oral reading, 181
Deliberative speaking, 323 ff.
  advocacy, 323, 347 ff.
  inquiry, 323, 324 ff.
Delivery, 190 ff.
  extemporaneous, 191
  impromptu, 190
  manuscript, 195
  means, 177
  memorized, 196
  poise and physical expression in, 236 ff.
  problems, 177
  rehearsal of, 197
  self-assurance in, 236
  self-confidence in, 195
  see also Presentation
Demonstration, 79
Demosthenes, 15, 78, 79, 131, 175
Description, 74, 103
Dewey, John, 337
  quoted, 196, 334
Dewey, Thomas E., 286
Diacritical marks, 214 ff.
Dialect, 232, 274
  regional, 232
  use of, in humor, 274
Dialogue, 273, 334
Diaphragm, 201
Dickens, Charles, 397
Diction, 173
  sense, 173
  sound, 174
Dictionaries, 44, 234, 235

Difference, the method of, 95
Differences in audiences, 114
  of age, 114
  of communities, 118
  of economic status, 119
  of education, 120
  of intelligence, 120
  of nationality, 118
  of occupation, 119
  of opinions, attitudes, and desires, 121
  of political beliefs, 120
  of race, 118
  of regions, 118
  of religion, 120
  of sex, 119
  of social position, 119
  of tensions, 122
Dillon, Douglas, 244
Diphthongs, 214 ff., 219
  chart of, 220
  defined, 219
  faulty, 219
Direct clash debate, 352
Directness, 108, 159, 247
  asking audience questions, 160
  creating a common feeling, 159
  using personal pronouns, 159
Discussion, 323 ff.
  contrasted with propaganda, 325
  critiques for, 345
  defined, 324
  group, 331
  leader of, 336
  member of, 340
  plan for, 337
  types of, 331
  see also Inquiry
Disposing, 379
Dispositio, 16, 17
Disraeli, Benjamin, 18
  quoted, 192
Dissimilarity, 291
Distinction, in style, 171
  diction, 171, 173
  felicity, 171, 174
  flexibility, 171, 174
  propriety, 171
Distortion, 11
Distraction, 9
Division, a method of informing, 73
Division of the assembly, 417
Divisions of a speech, 55, 57, 59
  illustration of, 55
  relation to the statement, 55
  wording, 55
Dooley, Tom, 288
Douglas, Helen Gahagan, quoted, 162
Douglas, Paul, 40

Douglas, Stephen A., 350, 365
  quoted, 159
Drafting a constitution and by-laws, 426
Drummond, Alexander M., 67n
Duration, 208

Eastman, Max, quoted, 401
Echo, 184
Economy, 161
Edison, Thomas A., 289
Educational debating, 351
Edwards, Jonathan, 19
Efron, Edith, 268n
Ehninger, Douglas, 308n
Eisenhower, Dwight D., 244, 287, 299, 356, 395
Eisenson, Jon, 204, 205, 217
Eliot, Charles W., quoted, 67
Elocutio, 16
Eloquence, 278
Emerson, Ralph Waldo, 248
Emotional appeals, 99
Emphasis, 151 ff.
  in language, 151, 155
  manifestation, 156
  position, 156
  proportion, 155
  structural, 187
Encyclopedias, general, 44
Engstrom, Warren C., 394n
Entertaining, 29, 259
  exercising good judgment, 274
  interest and stimulation, 260
  principles of, 259
  strengthening wit and humor, 273
  topics appropriate for, 29
  wit and humor, 263
Enthymeme, 90
Enumeration, plans of, 139
Errors in reasoning, 96
  in assumption, 96
  in cogency, 96
  of evidence, 96
Erskine, Thomas, 18
  quoted, 154
Essence, plans of, 138
  constituents, 138
  enumeration, 139
  illustration, 139
  location, 139
  succession, 138
Estimation, 287
  the appropriate, 288
  the beneficial, 288
  the continuous, 287
  the difficult, 287
  the first, 287
  the frequent, 287
  the honored, 288
  the last, 289
  the popular, 288
  the superlative, 289

Estimation (*cont'd.*)
  the unexpected, 287
  the unique, 287
Ethics of speechmaking, 6
  responsibilities of speech-
    making, 388
Ethridge, Mark, quoted, 281
Etiquette of speaking, 237 ff.
Eulogy, the, 300
Evaluation and criticism of
    speaking, 371
  criteria, 371
  standards, 371
  techniques, 371
Everett, Edward, 197
Evidence, 12, 88 ff.
  authority, 89
  circumstantial, 88
  direct, 88
  in support of propositions,
    87
  indirect, 88
  negative, 88
  refuting the, 97
Ewbank, Henry L., quoted, 400
Exclamatory expressions, 169,
  170
Exemplification, 76, 157
Exhalation, 201, 202
Experience, 106
Expert judge, 366
Explication, 75
  in introduction, 135
Exposing inconsistency, 98
Exposition, 62 ff.
  see also Informing
Expository speaking, 62 ff.
Extemporaneous speaking, 191
  adaptability and assurance
    in, 191
  hindrances of notes in, 192
  reading quotations in, 193
Extend debate, 418

Facts, sources of, 45
Fair play, 107
Fallacies, 96
  see also Errors in reasoning
Familiar, the, 102, 263
Familiarity, plans of, 139
Farewell, speech of, 296
Felicitative addresses, 294
  acceptance, 298
  commencement, 299
  congratulation, 296
  dedication, 299
  farewell, 296
  installation, 294
  introduction, 294
  presentation, 297
  response, 295
  stimulation, 297
  welcome, 295
Felicity, 173
Figures of speech, 270, 271, 272

Fix the time to which to ad-
    journ, 418
Flexibility, in style, 174
  adjusting to the occasion,
    175
  stylistic devices, 174
  vocabulary, 175
Folds, vocal, 203
Ford, Henry II, 300, 316
Fosdick, Harry Emerson, 104
  quoted, 280
Foster, William Trufant,
    quoted, 161
Fox, Charles James, 18
Franklin, Benjamin, 19, 342
Fricatives, 222 ff.
Frost, Robert, 182, 301
Fundamental interests, 102
Fundamental tone, 205

Gallup, George, 393, 395
  quoted, 394
General consent, 418
Generalization, 91
  methods of, 91
  tests of, 91
Genung, John F., 21
Gerber, John C., 308n
Gestures, 248 ff.
  communicativeness of, 252
  descriptive, 249
  for attitude or emotion, 249
  for emphasis, 249
  principles of, 251
  purposefulness of, 251
  restraint in, 252
  timing, 252
  use of whole body, 251
  visibility of, 251
Gladstone, William E., 18
Glenn, John H., Jr., 287, 296
Glides, 225
Glottis, 203
Goethals, George W., 283
Golden age of British oratory,
    18
Goldwater, Barry, 267
Good speech, 199
Goodrich, Chauncey A., 155n,
    165n, 169n, 170n
Grady, Henry W., quoted, 173
Graham, Billy, 246
Grammar, 173
Graphic aids, 79
Greek orators, 15
Grierson, Herbert J. C., quoted,
    62
Group discussion, the, 331
Gunderson, Robert G., quoted,
    393
Gurley, Fred G., quoted, 163
Gurowski, Count Adam,
    quoted, 397

Hale, John P., quoted, 248

Hall, Harry R., 315
Hamilton, Alexander, 19, 293n
  quoted, 160
Hammarskjold, Dag, 407
Hance, Kenneth G., 143n
Hand, Judge Learned, quoted,
    132
Hastings, William T., 74n, 310n
Havighurst, Robert J., quoted,
    75
Hayes, Helen, 288
Hazeltine, Mary E., 35n
Hazelton, Mayo W., *et al.,* 153n
Hazlitt, William, 264
  quoted, 115
Hearer, 100, 151
  see also Audience
Henry, Patrick, 19
  quoted, 156
Higginson, Thomas W., 248n
Hitler, Adolf, 88
Hobbes, Thomas, 264
  quoted, 146, 147
Holmes, Oliver W., 132, 288
Hone, Philip, quoted, 397
Hoover, Herbert, 374
  quoted, 77, 348
Hoover, J. Edgar, quoted, 308,
    309
Hortatory expressions, 169, 170
Hudson, Rock, 288
Hughes, Charles Evans, 280,
    293
Hull, Cordell, quoted, 279
Humor, and wit, 238, 263 ff.
  see also Wit and humor
Hunt, Everett, 20n, 67n
Hutchins, Robert, 395
Huxley, Thomas Henry, 65,
    78n, 350
  quoted, 149, 150, 350

Ideals, 279
Identification, 107
Illustration, 102, 167
  in introductions, 131, 135
  plan of, 139
Imagery, 103, 104
  auditory, 104
  gustatory, 104
  olfactory, 104
  tactual, 105
  visual, 103
Immediate situation, the, 133
Imperative expressions, 169,
  170
Implication, plan of, 142
Impressing, 278 ff.
  amplification, 286
  creating a unified program,
    286
  establishing a setting, 285
  minimizing, 293
  principles of, 278
  topics appropriate for, 30

Impromptu speaking, 190
Inaugural address, 356
Incidental motions, 418
Inconsistency, exposing, 98
Indexes, special, 42
Indiscrimination, 11
Inference, as augmentation, 292
Inflection, varieties of, 208
Informing, 62 ff.
  applicability, 64
  authority, 71
  beliefs, 69
  censorship, 70
  characteristics of, 63
  classification, 65
  complexity of, 69
  criticism, 78
  definition, 72
  demonstration, 79
  description, 74
  development, 66
  difficulty, 64
  distinctiveness, 63
  division, 73
  exemplification, 76
  explication, 75
  ignorance, 68
  imperfections of language, 70
  indifference, 68
  inertia, 69
  interpretation, 77
  methods of, 71
  narration, 74
  negation, 75
  obstacles to, 67
  prevalence, 63
  rationale of, 65
  significance, 64
  statistics, 77
  stupidity, 68
  taboos, 69
  unavailability, 70
  vested interest, 70
  wishful thinking, 70
Ingersoll, Robert G., quoted, 99, 174, 175
Inhalation, 201
Inhibition of activity, 240
Innuendo, 272
Inquiries, 41
Inquiry, 323 ff.
  characteristics of, 326
  critiques for, 345
  colloquium, 334
  debate forum, 333
  defined, 324
  dialogue, 334
  discipline, 330
  discursiveness, 329
  freedom, 326
  function, 327
  goal, 329
  group discussion, 331

imperfection, 331
  language, 344
  leader, 336
  lecture forum, 333
  limitations, 331
  oral presentation, 345
  panel, 332
  plans for evaluation, 346
  problem solving, 330
  procedures, 331
  public hearing, 334
  purpose, 328
  questions, 334
  symposium, 332
  types, 331
  unpredictability, 330
  value of discussion forms, 345
  see also Discussion
Installation, speech of, 294
Institutes of Oratory, 16
Integrity, 13, 106
Intellectual alertness, 387
Interest and stimulation, 260
  the antagonistic, 261
  the familiar, 263
  the problematical, 262
  the striking, 260
International Phonetic Alphabet, 214
Interpretation, 77, 188
Interviewing, 39
Intolerance, 9
Introduction, the, 132
  announcement, 134
  assertion or question, 134
  explication, 135
  illustration, 135
  personal reference, 134
  principles of, 132
  quotation, 134
  speech of, 294
  types of, 132
Inventio, 16, 17
Invention, 25
Irony, 269
Irrelevant, admitted, and waived matter in debate, 360
Isocrates, 15, 16
  quoted, 368
  theory of, 15, 16
Issues, 86
  discovering, 87
  in debate, 360
  stock, 361
  types of, 86

James, Henry, quoted, 3
James, William, quoted, 72
Jebb, Richard, quoted, 21
Jefferson, Thomas, 395
  quoted, 49, 396, 402
Jests, 264
Jesus Christ, 102

Johnson, Samuel, 74
Johnson, T. Earle, 314
Johnston, Alexander, 156n
Johnston, Eric, quoted, 99
Jones, Edgar Dewitt, 171
  quoted, 171, 197
Judgment, 106

Kant, Immanuel, 264, 265
Knapp-White murder case, 284
Kennedy, John F., 113, 266, 301, 318, 350, 356
  quoted, 180, 272, 273, 298, 386
Kenyon, John Samuel, 44, 229, 235
Keynote address, 356
Kipling, Rudyard, quoted, 271
Knott, Thomas Albert, 44, 229, 235
Knowledge and skill, 368
  application, 368
  principles, 368

La Rochefoucauld, François de, quoted, 24
Lange, E. E., quoted, 274
Language, 49, 146 ff.
  ages of, 14
  coherence, 153
  differentiating characteristics, 158
  of inquiry, 344
  of professional speeches, 320
  principles of, 146, 147, 151
  speaker's, 151, 165
  that interests and stimulates, 260
  unity, 152
Larynx, 203 ff.
  principal cartilages of, 204, 205
Lasswell, Harold, quoted, 399
Lateral, the, 224
Lay on the table, 418
Leacock, Stephen, 264
Leave to withdraw a motion, 418
Lecture forum, 333
Lee, Richard Henry, 19
Lee, Robert E., 292
Legislative address, 357
Legislative message, 356
Library, using the, 41
Lie, Trygve, 286
Likeness, plans of, 140
Limit (or extend) debate, 418
Lincoln, Abraham, 20, 274, 283, 301, 350, 358, 365
  quoted, 97, 152, 159, 171
Lincoln-Douglas debates, 97, 159, 350
Lindgren, Homer D., 167n
Lippman, Walter, quoted, 49
Listeners, *See* Audience

Listening, 3, 7 ff.
  accurate, 9
  critical, 10
  hindrances to, 9, 11
  suggestions to improve, 11 ff.
  to decide, 8
  to understand, 8
Literary criticism, 371
Location, plans of, 139
Lodge, Henry Cabot, quoted,
  290
Logic, formal, 91
Logical persuasion, 85 ff.
  cogency, 90
  errors in, 96
  evidence in support of propo-
    sition, 87
  finding the statement, 86
  issues, 86
Loose thinking, 12
Lothian, Lord, 295
Loudness, 203, 208
Lowell, James Russell, quoted,
  193
Loyalty, 106
Lysias, 15

MacArthur, Douglas, 287, 300
  quoted, 296
Macaulay, Thomas B., quoted,
  1
Maclean, Malcolm S., Jr., 394n
MacLeish, Archibald, quoted,
  292
Madison, James, 19
Magazines, 46
Magnus, Albertus, 17
Main motion, 419, 422
Major points of contention in
  debate, 360
Majority, 418
Malapropisms, 272
Manifestation of emphasis, 156
  asseveration, 156
  exemplification, 157
  repetition, 157
  restatement, 157
  striking phrase, 158
Mann, Horace, quoted, 192
Manuscript speaking, 195
  advantages, 195
  disadvantages, 195
  self-confidence in, 195
Mastery of content in speak-
  ing, 179
Material, finding and evaluating, 38, 39
  analyzing, 50
  organizing, 50
  recording, 46
Matthews, Brander, quoted,
  67
McBurney, James H., 143n
Mead, Margaret, 262, 277
Meaning, 14, 179 ff., 194

analysis by questioning, 180
and attitude, 187
concentration on, 188
interpretation of, 188
Memoria, 16
Memoriter speaking, 196
  advantages, 196
  preparation for, 196
Memorization, preparation for,
  196
Meredith, George, 264
Microphone, use of, 208
Mill, John Stuart, 94
Milton, John, 17
  quoted, 271
Minimizing, 293
Minutes, 418
  example of, 428
Monroe, Alan H., 143n
Mood, 187
Moot court, 351, 352
Morgan, Arthur, quoted, 161
Morley, Felix, quoted, 267
Morley, John, quoted, 177
Morris, Charles, 174n
Morse, Samuel, 14
Motions, 419 ff.
  incidental, 419, 423
  main, 419, 422
  order and precedence of,
    419, 422, 424
  privileged, 420, 422, 424
  related to voting, 419, 423,
    424
  renewal, 420, 423, 424
  subsidiary, 421, 423, 424
  tables of, 422, 423, 424
Motivated sequence, plan of,
  143
Motivation, plans of, 141 ff.
  argument and appeal, 141
  classical arrangement, 144
  implication, 142
  motivated sequence, 143
  problem solution, 143
  progression, 144
  reversal, 142
Mott, Frank Luther, quoted,
  240
Movement on the platform,
  252
Muggeridge, Malcolm, quoted,
  268
Murphy, W. B., 309, 310
Murray, Henry A., quoted, 310
Murrow, Edward R., 103
  quoted, 104
Mussolini, Benito, 330

Nafziger, Ralph O., 394n
Narration, 74, 103
Nasals, 224
Negation, 75
New concept, 183
New York Times Index, 43

Newspapers, 43, 46
Nightingale, Florence, 288
Nixon, Richard M., 348, 350
Nodel, Rabbi Julius J., 314
Nomination, speech of accept-
  ance or declination of,
  354
Norstadt, Lauris, 244
Norton, Charles E., 158n
Note card, sample, 46
Notes, 46, 192
  hindrance of, 192
  taking, 46
  use of, 192
Nott, Dr. Eliphalet, quoted,
  293
Novel, the, 102

Object, the, 148
Object to the consideration of
  a question, 419, 423, 424
Objectivity, 13
Observation, 39
Occasion, 126, 382
  ceremonial, 278
  policy forming, 353
  professional, 302
  relation of audience to, 126,
    127
  relation of topic to, 34, 133
  responsibility of audience at,
    126
  social, 275
O'Dwyer, William, 286
Officers, election of, 425, 427
Ofresh, Gabriel D., quoted,
  271
Oliver, Robert T., 354n, 355n
O'Neill, James M., 99n, 132n,
  354n
On Christian Doctrine, 17
Oral discourse, 159
Oral reading, terms used in,
  181 ff.
Oratory, 7
Order of business, 419
  example of, 428
Orders of the day, 419
Organization, steps in forming,
  425
Organization of material, 50
Originality in speechmaking, 48
  consulting a variety of
    sources, 49
  giving due credit, 49
  presenting your own point of
    view, 49
  recalling your own experi-
    ences, 49
  relating your own thought to
    investigation, 50
  using your own language,
    50
Otis, James, 19
Outline, trial, 38

Overstatement, 266
Overtones, 205

Paar, Jack, 288
Paderewski, Ignace, 288
Panel, the, 332
Parallelism, 167, 185
Parker, Theodore, quoted, 157
Parliamentary inquiry, 419
Parliamentary organization,
    procedures and forms, 425
Parliamentary procedure, 416 ff.
    basic tenets, 416, 417
    terms defined, 416 ff.
Parody, 272
Particulars to statement, 137
Patton, T. F., 299
Pause, 183, 194, 209
Paxton, Robert, 317
Pericles, 15
    quoted, 187
Periodicity, 168
Personal attributes, 282 ff.
    achievement, 283
    diligence, 283
    genius, 282
    nobleness, 282
Personal experience, 38
Personal persuasion, 105 ff.
    amiability, 108
    appeal to reason, 108
    attraction, 107
    attributes for, 105
    experience, 106
    fair play, 107
    identification with the group,
        107
    integrity, 106
    judgment, 106
    loyalty, 107
    means of, 107
    right timing, 108
    simplicity and directness,
        108
    sincerity, 108
    tact, 108
Personal pronouns, 159
Personal reference, 134
Personality, 103
Persuasion, 82 ff.
    characteristics of, 82
    differences from other arts,
        83
    habits of thought, 84
    logical, 85
    methods of, 85
    obstacles to, 84
    personal, 105
    prejudice, 84
    previous commitment, 84
    principles of, 83
    psychological, 98
    unity in, 83, 108
    universality of, 82
Peter the Apostle, quoted, 271

Peyre, Henri, 399
Phillips, Wendell, 27, 133, 160
    quoted, 161, 162, 193
Phonation, 202, 203
Phonetics symbols, 214 ff.
Phrase, 181
    the striking, 158
Phrasing, 183
Physical expression, 243
    bodily action, 236 ff., 243,
        245
    platform gestures, 243 ff.
Pitch, 207
    habitual, 207
    monotonous, 208
    optimum, 207
Pitt, William, 18
Plans of adaptation, 127 ff.,
    145
    essence, 138
    motivation, 141
    resemblance, 139
    selection, 136
    sequence, 137
    types, 137
Plato, 15, 264
    quoted, 390
Platonic, 15, 16
Plosives, 219, 222
Plurality, 419
Poetry reading, 193
    centering and phrasing, 193
    good timing, 193
    prolongation of sounds, 193
    rhythm, 193
Point of order, 419
Poise, 236 ff., 387
    acquisition of, 387
    adapting to the size of the
        audience, 238
    adjusting the length of the
        speech, 238
    avoiding apologies, 237
    beginning without stumbling
        and hesitating, 237
    behavior of poised speaker,
        237
    controlling the use of humor,
        238
    difficulties of acquiring,
        239 ff.
    exercising self-restraint, 238
    knowing when to talk, 239
    observing the customs of
        public address, 237
    occasions for, 242
    omitting perfunctory thanks,
        239
    planning the conclusion in
        advance, 239
    progressive adjustment, 242
    referring to personal rela-
        tionships, 238
    respecting the requirements
        of the program, 238

Policy-forming speeches, 349,
    353
    acceptance or declination of
        nomination, 354
    campaign, 354
    censure, 349
    critiques for, 366, 367
    denunciation, 349
    inaugural, 356
    keynote address, 356
    legislative address, 357
    legislative message, 356
    nomination, 353
    speech of public policy, 357
Popular lecture, 276
Popularizing, 302
Porter, Sylvia, 113
Position, 156
Postpone indefinitely, 419
Postpone to a definite time,
    419
Posture, 202, 248
Pound, Roscoe, quoted, 167
Precedence of motions, 419,
    422, 424
Preliminary survey of ideas,
    38
Prentis, Henning W., Jr.,
    quoted, 93
Presentation, 179, 190 ff.
    in debate, 364
    in discussion, 345
    methods, 190 ff.
    of humor, 273
    of professional speeches,
        321
Presentation, speech of, 297
Presiding officer, 417
    as leader of discussion, 336
Previous question, 419, 422,
    423, 424
Prior, James, 355n
Privileged motions, 420
Probability, in speechmaking,
    5, 13, 90
Problem solution, plan of, 143
Problem solving, 330
    in debate, 352
    in discussion, 337
Problematical, the, 262
Professional speaking, 302 ff.
    adaptability, 305
    adapting material to the au-
        dience, 320
    characteristics, 302
    choosing language that com-
        municates, 320
    critiques, 321
    demanding requirements, 306
    diversity, 305
    expectations of the profes-
        sional audience, 309
    individuality, 304
    inherent quality, 304
    necessity, 303

Professional speaking (*cont'd.*)
  needs of the lay audience, 311
  patterns of thought and behavior, 310
  practicality, 303
  presenting the speech, 321
  principles of, 306
  procedures in, 319
  relation of speaker to audience, 307
  significance, 303
  threefold nature, 305
  types, 313 ff.
Professional speeches related to specific professions, 313 ff.
  agriculture, 315
  business and industry, 315
  engineering, 317
  law, 313
  mass media, 319
  medicine, 313
  ministry, 314
  national defense, 318
  science and technology, 318
  teaching, 314
Program, 238, 286
  a unified, 238
  ceremonial, 286
  respecting the requirements of, 238
Program talk, 276
Progression, plan of, 144
Pronouncing Dictionary of American English, 44, 229, 235
Pronunciation, 226 ff.
  acceptable, 227
  pedantic, 228
  regional variations, 232
  standard, 227
  variations in, due to occasion, 234
Pronuntiatio, 16
Proof, 87
Propaganda, 325
Proportion, 155
Proposition, 87
  in debate, 348, 349, 351, 357, 358
Propriety, 171
  colloquialism, 172
  grammar, 173
  slang, 172
  triteness, 171
Psychological persuasion, 98
  emotional appeals, 99
  gaining and holding attention, 100
  narration and description, 103
Public address, customs of, 237
Public hearings, 334
Public opinion, 5
Public policy, speech of, 357

Puns, 271
Purpose in speaking, 124
  to entertain, 259
  to impress, 278
  to inform, 62
  to persuade, 82
Put the question, 420
Putnam, George Haven, 159n

Qualification, 186
Quality, vocal, 209
Question of privilege, 420
Questions for group discussion, 334
  fact, 335
  policy, 335
  value, 335
Questions of order, 420
Quintilian, 264
  quoted, 16, 289
Quips, 271
Quorum, 420
Quotations, 134
  books of, 45
  reading, 193

Raillery, 268
Ramus, Peter, 17
Random activity, 240
Rate, 194, 208
Rayburn, Sam, 287
Readers' Guide to Periodical Literature, 42
Reading a speech, preparation for, 180
Realization of meaning, 179, 188
Reasoning, 12
  analogy, 92
  causation, 93
  deduction, 90
  generalization, 91
Rebuttal, 363
Reconsider, 420
Reconsider and enter on the minutes, 420
Reduction to absurdity, 97
Reed, Thomas B., 171n, 173n
Refer to a committee, 420, 423, 424
Reference, 155
Reference books, 43
Reflective thought, pattern of, 337
Refutation, 96
  points of attack, 97
  rules of, 97
  special plans of, 97
Rehearsal of delivery, 197
Relevance, 153
Renewal motions, 420, 423, 424
Reopening nominations, 420, 423, 424

Repetition, 157
Rescind, 421, 423, 424
Resemblance, plans of, 139
  familiarity, 139
  likeness, 140
Residues, the method of, 95
  in refutation, 98
Resonance, 204
Resonators, 207, 213
Resources, 281
  experience, 281
  knowledge, 281
Respiration, 201
Response, speech of, 295
Responsibilities of speechmaking, 388
Restatement, 157, 184
Reston, James, quoted, 266
Restraint, in delivery, 238, 252
Reversal, plan of, 142
Reynolds, Senator, 355
Rhetoric, 4, 7, 17 ff., 259, 372
  as theory of an art, 4
  canons of, 16
Rhetoric, Aristotle's, 15, 21
Rhetorical criticism, 372, 381 ff.
  audience, 375, 376
  categories, 372
  occasion, 372, 374
  scope, 372
  speaker, 376, 377, 378
  speech, 378, 379
Rhetorical effectiveness, 380
Rhyne, Charles S., 313
Rhythm, 193, 194
Richards, I. A., quoted, 65
Ridicule, 267
Riesman, David, quoted, 39
Riley, Floyd K., 132n, 354n
Rives, William C., 397
Rodgers, Richard, 296
Rogers, Betty, 295n
  quoted, 274
Rogers, Will, 274
  quoted, 261, 268, 295
Romney, George, 316
Romulo, Carlos P., 286
Roosevelt, Eleanor, 389
  quoted, 285
Roosevelt, Franklin D., 20, 103, 158, 160, 284, 285, 287, 295, 301, 349, 354, 374, 375, 376, 377, 380, 381
  quoted, 168, 269, 354
Roosevelt, Theodore, 290
Root, Elihu, quoted, 293
Ruskin, John, 73

Salk, Jonas A., 289
Sandburg, Carl, 160n, 182, 301
Sarett, Lew, 161n
Satire, 267
Schirra, Walter M., Jr., 287
Schmitt, Francis O., quoted, 311, 312

Schopenhauer, Arthur, 264
quoted, 271
Schreiner, Herb, 400
Schweitzer, Albert, 288
Scott, Fred Newton, 21
Seaborg, Glenn T., 318
quoted, 281
Second, to a motion, 421
Secretary, 421
duties of, 421
electing a temporary, 425
Self-assurance, 236
Self-confidence, 195
Self-questioning, in analysis, 51
Sense, 173, 174
Sensory impressions, 103
Sequence, plans of, 137
combinations, 138
particulars to statement, 137
statement to particulars, 137
Setting, establishing a ceremonial, 285
Shakespeare, William, 17, 175
quoted, 236
Shaw, George Bernard, 72
quoted, 236
Shaw, Leslie M., quoted, 240
Sheen, Fulton J., quoted, 167
Sheridan, Thomas, 18
Sherman, Stuart, quoted, 74
Similarity, 291
Simplicity, 108, 160
choice of words, 161
economy, 161
straightforward sentences, 161
Sincerity, 108
Slang, 172
Slogans, 355
Smith, Alfred E., 354, 355
quoted, 191, 192
Smith, E. S. C., quoted, 65
Smith, George Barnett, 165n
Smith, Melancton, 19
Social program speech, 276
Social speaking, 259, 275
after-dinner speech, 275
critiques of, 277
Sophistic, 15
Sound, in language, 174, 194
Sounds of American English,
214 ff.
addition of, 229
consonants, 214, 219
diphthongs, 214, 219
in connected speech, 228 ff.
inappropriate stress, 230
omission of, 228
prolonging, in reading, 193,
194, 208
stress, 230
substitution of, 229
symbols for, 214
transposing of, 230
vowels, 214, 216

Speaker, 28, 124, 383
relation of topic to, 28
reputation, 124
Speaking, 3
criteria for appraisal, 371
extemporaneous, 191
from manuscript, 195
from memory, 196
impromptu, 190
uses and abuses, 386
Special indexes, 42
Specializing, 302
Specific, the, 102, 260
Specificity, 163
Speech for study, 393
Speech for criticism, 403
Speech mechanism, the, 213
diagrams of, 213
Speech patterns, 232
Speeches, current, 41
Speeches, material for, 38 ff.
finding, 38
sources, 39
Speechmaker, 146
Speechmaking, 4 ff., 21, 388 ff.
basic concepts, 4 ff.
basic principles, knowledge
of, 388
defensive use, 6
evaluation and criticism,
371
in ancient Greece, 15
in Ancient Rome, 16
in Britain, 18
in the Middle Ages, 17
in the United States, 19
instructional use, 6
necessity for, 6
normative use, 6
persistent questions in, 7
responsibilities, 388
significance, 5
technical use, 6
tradition, 14
uses, 5
Spellman, Francis Joseph, 316
Spencer, Herbert, 264
Spontaneity, in delivery, 255
St. Augustine, 17
Stage fright, 240 ff.
State the question, 421
Statement, 52 ff.
of fact, 86
of justification, 86
of policy, 86
phrasing the, 52, 86
testing the, 53
Statement to particulars, 137
Statistics, 77
Stephen, Leslie, quoted, 323
Stephens, Alexander H., 395
Stevenson, Adlai E., 80, 81,
164
quoted, 271, 280, 395, 403
Stevenson, Robert Louis, 64

Stimulation, speech of, 297
baccalaureate ceremony, 297
rally, 297
Stolidity, 10
Stout, C. F., 321
Straightforward sentences, 161
Strength, in style, 171
Stress, 230 ff.
inappropriate, 230
strong forms, 231
weak forms, 231
Striking, the, 260
concrete and specific language, 260
forceful and colorful language, 260
Strong forms, 231
Structural emphasis, 187
Structure of speech, 145
Studebaker, John W., quoted,
402
Style, 146, 159 ff.
adjusting to the occasion,
175
clarity, 162
directness, 159
distinction, 171 ff.
example of oral, 164
simplicity, 160
vigor, 168
Stylistic devices, 174
Stylistic humor, 272
Subdivisions, in analyses, 56,
57, 60
Subject, relation of topic to,
31
Subordinate idea, 185
Subsidiary motions, 421
Succession, plans of, 138
Sullivan, William C., 134
Summary, 131
Support, 25
Suspension of the rules, 421,
423, 424
Syllogism, 90
categorical, 90
disjunctive, 90
hypothetical, 90
rhetorical, 90
Symposium, 332
Syrett, Harold C., 160n
Systematic analysis for speech-
making, 57
Systematizing material, 320
Sweet, Henry, 374
Sweet, Ossian, 374

Taber, John, 271
Table a motion, 421, 423,
424
Tact, 108
Taft, Robert A., 128
quoted, 66
Taft, William Howard, 98
Take a recess, 421, 423, 424

Take from the table, 421, 423, 424
Taste, good, in humor, 274, 275, 278
Taylor, Gen. Maxwell D., 319
Tests of topics, 35 ff.
  audience test, 37
  occasion test, 37
  preparation test, 36
  purpose test, 36
  speaker test, 36
  subject test, 36
Thomas, Charles K., 232
Thomas, Lowell, 262, 277
Thomas, Norman, 102, 277
Thompson, Dorothy, quoted, 153, 154
Thonssen, Lester, quoted, 371
Thorndike, Ashley H., 74n, 75n
Thorndike-Barnhart Dictionaries, 235
Thought, the speaker's, 147 ff.
  the hearer, 151
  the object, 148
  the word, 147
Three-dimensional aids, 81
Thurber, James, 264, 393
Thyroid cartilage, 203 ff.
Timbre, 209
Timing, 108
  adjustments in, 238, 252
  in debate, 363
  in gestures, 252
  in presenting humor, 274
  in reading, 194
Title of a speech, 135
Toastmaster, functions of, 276
Tocqueville, Alexis de, 27, 397
Topics, 25 ff.
  choosing a, 25
  finding possible, 27
  in relation to audience, 33, 125
  testing, 27 ff., 35
Toth, Csanad, 300
Traditions of speaking, 14
Transition, 154, 186
Travesty, 272
Triteness, 171
Trivium, 17
Trueblood, Thomas C., 21
Truman, Harry S., 286
  quoted, 271, 285
Turning the tables, 98
Twain, Mark, 264, 274
  quoted, 166, 265, 266

U Thant, 244
Undergraduate course in speechmaking, the value of, 386
Understanding and judgment of speaking, 371

Understatement, 265
Unity, 151, 152
  completeness, 152
  in language, 151 ff.
  in persuasion, 108
  relevance, 153
Unusual, the, 262
Urey, Harold C., 298
Utterance, 199 ff.

Velum, 212
Vigor, 168 ff.
  active voice, 169
  climax, 170
  exclamations, 169
  hortatory expressions, 170
  imperatives, 170
  strength, 170
  vividness, 170
Visibility of gestures, 251
Visual aids, 79 ff.
  classes of, 79
  for social, program speech, 277
  graphic, 79
  techniques of using, 81
  three-dimensional, 81
Vital Speeches, as a source of current speeches, 41
Vividness, 170
Vocabulary, the speaking, 175
Vocal folds, 201, 203 ff.
  diagram of, 205
  photos of, 206
Vocal hygiene, 211 ff.
Vocal strain, 211
Voice, 199 ff.
  analyzing the, 207
  and emotion, 210
  loudness, 203, 208
  making the voice more expressive, 210
  pitch, 207
  production, 201 ff.
  quality, 209
  rate, 194, 208
Voice vote, 421
Volume, 203, 208
Vowels, 214 ff., 216
  back, 218
  central, 218
  chart of, 218
  front, 216, 217

Washington, Booker T., 299
Watson, Arthur K., quoted, 307
Watson, J. S., 265n
Weak forms, 231
Webster, Daniel, 20, 157, 160, 291, 299
  quoted, 284, 285, 302

Welcome, speech of, 295
Welles, Orson, quoted, 269
Wellington, Duke of, 149
Whan, Forest L., 365n
Whately, Richard, 19
Whistler, James McNeill, 72
Wilberforce, Bishop, 350
Wilde, Oscar, 72
Williams, Tennessee, 287
Williamson, Arleigh B., quoted, 401
Willkie, Wendell, 292, 355
Wilson, Harry Lean, quoted, 271
Wilson, James, 19
Wilson, Thomas, 18, 298
  quoted, 259
Wilson, Woodrow, 20, 41, 280, 282, 301
  quoted, 268, 269
Winans, James A., 21, 108n
  quoted, 179, 379
Winant, John G., quoted, 73
Wister, Owen, 341
Wit and humor, 263 ff.
  burlesque, 270
  dialect, 274
  dialogue, 273
  exercising good judgment, 274
  incongruous, the, 265
  irony, 269
  jests, 264
  jokes, 265
  overstatement, 266
  raillery, 268
  ridicule, 267
  sarcasm, 269
  satire, 267
  strengthening wit and humor, 273
  stylistic, 272
  timing, 274
  understatement, 265
  unexpected, the, 265
  wordplay, 271
Witherspoon, John, 20
Wolfe, Deborah Partridge, quoted, 307
Woodburn, James Albert, 156n
Woolbert, Charles Henry, 21
Woolson, Albert, 289
Wootton, Lady, quoted, 272
Word, 147
  choice of, 160
Wordbooks, 44
Wordplay, 271
Wren, Sir Christopher, 295
Wythe, George, 19

Yeager, Willard Hayes, 293n